Emancipating
Cultural Pluralism

D1527358

SUNY series
in
National Identities

Thomas M. Wilson, editor

Emancipating Cultural Pluralism

Cris E. Toffolo, editor
with an Afterword by M. Crawford Young

State University of New York Press

Published by State University of New York Press, Albany

© 2003 State University of New York

All rights reserved

Printed in the United States of America

For information, address State University of New York Press,
90 State Street, Suite 700, Albany, NY 12207

Production by Michael Haggett
Marketing by Michael Campochiaro

Library of Congress Cataloging-in-Publication Data

Emancipating cultural pluralism / Cris E. Toffolo, editor ; with an afterword by M. Crawford Young.
      p. cm. — (SUNY series in national identities)
   Includes bibliographical references and index.
   ISBN 0-7914-5597-1 (alk. paper) — ISBN 0-7914-5598-X (pbk. : alk paper)
   1. Multiculturalism. 2. Pluralism (Social sciences) I. Toffolo, Cris E. II. Series.

HM1271 .E45 2003
306—dc21   2002030974

10 9 8 8 7 6 5 4 3 2 1

For Charles,

*for teaching me so much about
identity, politics and pluralism,
and so many other things.*

Contents

Preface

This book brings together theoretical pieces and case studies on ethnicity and nationalism in an effort to take a step forward in conceptualizing these aspects of cultural pluralism. The chapters examine both the benign and harmful aspects of identity politics. Some look at ethnicity and nationalism at the microscopic level, providing detailed analyses of individual expressions of identity, while others critique our existing paradigm and theoretical frameworks. Whatever the approach, all of the contributions are united by two things. First, all of the chapters are the product of the same extended conversation, for they all were written during a 1997 National Endowment for the Humanities (NEH) summer seminar developed and led by Dr. Crawford Young at the University of Wisconsin-Madison, and ably assisted by Dr. Virginia Tilley. Second, the motivation for this book came from the group's sense that current scholarship was ripe for further development. The group developed the conviction that more attention needed to be paid to the normative issues associated with various expressions of cultural pluralism, for the ethical implications of the phenomena we were studying were too profound to be ignored. Thus while it is inevitable that any book that attempts to encompass so many different approaches and regions must omit much, and merely gesture toward arguments that require more space to be developed fully, the hope is that together these chapters will have the effect of taking readers beyond their current view of this subfield.

A brief note of clarification; at several places the authors in this book reference each other's chapters. The designation of *ECP*, followed by a page number, allows the reader to go directly to the source.

ACKNOWLEDGMENTS

All of the contributors are grateful to the NEH for providing the funding that was instrumental to this book's conceptualization. As well, I am grateful to the contributors for their patience and many helpful suggestions as I worked to bring this manuscript to publication. In addition, I am grateful to the University of St. Thomas for funding a sabbatical leave that allowed me to make substantial progress on this project. I wish to thank Elaine Robbins and my mother, Barbara Toffolo, who each helped in one stage of the preparation of this manuscript. Last, but in no way least, I especially thank Christine Igielski, without whose diligence and careful work this book would not have been completed.

Part 1

Introduction

Chapter 1

Overview and Critique of the Present Research into the Politics of Cultural Pluralism

Cris Toffolo

INTRODUCTION

Since Crawford Young (1976) placed the issue of cultural pluralism on the conceptual map, the literature on this phenomenon has exploded, as have debates about which theoretical framework is most fruitful. Until recently, three competing perspectives dominated empirical research: the primordialist, the instrumentalist, and the constructivist (Young 1993; Tilley 1997). Briefly, primordialists assume that ethnic and other forms of ascriptive identity are simply "given," they are the "natural" divisions of humanity. While many scholars have been labeled as "primordialists" by their opponents, including Clifford Geertz, today it is hard to find scholars who hold this position in its pure form. However, the rhetoric of many identity movements does project such a position (e.g., the claims about the biological determinacy of race made by racists). In contrast, instrumentalists explore and explain attachment to ascriptive identities (e.g., ethnicity, tribe, race, religion, language, etc.) by assuming that the present nature of these attachments is a function of the modern nation-state and the nature of the politics carried on within its borders. In short, ascriptive identities function as the tools of political elites in their competitions for power. Constructivists, along with instrumentalists, hold that identities are invented rather than primordial and natural, however, they question whether identities are merely tools easily manipulated by elites. Constructionists point to the symbolic nature of human understanding and to the difficulty of ever fully controlling the symbol systems through which we perceive the world. Increasingly constructivists are examining the role of narrative in producing group solidarity and defining the character of inter-group conflicts.

Much empirical work remains to be done by scholars working within each approach. Even so, these approaches are increasingly being called into

3

question. Currently debates rage about which approach, or which combination of approaches, best explains the continued existence of ascriptive identities, as well as the nature of the political and social dynamics they engender. These debates are not easily resolved, in part, because the approaches have different strengths and weaknesses: each provides adequate answers to some but not all of the issues at the center of the present research agenda. Furthermore, underlying and interacting with these debates are the broader epistemological clashes between the "modernists" and "postmodernists."

There are other important issues as well. Consider the topics that have comprised the research agenda: (1) the process of identity formation (through to political mobilization); (2) the links to modernization; (3) patterns of conflict and cooperation; (4) the connections between cultural pluralism and the nation-state; (5) the viability of the post–World War II nation-state system; and (6) the reasons for the intensity of the emotions surrounding nationalism.[1] While the first issue (i.e., the process of identity formation) is primarily phenomenological in character and, hence, amenable to an empiricist approach, all of the others, to a greater or lesser degree, also address important ethical issues. As such, researchers who explore these issues must come to terms with how to treat normative considerations, even as greater empirical information is being sought. Here phenomenological inquiry necessarily becomes entwined with normative concerns, for example, the moral status of identity claims, the proper structure, functioning, and role of state institutions, the justice of global patterns of development, and so on. There are also other crucial questions that are not on this research agenda, and many also raise troubling issues about the nature and status of truth claims within the social sciences, and about whether claims to being purely "scientific" can be justified.[2]

Given this confusing state of affairs, now is a good time to step back and reflect on the nature of present efforts to theorize identity politics and on how empirical research efforts are framed. This is necessary if we are to move forward on the levels of both theory and practice. These are the goals to which this book is devoted.

TERMINOLOGY AND HISTORY

Before proceeding, a brief word must be said about terminology. The terms *nationalism, ethnicity, cultural pluralism, communalism,* and *identity politics* often are used interchangeably.[3] Here no objection is raised to this practice, however, some attention must be paid to the history of how these terms have interacted in previous discourses, for there the differences were critical. Specifically, nationalism's agenda of nation building is antithetical to subnational identity politics. The fact that the terminology is more fluid today indicates just how much the theoretical terrain has changed, hence, the need for this book.

In particular, it is helpful to note some of the theoretical shifts, which have taken place since the end of World War II, that coincide with the beginning of the end of European colonization of the Third World and the simultaneous bid by the United States for global dominance. Most important here is the rise and fall of the modernization paradigm of political development, for although it is no longer the dominant theoretical paradigm, its central tenets continue to condition our understanding of cultural pluralism and its consequences for politics.[4]

After winning independence (in the course of which a form of anti-colonial nationalism was generated), many new states, working within the modernization paradigm, consciously set out to "build" nations: to generate a Western form of territorial nationalism capable of combatting parochial and ascriptive "primordial" identities. The idea was to generate the kind of homogeneous *gesellschaft* (i.e., rational cultural consensus based upon modern cultural precepts and structural organizational forms) that Western countries supposedly had done during their processes of industrialization. The argument was that modern societies required a culturally homogeneous form in order to function, because modern industry requires a mobile, literate workforce.[5]

While in the short run it was assumed that certain cultural symbols were important for identity formation (which itself was a necessary part of national integration), in the long run a gradual secularization of the political culture would, and should, accompany the socioeconomic structural differentiation which coincided with rising capacity. The final result was to be a unified "civic culture" characterized by trust of one's fellow citizens, consensus about the "outputs" that government should provide, and agreement on the proper basis of legitimate authority. It should also include a citizenry that saw itself primarily in terms of the nation-state and was capable of political participation yet still imbued with enough "parochial" and "subject" proclivities to maintain the "proper balance" between governmental power and governmental responsiveness to citizens. This in turn would allow elites the freedom they needed to govern (Almond and Verba 1963, 356-60, 529-41). In short, the nation-building approach to Third World political development, which was the first approach generated by the modernization paradigm, assumed that a conscious policy of symbol manipulation could produce the same effect as the gradual historical development that had unfolded unconsciously in the West. It also assumed that a unified, homogeneous symbol system was essential for a strong, modern state.

When this approach to political development got bogged down with various problems, the focus shifted to state building. This strategy concentrated power in the state and sought to develop sufficient "institutional capacity" to "contain" the social mobility that typically accompanies economic and political development (Huntington 1968). This was a more coercive approach founded upon suppressing rather than superseding identity politics. This strategy was no more successful than nation building, and after a few decades the salience of subnational identity groups was grudgingly recognized.

In some cases, new identity groups became relevant for the first time. In other cases, old identity groups gained a new lease on life because of the new conditions generated by the new state. In the latter instances, identity politics sometimes represents the success of state policies, as in cases where identity politics was successfully used to help consolidate democracy (e.g., linguistic identity in India). In other cases, however, the weakness or corruption of the state and/or economic sphere has produced a backlash by subnational actors who perceive their causes in identity terms.[6]

More recently we have seen an explosion of identity politics in the wake of the collapse of the Soviet Union and the communist regimes of Eastern Europe. The theoretical problems facing the leaders of these successor states are not very different from the ones faced by Third World post–independence leaders.[7] Ironically, the theoretical framework also is not very different. Despite the radical differences between communists and democratic-capitalist regimes on many fronts, and despite the awareness of national identities in early communist writings, in practice, both ideologies share an understanding of history in which ascriptive identities are assumed to be anachronisms that are destined to disappear: issues of language, ethnicity, religion, clan, and so on are irrelevant to political economy and, hence, the political logic of the new age. This means that while the experiences of the Eastern European states are important to consider in their own right, they do not fundamentally alter the development of the literature that was already unfolding in response to the shifting realities in other regions of the world. Primarily, the eruption of identity politics in Eastern Europe (and also in Western Europe and North America) has helped solidify the now generally acknowledged view that interethnic conflict and other forms of identity politics are an almost universal reality in our times.

The reason for presenting this brief summary of the modernization paradigm is to keep its assumptions in mind as we examine the contemporary literature on identity politics and cultural pluralism. Even though modernization literature has been thoroughly critiqued and has lost its preeminence, many of its assumptions (e.g., about modernity and tradition, etc.) still affect our understanding of both theoretical and practical issues. In the last thirty years or so since the modernization paradigm began disintegrating, we have witnessed an empirical moment in the study of identity politics. Having seen the grand theoretical edifices of the 1950s crumble so completely, scholars have turned to more modest empirical inquiries: categorizing different groups, generating typologies of different types of politically relevant identities, detailing case studies of particular ethnic groups, and so on. Disillusioned with the central theories, many scholars have been acting like naive Baconians, believing that the "facts" simply speak for themselves. Thus just when positivism was receiving heavy criticism from philosophers, those whose gaze was directed at the world were embracing a kind of primitive descriptivism. This has left the theoretical tenets of the modernization paradigm undisturbed, even if they are now well buried.

In addition to the modernization paradigm's presupposition of progress and its assumption that a unified, homogeneous symbol system was essential for a strong, modern state, it relied upon another tenet that we need to confront in order to move out of its theoretical orbit. I am referring here to its assumption about the opposition of tradition and modernity. While more muted today, this assumption is still a feature of the theoretical terrain. This continues to be the case, in part, because this supposition is intimately linked to another dichotomy upon which much Western political and philosophical thought is organized, namely, the distinction between the community and the individual. In Western thought, the individual is the criterion for defining other concepts and values and for determining how political time and space are divided up. Against the backdrop of an evolutionary understanding of history, the treatment of the individual becomes the standard by which historical ages are measured, with greater freedom and individuality associated with being more advanced. Because it is believed that an individual should be absolutely free to choose her or his life plan, "substantive values" are seen as problematic, for they "limit one's access to a wider field of possibility" (Kolb 1986, 6). Traditional communities, the bearers of such values, are seen as restrictive of individual freedom. It is this which lies behind the belief that to be modern is to shed the limitations imposed by traditional identities, values, and ways of life.

In other words, the dichotomy between the individual and the community is superimposed on the dichotomy between tradition and modernity, and these two dichotomies, along with the identification of other cultures with past eras of Western culture (that are themselves associated with tyranny), keep this "temporal" understanding of cultural pluralism (i.e., its transient historical significance) and its negative connotations in place even today. Even though scholars who do empirical studies of identity politics no longer overtly subscribe to these ideas, and even though some political theorists and philosophers have truly moved beyond this view, we are still only beginning to deconstruct the various philosophical and institutional edifices that are rooted in the temporal understanding of cultural pluralism and the related commitment to homogeneity and totality.

That the dichotomies of individual and community and tradition and modernity became so conflated may be understandable given the historical experience of some West European states, in which popular politics emerged partly for the sake of greater individual freedom and autonomy. However, this is not a universal development. In the East and the South, the dichotomy of individual versus community is not synonymous with the dichotomy of modernity and tradition. In Africa and Asia, the struggle for independence was the beginning not only of mass political mobilization but also of the reemergence of traditional communal identities. It was in the name of these identities that Third World peoples rejected colonialism. In the course of the independence struggles, however, what it was to be African or Indian or Muslim or Hindu changed. Members of such communities were now to be equal partners in the democratic polity that was to follow. Because traditional identities were reenergized within the context of mass-based liberation movements, a democratic dynamic was revived and/or injected into the traditions that went through such struggles. Today the political problem facing new states is to fulfill the democratic promises made at the time of independence. If they succeed, subnational identity groups can become the vehicles for participation, but if they fail, the shift in the locus of identity to ever smaller entities also may carry with it a repudiation of the normative demands of democracy as part of a general rejection of the status quo.

So when we talk about emancipating cultural pluralism, as we do in the title of this book, one of the things we are referring to is the need to examine the lens through which identity politics and cultural pluralism themselves are studied. We need to do this in order to delink examinations of cultural pluralism from the evolutionary view of history, its dichotomies of modernity and tradition and individual and community, and its assumptions about the anachronistic nature of ascriptive identities. If this is not done, our theoretical framework will remain essentially hostile to these phenomena.

If we are to find new ways of thinking about and working with cultural pluralism, it is also necessary to critically evaluate the perceived need for homogenizing projects, institutions, and processes (e.g., state building, melting pot metaphors, suppression of minorities, etc.). We need to question the assumption that community and tradition are intrinsically opposed to freedom, justice, and cultural plurality. Only when we truly are operating from principles that are no longer tied to a framework that was the product of the Western colonial project, and believed to be doing so by those engaged directly in identity politics, are we likely to find a new vision of the possible, as well as true resolutions for behaviors and practices that are unacceptable in themselves (and not because they are linked to identity politics).

Our contention is that identity politics are ubiquitous today, with nationalism and ethnicity being two versions of the same drive and conceptual framework, though played out by people differently situated with respect to power and state resources. We also see a proliferation of other forms of identity politics (e.g., linguistic, religious, indigenous, racial, etc.). These also need to be viewed in light of their relationship to the state, as well as in the global economic and cultural context. What also must be considered are the moral parameters within which identity politics operate. Therefore, rather than develop typologies of identity politics or delineate the unique features and histories of different forms of identity, future research must explore issues that until now have largely been ignored by students of cultural pluralism. Before we describe this further, however, let us consider some of the most recent areas of research for they provide some interesting new insights that will be helpful in reading this book.

POLITICAL IDENTITY IN BROAD BRUSH STROKES

In addition to the standard summary of the literature mentioned earlier (i.e., primordialism, institutionalism, and constructivism), another approach is gaining importance. It can be summarized nicely using the words of Emmanuel Levinas (1989, 236): "Contemporary thought is the thought to the nations among whom we live . . . [it] is the thought of a human society that is undergoing global industrial development, a fact that should not be treated lightly." This statement brings to mind research into global systems, and the growing importance of what Benjamin Barber (1992) calls the confrontation of "Jihad vs. McWorld." The very processes responsible for generating an increasing homogenization of cultures globally also are producing exaggerated and antagonistic forms of cultural difference.

This internationalist approach resonates with a branch of structuralist research that is coming to be known as "border theory." The latter argues that we should not discuss identity without also talking about borders and boundary setting, because the process of identity formation is highly interactive.[8] It is important to pay attention to how power operates at the boundaries between groups, and to the nature of the spaces that separate groups, both of which are constantly in flux.[9] As this process is very much impacted by the broader location, and by where and how power circulates, it also is important to examine the role played by the state. So rather than simply examine the cultural contents of various groups, we must understand who is located on the boundaries of the group. We also must examine how and why those particular boundaries are maintained, for we know that territories and populations that are associated with particular politically important identities can shift, because boundaries are as much ideological as territorial phenomena.

From this point of view, another important factor in identity politics is social mobility, in part because it is one of the central legitimizing claims in modern polities. While liberalism, at least theoretically, celebrates the social mobility of individuals, it largely ignores the fact that this often occurs as group mobility.[10] Identity groups do not remain in a fixed position within what typically remains a stratified system (even though most traditional principles of hierarchical ordering are no longer acknowledged to be legitimate).

Both the fluctuating locatedness of identity groups and frustrated aspirations to advance expose the officially denied hierarchy, and this creates tensions.

Finally, we must note that, like many scholars working within a postmodernist framework, many constructivist students of cultural pluralism are now focused on the role of discourse. They are examining legitimating discourses to explain how these help some identities to form, while disallowing others, and how these discourses regulate the types of interactions that can occur between groups, as well as the kinds of normative claims that can be made. That is, discourses establish their own communicative fields within which political identities, movements, and institutions are defined and legitimated, and around which boundaries are established (Apter 1997, 17), for it is through political discourse that moral principles and interests connect in politically significant (i.e., legitimating) ways. Hence, even though the processes of boundary setting and boundary maintenance are frequently associated with power expressed violently—in fact, a great deal of political violence centers around boundaries—even acts of sheer violence are regulated through political discourses that make moral appeals and call upon actors to "use their intelligence." In other words, "[p]eople do not commit political violence without discourse. They need to talk themselves into it" (Apter 1997, 2).

It also is increasingly recognized that we should regard conflict as a normal condition of politics. This claim is part of the broader rejection of the homeostatic views of society so prominent in the modernization literature and other strands of American political and social thought. Instead we need to start with the assumption that the normal condition of social systems is one of tension and intermittent conflict. "Such a view directs attention to the complexities arising out of conflicting, centrifugal tendencies in any society" and frustrates any effort to formulate simple explanations that stress only the integrative processes of a social system (De Vos 1975, 12). This view allows us to distinguish between the issues of conflict and violence. Furthermore, it also justifies the need to focus on the transformations of social identities that are constantly changing, often substantially, even in one generation.[11]

We must discuss as well why politics organized on the basis of cultural markers continue to have such appeal. Writers coming from an instrumentalist point of view argue that identity is just another resource used by "cultural entrepreneurs" to press their real or material claims, consolidate power, and/or gain access to resources. Another explanation points to the social dislocations caused by rapid modernization and population migrations: in times of rapid and confusing change, people cling to tested institutions and worldviews. While raising important issues, neither provides a complete explanation. Without discounting "rational" (i.e., strategic economic and political) reasons for the continued salience of "ascriptive" identities, we also must discuss such issues as the universal importance of myth, the nature of meaning, the role of discursive narratives, the nature of the human, and the psychological dimensions of individual identity and group solidarity. A metaphor, mentioned by George De Vos (1975, 377), of a California Indian sadly commenting on the death of his culture, helps capture what is at stake: identity is found in the "cup of custom" passed on by one's parents, from which one drinks the meaning of existence. It allows one to "taste" one's past and to plan and give meaning to one's future. Identity is a means and an end, something to savor. Once the cup is broken, one can no longer taste life.

De Vos goes on to say that in this metaphor further features of identity politics become evident. First, many forms of identity politics, including ethnicity, are linked to the myths that explain a group's origins and/or continuity. Such identity often is linked to religion, at least indirectly, as a central means of regulation and maintaining order. This has important implications:

> Origin myths establish who one is, and, because of one's progenitors, with which group one has rights and obligations. Such knowledge helps individuals resolve priorities of loyalty and allegiance in terms of a past frame of reference. It helps to integrate and regulate one's behavior. It defines the classes of persons to whom one can express affection or vent aggression. It indicates those who deserve respect and those who are to be derogated. (De Vos 1975, 358)[12]

This is an extremely important point to which we will return. Suffice it here to repeat Roberto Toscano's Levinasian argument that it is exactly the existence of such "partial ethics" that makes intergroup conflict possible. By this, Toscano means that at the root of violence toward "the Other" is the nonapplicability of ethical judgments to those considered beyond one's own group. In conventional morality, state-sanctioned group violence has not only been exempted from ethical stigma, it has been morally exalted; nothing should be considered wrong that defends the culture against outsiders. Indeed, this is a root of violent conflict between groups, for it is how the process of denying rights of others is justified (Toscano 1998, 63–81).

The enlightenment tradition attempted to overcome this approach to ethics, however, it is precisely its roots and suppositions that are called into question today by the continuing relevance of identity politics. The challenge, therefore, is to explore other approaches that take seriously cultural locatedness. Such approaches must address the fact that the rituals that reaffirm myths of origin often center on ancestral sufferings and triumphs. Out of these, future purpose is born (De Vos 1975, 358). In ethnic identity (as in other politicized identity), there is a commitment to endure suffering. Each group thinks that in maintaining itself, it has to undergo unique suffering not experienced by others. This commitment to endure suffering, combined with partial ethics, can become the basis upon which denials of the humanity of others are justified. When the group is under stress, the myth about surviving past harms can be transformed into a justification for inflicting harm on other groups. This, however, is the perverse side of identity politics. Its positive side, and raison d'etre, is to express meaning, uniqueness, connectedness—in short, to define one's humanity.

The linkage between myths of origin and religion shows that identity politics exist in a moral universe and are experienced as a moral commitment. This very important and much overlooked fact needs to move to the forefront of research and theoretical writing, as indeed is beginning to occur in some of the recent publications (see, e.g., Weiner 1998; De Vos and Romanucci-Ross 1975; Gladney 1998; Apter 1997; Brass 1996; Fearon and Laitin 1996).

WHAT TO INVESTIGATE AND HOW TO INVESTIGATE

The title of this book, *Emancipating Cultural Pluralism*, alludes to three different dimensions that must be part of the reorientation of scholarship that is now beginning to take place. First, we need to interrogate, and by this process emancipate ourselves from, the paradigm through which we understand identity politics as "the Other" of rationality and modernity (i.e., as anachronistic). One dimension of this was already noted earlier when discussing the evolutionary view of history and the interlocked dichotomies of tradition/modernity and individual/community. Identity politics exists in a world both created and hemmed in by these notions.

More broadly, we must emancipate our understanding of the nature of modernity, the "modern project" and its problems, for ethnicity and other forms of identity politics implicitly expose the limits and failures of existing understandings. These dynamics raise serious questions about the nature of reason per se, about its role in the social world in general, and about its role in identity construction and group solidarity in particular. It also raises questions about the continuing importance of symbolic and mythopoeic dimensions of the human.

Another aspect entails seeing identity politics as normal politics. With Patha Chatterjee, we advocate a more political view of politics generally.[13] By its volatility and unpredictability, identity politics exposes this truth, thus encouraging us to emancipate ourselves from a view of politics that remains tethered to key tenets of positivism as well as to technologized and bureaucratic theories of politics.

In contrast to traditional approaches to cultural pluralism, we argue that the basic problem of politics needs to be redefined, away from the problems of the peaceful aggregation of individuals and the development of cultural homogeneity and strong state institutions, to the problem of how a plurality of cultural groups can coexist without domination. In short, rather than being an interesting anomaly, identity politics define the central theoretical and institutional issues of our times.

We also intend emancipation in the sense that Crawford Young mentioned in his first work on this subject: finding formulas "for the preservation of intercultural harmony"(1976, 11). Broadly understood, this is emancipation from specific violent acts and practices that cause pain, harm and fear. It is of the utmost practical importance to demonstrate how new scholarship into identity politics, which takes the above-mentioned theoretical considerations seriously, can generate the kinds of knowledge that can help decrease the amount of harm (both to individuals qua individuals and to whole peoples) associated with identity politics. This suggests that the research agenda should include questions such as the following: How might we effectively address aggressive expressions of identity politics? Is it useful to distinguish between movements which (or moments when) intentions are emancipatory rather than predatory? For instance, is there something fundamentally different about the kind of ethnicity that is behind a regime that engages in ethnic cleansing and that of indigenous peoples' movements that are resisting state incursions into their homelands? What about movements whose participants are seeking to redefine their political position within an already segmented political community? Are all of these diverse expressions of identity politics ontologically and/or normatively equivalent? How might the answer to this question influence policy? Does it matter whether a particular expression of cultural politics is the product of the maneuvering of those in power, or whether it is a "grassroots" attempt to overcome the new forms of alienation and oppression produced by modernization, the integration into the global economy, and the growth of bureaucratic-authoritarian state institutions? Finally, how can we extend the legal meaning of the term *harm* to encompass cultural wrongs and thereby extend institutional protections?

To do all of the above, we need to more thoroughly expound an epistemology rooted in a social and cultural definition of the human that can articulate a reconceived vision of the rational: an epistemology compatible with the continuing existence of culturally defined identities and the continued importance of cultural politics. We need an epistemology that is engaged and contextualized, whose questions come openly from a committed stance, for it is on this basis that a transformation in the way that the social sciences approach identity politics can be achieved. Much work has already been done in this area, but it is not always accessible, and its practical implications are not always apparent.

Ultimately, this book's aim is to be counted among those recent works that are developing new strategies for approaching cultural pluralism. It will have achieved its goal if it contributes to any of the following tasks: (1) identifies ways in which hegemonic projects themselves generate some of the forms of violence and unrest associated with cultural pluralism; (2) focuses attention on the emancipatory possibilities inherent in some instances of cultural pluralism; and (3) elaborates on ways to prevent or resolve the kinds of harms that have been associated with cultural pluralism. In short, the approach we will be developing begins by asking what the study of cultural pluralism would look like if it were carried out by those with a commitment to what Habermas called the "emancipatory interest" (see note 2 in this chapter).

ELABORATIONS ON THE THEME

In addition to this introduction and Crawford Young's concluding chapter, this book has three main sections. The first addresses underlying epistemological, theoretical, and ethical issues. More specifically, the first chapter in Part 2, "A Propaedeutic to the Theorizing of Cultural Pluralism," by Jeff Hoover, argues that we should conceive of identity movements as answering the basic needs of human subjectivity. However, Hoover rejects the primordialist view of identity groups as expressing essential differences between human groups, nor should identity groups be conceived of as the residue of premodern ways of life, or as the instruments of elites. Rather, identity movements are a historically constructed means of satisfying the conditions for the flourishing of human subjectivity. As such, cultural pluralism belies an emancipatory interest, hence, theorizing about cultural pluralism should include an exploration of the role of identity movements in producing, for their members, such goods as self-awareness, security, and social space, as shaped by the reciprocity of aid and protection. From this vantage point it is possible to suggest ways of avoiding harm to nonmembers.

The next two chapters revise our way of approaching international and institutional issues. In chapter 3, "The Ethnic State," Virginia Tilley analyzes the way in which the state impacts on identity politics. Rejecting the prevailing wisdom that the state is ethnically neutral, hence, able to play the role of a mediator vis-à-vis ethnic conflict, she argues that the state itself plays a key role in fostering ethnic conflict, due to its unique function in connecting international security concerns to the domestic ethnic environment. The state does this routinely by translating international norms regarding nation building into domestic nationalist discourses that are invariably imbued with ethnic logics. Moreover, the state often takes on an "ethnic" identity in crafting its security concerns and, hence, its allies. This has a negative impact on domestic diversity. By identifying how ethnic interests are built into the state itself, this chapter questions whether we should continue to rely on the modern state as the main mitigator of ethnic conflict.

In chapter 4, "Cleansing Ethnicity," Thomas Simon develops this book's third goal (to prevent harms associated with cultural pluralism) by developing an alternative to the two main approaches to understanding ethnicity that currently inform policy formation (i.e., the identity and strife views). Simon argues that these views lead us to believe that all ethnicity is either valuable or harmful, and thus policy makers ignore the political dynamics that make ethnic identification contingent and malleable. To improve upon this situation, Simon articulates an alternative "group harm" view that focuses on the harms frequently associated with ethnicity, for example, discriminatory policies, apartheid, genocide, and so on. A key aspect of Simon's view is to point out a common sequence of stages (designation, discrimination, and brutalization) that typifies many instances of group harm. He then demonstrates the usefulness of this approach by applying it to the Yugoslavian and Rwandan cases. In so doing, he makes the case that in order to generate policies that might prevent group harms, policy makers should track the severity of harms, beginning with the initial designation of group identifications.

After Simon has shifted our attention to the harms associated with cultural pluralism, Part 3 presents several other profoundly disturbing expressions of cultural pluralism. Robert Buffington's chapter, "Forjando Patria," forces us to consider complex and often unforeseen problems associated with efforts to justly accommodate cultural pluralism. Specifically, he examines the unforeseen consequences of competing discourses within a state and shows how even well-intentioned efforts can be undercut by strands of cultural discourse that at first appear to be unrelated to matters of ethnic inclusion. Examining the case of the Mexican Revolution, Buffington argues that its failure to create a truly inclusive society can be traced in part to perceptual and discursive causes. The first of these is the intersection of anthropological discourse and eugenics that stressed the biological and cultural "improvement" of the indigenous peoples while it depreciated their current state. Second is the intersection of anthropological and criminological discourses, for even as radical anthropologists were attempting to revalue indigenous cultures, as part of an effort to incorporate indigenous peoples into a broader vision of citizenship, criminologists were defining the terms of acceptance in ways that undermined this effort. In raising issues about how knowledge is created and about how disciplines interact, Buffington goes to the heart of the epistemological problems that underlie any effort to emancipate cultural pluralism. In fact, as more and more states enact inclusive cultural policies, the perceptual and discursive issues that are raised here become increasingly relevant.

Ismail Abdalla, in chapter 6, "The Shari'a State," attempts to get us to think outside of the Western paradigm by examining the Islamic regime of General al-Bashir in Sudan. He examines the ideas and actions of the Sudanese Brotherhood's leader and ideologue, Dr. Hasan Abdallah al-Turabi, who is the main intellectual force in contemporary Sudanese politics. This chapter defines the essential features of the Sudanese Islamic paradigm and situates its discourse within the ideology of contemporary self-conscious political Islam. It also attempts to identify some salient features in this case that may enable us to establish some general theoretical formulations useful in understanding similar experiences elsewhere.

Manfred Steger, in chapter 7, "Mahatma Gandhi: on Indian Self-Rule," returns to the debate about which theoretical approach works best for cultural pluralism by arguing that any purist answer is unsustainable. He argues that the various approaches are not mutually exclusive and goes on to state that a more promising way to analyze the potency of nationalism is to explore how various instrumental, symbolic, and psychological elements contribute to its construction and perpetuation. To make such an approach manageable, Steger adopts a micro-level analysis of a specific text in its context(s). Assuming that nationalist leaders play a vital role in this process, he develops his argument by focusing on Mahatma Gandhi's seminal work, *Hind Swaraj*, in which Gandhi developed his influential views on *swaraj* (self-rule, independence), Indian civilization, and *ahimsa* (nonviolence). In this unique hermeneutic, Steger identifies and accounts for the various instrumentalist, ethno-symbolic, and psychological aspects that give Gandhi's nationalist discourse its unique gestalt and power. While the analysis in this chapter is focused on one unique source, the lessons learned from engaging in the exercise have much broader implications, most importantly perhaps for those who are working to counter the efforts by those in India today who are attempting to reconstruct Indian nationalism into a politically reactionary force.

In chapter 8, "Here We Do Not Speak Bhojpuri," Beth Simon's work, which also focuses on India, picks up on some of the themes raised earlier by Toffolo, Hoover, and Steger about the connection between individual identity negotiations and the construction of communal identities. Analyzing a set of real-time conversations about language and identity through the lens of speech act theory, Simon explains the dynamic connections between individual instances of situated language use and ongoing group processes of constructing communities. Her analysis reveals these connections as social practices and activities that are individually instigated and enable certain symbolic identities while demonizing others. She thus raises normative issues concerning the basic notions of identity, individual, and social group. Simon's type of close analysis in an empirical investigation is crucial in providing a foundation for the theoretical and methodological debates embroiling cultural pluralism.

In chapter 9 "Reclaiming Sacred Hindu Space at Ayodhya," Ellen Christensen expands on themes raised by Steger and Beth Simon by exploring the symbolic and ritualistic mechanisms by which the Hindu right mobilized the population in order to reconstruct Indian nationalism as an exclusive form of Hinduism that portrays Muslims as the dangerous and demonized "Other." Through her analysis, we see not only how the manipulation of traditional symbols has astonishing power to move people to action, but that this effort is being undertaken both to obtain and further modern aims, and as a response to modern conditions. This case study takes seriously the central importance of symbols and rituals, and their continual reinvention and manipulation. In the instance recorded by Christensen, this is being done for exclusivizing and excluding ends (i.e., asserting Hindu dominance and deepening the division between Hindus and Muslims), however, the lesson to be drawn is not the necessary association between symbol manipulation and reactionary identity construction but that symbolic manipulation is central to any identity construction. The implication is that those who seek to strengthen emancipatory forms of cultural pluralism also need to utilize symbols. As long as we see modernity as opposed to tradition, with reason versus the mythopoeic as the measure of that divide, then the power of the symbolic will remain solely with those who consciously link identity with tradition. It is possible though to imagine ways to use the symbolic to create a liberating form of cultural pluralism. In other words, the classic liberal modernist answer of juxtaposing universalistic identities to counter parochialism unravels, for it refutes nothing, and creates nothing. So emancipating ourselves from violent forms of identity by its methods is a hollow victory indeed. Rather, what these studies of India suggest is the need for a new form of symbolic interaction that picks up inclusive symbols and posits moral discourses, where the other is constructed via reference to moral categories (ala the rhetoric of Gandhi or Martin Luther King).

Part 4 turns to an important set of institutional questions. Specifically these chapters examine various attempts to devolve power as a means to address the demands made by those adhering to identity politics in culturally plural political systems. In chapter 10, "Self-Government in the Darjeeling Hills of India," Selma Sonntag reports on the Darjeeling Gorkha Hill Area Council of West Bengal. She shows how this model is informed by principles of liberalism, federalism, and democracy, and she discusses the potential of autonomous councils to successfully accommodate the plurality needs of culturally distinct minorities (rather than simply viewing the practice as a last resort to avert secession and civil war). She also discusses both the virtues and limits of "muddling through" as a strategy for dealing with cultural pluralism.

Paul Adogamhe, in chapter 11, "Politics of State Creation and Ethnic Relations in Nigeria," gives a critical and an ambivalent assessment of decentralizing power in his examination of Nigeria's effort to reduce ethnic conflict by carving larger states into smaller, more homogeneous units. His conclusion is that this effort has not lessened but has increased ethnic competition, which in turn has produced an increase in the level of intercommunal tensions. These conclusions are reached by focusing on how these changes have affected that part of eastern Nigeria formerly incorporated as the state of Bendel. Adogamhe points out that emancipating cultural pluralism cannot simply mean increased governmental autonomy or separate governing units. Rather, attention also needs to be paid to the sum of the parts and to the nature of the division of resources nationally.

Assefaw Bariagaber, in chapter 12, "Ethnicity and Constitutionalism in Ethiopia," concludes the discussion on devolving power by examining the effects of Ethiopia's 1995 constitution on its politics of cultural pluralism. With this constitution, Ethiopia claims to have transformed itself from a centralized state into a federation of ethnically defined territories that have a unique constitutional right to secede under certain circumstances. Comparing the current federalism to Ethiopia's previous arrangement, Bariagaber discusses why the federal approach is a better alternative, and also why the devolution of power in the context of an extreme multiparty system, with segmented ethnicity, makes sense.

In Part 5 our efforts to develop an alternative, emancipatory approach to cultural pluralism are reviewed and critiqued by Dr. Crawford Young, in chapter 13, the concluding chapter of this book. As the convener of the National Endowment for the Humanities seminar, out of which this work grew, and as one of the first to recognize the importance of cultural pluralism and identity politics, Young is well positioned to evaluate and critique our efforts.

NOTES

1. This list was generated from a survey of the existing literature by Crawford Young. It served as an organizing framework for a National Endowment for the Humanities seminar on "Nation, State and Cultural Pluralism," held at the University of Wisconsin at Madison in 1997.

2. These debates came to the fore in the late 1970s and are nicely captured in various places, including Dallmayr and McCarthy (1977). Habermas (1968) argued that knowledge is always generated out of some interest (for the sake of some end, pursued by some group). Most academic research pursues either "technical" or "practical" interests. The former is utilized mainly in the natural sciences, which seek to explain the world in order to control it more efficiently. The latter is used in the humanities, which interpret the meaning of ancient texts, unique human events, and other epochs. The goal of this hermeneutic approach is to generate mutual understanding. While the technical and practical interests generate much useful information, neither should be at the center of the social sciences. Given that their subject matter is human beings, it is not enough either to take account of regularly recurring events and structures or to explore the meanings of such phenomena. It also is necessary to generate normative judgments and the type of knowledge that will allow us to escape from pseudo-natural constraints and to thereby transform our culture and institutions, to make them less oppressive. This is the "emancipatory interest," and it coincides with the unique human trait to seek self-enlightenment.

3. According to Young (1976, 12, 16) "cultural pluralism" should be defined in terms of three basic components: "(1) Plurality is with relationship to an authoritative arena, the sovereign territorial state . . . which provides sharply demarcated boundaries within which groups define themselves and each other, and their interaction occurs; (2) Two or more socially and politically significant aggregates, differentiated by cultural criteria . . . whose competition, interaction, and conflict constitute one important ingredient in the overall pattern of political transactions in the polity; (3) The bases for these solidarity groupings are commonalities or affinities of ethnicity, language, race, caste, assumed blood tie, custom, and/or territory." For an excellent description

of the unique dimensions of each aspect of cultural personalism, see Young's conclusion in this book.

4. Good overviews of the modernization literature include S. N. Eisenstadt (1974, 225–53). Robert A. Packenham (1973), and Stephen Chilton (1988).

5. Central to the West's view of itself is a series of conceptual dualisms, including the one between traditional and modern society. That distinction grounds sociology, which developed as a discipline by using this distinction to understand and critique the shifts being caused by the Industrial Revolution. While Marx's and Weber's work also are of central importance, it was the work of Tonnies that served as the template for how this distinction is conceived. Tonnies conceived of the difference as a distinction between *Gemeinschaft* (community) and *Gesellschaft* (society). The former is like a living organism. It is the natural condition of humanity in traditional society and arises because human wills are linked by connections of kinship, locality, and mind. These give rise to an instinctive, paternalistic tenderness among the strong for the weak members of the community, which is the basis of feudalism. In contrast, modern bourgeois society (*Gesellschaft*) is characterized by a spirit of "apartness." In this social form, people remain separate, held together only by convention and law. All busily seek their own interests and are devoid of familial relationships. Durkheim went on to argue that the distinction is rooted in differing levels of labor division. *Gemeinschaft* is rooted in a low social division of labor and is expressed by the homogeneity of individuals. As the division of labor increases, a new form of "organic solidarity" becomes the unifying principle. Each person comes to fill a different function, so that individuals can no longer be easily separated. Individuals are now no longer grouped according to lineage but according to the nature of the social activity they perform. Durkheim's functional differentiation is analogous to Darwin's account of the differentiation of species within a given environmental niche. Thus when the tradition-modern distinction collided with social Darwinism, as it did in the modernization literature, the distinction between traditional and modern society, which originated as a heuristic device for critiquing modern society, came to be seen as evidence that confirmed the superiority of modern social organization (see Tonnies 1957, 47, 53, 66, 74; Durkheim 1933, 130, 148, 172, 180-81).

6. Victor Uchendu has summarized this point nicely: some ethnic revivalist movements are defenses against extinction, which is threatened when an externally imposed ruling polity seeks to secure the ultimate loyalty of all those it governs by annihilating local cultural symbols and practices. Other identity affirmations counter the effects of population dispersions or degradation by evoking old images and emblems around which members can rally to shed shame, renew pride, and gain a sense of self-acceptance.

7. In the conclusion of this book, Crawford Young explores these issues further.

8. This has been a persistent thesis in various strains of the literature, going back to Barth (1959). It is seen not only in the psycho-cultural theories of ethnic identity but also in more postmodernist/discursive views. More recently, border theory has become a field of inquiry in its own right, with its own organizing presuppositions. According to Michaelson and Johnson (1997, 10–12), who draw upon the work of Todorov, Jean-Luc Nancy, Homi Bhabba, Hicks, and Anzaldua, the central assumptions

of border theory can be summarized as follows: (1) The difference between modern and premodernism is that in modernity, border crossings are common and welcome, but in the premodern world, distinct cultures lived separately; (2) This body of literature is morally committed to saving all cultures; (3) Cultural isolationism is dangerous, and border crossing will be our salvation; (4) The latter is the case, because cultures are now forced to be in increasingly complex relationships with one another; and (5) Indigenous people can help heal the modern world, which suffers from fragmented subjectivities.

9. Friedman (1998) discusses the shifting back and forth between being somewhat permeable "borderlands" and being more impenetrable boundaries.

10. Examples from the United States include the migration of African Americans from the rural South to the urban North and the rise of the Irish through control of big-city politics. An example from Pakistan is the capture of state institutions by Punjabis. This has greatly improved the fortunes of many individuals belonging to this ethnic group.

11. This is increasingly the case, perhaps due to the fact that today there is a growing amount of social mobility (related to individual achievement), as well as an increase in geographic mobility (due to shifting labor markets). Additionally, all groups today, no matter how committed to traditionalism and/or orthodoxy, find it necessary to make self-conscious, repeated articulations of their supposedly unchanging, primordial claims. It also may be a product of the fact that today no group is content to remain mute (De Vos 1975, 16, 17).

12. In a rather alarming development, David Miller (1995) has developed an exclusivist ethnic ethics on the basis of just such an argument.

13. Chatterjee (1993, vii) notes that "it is remarkable how seldom political theorists have taken seriously the fact that 'politics' necessarily operates in an ideological world . . . where choices are strategic and relative, not univocal and absolute."

References

Almond, Gabriel A., and Sidney Verba. 1963. *The Civic Culture*. Princeton: Princeton University Press.

Apter, David E., ed. 1997. *The Legitimization of Violence*. New York: New York University Press.

Barber, Benjamin. 1992. "Jihad vs. McWorld." *The Atlantic* 269:3 (March): 53–62.

Barth, Fredrik. 1959. *Leadership Among Swat Pathans*. London: University of London, Athlone Press.

Brass, Paul R., ed. 1996. *Riots and Pogroms*. New York: New York University Press.

Chatterjee, Partha. 1993. *Nationalist Thought and the Colonial World: A Derivative Discourse?* Minneapolis: University of Minnesota Press.

Chilton, Stephen. 1988. *Defining Political Development, GSIS Monograph Series in World Affairs*. Boulder and London: Lynne Rienner.

Dallmayr, Fred, and Thomas McCarthy, eds. 1977. *Understanding and Social Inquiry.* Notre Dame: University of Notre Dame Press.

De Vos, George. 1975. "Ethnic Pluralism: Conflict and Accomodation." Pp. 5–41 in *Ethnic Identity: Cultural Continuities and Change.* Edited by George De Vos and Lola Romanucci-Ross. Palo Alto: Mayfield.

Durkheim, Emile. 1933. *The Division of Labor in Society.* Translated by George Simpson. London: The Free Press of Glencoe, Collier-Macmillan Limited.

Eisenstadt, S. N. 1974. "Studies of Modernization and Sociological Theory." *History and Theory* 13:3: 225-53.

Fearon, James D., and David D. Laitin. 1996. "Explaining Interethnic Cooperation." *American Political Science Review* 90:4 (December): 715-35.

Friedman, Susan. 1998. Talk given to NEH Seminar, University of Wisconsin-Madison (Summer).

Gladney, Dru C., ed. 1998. *Making Majorities: Constituting the Nation in Japan, Korea, China, Malaysia, Fiji, Turkey, and the United States.* Stanford: Stanford University Press.

Habermas, Jurgen. 1968. *Knowledge and Human Interest.* Boston: Beacon Press.

Huntington, Samuel P. 1968. *Political Order in Changing Societies.* New Haven: Yale University Press.

Kolb, David. 1986. *The Critique of Pure Modernity: Hegel, Heidegger, and After.* Chicago: University of Chicago Press.

Kymlicka, Will. 1989. *Liberalism, Community, and Culture.* Oxford: Clarendon Press.

Levinas, Emmanuel. 1989. "Ideology and Idealism." In *The Levinas Reader: Emmanuel Levinas*, ed. Sean Hand. Cambridge: Basil Blackwell.

Michaelson, Scott, and David E. Johnson, eds. 1997. *Border Theory.* Minneapolis: University of Minnesota Press.

Miller, David. 1995. *On Nationality.* Oxford: Clarendon Press.

Packenham, Robert A. 1973. *Liberal America and the Third World: Political Development Ideas in Foreign Aid and Social Science.* Princeton: Princeton University Press.

Rawls, John. 1993. *Political Liberalism.* New York: Columbia University Press.

Tilley, Virginia. 1997. "The Terms of the Debate: Untangling Language about Ethnicity and Ethnic Movements." *Ethnic and Racial Studies* 20:3 (July): 497–523.

Tonnies, Ferdinand. 1957. *Community and Society (Gemeinschaft and Gesellschaft).* Translated and edited by Charles P. Loomis. New York: Harper Torchbooks, The Academy Library, Harper and Row.

Toscano, Roberto. 1998. "The Face of the Other: Ethics and Intergroup Conflict." Pp. 63–81 in *The Handbook of Interethnic Coexistence,* ed. Eugene Weiner. Foreword by Alan B. Slifka. An Abraham Fund Publication. New York: Continuum.

Weiner, Eugene, ed. 1998. *The Handbook of Interethnic Coexistence.* Foreword by Alan B. Slifka. An Abraham Fund Publication. New York: Continuum.

Young, Crawford. 1976. *The Politics of Cultural Pluralism*. Madison: University of Wisconsin Press.

————, ed. 1993. *The Rising Tide of Cultural Pluralism: The Nation-State at Bay?* Madison: University of Wisconsin Press.

Part 2

Transforming the Conceptual, Theoretical, and Methodological Terrain

Chapter 2

A Propaedeutic to the Theorizing of Cultural Pluralism

Jeff Hoover

It is commonly noted that even while political democratization appears to be on the march globally, there also is a groundswell of movements emphasizing distinctions and differences among humans. These particularist distinctions, which are ethnic, racial, linguistic, nationalist, or religious in nature, are asserting themselves with new vigor both in democratic and nondemocratic societies. As was noted in the introduction to this book, those who take note of this simultaneous advance of democracy and particularism often view this as a theoretical conundrum, since much current social and political theory tends to assume that under the conditions of democracy and increased modernization, particularist identifications should come to have less of a grip on individuals. They presume, accordingly, that as societies democratize (as equality of rights and access to decision making are maximized), distinctions between persons due to culture, race, faith, or ethnicity will be deemphasized. Moreover, it is assumed that the processes of modernization in general (increasing urbanization, social mobility, awareness of other cultures, and access to education) will result in a shift in primary group identifications, away from local and particularist forms of identification, to the more general, abstract, and voluntary forms of association.

However, these assumptions reveal a misunderstanding of the function of particularist identifications. If we view group identification in light of its role in human flourishing, we can understand more clearly why these identities continue to assert themselves. More importantly, we also will be in a position to anticipate the manner in which these identifications could serve emancipatory functions.

The following discussion seeks to reorient our theoretical assumptions about identity movements. This proposed reorientation takes its departure from a claim about the function of identity group membership in the development of subjectivity (i.e., the capacity for self-awareness). Taking this function of identity group membership into account discloses the possibility of a broadly emancipatory role for such groups. In recognizing the broadly emancipatory possibilities, moreover, there are important distinctions to be made regarding the kind of emancipatory roles that identity groups might serve. The ensuing analysis does not seek to establish a detailed theoretical framework for understanding, explaining, and analyzing identity movements but aims at a new propaedeutic for such work by outlining the basic commitments of a new theoretical framework.

Unlike either ideological groups or secondary associations, where membership is voluntarily chosen, membership in identity groups originates in ascription (i.e., individuals are ascribed membership to these groups by others). But mere ascription of individuals to a group is insufficient to establish identity. An identity group is one in which this ascribed membership becomes fundamentally constitutive for the self-understanding of its members. These group ascriptions must be accompanied by a felt affinity, a perceived commonality, if membership is to be fundamentally identity forming for members. What defines identity group membership is not merely the common allegiance to a particular chosen political position (as in ideological groups), nor the presence of a shared interest or activity (as in voluntary or secondary associations), but something very basic to the self-conceptions of individual members. The affinities among members of identity groups tend to be comprehensive, including not only commonalities of beliefs, values, and lifestyles but also commonalities of tangible, everyday elements including language, calendar, eating habits, or the manner in which the body is presented or comported—it is a shared way of being. Identity groups, then, produce unique "cultures" that give expression to these identities. To be sure, not all individuals ascribed to such groups have affinities for others in the group, or develop the requisite cognitive and affective identification with the group. For such individuals who lack these identifications, the group to which they are ascribed does not serve as their identity group. Furthermore, under this conception of identity groups, it is not necessary that all members have something in common—it is necessary only that members of an identity group *perceive* that there is an affinity rooted in a commonality.

As already noted, the continued assertiveness of identity groups is contrary to the expectations of current social and political theory, yet the expectation that the trajectory of human development would be in a direction away from particularist identity would appear to be mistaken. Indeed, it would seem that increased democratization and modernization are not only compatible with particularist identity movements, but in the current tide of particularist assertions of identity, they are implicated as contributing factors. By placing relatively local and traditional forms of identity at risk, the conditions of democracy and modernization may produce a heightened need for identification. Prior to these modernizing influences, built-in systems of identification, such as kinship or class structures, provided individuals with an automatic, unremarked means for identification. Moreover, premodern communities tended to present individuals with a near-totalizing context for constructing their identities. Such communities offered a high degree of cultural homogeneity, value consensus, and stability in social relations—with repeated interaction with familiar individuals. In addition, premodern communities often adhered to a relatively unquestioned metaphysical and religious framework that provided preestablished meaning and purpose to one's choices (Calhoun 1994, 10ff.).

Charles Taylor has reconstructed a cultural history of modern demands for identity that attempts to explain why demands for recognition have become particularly salient within late modern democratic societies. According to this account, the democratization of society itself has made identity problematic for moderns. In predemocratic society, identity was determined for one by one's society, beginning already at birth according to the relatively fixed position of one's family within the social categories that were widely acknowledged and uncontested. But as these hierarchical categories began to erode through democratization, individuals came to experience their identities not so much as something projected onto them by their society but as something innerdirected and more individualized than the broad social classifications of premodern castes. This sea change in the way in which identity is understood has made the role of recognition much more important for modern selves—the stakes that individuals have in their identities have been raised. Identity is now personal, therefore, to fail to receive recognition is to experience personal harm. Moreover, at the same time that the stakes have become higher, it also has become more difficult to secure recognition, since one's identity is no longer fixed by the hierarchies that were taken for granted in premodern and predemocratic society (Taylor 1994, 1992, 1989). Instead, under democratic conditions, securing an identity must be worked out along with others, including those who do not belong to one's particular group. This means that often there is a broader range of individuals with whom one must negotiate one's identity (Calhoun 1994, 1–2).

Democratic conditions contribute to heightened identity group mobilization and conflict in yet another way, especially in new democracies. In many emerging democracies, ethnic and territorial divisions that had once been contained by authoritarian politics are now on display. Under democratic politics, these ethnic and territorial groupings are given the opportunity to form competitive interests within an electoral process. This tends to raise expectations for gaining recognition within the emerging democratic processes on the part of various group interests (Glickman 1995). Yet in many fledgling democratic regimes, minority groups find themselves outnumbered and facing the prospect that their interests will always be outvoted and thus permanently excluded. For these reasons, ethnic and territorial conflict is sometimes exacerbated by democratic politics.

If democratization and modernization themselves are enabling conditions for the production of particularist identity movements, then the group identities that emerge under these conditions are, at least in part, artifactual. Arising under specific social and historical conditions of modernization and democratization, these identity movements do not necessarily reflect "natural" or primordially determined divisions of humanity. Instead, they reflect the results of these new conditions. Even if some of these identities hearken to premodern and predemocratic social classifications, the specific form and virility of these identifications, under the conditions of modernization and democratization, are not to be understood apart from those conditions. When identity groups come under pressure from these modern or democratic conditions, often they react by attempting to reproduce an identity or a common culture with renewed vigor.

In some cases, group identities that would appear to express premodern identities are reproductions of identities in yet another sense. Some identities are recent artifacts constructed to call forth the assumption of a premodern history that is, strictly speaking, fictional. For example, current African tribal identities, even while appearing to have precolonial roots, often fail to express long-standing cultural divisions, but instead express divisions that are a product of colonial and postcolonial developments (Vail 1989, 1–19; Glickman 1995, 10ff.). Then there are the so-called "identity" movements associated primarily with Western liberal societies that do not attempt to reproduce premodern or predemocratic identities at all, for example, the women's movement, black power, and the gay and lesbian movement. These groups are rooted in the shared experiences of oppression, marginalization, or discrimination within societies that professes inclusion. Identities such as these ought also to be understood as artifactual rather than primordial.

In general, then, whether they arise in social contexts currently undergoing the processes of modernization and democratization, or in social contexts where these processes are long underway, identity movements tend to appear as a dialectical response to the advancement of the conditions of modernity and democracy. In which case, one cannot view the identities at the heart of these movements as relics of premodern and predemocratic realities. Indeed, no identity group can be understood apart from the historically contingent context and specific circumstances in which it appears and as such must be considered an artifact of that social and historical reality. This claim should not be taken to mean, however, that there is no more fundamental explanation of these identities than the sheer accidents of collective discourses and practices (constructivism) or the aims of elite members of a population who manipulate these identities (instrumentalism). Even if the specific expression of the identities is read as artifactual and constructed under particular historical conditions, in order to best explain the persistence generally of identity groups under modern social conditions, they must be understood as answering to basic needs of human subjectivity. Modern institutions and social groups often fail to generate a form of identification that is substantive and may at times even exacerbate the need for such identifications. Thus these conditions provide occasion for identity groups, whether old or new, to step into the breach and play a meaningful role for some individuals.

Specific identities, then, may be conceived of as artifactual and historically contingent, but the fact that there are any such group identifications would appear to be less artifactual, since some form of identity group membership would seem to be central to the development of all forms of human subjectivity. It is doubtful that humans can flourish as self-conscious forms of life within a populous social environment and engage in collective pursuits without the presence of particularist group identities that define them in contradistinction to other groups. An identity, by its nature, locates an individual within a known social horizon, thus an identity that gives no more specific location than the social horizon itself (e.g., "human") would fail as a satisfactory identification. Identification would seem to require marking relative differences between groups within a broader social environment. The most general social classifications, then, will fail to be good social locators.

The development of identity in the course of our natural lives would appear to begin with middle-sized groups. It begins neither with the largest groups, say "human," or "European," nor with the most particular and unique identifications, those that would single one out as a member of a group of one. We tend to belong first to family and neighborhood. We later add larger group identifications such as ethnicity or religion, and perhaps still later, the identifications that might arise from the likes of profession, nationality, and ideology. While some of our identifications change as we mature, middle-sized groups continue to serve as primary anchors of identity throughout our lives. Just as our physical ontology is anchored by middle-sized objects in our physical environment (persons, tables, and chairs), and not the micro- or macro-entities of physics, so too, our social ontology is anchored by mid-range entities, and our identity is dependent upon our social location relative to such entities. When we come to learn that the middle-sized objects of the physical world are actually clouds of subatomic entities, they do not become any less useful to us nonphysicists, nor is their fundamental role in our daily lives altered. Likewise, when we come to view the groups with which individuals have primary identifications as artifactual, the important role they play in providing social location is not necessarily thereby altered.

It is difficult to envision human society (except in the abstract) as developing into a social arrangement that did not prominently feature middle-sized groups as anchors for identity. A social order that was not demarcated by such things as locale, language, religion, and so on cannot plausibly be embraced. The humanist dream in which allegiances to middle-sized groups cease to be compelling and are replaced by universal and cosmopolitan sentiments would appear to be a misplaced hope. Even the modernist version of this dream, where identification and primary allegiance comes to lie not with humanity in general but with large states, seems an untenable prospect for global realization. The claim here is not to be confused with the assertion that all individuals have strong identifications with middle-sized groups, nor that all individuals will have strong nationalist or ethnic identities. Indeed, there are cosmopolitans among us—individuals who have no strong national or cultural affinities, and who relish the experience of diverse cultures. Rather, what is being asserted is that a vision of a society of only cosmopolitans is not a coherent ideal. In a thoroughly cosmopolitan society, there would be no national, cultural, or ethnic identifications relative to which one could be cosmopolitan—there would be only a sea of individuals. Some individuals can be cosmopolitan only because others remain rooted and develop primary group identifications larger than family and locale, yet smaller than humanity in general.

As should already be evident, however, this is not a case for the primordialism of identity groups. Identity groups (even gender and race) do not necessarily reflect natural divisions within humanity. First, they mark differences that are not *permanent* but arise under specific, historically appearing conditions. Even those divisions that might appear relatively perennial, such as gender, have cognitive and affective content associated with them that is altered over time and can always be reconstructed to reflect different meanings. The social boundaries of identity groups, who is included and excluded, are constantly subject to change. Social boundaries may even cease to be important at all, which is to say, an identity group might disappear. Second, these group identities do not mark *essences*, since there is no single attribute or set of attributes that all members of such groups possess.

Accordingly, the best explanation of the continued vitality of particularist identity movements in general is not that they are the residue of primordial social classifications, nor is it that they are accidental, collective constructs or the result of the instrumental aims of an elite. Rather, this vitality is best explained by reference to the function of these identities in human development and flourishing, especially the flourishing and development of subjectivity (i.e., self-conscious capacities). Identity groups would seem to serve needs beyond those of material flourishing. Indeed, even if we were to imagine the optimum social conditions for human development, where conditions of universal freedom and material well-being were met, we could expect that middle-sized group identifications would continue to play a significant role. Identity groups are to be conceived of not as primordial but as primary—they are historically constructed groups that tend to be fundamentally constitutive of their members' subjectivity.

One conclusion to be drawn from this may be that identifications with groups of a mid-range size are ineliminable from human society. Rather, these identifications must be understood as a potentially positive force. Granted, this claim cannot be established a priori, by argument on the basis of having divined some "essence" of humans for which middle-sized groups are necessary. Instead, the claim about the significance of intermediate associations for human flourishing must rely on its being consistent with our best attempts to make sense of sociological, anthropological, and psychological data. If this claim for the "primary-ness" of intermediate group identities is plausible, then group differentiation is not something to be merely tolerated within contemporary societies, nor something to be corrected for, as our societies march toward the assimilation of their minorities. Rather than assuming that human society will outgrow the need for identity groups, the groups' presence must be affirmed and the constituent affinities understood in relation to the needs and interests they serve. In forsaking the assumptions of modernization, namely, that particularist identities will ultimately subside, and that these identities do not fulfill an essential role in future human development, we also must forsake a theoretical approach that takes as its goal the elimination of particularist identities and their ensuing conflicts. Instead, what is needed is a theoretical framework that anticipates conflict and struggle and provides a means for competition among groups but at the same time avoids violence and oppression.

In affirming a primary role for identity groups in the development of human subjectivity, we need not be indiscriminate in embracing group identifications. Indeed, many particularist identifications clearly frustrate basic human needs. The challenge is to sort out the kinds of identifications that are consistent with human flourishing from those that are not, in order to be able to effect the promotion of the former over the latter. Conceived of in this manner, the theorizing of cultural pluralism takes on an emancipatory interest.

However, the emancipatory interest that informs such an approach is "broadly" emancipatory. Approaching cultural pluralism from this theoretical starting point does not imply acceptance of any particular tradition of emancipation or specific conception of human interests. It assumes merely that the promotion of human emancipation in its broadest sense (i.e., the reduction of force and harm and the promotion of human flourishing) is a good. It does not even require, ala Habermas and Benhabib, that we adopt some minimum standard for freedom that is to be universally acknowledged, such as a set of rights or procedures. In fact, modern liberal notions of emancipation may not be the most useful measure of the potential of identity groups for aiding human flourishing, since they place a high value on a form of subjectivity that involves choice, self-expression, and autonomous self-direction. Other elements of subjectivity such as a sense of belonging, a secure social location, or self-esteem may all be argued to be more basic to the flourishing of humanity in the broad sense. Since identity groups are seen as promoting these latter elements of subjectivity rather than the former, they are not commonly viewed within the liberal tradition as having emancipatory potential. As noted earlier, identity groups are built on ascriptive identities, so that one's membership is not simply a matter of choice but originates in the ascription by others, and often by a given fact of one's existence, such as one's ancestry, place of birth, and so on. Identity groups are different in kind, then, from ideological groups or secondary associations of a voluntary sort. Within liberal theory, this ascriptive nature of identity groups causes them to be viewed with much more suspicion than ideological or interest groups. Unwilling to give a political role to groups that do not reflect individual rational choices, identity groups usually are relegated to a private sphere within liberal theory. Due to its commitment to a certain conception of emancipation, then, liberalism has been unable to appreciate the emancipatory potential of identity groups.

Emancipation can involve the removal of limitations and barriers placed on the exercise of one's will or choices, and this is how it often is understood within the liberal tradition. But in its most basic form, emancipation is the release from harm and the threat of harm. The search for identity—that is, the struggle to secure recognition for one's way of being—is the struggle for emancipation in this latter sense. Identity movements, insofar as they are *identity* movements and not liberation or rights movements (which they so often are as well), are a struggle against harm—and not only physical harm, but also the harm of a truncated subjectivity, a diminishing of one's capacities for self-development and self-understanding. The issue is not simply the barriers to the exercise of the will or self-expression but the conditions of will formation and self-formation. Subjectivity, which develops only through interaction with others, is fundamentally dependent on the social context in which it is situated. The good of identity groups is actualized through the role they play in facilitating subjectivity—providing individuals with a sense of belonging, self-esteem, self-knowledge, a secure social location, and a social space that is shaped by their own needs. (These potential benefits to subjectivity are in addition to the material benefits, such as reciprocity of aid and the protection of interest, which are realized in many forms of group memberships.) To marginalize a group with which individuals have primary identifications, or to otherwise limit the ability of such groups to enjoy a social space shaped by the needs of that group, is to pose the risk of harm to those individuals' subjectivity.

Of course, these "goods" associated here with identity groups might be provided within the context of a group identity that is fundamentally at odds with the freedom and flourishing of members of other groups. The "Aryan Nation" may provide some disaffected North Americans with the elements for developing a sense of self that are denied them in the larger society—they may find fraternal support, pride, and a social space that is shaped to serve their needs—but at the same time it poses the threat of harm to black, Gay, and Jewish nonmembers. Accordingly, such groups cannot be considered emancipatory.

The greatest threat of harm that identity groups such as these pose is physical attacks and even murders perpetrated against these groups' targets of hate. But in addition to this physical violence, such groups are harmful to other groups by virtue of their very identity. This is because their self-definition entails the negation of the subjectivity claims of others (thus the appropriateness of the label "hate group"). For example, part of the core identity of the Aryan Nation as a group is the denial of a secure, self-defined social location within American society for blacks, Gays, and Jews. However, it is exactly the feeling of negation and the experience of a lack of social space that groups such as the Aryan Nation use to justify their own right to exist in the first place. That is, it is the denial of social space and the lack of recognition and support by others that lead individuals to join these groups—witness their frequent and imploring use of metaphors of "siege," "loss," and "threat," or their appeal to their "underdog" status. It is the experience of marginalization, and the harms associated with that experience, that leads to the formation of such groups in the first place and undergirds their claims for legitimacy. If we apply the broadly emancipatory requirements that take into account the basic needs for subjectivity, it becomes clear that hate groups undermine their own legitimacy as an identity group when they target the existence and flourishing of other groups. The Aryan Nation is rooted in the experience of perceived threats to its members' social location and social space and is mobilized to prevent such harms and to recover a sense of self-esteem and pride for its members. The Aryan Nation is therefore organized to prevent the very harms that it would visit on others and to secure for its members goods that it would deny others. Thus it is the logic of hate groups' own self-justifications that provides the grounds for denying them moral legitimacy or public support. Consequently, those who are not members of the Aryan Nation are under no obligation to sanction, support, or provide space for it.

There also are identity groups whose self-conception does not necessarily entail harms to other identities but whose attempt to foster the development of their own self-awareness negatively impacts on other groups. The identity of the Sons of Confederate Veterans, for example, may be grounded primarily in honoring a shared struggle for autonomy among the Southern states, and also in restoring pride in the cultural and military history of the American South. This identity does not strictly entail a condonement of slavery as part of that history, nor of racism as part of contemporary society. However, when this group promotes the display of the Confederate flag over public buildings and spaces, thereby championing a symbol whose primary meaning for African Americans is its association with slavery and racism, it clearly poses harm to the subjectivity of others. A broadly emancipatory approach to identity groups can in no way allow public sanction or support for such harmful elements of a group's identity, even if the group itself has a legitimate identity claim.

One of the first and most basic considerations in determining the emancipatory potential of identity groups, therefore, is to determine the extent to which these groups and their expressions of identity pose a harm or threat of harm to nonmembers. There is nothing inherently nonemancipatory in maintaining group differences based on a commonality of ethnicity, region, language, faith, and so on. However, since such identities are capable of much harm to nonmembers, each must be examined with respect to its impact on the flourishing of nonmembers, that is, each must be examined individually with respect to broadly emancipatory concerns.

There is yet another class of potential harms that identity movements pose that must be considered from the standpoint of broadly emancipatory expectations. The concerns over potential harms touched upon in the aforementioned examples center on the relation of identity groups to nonmembers, specifically to individuals who stand in an external relation to the identity group. However, the impact of identity groups on their own members, and their own internal minorities, also must be considered. Many identity movements around the world are associated with projects that have nationalist or at least culturally hegemonic aims. These groups tend to harbor aims of establishing a self-determined social order (often a political order as well) that would encompass an ethnic, a religious, or a cultural homogeneity. Thus these identities often eschew pluralism and display intolerance for groups perceived as competitors to their own attempt to secure hegemony. This is yet another reason liberal theory has long been suspicious of identity groups. These groups are seen not only as having an ascriptive, nonvoluntary nature as limiting the autonomy of individuals who fall under their sphere of influence.

Can an identity group that fails to embrace either pluralism or democratization be understood as being compatible with broadly emancipatory ends? An approach to this question can be made by evaluating identity groups according to their ability to serve members' sense of belonging, self-esteem, self-knowledge, and security of social location, and to provide members with a social space shaped by their own needs. For members whose identities are consistent with those of the identity group, a lack of diversity and openness to other identities would not seem to threaten their sense of belonging, social location, and so on. However, the concern is over those individuals whose identity is not consistent with the homogeneity sought by the identity group in question. Of critical importance, therefore, is whether such individuals can readily exclude themselves from the authority or expectations of the would-be homogeneous order of the identity group in question, or whether the identity group claims a political hegemony over a population (i.e., can such individuals "convert out" of the group identity). This is not a matter of whether such individuals are in a position to make authentic choices between life alternatives—certainly many conservative religious or otherwise strictly bounded groups provide their members with a very limited choice in this sense. The issue is a more basic one of whether they have the freedom to legally and politically opt out. If there is a claim to political hegemony, then internal minorities must be granted the room to develop their own identities and express them in a manner consistent with the conditions of emancipation. For example, since the Taliban would claim political hegemony in Afghanistan, it must embrace pluralism and allow for internal minorities within its sphere of authority if it is to be consistent with broadly emancipatory requirements. But the Amish, who, like the Taliban, do not actively teach or expose their children to other ways of life, nor provide them with the intellectual or emotional tools to opt out of the group identity, are nonetheless in accordance with broadly emancipatory requirements, because they do not claim political hegemony over any territory. According to the demands of avoiding harm and threat of harm, there is no necessary requirement that a group which is not a threat to others, or its own members, must embrace pluralism or democracy.

In conclusion, then, identity groups should be understood in light of their emancipatory role in providing for the conditions for the development of subjectivity. This emancipatory potential, moreover, must conform to the broadly emancipatory requirements of avoiding harm and the threat of harm to others—both members and nonmembers. Harm is not to be conceived of solely in terms of physical well-being but also in terms of the impact on individuals' subjectivity. Therefore, identity groups can be measured not only by harms of violence or exploitation but also by harms to subjectivity, that is, the risk that they pose to either members' or nonmembers' sense of belonging, self-esteem, and secure social location, or their capacity to live in a social space that is shaped by their own needs.

The framework proposed here for acknowledging the emancipatory potential of identity groups is both broad and abstract. Its abstractness means that it is unsatisfactory as a theory in its own right and remains only propaedeutic to theory construction. Its breadth (i.e., its consideration of all identity movements whether or not they are consistent with liberal expectations) is essential if it is to escape the fault of universalizing culturally specific conceptions of emancipation.

REFERENCES

Calhoun, Craig. 1994. "Preface." Pp. 1–7 in *Social Theory and the Politics of Identity*, ed. Craig Calhoun. Cambridge: Blackwell.

———. 1994. "Social Theory and the Politics of Identity." Pp. 9–36 in *Social Theory and the Politics of Identity*, ed. Craig Calhoun. Cambridge: Blackwell.

Glickman, Harvey. 1995. "Issues in the Analysis of Ethnic Conflict and Democratization Processes in Africa Today." Pp. 1–31 in *Ethnic Conflict and Democratization in Africa*, ed. Harvey Glickman. Atlanta: The African Studies Associated Press.

Taylor, Charles. 1989. *Sources of the Self: The Making of Modern Identity.* Cambridge: Harvard University Press.

———. 1992. *The Ethics of Authenticity.* Cambridge: Harvard University Press.

———. 1994. "Politics of Recognition." Pp. 25–73 in *Multiculturalism: Examining the Politics of Recognition,* ed. Amy Guttman. Princeton: Princeton University Press.

Vail, Leroy. 1989. "Introduction." Pp. 1–19 in *The Creation of Tribalism in Africa,* ed. Leroy Vail. Berkeley: University of California Press.

Chapter 3

The Ethnic State

The Structural Generation
of Ethnic Conflict
by the International System

Virginia Q. Tilley

As has already been noted in the preceding chapter, social scientists have puzzled over the persistence of ethnic conflict in the "modern" world. Since the late nineteenth century, it has been believed that "modernization"—of societies, of governments—would lay such conflicts to rest. Especially in the 1950s, after World War II and the horrors of the Nazi Holocaust and of Japanese racist imperialism in Asia, prevailing intellectual thought and official nationalist doctrines in North America and Europe swung away from ethnic and racial nationalism and toward ideas of *civic* nationalism, in which all ethnic and racial groups within a state's borders would share equal protection and opportunities under a common set of laws (Barkin and Cronin 1994). In this new, modern (and supposedly more "rational") climate, many political theorists shared a new optimism that ethnic passions and rivalries surely would lose relevance and subside.

Instead, those passions and rivalries persisted. In the post–Cold War era, they even seem to be proliferating. Efforts by social scientists to explain this persistence have generated a myriad of studies examining a gamut of culprits: group psychologies, culture, biased electoral systems, race-based labor systems, and self-serving ethnic leaderships, to name just a few. Many of these studies have offered valuable insights into the dynamics of particular ethnic conflicts. Still, one factor has remained neglected in all of them: the role of the state.

Scholars of ethnic conflict generally assume, without giving it much direct attention, that the state itself is ethnically neutral. Of course, in making this observation, I do not use "state" to mean *government*. We all recognize that a state's government may be "captured" by an ethnic group and used to prejudicial ends.[1] And clearly, within many countries, governments foster racial and ethnic discrimination, whether such effects are intended or not. It also is the case that some governments are so weak that they seem to have little or no role in a local conflict. Especially in some Third World regions and in some post–Soviet states, power is so diffused and fragmented (among capitalist entrepreneurs, local strongmen, or various patronage networks) that the "state," in any coherent governmental sense, seems a mere fiction. Some historians and anthropologists, grappling with difficult conditions in such states, can get rather testy at the mere mention of the "state" for this reason. Political scientists in the same conditions, having faith in the potentials of the "civic nationalism," mentioned earlier, may readily identify "state weakness" as a key factor in the outbreak of ethnic conflict.[2] Their policy prescriptions, therefore, often advocate stronger and more effective "state" institutions.

In this chapter, I refer to the state in its external or international sense: as the sovereign boundary for state politics; the legal demarcation of the territory in which national politics play out; a kind of international-institutional shell in which governments take shape and may change over time. The state in this sense—as a unit of the international system—is the outward face of entities such as "Russia" and "Nigeria"; domestically, it is the territorial sovereign frame for national politics, and it can embrace very different kinds of government. It is in this abstract, background sense that the state is generally ignored, as being too sterile, "rational," and/or "universal" to sustain any ethnic quality or bias of its own. Its only role in ethnic conflict would appear to be in defining a particular territory as a single political arena, a condition that creates a central government that groups may then compete to control (see, e.g., Ganguly and Taras 1998).

I argue, however, that the modern state is not so neutral, or simply a backdrop or passive boundary framing the domestic political arena. Rather, the state can have ethnic effects in at least three ways. First, all states today conform to a kind of *institutional template*, imposed by international criteria, whose design affects the selection of state elites and also contributes to those elites' own ethnic ideas. Second, the state's own security concerns compel *national integration*, a project notorious for its ethnic tensions. Third, as international actors, some states obtain *"ethnic" identities* as state elites negotiate the state's alliances and other relations on the international stage. Together, these ethnic effects make the state a contributor to what I call the *ethnic environment*: the body of (often competing) perceptions, ideas, doctrines, and values, playing out in the national political arena, which establishes ethnic and racial identities that accompany and rationalize their power relations and determine what ethno-political claims can be made effectively, by any actor, in national politics.

This analysis of the state is drawn from studies of specific cases of ethnic conflict, but in the discussion that follows I will cite such cases only briefly, as illustrations and to suggest further debate. My central argument is more general: identifying the state's role can help identify certain political avenues for mitigating some of the conditions that foster ethnic conflict.

"SOCIALIZATION" AND ETHNIC CONFLICT

When we look at a map of the world today, we see that it is entirely divided up into territorial units called "states." Furthermore, we understand something fairly specific about these "states." To survive in its international environment—even to exist as an entity—every state must sustain a basic set of institutions that allows it to function as a state and be recognized as a state by other states. Once recognized, each state then enjoys the juridical status of "state": that is, it operates according to the same body of international laws, rules, and norms regarding its sovereignty, privileges, and obligations. This homogeneity allows realist and neorealist theorists of international relations (IR) to treat states as "like units": constituted as the same kind of entity whether large or small, weak or strong, facing the same conditions in the international system, and motivated primarily by concerns for their own security and survival (Carr 1939; Waltz 1979). The same idea supports more liberal IR theory as well, which views states as roughly analogous to individuals who form the world "community" or a "society" of states, through negotiations and rule making (Bull 1977; Watson 1992).

The state's institutional homogeneity did not come about overnight. In Europe, the modern nation-state evolved through centuries of war, rule making, institution building, legal thought, and philosophical debates related to intensifying production and long-distance trade (C. Tilly 1985; Spruyt 1994). Nor does the state's global scope as a single model, or template, represent the historical culmination of some voluntary global negotiation among equals. European powers exported their (evolving) ideas, rules, and norms about statehood (and eventually nationhood) to the rest of the world through the pressures and outright military force associated with colonialism and imperialism. Local systems of governance that did not match Europe's criteria were not granted recognition and admission to the "family of nations" (Gong 1994). In other words, they lost control over their territory and came under European control.

The experience of this pressure inspired elites all over the world to try to emulate Europe's standards for statehood: that is, to manifest as a "civilized" society by European standards, with an effective central government capable of sustaining the conditions that European powers demanded for international trade (laws, security, courts, a reliably functioning port, and so forth). But as these demands became more institutionally complex in Europe, the project of matching Europe's "standard of civilization" became more complicated, exact, and demanding, and most non-European peoples and elites

ultimately failed in the attempt. Europe eventually carved up all of the
Americas, Africa, and South and Southeast Asia on the "legal" justification
that they lacked coherent governments and therefore were "empty lands," or
they were suffering in anarchy, backwardness, and "darkness." Most of those
regions gained independence in the mid-twentieth century only by accepting
European terms for decolonization, which now included very elaborate European models of nation-statehood. Those who clung to divergent paths—for
example, the tribes of nineteenth-century Iran (Arjomand 1988), or Native
Americans (Berman 1992)—generally lost territory, power, and sometimes
even a place in history.

This great convergence of a formerly diverse world into a single state
model has been called "socialization" in the IR literature (Ikenberry and
Kupchan 1990). Socialization has had several lasting effects on the persistence of ethnic conflict. First, it has had a powerful effect in selecting political
elites. Under the conditions of European pressure, only those peoples (or, in
practice, their educated classes) capable of mastering the modern state's design could successfully retain or obtain state power. Some elites reconfigured
themselves to suit these criteria: for example, in Japan, the Meiji Restoration
reformers recognized the urgency of meeting the narrowing European standards and, in a few decades, redesigned their entire governing system, even
their entire society. Other elites were cultivated by Europeans to assume
control of newly independent states (designed, of course, in accordance with
European standards), for example, the Tutsi in Rwanda. Alternatively, the
Sabaah family of Kuwait and the al-Nahayan family of Abu Dhabi, both
comprador families, were selected by the British to become "princes" (emirs)
of governments already built of British design and even sustaining a continuing British staff presence (Abdulla 1984).

Despite a difficult and violent past, some observers might view this "socialization" of state elites as ultimately beneficial, because today it allows for
improved communications and the hope for global accord. Unfortunately, the
selection process also has created "losers": a range of conflicts reflecting the
bitter resentments of those *not* selected—for example, the Hutus, the Pales-
tinians, the Kurds, and the Tamils—whose enduring resentments and ambitions to regain sovereignty over lost territory have fueled many of our most
violent conflicts. Less obvious is the situation of those peoples whose claim
to sovereignty was lost through a more subtle method: their redefinition as
other kinds of actors, such as "ethnic groups." The U.S. context offers an
example of how the sovereignty of such peoples disappeared as the modern
state took shape. Many native peoples in North America were recognized in
British and French diplomacy as "nations" through the early eighteenth century, as the diplomatic record has confirmed (Berman 1992); "Indian treaties"
were understood as international treaties, negotiated in accordance with the
Law of Nations. That earlier sovereign status actually was acknowledged

when "the Indians" were redefined by the U.S. Supreme Court, in the 1830s, as "domestic dependent nations" to explain their effective absorption by the United States.[3] But as time passed, this diplomatic standing was obscured and forgotten, and native peoples were considered *never to have been nations*. In 1890, the U.S. Supreme Court declared that the Native American peoples had never enjoyed true sovereignty, and that the "nation" label had merely been a rhetorical device to placate them, to facilitate their removal and subjugation.[4] Thus the idea that Indian peoples are inherently *incapable of* state sovereignty became retroactively naturalized in law and also in political theory, as part of the larger framework that rationalized the modern state. For this reason, Native Americans—and indigenous peoples generally—today must struggle against the ideas, presumptions, and values that support the entire modern state system in their efforts to regain some control over their territories, societies, and lives.

A third effect of socialization has been to influence how state elites understand domestic cultural diversity. First, the close rivalries among ethnic groups for state power have triggered new discourses about identity, which serve competing agendas. For example, in Burundi and Rwanda, "Tutsi" and "Hutu" are identities that are now understood quite differently—and more rigidly—than they were prior to state formation. Second, concerns to be "civilized" continue to affect state elite thinking—so we find among them certain common language about, and concepts of, "backwardness," hence, the extensive debates among state elites in Africa, Asia, and Latin America about their "backward" populations and worries about any "primitive" elements in the nation—for example, the "Indian problem." Such concerns have translated historically into dismissive treatment, deliberate marginalization, or forced assimilation projects that have left a legacy of bitter resentment and resistance among groups so targeted. That same resentment has fed the new wave of movements by "indigenous and tribal peoples," launched in the 1980s, such as those of the Guatemalan Mayan peoples, the Ecuadorean confederations, the Australian Aborigines, the New Zealand Maoris, some African nomadic peoples such as the Namibian San, and numerous "tribal" groups in South and Southeast Asian states.[5] The growing political clout of such movements has been startling to many observers who, uncritically accepting the rhetoric of state elites and the tenets of modernization theory, had supposed such groups to be ethnically irrelevant, or nearing extinction.[6]

A fourth ethnic dimension of socialization is its effect on ethnic biases within government bureaucracies. To operate successfully in international affairs, government institutions must be more or less congruent with those of other states: for example, they must abide by the codes and norms of international diplomacy and fit into the demands of international finance and trade (Finnemore 1996). Because of this necessity, international standards feed into the state's domestic institutional design and bureaucratic culture in ways that may generate ethnic biases even where prejudice or ethnic conflict is not intended.

To explore this point, we must consider that ethnic differences in a country may include different meaning systems that can clash with one another. For example, today, white ethnic groups in the United States differ in some ways (or they would not self-identify as "ethnic"). But particularly in the middle and upper classes, people from different U.S. white ethnic groups generally share a very similar worldview and most popular culture, and so they can work together without much cultural friction. In contrast, some ethnic identities are more deeply rooted in the group's social system: for example, nomadism, consensus-based decision making, or profoundly different ideas about such social basics as time, gender, "face," or language. In these cases, the government's bureaucratic culture will tend to filter access to public or even higher-level private employment to certain groups. To gain such access, minority individuals must assimilate, which is a burden. Some individuals will succeed in such projects, but many will find the task varyingly difficult (depending on the cultural distance to be crossed), and some may avoid it altogether, on personal but also possibly on political grounds. Although bureaucracies can be modified to be more flexible about such matters, no bureaucracy can absorb the full gamut of human cultural norms. Such embedded ethnic or racial biases in government are old news to students of ethnic and racial conflict. Important here, however, is that such filters are not generated solely by domestic factors—such as the ethnic identity of the elite— but also by the international norms that have compelled the state's institutions to assume a certain configuration, and therefore have infused the bureaucratic culture with particular cultural biases (and helped select that elite).[7]

In all of these ways, socialization has influenced ethnic tensions and conflict in each state's own domestic arena. In other words, the international criteria for statehood have contributed to the norms, ideas, and values, and therefore the politics, of the domestic ethnic environment. The ethnic environment is so important to the "who gets what" of politics that controlling it is a state project in itself. We can examine that project through a different lens by looking at one prominent dimension: the politics of nationalism and national integration, in which, again, we can identify the state's contribution.

NATIONALISM AND NATION BUILDING

Social scientists have long recognized that nationalism can foster ethnic conflict in several ways. Classically, nationalisms are "imagined" by intellectuals and state builders (Anderson 1991; Hobsbawm 1990) whose own cultural biases and assumptions infuse their political thinking about the national identity.

Such thinking may include general concepts of "civilization," which have their own biases (e.g., against "primitive" cultures, as discussed earlier). Usually though biases are much more ethnically specific. Whether intentionally or unintentionally, nationalists tend to propose their own ethnic symbols and traditions as being fundamental to the national ideology, and so they give the imagined "nation" a particular ethnic configuration centered on themselves, hence, U.S. schoolchildren hear about the "Pilgrim Fathers" and so forth. In earlier eras, theorists and philosophers celebrated the glories of such *ethno-nationalist* discourses. Post–Cold War theorists have tended toward greater sensitivity to the cost. Where ethno-nationalist doctrines too severely elevate one domestic group at the expense of another, they have contributed to ethnic resentment and conflict (Smith 1986).

Liberal response to such problems has been to target the nationalist doctrines and perhaps to blame the shortsighted policies of ignorant, prejudiced, and/or self-serving elites. The liberal answer, as noted in this chapter's introduction, is to promote *civic* nationalism that can supposedly bridge ethnic differences and defuse ethnic tensions.[8] It is in this light that the modern (civic) nation-state appears to many liberal thinkers as the logical forum for *resolving* ethnic conflict because, at least theoretically, it provides the neutral forum in which ethnicity can become irrelevant to the individual's civil liberties and protections. Classic liberalism focuses on the rights of individuals in this setting, but *group rights* also can be addressed in liberal thought, under the rubric of cultural pluralism. These approaches hold that if properly recognized and granted a political voice and perhaps a few symbolic concessions, ethnic tensions will find reconciliation and eventually lose public force (see, e.g., Young 1976; Horowitz 1985; Vail 1989). All of these approaches assume that while the state might be "captured" by a particular dominant ethnic group, the state at root represents a neutral framework in which competitive group claims can be fairly negotiated. And certainly a significant number of successes can support faith in the nation-state in this respect.

Yet a myriad of failures has dampened such optimism, and some recent literature has raised the question of whether nation building can ever be fully divorced from ethnic bias. Anthony Smith (1986) and others have pointed out that nationalism almost necessarily entails ethnic biases because national institutions and ideologies always incorporate ethnically biased features, such as an official language. Will Kymlicka (1994) has observed that actual *cultural diversity*—differences in meanings and values, and in how groups are internally organized—may prevent a system from being truly inclusive. For example, Canadian law does not embrace and protect the system of collective land use employed by Canada's native peoples, although it fully serves the property needs of another Canadian ethnic group, the Quebecois.

Yet even these corrective studies overlook the fact that nationalism also reflects the state's own agendas regarding its domestic environment. Of course, states are not sentient actors, but they can have independent agendas in the sense that in order for the state to survive some key conditions are imperative. Such state "imperatives" inform and constrain the choices of state elites, who must adopt those imperatives in assessing and deciding on state policy or risk losing control of state power (Young 1994). In this sense, the state is an interested "actor" in its own arena, in two senses.

First, unless it is entirely dependent on some foreign power for protection, a state must maintain some capacity to defend itself militarily. Furthermore, to avoid fragmentation and collapse, it must maintain some kind of force to put down internal rebellions and secessionist groups. To do this, the modern state needs two things: people to staff its security forces and funds to pay and supply them. For most states, such funds come from taxes. Both people and taxes can be obtained through compulsion, but not efficiently. For most modern states, security is therefore closely tied to popular cooperation—at least by a significant percentage of the population—with military service and perhaps with the tax levies necessary to support security forces and other government institutions. Domestic hegemony in these spheres thus becomes an agenda of the state itself, adding weight to the nation-building project. However weak, poor, or hated the government, most state nationalisms have accomplished surprising degrees of success in this project, when judged by the standards of popular belief in the legitimacy of the state as defender of the nation and willingness to serve militarily in risky situations. Even where a citizenry is widely disillusioned and cynical about the government, a sense of belonging to that state usually will persist.

Second, the international standing of the modern state rests partly on its ability to manifest as a "nation-state": that is, a territory embracing a population unified at least by the common will to be under one government (which, from the perspective of the state elite, is the one it controls). In practice, of course, few states enjoy total unity in this sense. A few so-called "nation-states" exist more as diplomatic fictions than as facts—that is, they are "juridical" rather than "empirical" (Jackson and Rosberg 1982); many more enjoy the support of only some portion of the population, and most have some groups or peoples whose acceptance of the state's sovereignty is only contingent on the absence of alternatives. But even *fictional* unity is key to states, because it supports the basic diplomatic premise that the state's diplomatic corps truly represents and can defend and advocate for the state territory's population in international forums and, even more important, that the state's government will ensure that population's adherence to its international agreements.

For this reason, state elites normally are concerned with the state's international *image* of unity. Therefore, even if they might otherwise not care much about actual ethnic divisions, an ethnic conflict that undermines the government's international credibility as the representative of the territory will inspire state elites to act. Some actions are violent—genocides or mass expulsions—although the international influence on these practices may be difficult to separate from their domestic motives. Other tactics, however, are more clearly oriented toward international pressures, for example, when state representatives offer rhetorical defenses against charges of human rights abuses by human rights organizations (such as Amnesty International), in forums such as the United Nations Commission on Human Rights. Typically in such settings state spokespeople argue that ethnic divisions actually are inconsequential (Lemarchand 1996), or that they are anachronisms, remnants of earlier (colonial, imperial) interventions that the hapless, decolonized state has yet to overcome, or that they are being pumped up by agitators ("ethnic entrepreneurs") and have no real social substance. A government also may draw on "civilization" discourses to define some group as "backward," "irrational," "primitive," or otherwise unqualified to challenge the state's legitimacy.

Important here is that such claims are part of official state policy, to the international community, about domestic ethnic identities and relations within the country. They therefore reinforce the state's posture in its domestic ethnic environment as well. For example, responding to international human rights critics, the Algerian government has long claimed that the Berbers are assimilated to Arab cultural norms, and that no significant ethnic conflict exists there. This claim is an impediment to any official state recognition that Berber ethnic sentiment remains strong and to the state's willingness to accommodate Berber ethnic demands through even minor reforms. In this case, concern for the image of national unity has aggravated ethnic tensions (partly because unity is attached to the state's identity, as discussed later). On the other hand, international scrutiny in cases of ethnic conflict can be crucial to limiting government repression and violence, largely because of the potential damage to the state's international prestige. For example, the premise of an ethnically pluralist, unified nation has restrained Mexican state security forces from unlimited attacks on the Zapatista movement in Chiapas. Too much violence would establish the Mexican state, in international eyes, as maintaining its hegemony by force and would demolish the (already shaky) idea that the nation is unified.

To undo these ethnic tensions in the "nation-state" concept, the rigid association of states with unified nations would have to be softened or abandoned. For this reason, ethnic movements such as those of the Guatemala Mayan and Ecuadorean indigenous peoples have proposed that their states be reconceptualized as "multinational states." These projects are resisted by the dominant societies in these countries first, and most obviously, because a state built on multinationalism might not serve elite interests so well. But broader questions also are raised, which are harder to answer, for if the state is merely a territorial authority, embracing several "nations," what central core of principles would determine the state's policies? Indeed, if they do not represent unified nations, what is the moral justification for states—at least as is presently understood?

These difficult questions also have international implications, because the mechanisms for international diplomacy and trade assume that state territories speak with one voice and will form alliances and enter into trading blocs in predictable, consistent ways. In this sense, for international purposes, states are assumed to have certain "identities," that is, certain policy tendencies that help stabilize their security and trade relations.

To consider how international concerns about state identities translate into ethnic effects in the domestic ethnic environment, we need to address yet another dimension of the state. In an earlier discussion, we examined the state in its more liberal and institutional senses. We saw how its ethnic biases emerge from its function as a shell for the domestic arena: that it is an institutional template, historically biased toward European standards of civilization, still exclusive of certain cultural variations, and structurally compelled by its international environment to undertake national integration. But the ethnic environment also is affected by the kind of "identity" that is attached to the state's international relations. This matter brings us to consider the ethnic state in a more classically realist IR sense, as a strategic, unitary actor in the international system.

STATE IDENTITY POLITICS

"Identity" is a concept that is under increasing scrutiny by international relations theorists. How the *national* and *state* identities overlap and interplay is our focus here. As discussed earlier, *national* identity is an old and a much-labored subject of attention in studies of ethnic conflict. National identities, as understood here, are bodies of concepts developed domestically, over time and by many thinkers (philosophers, artists, poets, newspaper editors, politicians), to define the collective character and common will of the polity. National identities typically include a formative history, ethnic components such as dress and language, and ideas about collective political values. As many theorists have observed, developing the national identity is a project intimately connected to the more material dimensions of national integration (road building, imposing a single language, establishing effective policing and courts, ensuring military service, and so forth). Over time, if successful, the national identity naturalizes in popular thought as a kind of perceived "given": that is, while its exact details may be fluid, "Canadian" and "American"—or even more tortured identities such as "Salvadoran"—remain identities that most citizens internalize into their sense of themselves.

But *state* identity formation, as understood here, is a distinct concept: a quality, or set of qualities, symbolically ascribed to the state by elites, meaningful to the international community, and understood to determine the state's *foreign* policy orientation. State identities can be built on any set of principles. For example, in the Cold War era, an identity such as "buffer," or "non-aligned" would signal a state's position in relation to the U.S.–Soviet rivalry. In the post–Cold War period, an identification such as "liberal" and "democratic" has helped some former Soviet states reorient and solidify their alliances toward Western Europe and the United States. A state's identity also may be defined for it by other states, to justify sanctions or reprisals (e.g., "terrorist" or "outlaw" states). That such identities are contested, and to some extent fluid, does not diminish their importance. Indeed, they often are hotly debated, precisely because they are both fluid and important, particularly in defining the state's trade and security communities. For example, major economic interests drive the ongoing debates about which states belong in "Western," "Central," or "Southern" Europe, or whether "Europe" can expand to include historically "non-European" states, such as Turkey.

When state identities are conceptually associated with traits such as race (e.g., "black Africa," or "white" settler colonial states), language (e.g., Arabic, Francophonie), religion (e.g., Christianity, Islam, Confucianism), or more general ideas about "culture" (e.g., "Arab," "European," or "Latin American"), they become more "ethnic." Such identities often are regional, but not solely so: indeed, they may jump over considerable distances, as in the case of "white Australia" (discussed later). The exact meanings of all of these identities—are fluid and contested (by insiders and outsiders). Also, like people, states may have multiple identities: for example, Chile is simultaneously a "western," "Latin American," "southern Cone," and "Pacific Rim" state, with all of these identities being important in different settings (and sometimes in conflict, around questions of, say, which trading bloc to join).

Most importantly, for our purposes here, a *state's* "ethnic" identity forms in response to its external environment. Therefore, although it will certainly draw on domestic ethnic and racial conditions and the nationalist identity, the state identity may differ in some ways from the national identity as it is articulated in domestic settings. A state's identity strategy can therefore impact on the domestic ethnic environment in several distinct ways. First, when a state elite claims a particular identity for the state, such as "Arab," the international importance of that claim may alter the political significance of any group inside of the country that undermines the claim. For example, we noticed earlier that Algeria denied Berber ethnic efforts to gain some concessions from the state to support Berber ethnic agendas. That policy, however, was not merely concerned with affirming Algeria's national unity. Algeria's postindependence policy toward the Berbers took shape in the 1960s in the context of Arab nationalism, a regional identity that attracted immense political passions and energies associated with decolonization. Embracing about twenty states, this "Arab" state identity was the normative basis for the Arab

League, convened as a security community. Hence, it was an interplay of security and identity concepts, gelling around the concept of "Arabness," which inspired and guided the Algerian elite's efforts to launch the "Arabization" program that eliminated long-standing Berber language rights. Because they corroded the "Arabness" of the country, Berber ethno-political aspirations manifested to state elites as sedition, which the regime then forcibly suppressed (Stone 1997).

Australia offers a second example of how an international identity strategy can feed into changing domestic ethnic politics. From its conversion to commonwealth status (in 1901) through the 1970s, Australia maintained a deliberately "white" or "Anglo" state identity. Clearly concerned with domestic ideas connecting whiteness to democracy and British political values generally (Kane 1997), this "white Australia" policy also served to confirm the country's "natural" (cultural, ethnic, and racial) ties to Britain and to the United States—ties clearly vital to Australia's trade and security. One policy mechanism serving this identity strategy was Australia's "white-only" immigration laws, which excluded "Asian" immigration (Jupp 1997). Since the mid-1970s, however, Australia has faced very different international conditions. The "Asia-Pacific" has boomed economically, and closer trade ties have become increasingly important to Australia's economic security. To enter into close coordination with "Asian" states and to join "Asian" trading blocs, Australia has had to mitigate its ostentatiously "Anglo" image. One measure has been to modify its laws to allow more Asian immigration. The consequences of this shift for state policy and domestic ethnic relations in Australia have run both ways. On the one hand, a more open immigration policy has permitted a small but socially significant increase in Australia's Asian population (mostly Chinese). On the other hand, that small increase has contributed to a white racial nationalist backlash, given political clout in 1999 through recent electoral advances of the "One Nation" party led by Pauline Hanson. Of course, immigration often raises such tensions independently of external state-identity concerns. Still, Australia's new external posture as an "Asia-Pacific" state both informed and reinforced this shift in state immigration policy (Hudson and Stokes 1997).

A third example of "ethnic" state identity politics is the concept of complete racial mixture, or *mestizaje* (often labeled simply "la raza" or "the race"), which has become part of the "Latin American" state identity discourse. The historical, geostrategic origins and motives of this popular idea often are overlooked. In the late nineteenth and early twentieth centuries, British and U.S. racial theorists were promoting the superiority of "whites" over a descending order of progressively darker "races." These racial "sciences" took shape in their own corner of academia and were not always explicitly political. But they were closely tied to, and certainly used for, international political concerns: justifying British and U.S. imperialism, by explaining the innately limited capacity of darker peoples to "civilization" and "progress." Concerned with avoiding European and U.S. hegemony, or even colonial conquest, Latin American intellectuals first reacted to this new "science" with various calls to "whiten" their nations—for example, by encouraging white immigration. By the 1920s, however, the impossibility of "whitening" Latin America, coupled with some fresh anthropological ideas about "race" itself, generated a counter discourse. Intellectuals such as Manuel Gamio (1916) and Jose Vasconcelos (1925) argued that "Latin" America actually represented a superior racial type, because it was a hybrid of the indigenous peoples with all of the immigrant European races, therefore it fused the best qualities of each race into a new and glorified "cosmic race." This idea of racial mixture—mestizaje—became a key ingredient in crafting the new, anti-hegemonic, "Latin American" identity bloc and became attached to many "Latin American" member states' national ideologies.

The same idea reflected inward to affect the ethnic environments in profound ways. First, although it symbolically celebrated the Indian of the Conquest era, the new "Latin American" identity emphasized its racially "Latin" element: that is, the Spanish and French origins of the settler society. In sustaining this Eurocentric orientation, mestizaje actually devalued living indigenous cultures as "primitive" and "backward." Second, mestizaje essentially "undefined" formerly distinct racial groups. This move actually helped support the eradication of long-established indigenous group privileges, such as collective land rights (Adams 1967; Gould 1998). It also seemed to make unnecessary any public need to address embedded racist attitudes toward "Indians" and blacks, because racial divisions supposedly had been eliminated. Today, both indigenous peoples and Afro-Latinos face major battles to simply gain public confirmation of enduring racial discrimination in their societies—an admission that is a necessary prerequisite to any talk of reform. Thus mestizaje, designed partly to serve foreign policy and actually at odds with domestic conditions, has altered the terms by which domestic ethno-racial politics in Latin America can be imagined and pursued.

The aforementioned examples illustrate how "ethnic" state identity politics can affect domestic ethnic conflict in several ways. First, it can contribute to state elite understanding (and valuing) of ethnic and racial identities, both of domestic groups and of the nation as a whole. Second, by doing so, a state identity shift can alter the ethnic environment for domestic groups by effecting changes in policy and attitudes. Third, "ethnic" state identities create enduring links between a state's foreign policy and domestic conditions, by connecting the *state* identity to the *national* identity. Fourth, it can trigger counter-discourses by domestic groups and contribute to their specific arguments.

CONCLUSION

Presumptions that the modern state is ethnically neutral are gravely misplaced. The modern state is heavily implicated in ethnic conflict: in its institutional design, in its pressures on the domestic "national" environment, and sometimes through its identity politics, reflecting its own security imperatives. I do not argue here that state interests determine ethnic politics, or that the state's international concerns always trump domestic ethnic interests. Rather, I propose that the state generates various ethnic effects that contribute unevenly and inconsistently to elite policy choices and ethnopolitical strategies, and so are best treated as variables. But that contribution can be potent, and the degree and nature of the state's role certainly should be considered in any careful study of ethnic conflict.

So is the modern state the secret villain in the perpetuation and proliferation of ethnic conflict around the world? Yes and no. The modern state establishes conditions that foster ethnic conflict, and we should stop being surprised that ethnic conflict is so prevalent. But the state's evaporation or dissolution, which some people think is now happening with "globalization," would not solve the problem. Certainly transnational movements can undercut the power of state elites and help provide long-denied resources to marginalized groups; but transnational movements also can develop hegemonic biases that discriminate against weaker players. Local autonomy to ethnic groups can restore more meaningful and appropriate self-government to communities and peoples, but greater local power also may trigger intergroup jealousies, reduce motives to cooperate, and lead to greater tension. Global human rights can foster a more pluralistic idea of the "nation" and restrain governments from acting brutally, but in practice, human rights regimes are still heavily dominated by first-world groups and cosmopolitan upper classes, and so are not immune to their own biases or to developing new "standards of civilization." The ethnic effects of the modern state are likely to mutate into these new systems rather than to disappear entirely, and many ethnic tensions may still be unaddressed.

Still, to address ethnic conflict effectively, a fuller appreciation for the modern state's complicity in ethnic conflict is vital. At a minimum, political scientists should not uncritically call for "stronger states" as a solution to ethnic conflict in developing regions. If the ideas presented here are sound, a much more complicated treatment of the state's role is necessary if we hope to resolve ethnic conflicts, or perhaps simply to soften their violence and reduce their number.

NOTES

1. For example, see Marx (1998) for a recent comparative study of how the state is enlisted to uphold a racial or an ethnic order in Brazil, the United States, and South Africa.

2. See, for example, Posen (1993), Synder (1993), and Lake and Rothchild (1998).

3. *The Cherokee Nation* v. *The State of Georgia*, 30 U. S. (5 Pet.) 1 (1831).

4. *Cherokee Nation* v. *Southern Kan. Ry.*, 135 U. S. 641 (1890), 654.

5. For a valuable collected volume on the politics of indigenous and tribal peoples, see Van Cott (1995). On Latin American peoples, see Urban and Sherzer (1990). For analyses attempting a global scope, also see Aga Khan and bin Talal (1987) and Burger (1987).

6. A prominent example of this assumption was the canon on democratization in Latin America, which long ignored even glaring ethnic issues: see, for example, articles in Linz and Stepan (1978), Collier (1979), Diamond, Linz, and Lipset (1989), and O'Donnell and Schmitter (1986). More recent standard survey texts continue to omit such politics and to conflate indigenous and peasant issues: see treatments of Guatemala, Ecuador, and Peru in Wiarda and Kline (1996) and Skidmore and Smith (1997). Literature on social movements began to correct the hegemonic omission, but only unevenly: see, for example, Eckstein (1989) and Escobar and Alvarez (1992).

7. On the Maya, see especially Warren (1998).

8. On optimistic views of civic nationalism, see, for example, Steinberg (1989). On the difference between civic and ethnic nationalisms, see Smith (1986). On the ascendance of civic nationalism as a conceptual corollary of the post–World War II concept, that state legitimacy rests on territorial rather than ethno-national cohesion, see Barkin and Cronin (1994).

REFERENCES

Abdulla, Abdulkhalek. 1984. *Political Dependency: The Case of the United Arab Emirates.* Unpublished dissertation, Center for Contemporary Arab Studies, Georgetown University, Washington, D. C.

Adams, Richard. 1967. "Nationalization." *Handbook of Middle American Peoples*, vol. 6. Austin: University of Texas Press, 469–89.

Aga Khan, Sadruddin, and Hassan bin Talal. 1987. *Indigenous Peoples: A Global Quest for Justice.* London: Zed Books.

Anderson, Benedict. 1991. *Imagined Communities.* London: Verso.

Arjomand, Said Amir. 1988. *The Turban for the Crown: The Islamic Revolution in Iran.* New York and Oxford: Oxford University Press.

Barkin, J. S., and Bruce Cronin. 1994. "The State and the Nation: Changing Norms and the Rules of Sovereignty in International Relations." *International Organization* 48:1: 107–30.

Berman, Howard. 1992. "Perspectives on American Indian Sovereignty and International Law, 1600 to 1776." Pp. 125–88 in *Exiled in the Land of the Free*, ed. Oren Lyons et al. Santa Fe: Clear Light Publishers.

Brown, Michael E., ed. 1993. *Ethnic Conflict and International Security.* Princeton: Princteon University Press.

Bull, Hedley. 1977. *The Anarchical Society.* New York: Columbia University Press.

Burger, Julian. 1987. *Report from the Frontier: The State of the World's Indigenous Peoples.* London: Zed Books.

Carr, Edward Hallett. 1939. *The Twenty Years' Crisis, 1919–1939.* New York: Harper Torchbooks.

Collier, David, ed. 1979. *The New Authoritarianism in Latin America.* Princeton: Princeton University Press.

Diamond, Larry, Juan J. Linz, and Seymour Martin Lipset, eds. 1989. *Democracy in Developing Countries: Latin America.* Boulder: Lynne Rienner.

Eckstein, Susan. 1989. "Power and Popular Protest in Latin America." Pp. 1–60 in *Power and Popular Protest: Latin American Social Movements*, ed. Eckstein. Berkeley and Los Angeles: University of California Press.

Escobar, Arturo, and Sonia E. Alvarez, eds. 1992. *The Making of Social Movements in Latin America: Identity, Strategy, and Democracy.* Boulder: Westview Press.

Finnemore, Martha. 1996. *National Interests in International Society.* Ithaca: Cornell University Press.

Gamio, Manuel. 1960 (1916). *Forjando patria.* Mexico: Editorial Porrúa.

Ganguly, Rajat, and Raymond C. Taras. 1998. *Understanding Ethnic Conflict: The International Dimension.* New York: Longman.

Gong, Gerrit W. 1984. *The Standard of "Civilization" in International Society.* Oxford: Clarendon Press.

Gould, Jeff. 1998. *To Die in This Way: Nicaraguan Indians and the Myth of the Mestizaje 1880-1965.* Durham: Duke University Press.

Hobsbawm, Eric J. 1990. *Nations and Nationalism since 1780: Programme, Myth, and Reality.* Cambridge & New York: Cambridge University Press.

Horowitz, Donald L. 1985. *Ethnic Groups in Conflict.* Berkeley: University of California Press.

Hudson, Wayne, and Geoffrey Stokes. 1997. "Australia and Asia: Place, Determinism, and National Identities." Pp. 145–57 in *The Politics of Identity in Australia*, ed. Geoffrey Stokes. Cambridge and Melbourne: Cambridge University Press.

Ikenberry, G. John, and Charles Kupchan. 1990. "Socialization and Hegemonic Power." *International Organization* 44:3, 283–315.

Jackson, Robert H., and Carl G. Rosberg. 1982. "Why Africa's Weak States Persist: The Empirical and the Juridical in Statehood." *World Politics* 35:1–24.

Jupp, James. 1997. "Immigration and National Identity: Multiculturalism." Pp. 132–144 in *The Politics of Identity in Australia*, ed. Geoffrey Stokes. Cambridge and Melbourne: Cambridge University Press.

Kane, John. 1997. "Racialism and Democracy: The Legacy of White Australia." Pp. 117–31 in *The Politics of Identity in Australia*, ed. Geoffrey Stokes. Cambridge and Melbourne: Cambridge University Press.

Kymlicka, Will. 1994. *Multicultural Citizenship: A Liberal Theory of Minority Rights*. New York: Oxford University Press.

Lake, David A., and Donald Rothchild, eds. 1998. *The International Spread of Ethnic Conflict: Fear, Diffusion, and Escalation*. Princeton: Princeton University Press.

Lemarchand, René. 1996. *Burundi: Ethnocide as Discourse and Practice*. New York: Cambridge University Press.

Linz, Juan J., and Alfred Stepan. 1978. *The Breakdown of Democratic Regimes: Latin America*. Baltimore: Johns Hopkins University Press.

Marx, Anthony W. 1998. *Making Race and Nation: A Comparison of the United States, South Africa, and Brazil*. Cambridge: Cambridge University Press.

O'Donnell, Guillermo, and Philippe C. Schmitter. 1986. *Transitions from Authoritarian Rule: Tentative Conclusions about Uncertain Democracies*. Vol. 4. Baltimore and London: Johns Hopkins University Press.

Posen, Barry. 1993. "The Security Dilemma and Ethnic Conflict." Pp. 103–24 in *Ethnic Conflict and International Security*, ed. Michael E. Brown. Princeton: Princeton University Press.

Skidmore, Thomas E., and Peter H. Smith. 1997. *Modern Latin America*. 4th ed. New York and Oxford: Oxford University Press.

Smith, Anthony. 1986. *The Ethnic Origins of Nations*. Oxford: Blackwell.

Spruyt, Hendrik. 1994. *The Sovereign State and Its Competitors: An Analysis of Systems Change*. Princeton: Princeton University Press.

Steinberg, Stephen. 1989. *The Ethnic Myth: Race, Ethnicity, and Class in America*. Boston: Beacon Press.

Stone, Martin. 1997. *The Agony of Algeria*. New York: Columbia University Press.

Synder, Jack. 1993. "Nationalism and the Crisis of the Post–Soviet State." Pp. 79–101 in *Ethnic Conflict and International Security*, ed. Michael E. Brown. Princeton: Princeton University Press.

Tilly, Charles. 1985. "War Making and State Making as Organized Crime." In *Bringing the State Back In*, edited by Peter B. Evans, Dietrich Rueschemeyer, and Theda Scocpol. New York: Cambridge University Press.

Urban, Greg, and Joel Sherzer. 1990. *Nation-States and Indians in Latin America (Symposia on Latin America Series)*. Austin: University of Texas Press.

Vail, Leroy, ed. 1989. "Introduction." Pp. 1–19 in *The Creation of Tribalism in Southern Africa*, ed. Lewy Vail. Berkeley: University of California Press.

Van Cott, Donna Lee, ed. 1995. *Indigenous Peoples and Democracy in Latin America*. New York: The Inter-American Dialogue.

Vasconcelos, José. 1925. "La raza cósmica." In *José Vasconcelos,* ed. Justina Sarabia. Madrid: Ediciones de Cultura Hispánica.

Waltz, Kenneth. 1979. *Theory of International Politics.* Boston: Addison-Wesley.

Warren, Kay. 1998. *Indigenous Movements and Their Critics: Pan-Maya Activism in Guatemala.* Princeton: Princeton University Press.

Watson, Adam. 1992. *The Evolution of International Society.* London: Routledge.

Wiarda, Howard J. and Harvey F. Kline. 1996. *Latin American Politics and Development.* 4th ed. Boulder: Westview Press.

Young, M. Crawford. 1976. *The Politics of Cultural Pluralism.* Madison: University of Wisconsin Press.

———. 1994. *The African Colonial State in Comparative Perspective.* New Haven and London: Yale University Press.

Chapter 4

Cleansing Ethnicity

Taking Group Harms Seriously

Thomas W. Simon

Ethnic groups have become main actors on the international stage, and ethno
violence has made its way to the top of the international political agenda.
Ethnic issues require political action, but effective and just responses must
stem from a sound conceptual base. Unfortunately, the existing paradigms
that explain ethnicity make unwarranted assumptions about its nature. The
two policy approaches that have emerged as a result (i.e., the ethnic "Identity
view" and the ethnic "Strife view") proceed from questionable theoretical
foundations and have led policy makers down dangerous roads. In a sense, by
prejudging ethnicity as either valuable or harmful, the prevailing views take
ethnicity too seriously and do not give due attention to the political dynamics
that make ethnic identification contingent and malleable. Further, they fail to
assess, normatively, political developments connected to ethnicity. This chapter begins to do this by developing an alternative "Group Harm" view of
ethnicity. Its advantage is that it provides a clearer, more politically oriented and
normatively defensible position on ethnicity. Examples from the Balkans and
Central Africa are used to demonstrate the value of this Harm perspective.

Within a Harm framework, analysts care little about the origins of an
ethnicity; they do not need to take a position on whether ethnic identification
is good or bad. Their concerns lie elsewhere—with harms associated with
using ethnic labels, with discriminatory policies and actions aimed at ethnic
groups, and with the more brutal harms inflicted on ethnic groups. Furthermore this view assumes that each of these events tends to happen in a sequence of stages: defining a group *(the designation phase);* discriminating against
a group *(the discrimination phase);* and, finally, attempting to exterminate the
group *(the brutalization phase).*

The Harm view further assumes that ethnic designations become important as they solidify defensively, relative to perceived or actual harms directed
at a group and its members. It therefore becomes critical to track political

developments as they unravel during a "group designation phase." Moral concerns emerge in the second "discrimination phase." Policy makers outside of the state wherein group discrimination is taking place have a moral obligation to attend to discriminatory harms, particularly when these harms become embedded in a system of apartheid. The idea of coupling policy and morality at some point during a discrimination phase intuitively makes more sense in the context of the final "brutalization phase." When brutalizations reach to the level of group extermination, moral actions should motivate policy. Analogously, when discriminations reach a stage of institutional apartheid, moral condemnation should dominate policy.[1]

Before the presentation of arguments for the claims underlying the Harm framework, the obvious play on words contained in the title (i.e., "cleansing ethnicity") calls for an explanation. "Cleansing ethnicity" tries to accomplish conceptually what "ethnic cleansing" (the systematic removal of individuals from their residences because of their perceived ethnic identity) aims to do physically and socially. The play on words suggests itself, because the more ruthless forms of ethnic cleansing attain their foothold in part because of prior conceptual legitimizations of negative and positive valuations of ethnicities. Moreover, the use of the adjective "cleansing" to describe the barbarity of the forceful removal of people represents a scourge on language. Cleansing the concept of ethnicity of its valuations and reifications reveals and differentiates the harms that fall under the label "ethnic cleansing."

The goals of this analysis, however, are more ambitious. Examinations of past ethnic conflicts demonstrate the need for policy makers to construct early warning systems cautiously, to attend to the political aspects of group formations, to establish ways to effect moral condemnation of group discrimination, and to implement rapid moral responses to the more severe kinds of group brutalization. The task ahead is to clarify and support these claims.

RECONCEIVING THE CATEGORIES: THE CASE FOR "DEFENSIVE ETHNICITY"

So far the discussion has purposefully interchanged the terms *ethnic* and *group* as a signal that this critique applies to other group designations as well (e.g., "race"). Cleansing ethnicity (conceptually clarifying the term *ethnicity*) involves relating it to associated terms such as *race* and *ethnos* (Fenton 1999). Not only should the use of particular ethnic labels be problematized but so should the general label "ethnic" when it is used to categorize identities, issues, problems, conflicts, and violence. A so-called "ethnic problem" may begin with the use of the adjective "ethnic" and the noun "ethnicity" (or their surrogates) to describe a situation. Let us call the seemingly innocent analytical process that uses ethnic labels *ethnization*. A threefold strategy serves to undermine confidence in seemingly neutral labels such as "ethnic." The first step involves revealing problems associated with any use of the related term *race*. The second task includes demonstrating how the same problems that plague uses of race carry over, *mutis mutandis*, to the use of ethnic. The final prong of the argument consists of describing how past uses differ from present uses. Ethnization assumes that ethnicity is a natural category. It assumes a preanalytic sense of ethnicity that avoids value judgments. The arguments against ethnization do not imply that theorists and policy makers should completely cleanse their conceptual schemes of this category, but they do urge caution when using these concepts. To understand why, it is helpful to consider ethnicity in light of the related concepts of race and ethnos.

Modern analysts, amidst sorting out the complexities of the ethnicities in the Balkans, sometimes bemoan the fact that ethnicities are not as easily identified as races. They regard race as an analytically superior concept, since it is commonly believed that race refers to tangibles, physical characteristics (phenotype), and biological factors (genotype)— whereas ethnicity denotes less tangible items, including those that fall under the vague heading "culture." Despite these predilections, it might give the theorists of ethnicity some solace to know that the idea of race has been just as contested as that of ethnicity, to the point that Hollinger argues that while racism is real, races are not (1995, 39). Race does not have any firmer scientific basis than ethnicity. One distant black relative ("one drop of blood") places an individual in the black racial category, yet a near white relative does not put an individual into the white racial category. The "one-drop" rule in the infamous 1896 U.S. Supreme Court case, *Plessy v. Ferguson,* is a case in point. Plessy established the "separate but equal" doctrine that governed race relations until *Brown v. Board of Education* in 1954. In his initial pleadings, a blond haired, blue-eyed, Homer Adolph Plessy claimed that the statute barring Negroes from white trains did not apply to him, for he denied he was a Negro. As evidence, he cited the "fact" that he had only one black great-grandmother, making him, at most, one-eighth Negro. The Court quickly brushed aside Plessy's plea by defining a Negro as a person who had any remnant of black ancestry. The one-drop rule still has legal validity in the United States (Davis 1991). In *Jane Doe v. Louisiana* (1986), Mrs. Susie Phipps was denied a passport, since she had designated her color as "white." She asked the Louisiana courts to change the color designation on her deceased parents' birth certificates. The state presented genealogical evidence of her great-great-great-great-grandmother's black race. According to the state, "black" meant "having more than one-thirty-second black ancestry." On the opposite side, former dictator of Haiti, "Papa Doc" Duvalier, informed a dumbfound American journalist that Haiti had a 90 percent white population based on Haiti's one-drop-of-white-blood rule. Haiti allegedly defined its citizens as white if they had one drop of white blood. These examples show that race was, is, and will be a politically contested means of classifying individuals. In short, race does not provide a politically uncontested exemplar for students of ethnicity to use. And just as race does not have a physical or biological existence prior to and apart from politics, neither do ethnic groups exist prior to and apart from politics.

The history of the related concept ethnos exposes further impurities in the concept ethnicity. The Greek origins of ethnos, as analyzed by Tomkin and others (1989, in Hutchinson and Smith 1996), have some telling features. Initially, ethnos simply referred to any grouping. (Homer wrote of *ethnos hetrairon*, a band of friends.) Then, ethnos began to connote not just any grouping but a particular type of collectivity. (Homer wrote of *ethnos melisson*, a swarm or throng of bees, and *ethnos ornithon*, a multitude of birds.) From these and other examples, it is unclear whether any assessment is being made about the group (i.e., a "swarm" of bees does not seem bad). Eventually, ethnos took on more explicitly negative connotations—denoting chaotic groups. In a transition period, Aeschylus used ethnos for the Furies and for the Persians. For Pindar (*Pythian Odes* 4.448), ethnos referred to "the husband-killing women of Lemnos." Then, ethnos began to be used in clearly negative ways, for foreign and barbarous groups, which stood in sharp contrast to the Greeks, themselves the genos Hellenon (Aristotle *Politics* 1324.b.10). This history serves as an interesting context for current debates. A positive sense of ethnos is a modern invention. For ethnic identity theorists, an ethnos denotes a group deserving social respect and state protection. The Strife Sense of ethnos also is particularly modern. For Strife theorists, ethnos situates those groups that often end up despising and fighting one another.

This brief excursion into etymology holds an important lesson for theorists and policy makers. The concept of ethnicity does not have a clear definition and, hence, it cannot yield any valid classification scheme. Further, ethnicity comes with built-in assessments and valuations. Take, for example, the classic anthropological study by Colin Turnbull of the Dodo and the Ik. In it, he "scientifically" describes the Dodo as "a tall, large people," noting that "they carried themselves with a *pride* that is almost *haughty* and *aggressive*, although they are a *gentle* and *friendly* people" (Turnbull 1972, 55). He then describes the Ik as "small, around five feet tall," who "do *not* wear the elaborate mud packs or headdresses *of their pastoral neighbors* [the Dodos]" (ibid., emphasis added). By making the comparisons in the way that he did, Turnbull made value judgments about Dodos and Iks. (A positive assessment of an ethnic group includes a set of positively evaluated qualities such as physical appearances, cultural practices, language, etc.) In short, neither positive nor negative evaluations of an ethnic group have a purely descriptive basis despite scholarly claims to the contrary. Any analysis that uses the concept of ethnicity as an unanalyzed conceptual starting point eventually will have to face the often hidden value judgments underlying the concept. Thus analysts do not have the luxury of constructing a theory of ethnicity that begins with the relatively innocuous concept of ethnicity. To avoid inadvertently smuggling unexamined value judgments about groups and group conflicts into an analysis, ethnicities should be taken as contingent, political data. This means making our political and moral commitments explicit at the beginning and then building these commitments into our theoretical and policy efforts. What might this mean? Instead of utilizing a supposedly neutral category such as ethnicity, why not use a more circumscribed concept—"defensive ethnicity?" This concept is conceived of with an awareness of group harms in mind.

In 1955, David Riesman, a renowned American sociologist, was the first to use the word "ethnicity." He did so in the context of exposing a crucial factor underlying ethnic issues, namely, group harm, which provides a key ingredient for a conceptually clear sense of ethnos and ethnicity. Riesman's concern was to articulate a sense of group harm by arguing for the acceptance of the notion of group libel as a legally recognized harm on the grounds that words hurt vulnerable groups in a manner similar to the way words hurt individuals.

And the devastating harm caused to racial or cultural minorities— to Negroes, to Jews, to American Indians, to Poles—as a result of systematic defamation needs no underscoring here; no member of these groups escapes some psychic or material hurt as a consequence of the attacks upon the groups with which he is voluntarily or involuntarily identified. (Riesman 1942, 770–71)[2]

To incorporate the group harm component, as highlighted by Riesman, let us offer yet another sense of ethnos—that is, a group identity constituted, in part, as a response to harm directed against a group ("a reactive or defensive group identity"). This sense challenges the sense of ethnos used by both Identity and Strife theorists. Unlike with the other views, within a Harm framework, ethnos becomes a historically contingent political phenomenon that solidifies primarily in reaction to hostile political forces. Identity theorists, lured by the positive features of ethnic identity, tend to ignore reactive aspects of ethnic identity formation. Strife theorists fail to see how members of a group have an ethnos thrust upon them. To use the vocabulary of one influential commentator, being (or becoming) a self-ascribed member of a group or adopting "a positive life-script" arises in response to negative scripts thrust upon individuals by a dominant culture (Appiah 1994, 159–60). Or, as another commentator put it:

The need for ethnic solidarity arises only when strange, threatening, competitive outsiders must be confronted. Only then are distinctions between "us" and "them" noted, explained, and evaluated to reinforce internal coherence and to signal and explain differences with outsiders and competitors. Only then does the need for internal solidarity and discipline become evident. (Easman 1994, 13–14)

Appiah and Easman seem to think that ethnic identity forms *only* defensively. While this judgment is too sweeping, they have uncovered a critical aspect of the process of ethnic identification; ethnic identities often solidify defensively, under negative pressure from outsiders. Some Holocaust survivors, for example, recount how they had little or no self-conscious identity as Jews until the rise of Nazism. "What has held the Jewish community together in spite of all the disintegrating forces is . . . the fact that the Jewish community is treated [negatively] as a community by the world at large" (Wirth 1949, 493). As detailed in a later section of this chapter, the Nazis classified some individuals as Jews who had no past self-identification as Jews; they refused to identify other individuals as Jews, even if they had a history of self-identification as Jews, and they failed even to consider the possibility that some individuals who did not fit their criteria might have been practicing religious Jews. Gross, macro, determinative qualities often suffice to classify a person as a member of an ethnic group when outsiders look down on a group. Outsiders who politically attack groups find ways to identify group members, even if their criteria for identification make little sense. A Harm framework focuses on this sixth sense of ethnos that interprets ethnic identification as a defensive political phenomenon. Defensive ethnic identity, therefore, will serve as a key concept in a Harm analysis.

THEORIZING ETHNICITY IN LIGHT OF STATUS HARMS

A Harm framework should be further situated within theoretical debates about ethnicity (Ganguly and Taras 1998). The Identity view sees ethnic groups as providing a crucial framework for human expression. Identification with an ethnic group enables individuals to find meaning in their lives. Accordingly, ethnicity has an intrinsic value that rights (both individual and group) should protect (Kymlicka 1995; Hoover, *EPC*). In contrast, the Strife view looks at ethnicity more negatively, as a major cause of conflict, strife, and violence (Ignatieff 1997). On the Strife account, the promotion of ethnicity "almost inevitably" leads to divisions among groups that eventually will mean strife and conflict (Kaplan 1994). It seems as though the choice is either that ethnicity leads to greater human fulfillment or to increased group conflict. Thus by adding either richness to culture or fuel to strife, Janus-faced ethnicity pulls in irreconcilable directions.

From the discussion so far, it might appear that one could either adopt an optimistic or a pessimistic view of ethnicity, but these blanket assessments are not the only options. Both views contain elements of truth, yet they both leave out critical political and moral elements. The ethnic identity view looks at the (largely positive) social and cultural aspects of the process and product of ethnic formation. This Identity view has many variants, but it is most often associated with primordialist and perennialist approaches. Primordialists conceive of ethnicity as something deeply ingrained in human biology. Perennialists view ethnicity as a recurring cultural phenomenon. However, whatever the variants, an Identity perspective woefully underestimates the role of ethnicity in conflict, which of course serves as the basis for the competing Strife model.

The Strife view, seeing a world riddled with ethnic conflict, places great emphasis on the largely negative effects of ethnicity. It is most often associated with instrumentalism, which interprets ethnicity as a tool available for manipulation by elites. Yet while ethnic strife is evident throughout the world, the Strife perspective exaggerates and underestimates the role of ethnicity in conflict. Often, politicians outside of a conflict overplay the ethnic card to justify their inaction, and they overlook the relatively recent ways that political developments have changed and molded ethnic identifications. In summary, those working within an Identity view underestimate the role of ethnicity in conflict, while those adopting a Strife view overestimate its role. In keeping with the operative metaphor, the Identity and Strife perspectives should be cleansed of their intrinsic valuations of ethnicity. Ethnicity has no intrinsic positive or negative value. Apart from particular political contexts, ethnicity deserves neither praise nor blame. Ethnicity demands attention, however, whenever and wherever it becomes entangled in seriously harmful actions.

A Harm framework rules out moral claims made about individual character or about forms of social organization. Instead, it directs moral analysis to harmful consequences of actions associated with ethnicity. Ethically, a Harm perspective is consequentialist. It holds actors accountable for depriving individuals of liberty and welfare because of their status (discrimination), and for physically or otherwise hurting them (brutalization). The analysis focuses on group harms. While it might seem obvious that genocide is immoral, spelling out the reasons helps establish why group harms in general have a distinct moral status. Overall, individuals are treated prejudicially (labeled, designated), discriminated against, and brutalized simply because of their perceived group identity or group status. Societies make efforts to combat social forms of prejudice, and governments legislate against discrimination. Generally, legislators have no difficulty criminalizing the more severe forms of these harms (the brutalizations). Internationally, brutalizations should have a special legal and moral status, especially with respect to probably the most extreme form of brutalization, genocide. Brutalizations are carried out against individuals for a particularly bad reason, namely, because of individuals' group status. Certainly many individual murders are committed for bad reasons, but killings against members of a group become even more heinous because, by definition, they do not stop with a single individual.

The following studies use the political concept of "defensive ethnicity" and the moral category of "status harms." These analyses of past cases within a Harm framework provide policy guideposts for future cases where harms associated with ethnicity might arise.

THE SEQUENCE OF STAGES:
DESIGNATION, DISCRIMINATION, BRUTALIZATION

However valuable it is to explain and understand the complex dynamics of ethnic group formation, it is crucially important to single out harms connected to ethnicity. One reason for giving primacy to group harms is that less severe forms of harms directed at groups and their members can lead to probably the worst harm imaginable, namely, genocide. The history of anti-Semitism in Nazi Germany followed the threefold path, mentioned above, from defining a group (designation), discriminating against a group (discrimination), and then attempting to exterminate the group (brutalization). Raul Hilberg, in his seminal study *The Destruction of the European Jews*, described the "inherent pattern" of the Nazis' "machinery of destruction": "no group can be killed without a concentration or seizure of the victims, and no victims can be segregated before the perpetrator knows who belongs to the group" (Hilberg 1985, 267). If the history of anti-Semitism is any indication, the first signs of group harm occur when individuals, once classified (designation phase), are denied social goods, including employment and education (discrimination phase), because of their perceived or actual group affiliation. As discussed in the first section of this chapter, race classification systems have built-in illogical asymmetries among the designated groups, and the criteria for "membership" are commonly inconsistently and nonsensically applied. Hilberg traced the difficulties the Nazis first faced in promulgating precise definitions of Jews. The Nazis divided non-Aryans into Jews and *Mischlinges*. They further differentiated Mischlinges into Second Degree (those with one Jewish grandparent) and First Degree, or half Jews (those with two Jewish grandparents but not belonging to a Jewish religion). In one court case, the petitioner, a half-Jew who had married a half-Jew and attended a synagogue with her father, had designated her religion as "Jewish" on an employment application to a Jewish community organization. The Reich Administrative Court interpreted "belonging to a Jewish religion" as an attitude. The court noted that her father had undoubtedly dragged her to the synagogue, and that her self-identification as Jewish stemmed from economic need. Yet in another case, the Nazi court (unlike the American court's reasoning in *Plessy*) classified a petitioner with four German grandparents as a Jew, because the latter felt bound to Jewry despite his Aryan blood.

The classifications determined which marriages would be permitted and which ones would be prohibited. Second-Degree Mischlinges could marry Germans, but they could not marry Jews. First-Degree Mischlinges could not marry Second-Degree Mischlinges or Germans, except with special permission, but they could marry other First Degree Mischlinges and Jews. Further, Hitler decreed that, regardless of race, men (but not women!) could be punished for the serious crime of *Rassenschande* (race defilement), that is, having extramarital intercourse with a Jew.

As illustrated by the inconsistent judicial classifications made in the early stages of Nazi rule, the relatively detailed distinctions that accompany discriminatory harms become blurred as the genocide engines ignite and accelerate. The road to genocide can sometimes (but not always!) be traced to a point that begins with an externally imposed definition of a group—racial, ethnic, or whatever. Classifications of groups, even if innocently intended, are not easily divorced from evaluations of groups. The first phase of the Harm model is called the "designation phase." Hilberg notes two subsequent and more explicitly harming phases, a "discrimination phase" and a "brutalization phase." Discrimination and brutalization constitute group harms. Group harms affect, directly or indirectly, all of those deemed group "members." Often, the most severe group harms have precursors in other, less severe forms of harm. Isolated incidences of violence directed toward individuals because of their perceived group affiliation (e.g., hate crimes) may constitute a precursor to more severe, brutalization harms. Discrimination, in its many forms, then, may serve as a general precursor to brutalization. The sequence, from discrimination, to ethnic cleansing, to genocide, sometimes runs concurrently. However, as the cases that follow show, if policy analysts base early warning systems too rigidly on a sequence going from designation to discrimination to brutalization, they may miss other signs of group harm erupting that demand immediate action (Szayna 2000).

It seems that the Balkans and Central Africa provide quick and easy examples of the three phases set forth in the Harm model. Comparisons of the plight of Bosnian Muslims, Albanian Kosovars, and Rwandan Tutsis, however, show that the phases do not always follow in neat, chronological order. The designation (political solidification) may be relatively recent and short lived. While long-term, severe, and institutionalized discrimination may signal impending brutalization (as in the case of Rwandan Tutsis), discrimination may not clearly evolve into brutalization (as in the case of the Albanian Kosovars). Brutalization may occur with relatively little prior discrimination (as in the case of the Bosnian Muslims). Despite these counter-instances, the sequencing of the phases offers valuable guideposts for policy makers. More importantly, each phase stimulates questions that might not otherwise be raised. By treating group designations as problematic, the contingent and political factors underlying the processes of designation surface. The complexities of the histories associated with Bosnian, Kosovar, or Tutsi identity become less important than the harms stemming from the recent political solidifications of these identities, through brutalizations committed against them. Analyses of the designation phase also provide a clearer picture of recent and current political complexities. They help forge connections among groups within different states. For example, the Tutsis are not only in Rwanda but also in Uganda and the Democratic Republic of the Congo (former Zaire). The discrimination and brutalization phases of inquiry stimulate the search for links between the two forms of group harm. Discrimination takes on a new importance when seen as potentially sowing seeds for brutalization. The potential discrimination-brutalization link further creates an opening to elevate certain forms of discrimination (e.g., apartheid in Kosovo and Rwanda) to a level of universal moral condemnation. In addition, analyses of the brutalization phase bring up issues regarding different kinds of brutalization, thereby raising serious moral questions about international reactions to these differing degrees of harm. Finally, the Harm framework places genocide within the same domain of inquiry as ethnic designation and ethnic discrimination. And, most importantly, the adoption of a Harm framework forces political and moral confrontations with the scourge of genocide as a sadly unexceptional phenomenon.

THE BALKANS

I come from a Land of Blood Groups. There the dedicated blood-cell counters noted each of my blood cells. As a result I became . . . no one. Write no one, I say to the officials in the booths each time they ask me my nationality, and they ask me often. Hurry up, they say, tell us what it is. Nationality: no one. Citizenship: Croatian, I repeat. We don't have no one of yours in the computer, they say. The right to be no one is guaranteed to me by the constitution of this country. Citizens are not obliged to declare their nationality if they do not want to, I say. In real life it's different, they say, everybody is obliged to be someone. That's just why we have wars, I say, because everyone agreed to belong to their own blood group. That's why we have wars, they say, because people like you wanted us all to be no one. (Ugresic 1998, 237–38)

There is no safe way to begin to discuss the Balkans. Even the term *Balkans* proves troubling. Is Slovenia part of the Balkans? Is the eastern or "European part" of Turkey included within the Balkans? Whatever territories make up the Balkans, analysts seem to agree that the region contains distinct and factious ethnic groups. From a Strife perspective, the crises in the former Yugoslavia stem from ancient ethnic and religious hatreds: Serbs against Croats, Serbs and Croats against Bosnians, Eastern Orthodox Christians against Catholics, and Christians against Muslims. The Balkans seem to contain nothing but rival ethnic groupings. The habit of describing the region in ethnic terms continues today. Political discussions uncritically use the following state and cultural designations interchangeably: Slovenians/Slovenes, Croatians/Croats, and Serbians/Serbs. Recent brutalizations have taken place around two designations, namely, Bosnian Muslims and Albanians.

Bosnian Muslims

Consider how to define Bosnian Muslims, who speak Serbo-Croatian and are considered to be Slavs, (e.g., Serbs, Croats, and Slovenes). Bosnian Muslim identity politically solidified only recently as a response to the increasingly severe harms inflicted upon this group after the former Yugoslavia unraveled. The political and legal history of the former Yugoslavia demonstrates that Bosnian Muslims constitute a reactive or defensive identity (Bringa 1995, 25–27). The 1946 Constitution used a three-tiered classification system for citizenship, which was implemented and interpreted in distinct ways throughout Yugoslavia's history. The three types of citizens were: "nations" or *narodi* (Serb, Croat, Slovene, Macedonian, Montenegrin, and Muslim); "nationalities" or *narodnosti* (those with "national homes" outside of Yugoslavia, such as Albanians); and "other nationalities and ethnic minorities" (Jews, Yugoslavs). "Everyone held 'Yugoslav' citizenship but no one held Yugoslav nationality," except in a census (Bringa 1995, 27). In a census taken every ten years, individuals could designate their national identity under one of the six nations, or as Yugoslavs. National identity never appeared on an individual's passport, although it did appear on the Yugoslav Peoples Army's identity cards. The 1946 Constitution recognized Serbs, Croats, Slovenes, Montenegrins, and Macedonians as nations. It did not recognize Bosnian Muslim as either a nation or a nationality. In the 1961 census, Bosnia Muslims became a nationality (formalized in the 1963 Constitution), and in the 1971 census, they became a nation (formalized in the 1974 Constitution). That is, Muslims then had a national home in the republic of Bosnia-Herzegovina. In the 1974 Constitution, Bosnia-Herzegovina became one of the six primary republics, but the constitutional drafters only defined Serbo-Croatian, Slovenian, and Macedonian as official languages. This is not to say that the idea of Bosnian Muslims appeared out of thin air. The late 1970s saw a campaign to redesignate Bosnia a Muslim Republic and to authorize mosque building. During that same period, Yugoslavs also saw Bosnian Muslims as the hope for constructing a national Yugoslav identity. This brief history shows the designation "Bosnian Muslim" as a distinct, contested, changing, and not yet solidified classification.

Sarajevo, the main city of Bosnia, symbolized (perhaps falsely) the hopes for a flourishing, multiethnic community in Federal Yugoslavia, as evidenced by its notably high interethnic marriage rate. Srebrenica, another city in Bosnia-Herzegovina, came to symbolize the horror of ethnic conflict when Bosnian Serb forces massacred some 5,000 Muslims under the helpless eyes of United Nations soldiers from the Netherlands. What accounts for the gap between the flourishing of multiculturalism in Sarajevo and the brutalization in Srebrenica? In terms of the phases set forth in the Harm model, the first phase in which Bosnian Muslim identity was solidified politically, occurred relatively recently. Further, there was comparatively little discrimination against Bosnian Muslims before their brutalization. Despite portrayals to the contrary, "Bosnian Islamic identity has historically been moderate and opposed to clericalism and strict religious observance" (Sofos 1996, 272). Although there was prejudice against Bosnian Muslims, as Slavs who had converted to Islam under Ottoman rule, discrimination against them was not particularly widespread or severe. Most importantly, the discrimination was not institutionalized or legally sanctioned. Widespread discrimination, therefore, does not always reliably forecast severe brutalization. Formal political parties, organized along avowedly ethnic lines, did not emerge until late 1989 in Bosnia-Herzegovina. The Bosnian Muslims had two major parties, the more secular Muslim Bosniak Organization (MBO) and the Muslim Party of Democratic Action (SDA). The SDA was, until recently, led by Alija Izetbegovic, who promoted an Islamic Muslim civic identity in contrast to the more religious, fundamentalist wing of his party. From 1990 to 1991, Serbian politicians tried to woo the SDA. After that, the solidification of Bosnian Muslims came quickly and feverishly, as a reaction to the enmity of Serbian (and, to a later and lesser extent, Croatian) nationalism that suddenly turned violent (Doubt 2000, 30).

Policy makers, for the most part, wrongly pinpointed the solidifications of the groups and failed to appreciate the disparities of harms inflicted on each group in Bosnia. According to a 1993 U.S. State Department assessment, the Balkans pose "an intractable 'problem from hell' that no one can be expected to solve . . . less a moral tragedy . . . and more a tribal feud that no outsider could hope to settle" (Warren Christopher, cited in Friedman, 1993). The ancient-hatreds thesis proved to be part of the problem. Many policy analysts now agree that an unwillingness to abandon the Strife view, which saw the Balkans populated by intractable ethnic groups with long-standing hatreds, posed the "primary obstacle to action" in Bosnia (Woodward 2000, 153). If the political solidification of Bosnian Muslim identification is of relatively recent origin, the ancient-hatreds thesis appears disingenuous at best. This is not to say that historians and polemicists cannot point to past conflicts among groups in the region, but these ancient group conflicts have highly tenuous connections to modern ones. Further, the ancient-hatreds thesis implies a leveling of group harms. Victimization claims of past and current harms become analytically incomparable and politically intractable. Initially, the United Nations peacekeeping forces saw each of the sides as having legitimate and roughly comparable claims about their past and current victimizations. Yet brutalizations seldom come in equal doses. A Harm framework demands assessments and rankings of competing victimization claims on some sensible scale using severity of harms as a standard. Throughout the 1970s and 1980s, the Serbs made victimization claims. They saw Tito's reform efforts, particularly as manifested in the 1974 Constitution, as harming Serb (which overlapped with "Serbia's") interests. If harms against Serbs occurred largely in past history, and if Serbs inflicted relatively more severe harms against Bosnian Muslims recently, then Bosnian Muslim victimization claims should have taken precedence over Serbian ones. Although it is difficult to demonstrate fully, some analysts claim that the peacekeeping forces favored certain groups over others. They charge that the United Nations' refusal to see that brutalizations were disproportionately committed against Bosnian Muslims stemmed from key leaders having a more negative evaluation of Muslims than they did of other factions.

In summary, a Bosnian Muslim group solidified defensively primarily after 1990. The recent, short-lived designation phase quickly devolved into fairly severe brutalizations (forced removals, rapes, and exterminations) with relatively little preceding group discrimination. Within the former Yugoslav federation, this made the political designs, decisions, and developments even more crucial than under other crisis conditions. When the state dismantled, outside actors confronted crisis conditions that demanded swift and definitive actions. External interventions became morally mandated as soon as the peacekeepers knew of the more severe brutalizations inflicted on Bosnian Muslims.

Albanian Kosovars

A Harm analysis of Albanian Kosovars deviates in important ways from the analysis of Bosnian Muslims. Constitutional design and designations again prove helpful. The 1946 Constitution designated the region of Vojvodina, with its majority Hungarian population, as an Autonomous Province. Kosovo (more accurately, Kosovo-Metihija) became an Autonomous Region, a decidedly lower designation because, unlike Vojvodina, it did not have an independent legislature or a supreme court. The 1963 Constitution upgraded Kosovo to the same status as Vojvodina, but this Constitution decreased the powers of autonomous provinces. With the 1974 Constitution, Kosovo became a full constitutive member of the Yugoslav Federation, as one of eight federal units. However, unlike Bosnian Muslims, who by that time had attained nation status, Albanians remained in the lower category, a nationality. From this constitutionally mandated design, and Yugoslavia's demographics, two critical observations emerge. First, Albanians remained second-class citizens (a nationality), "despite their numerical superiority over less numerous Slav nations of Yugoslavia, which did have their own republics within the federation" (Vickers 1998, 217). Second, the creation of the autonomous provinces of Vojvodina and Kosovo meant that "21% of the Serbs in Serbia were not under the jurisdiction of Belgrade" (ibid., 179).

Legally, Albanians in Kosovo solidified their identity earlier than Bosnian Muslims. Constitutionally, Albanians achieved nationality status in 1946, whereas Bosnian Muslims did not do so until the 1960s. From the 1974 Constitution to the 1989 constitutional crisis, when Serbia amended its republic constitution to undermine Kosovo's autonomy, "the Albanians of Kosovo had a better situation in terms of representation and cultural autonomy than they had known at any time since the end of the Ottoman Empire and arguably in their entire history" (Vickers 1998, 217). Up until 1990, when Serbia removed Kosovo's autonomy and imposed repressive emergency measures, Albanians had coexisted with Serbs in Kosovo. In fact, in 1389, members of the two populations fought together as allies on both sides of the infamous battle of Kosovo, celebrated by Serb nationalists (Malcolm 1998, xxix). The two populations are divided along religious lines (Islam and Christian Eastern Orthodox), yet the designation "Muslim Albanian Kosovars" is highly misleading. For example, in a situation similar to that experienced by Bosnian Muslims, "the Albanians of Kosovo today are in many ways a politically mobilized people, but religion has played almost no role at all in that mobilization" (Malcolm 1998, xxviii). Further, if religion constituted the critical signal of impending conflict, then one would expect more similarities between the treatment of Bosnian Muslims and Kosovar Muslims. Recent history, however, reveals more severe discrimination against Albanian Kosovars than against Bosnian Muslims, but more severe brutalizations against Muslims in Bosnia than against Albanians in Kosovo.

The Albanian Kosovars, unlike the Bosnian Muslims, could point to a period of severe discrimination from roughly the 1980s through the 1990s. The Albanians rioted in 1981, 1989, and 1990. In reaction to each incident, Serbia imposed increasingly repressive measures. Elections, boycotted by the Albanians, became part of the repression. Given his past criminal record and future role as a paramilitary leader in Bosnia, it is a sad irony to note the election of Arkan to the Serbian assembly to represent a Kosovo constituency. After his election, Arkan proposed that the 1.5 million Albanians, whom he claimed had emigrated from Albania to Kosovo, be treated as "tourists" (Malcolm 1998, 351). The repressive actions caused the Albanians to form an underground government and society—a clear manifestation of a defensive group formation. For example, 18,000 Albanian teachers taught 335,000 students in an unofficial education system. Thus having in some sense solidified their identity earlier than the Bosnian Muslims, the Albanians, under the nonviolent leadership of Ibrahim Rugova, established a parallel state. The U.S. State Department, Amnesty Intentional, and others documented the severe and widespread human rights abuses carried out against the Albanians. By 1996, the severity of discrimination against Albanians in Kosovo reached apartheid levels.

To appreciate the emergence of morality during the discrimination phase, we need to project ahead for a moment to Rwanda. Events there support the contention that, in general, humanitarian intervention becomes more justifiable the more the brutalizations approach the extreme of genocide. International jurists generally accept the argument that genocide constitutes so severe a crime that state immunity is inapplicable, and perhaps humanitarian intervention is mandated. In parallel fashion, the Kosovo case supports the claim that international moral condemnation and external policies become more justifiable as the severity of discrimination approaches the level of apartheid. It is difficult to defend the legitimacy of any state that keeps a majority of its population so oppressed that they become noncitizens. Apartheid conditions were applied with increasing severity to Albanians in Kosovo over a relatively extensive period, whereas the same cannot be said of Bosnian Muslims.

Further comparisons of the Bosnian and Kosovo cases reveal a crucial difference in their brutalization phases. Unlike the Bosnian Muslims, who speak the same language as the Serbs who inflicted brutalities against them, the more impoverished Kosovar Albanians speak a different language than their nemesis, the Serbs. Given these differences, one might have predicted that greater brutality would have been unleashed against the "more different" Albanian Kosovars. Yet while it remains difficult to compare fully the two brutalizations, the swift and severe aspects of the harms suffered by the Bosnians are more readily apparent than the afflictions suffered by the Kosovars.

Decisions about humanitarian intervention involve assessments of brutalizations. On June 25, 1999, President Clinton defended the bombing of Kosovo as a way to stop "deliberate, systematic efforts at . . . genocide" (quoted in Layne and Schwarz 2000, 21). Yet prior to the bombing campaign, less than 2,000 Albanians and Serbs had been killed in fifteen months of warfare; after the bombing, the United Nations managed to confirm only about 2,000 civilian victims (ibid.) Further, policy analysts also had come to see that swifter intervention could have averted some of the brutalizations committed in Bosnia. In contrast, a strong case can be made that "Belgrade did not turn from conducting counterinsurgency against the KLA to uprooting the province's ethnic Albanian population until several days after NATO began its bombing campaign" (ibid.).

Some fascinating aspects of group identity contestation in Kosovo support the view that identity is highly malleable. The status of Turks in Yugoslav Kosovo provides a striking contrast to the brutal consequences that flowed from a designation as "Turk" by Serbs. In Kosovo, even though the percentage of the Turk population decreased, Albanians tried to assimilate Turks, while Yugoslavs promoted the Turk minority. Unlike Bosnian Muslims, whom Yugoslavs perceived as good candidates for national identity, the Yugoslavs tried to treat the Turks as a national minority, just like the Albanians. A second example proves even more troubling, since it challenges the tendency to see ethnic and religious identities as natural and immutable. According to one historian, throughout the 1990s, Albanians seriously entertained converting from Islam to Roman Catholicism "as a first step towards incorporation into Western civilization and national unity as Albanians" (Vickers 1998, 248). Among other things, the analysis supports the claim that the defensive identification of Albanians did not completely solidify until 1996.

In summary, Albanian identity in Kosovo formed more solidly and more quickly than Muslim identity in Bosnia. The role of group identity as a shield against institutionalized discrimination became much more critical for Albanians than it did for Muslims. Sovereign immunity applies as a defense in international law against humanitarian intervention to end apartheid, however, the nature of apartheid makes it a matter of international moral concern. Apartheid consists of structurally embedded harms often directed at a majority group within a single, statelike system. The international condemnation of, and policies implemented against, apartheid in South Africa had political and moral dimensions. The situation faced by Albanians in Kosovo amounted to apartheid and should have stimulated foreign responses similar to those mobilized against apartheid in South Africa. Policy analysts, however, did not point to apartheid in Kosovo as playing any role whatsoever in justifying the humanitarian intervention carried out there. Beyond these speculations, the analysis supports the contention that severe discrimination against groups warrants international moral condemnation. Further, if strong international policies against apartheid in Kosovo had been mobilized and implemented, perhaps the brutalization phase would not have occurred. The brutalizations aimed at Albanian Kosovars were less severe than those directed at Bosnian Muslims but, regardless of many other reasons, the truth remains that the international community launched a quicker and stronger humanitarian intervention in Kosovo than in Bosnia.

RWANDA

One does not have to search far beneath the allegedly neutral descriptions to find harsh judgments of entire groups in Rwanda. The colonialists in Rwanda passed value judgments on the Hutus and the Tutsi (the Twa in Rwanda seldom receive mention). At first, the Germans and then their successors, the Belgians, had a more favorable view of the Tutsis than of the lowly Hutus. In his 1863 journal, English explorer John Hanning Speke found little hope for "the true curly-head, flab-nosed, pouch-mouthed negro," whose breed seemed destined for perdition (Gourevitch 1998, 51–52). The anthropological literature incorporated these non-neutral descriptions. Value-ladened descriptions of physical features can be detected even in the current literature. Philip Gourevitch, an ardent defender of the current Tutsi regime in Rwanda, gives the following account: "But nobody can dispute the physical archetypes: for Hutus, stocky and round-faced, dark-skinned, flat-nosed, thick-lipped, and square-jawed; for Tutsis, lanky and long faced, not so dark-skinned, narrow-nosed, thin-lipped, and narrow chinned" (1998, 50).

European explorers helped solidify the race categories by conjecturing, on the basis of slim evidence, that the "superior" Tutsis originated in Ethiopia. Anthropologists, relying on this Hamitic "scientific" theory, classified the Tutsis as being from "the primordial red race," or "Europeans under a black skin." All forms of civilization in Africa were deemed to have come from the Hamitic race, implying that anything civilized found in Africa must have come from outside of Africa. According to the biblical account in Genesis, Noah cursed the progeny of his youngest son, Ham, who saw Noah naked. The colonizers discovered a group of superior Africans, the Hamites, or "white-coloreds," who represented the missing links between the white Caucasoid and black Negroid races. While appearing more refined during the early part of the twentieth century, the descriptions never lost their value-burdened origins. Father Pages, in 1933, identified the Tutsis as a lost tribe of Christendom, which had lost its Ethiopian Coptic Christian roots during its migration. In 1933, the Belgian colonial rulers required Tutsi and Hutus to carry identity cards, first introduced in 1926. Rwanda's Belgian rulers first favored the Tutsis. Then, in 1962, just before granting independence to Rwanda, they bequeathed power to the Hutus. The colonialists' sharp differentiation between Hutu and Tutsi has been contested on historical grounds. According to a currently popular interpretation, prior to colonialization, the region's group classifications were fluid and permeable, permitting individuals to change, depending on economic status and occupation. The historical debates are interesting, but the important classifications lie in the dynamics of modern political group formations. Rwanda's more recent political history uncovers a pattern similar to the one set for groups in Nazi Germany—designation, discrimination, and brutalization.

Hutus and Tutsis, inside and outside of Rwanda, are Banyarwandan (speakers of Kinyarwanda who number over 10 million) who practice the same religion and have similar cultural habits. Within Rwanda, however, Hutus and Tutsis have constituted radically different political identities. Rwandan independence ushered in varying waves of discrimination against the Tutsi minority under two Hutu-led regimes. The system put into place in the First Republic (1961–1975), under Gregoire Kayibanda (president until a 1973 coup), functioned as an apartheid system, placing quotas on Tutsis in education and government jobs. International protection against apartheid in Rwanda was largely muted. Rwanda's First Republic ended with massive slaughters of Tutsis. During the First Republic, Rwanda lost over one-half of its Tutsi population to refugee flight to Uganda and other neighboring countries. Kayibanda's army chief of staff, General Juvenal Habyarimana, seized power and ended the anti-Tutsi pogroms. As president of the Second Republic, Habyarimana ended the First Republic's "national Hutuism" and granted citizenship to resident Tutsi, but not to those Tutsis who had fled mainly to Uganda. In 1986, the Museveni regime in Uganda changed citizenship requirements from ancestry to residence. The Ugandan diaspora group formed the bulk of the Rwandan Patriotic Front (RPF). However, the Museveni government, for internal political reasons, reversed the citizenship policy and made members of the RPF refugees in Uganda. "The Tutsi guerrilla fighters . . . found themselves between the Rwandan devil and the Ugandan deep sea. The [RPF] invasion of 1990 was their attempt to escape the closing scissors of a postcolonial citizenship crisis in Rwanda and Uganda" (Mamdani 2001, 38). The 1993 Arusha Accords, designed to end the civil war brought about by the 1990 RPF invasion, required the repatriation of Tutsi refugees. This brief account demonstrates the critical aspects of the political solidification of Tutsi identity over a roughly thirty-year period.

The brutalization phase in Rwanda distinguishes it from the brutalizations carried out in Bosnia and Kosovo. The extent and severity of the harms perpetrated against Bosnian Muslims and Albanian Kosovars pale in comparison to those inflicted on Tutsis. There were ample, immediate warning signs of a genocide brewing in Rwanda. In 1990, President Habyarimana assembled the Interahamwe, an armed militia that later carried out systematic massacres of Tutsis. Rwanda's three major radio stations played instrumental roles in solidifying and politicizing the identities and engendering the hatred of Hutus for Tutsis by utilizing the Hamitic theory designating Tutsis as Northern invaders. A prosecution for the international crime of genocide requires a showing of intent. Few analysts deny that the 1994 Rwandan genocide, where Hutu militants massacred 800,000, mostly Tutsis, children, women, and men within 100 days, met the intent requirement. According to the United Nations (UN) Commission of Experts, "There exist[s] overwhelming evidence to prove that the acts of genocide against the Tutsi ethnic group were committed by Hutu elements in a concerted, planned, systematic and methodical way" (submitted to the Security Council on December 4, 1994). The report marked the first time since adopting the 1948 Genocide Convention that the UN identified an instance of genocide. The evidence further shows that the genocide was organized at the governmental level. It takes an incredible mobilization at the state level to carry out a genocide of this proportion. The ethnic identity cards, first instituted by the Belgians, proved highly useful. Hutu extremists played the tribal card of ethnic identity with ruthless vengeance.

Policy makers outside of Rwanda also played their version of the ethnic identity card during the "crisis," which lasted from April 6 to July 26, 1994. On April 29, 1994, Secretary General Boutros-Ghali saw the situation in Rwanda as "Hutus Killing Tutsis and Tutsis Killing Hutus" (*African Rights* 1995, 1126). In May 1994, the United States pressured the UN to replace the word "genocide" in a resolution on Rwanda to "systematic, widespread and flagrant violations of humanitarian law," that is, human rights abuses. On June 10, 1994, the U.S. State Department's spokeswoman, Christine Shelly, assessed the ongoing atrocities in Rwanda: "Although there have been acts of genocide in Rwanda, all the murders cannot be put in that category" (*International Herald Tribune*, June 13, 1994). On June 14, 1994, the U.S. ambassador to Rwanda, David Rawson, described the situation as one of brother against brother, "Cain and Abel all over again." The policy advocates in each of these examples characterize the situation as a conflict between two equally blameworthy, prepolitical ethnic groups. To have applied the word "genocide" to Rwanda not only would have meant the acceptance of certain obligatory action according to international law, it also would have meant accepting a politicized version of the ethnic groups and an assessment that an egregious moral wrong was being committed.

The failure to differentiate among group harms had serious consequences. In the civil war in Rwanda in the early 1990s, some nongovernmental organizations had labeled various killings of hundreds of Tutsis as genocide. They also equated civilian war deaths with genocide. "The linking of the deaths of 'only' hundreds to the terms apocalypse and genocide throughout the civil war period diminished their impact as warnings" of an impending genocide (Suhrke and Jones 2000, 256). After the 1994 genocide, policy makers invoked the strategy of considering the different group harms as roughly equal. If all instances of group harms stood on par, then political leaders had no pressing grounds for taking measures to act on the worst harms. Although we should be wary of any comparisons, consider the following. If genocide means the intentional killing, in whole or in part, of members of an ethnic group, then despite difficulties finding reliable numbers, the genocide toll from the former Yugoslavia probably falls within the order of tens of thousands, whereas the count from Rwanda falls into the order of hundreds of thousands. A great deal of (but certainly not all of) what went under the heading of genocide in Bosnia and Kosovo consisted of uprooting ethnic groups from their homes (so-called "ethnic cleansing") and military combat-related deaths ("war crimes" and "crimes against humanity"). The Rwandan genocide meets the narrow, legal definition of genocide. About one-third of all Tutsis were intentionally and systematically eliminated. The Rwandan genocide occurred after ethnic cleansing attracted international attention in Bosnia. Rwanda became second more than in time. "More people were killed, injured, and displaced in three and half months in Rwanda than in the whole of the" Bosnian campaign (Gourevitch 1998, 169). Perhaps, the Rwandan Patriotic Front "had effectively been the only force on earth to live up to the requirements of the 1948 Genocide Convention" by acting to stop an ongoing genocide (Gourevitch 1998, 219).

Reflection upon a highly disturbing incident helps to undermine the misleading impression left so far by the analyses of the Bosnian and Kosovo cases. Identity formation, while recent and largely defensive in Bosnia and Kosovo, appears to have come about largely from above, that is, at the initiation of political, military, and other leaders. In many ways, some of the more brutal incidences occur when an identity is forced upon individuals from below.

> Kodjo Ankrah of Church World Action recounted to me what happened when soldiers entered a church in Ruhengeri and asked that Hutu step on one side, and Tutsi on another: "People refused; when they said, Tutsis this side, all moved. When they said Hutus that side, all moved. Eventually, soldiers killed them all, 200 to 300 people in all." (Mamdani 2001, 219–20)

The Rwandan case comes the closest to matching the experience of Jews under the Nazi regime in terms of the sequence and severity of harms, within sequenced phases. However, the case of the Tutsis also breaks rank with that of the Jews in Nazi Germany. The plight of the Jews became continuously and increasingly serious through the designation, discrimination, and brutalization phases. The plight of the Tutsis did not follow the same, continuously downhill descent into the hells of brutalization. Tutsis fared better under Rwanda's Second Republic than they did under the apartheid of the First Republic. Further, brutalizations occurred on the heels of outside policy makers imposing a quota system for Tutsis. Well-intentioned policies, especially when they solidify ethnic categories, often have adverse affects. The results of the Arusha Accords now haunt its promoters. An assessment of the results of the Dayton Accords for Bosnia remains open.

In any event, severe group brutalization does not always follow from increasingly severe group discrimination. Brutalization may erupt after discrimination seems to have abated. The Rwandan case illustrates one clear lesson. Patterns of severe group brutalization, most prominently of genocide, demand swift and immediate humanitarian intervention to stop them. Sovereign immunity does not apply, legally or morally. The final cleansing of ethnicity consists of removing any remnants of ethnicity that impair the effective implementation of an international moral mandate to stop genocide.

CONCLUSION

A Harm framework provides a politically defensible and morally justified way of organizing a policy analysis of group conflict. It places academic and political debates over the value of ethnicity to the side. It demands a central focus on something that should concern everyone who addresses ethnic issues, namely, on the harms associated with ethnicity. Unfortunately, the critique presented here does not produce a neatly ordered, early-warning sequence. Ethnic violence often does not proceed on a predictable and continuous path, beginning with prejudice against a group, and then proceeding through institutionalized forms of group discrimination, to attempts to exterminate the group. The proposal, in fact, challenges overly simple, early-warning models. However, the Harm framework provides an easily manageable set of three phases—designation, discrimination, and brutalization. In each phase, the policy maker should track the severity of harms. In the designation phase, political developments over a relatively short period loom large. The analysts should search for group identifications that primarily function defensively, to protect individuals from forces forming against their interests. Then analysts should track various institutionalized forms of discrimination and assess their severity, politically and morally. The discrimination phase might be skipped altogether, as in the Bosnian case, or severe institutionalized group discrimination might develop, as illustrated by the apartheid regimes experienced by Albanian Kosovars and Rwandan Tutsis. The implementation of apartheid, a particularly severe form of group discrimination, calls for international moral condemnation. The policy analysts should look for discrimination that turns into brutalization. As the Kosovo case cautions, analysts should be wary of seeing a situation as jumping quickly from the discriminatory to brutalizing harms. Yet as the Bosnian case teaches, just as analysts should not ignore the severity of harms operating under the auspices of the state during a discrimination, they should not become so focused on looking for discriminatory harms that they ignore the rapid eruption of severe brutalization in the absence of preceding discrimination. Finally, analysts should compare perceived and actual brutalization activities directed against groups and their members. Let us characterize these brutalizations as incidences of status harms, whereby perpetuators kill individuals because of their perceived ethnic or racial identity.

It proves too convenient to end with a final cleansing of ethnicity. A clarion call to eliminate all uses related to "ethnicity" would imply discarding otherwise valuable protection devices for groups (such as minority rights). However, this discussion should make us wary of efforts to institutionally reify groups. Before taking up these complexities, we must first address harms, at least in their most severe, group-related manifestations.

Notes

1. While each phase (designation, discrimination, and brutalization) raises different concerns, their seeming sequential ordering serves only as a possible unfolding in any given case. In fact, the increasing severity of the harms unfolding within each phase provides a politically more reliable and a morally sounder signal of action than do sequential developments through each of the stages.

2. The State of Illinois enacted legislation that reflected Riesman's views on group libel. The case of *Beauharnais v. Illinois* tested an Illinois group libel statute. In January 1950, Beauharnais, the president of the White League of America, distributed a leaflet urging action to keep Negroes from moving into Chicago's white neighborhoods. The leaflet proclaimed that if "persuasion and the need to prevent the white race from being mongrelized by the negro will not unite us, then the rapes, robberies, knives, guns and marijuana of the negro surely will." The state convicted Beauharnais of violating the Illinois criminal group libel law prohibiting the public display of any publication that "portrays depravity, criminality, unchastity, or lack of virtue of a class of citizens, of any race, color, creed, or religion to contempt, derision, or obloquy, or which is productive of breach of the peace or riots." The U.S. Supreme Court, in 1952, upheld his conviction. Justice Felix Frankfurter noted that Illinois had a long history of "exacerbated tension between races, often flaring into violence and destruction." He reasoned that since the fighting words doctrine (upheld in *Chaplinsky v. New Hampshire*) would not protect the same speech directed toward individuals, then the judiciary should not second-guess the Illinois legislature when it prohibited these words directed toward groups.

References

Amit-Talai, Vered, and Caroline Knowles, eds. 1996. *Re-Situating Identities: The Politics of Race, Ethnicity, and Culture*. Peterborough, Ontario: Broadview.

Anderson, Benedict. 1983. *Imagined Communities: Reflections on the Origins and Spread of Nationalism*. London: Verso.

Appiah, K. Anthony. 1994. "Identity, Authenticity, Survival." Pp. 149–64 in *Multiculturalism*, ed. Amy Gutman. Princeton: Princeton University Press.

Bringa, Tone. 1995. *Being Muslim the Bosnian Way*. Princeton: Princeton University Press.

Davis, F. James. 1991. *Who Is Black?* University Park: Pennsylvania State University Press.

Doubt, Keith. 2000. *Sociology after Bosnia and Kosovo: Recovering Justice*. Lanham, Md.: Rowman & Littlefield.

Easman, Milton J. 1994. *Ethnic Politics*. Ithaca: Cornell University Press.

Fenton, Steve. 1999. *Ethnicity: Racism, Class, and Culture*. Lanham, Md.: Rowman & Littlefield.

Friedman, Francine. 1996. *The Bosnian Muslims: Denial of a Nation*. Boulder: Westview Press.

Friedman, Thomas L. 1993. "Bosnia Reconsidered: Clinton Administration Recasts a Conflict from a Historical Crime to an Ancient Feud," *New York Times* (April 8), A1.

Ganguly, Rajat, and Ray Taras. 1998. *Understanding Ethnic Conflict: The International Dimension*. New York: Addison Wesley Longman.

Gourevitch, Philip. 1998. *We Wish to Inform You That Tomorrow We Will Be Killed with Our Families*. New York: Farrar, Straus and Giroux.

Hilberg, Raul. 1985. *The Destruction of the European Jews*. New York: Holmes & Meier.

Hollinger, David A. 2000. *Postethnic America: Beyond Multiculturalism*, 5th ed. New York: Basic Books.

Horowitz, Donald. 1985. *Ethnic Groups in Conflict*. Berkeley: University of California Press.

Ignatieff, Michael. 1997. *The Warrior's Honor: Ethnic War and the Modern Conscience*. New York: Henry Holt.

Judah, Tim. 1997. *The Serbs: History, Myth, and the Destruction of Yugoslavia*. New Haven: Yale University Press.

Kaplan, Robert D. 1993. *Balkan Ghosts*. New York: Viking.

———. 1994. "The Coming Anarchy." *Atlantic Monthly* (May): 44–76.

Kymlicka, Will. 1995. *Multicultural Citizenship*. Oxford: Oxford University Press.

Layne, Christopher, and Benjamin Schwarz. 2000. "Kosovo, One Year Later." *The Washington Post National Weekly Edition* (April 3): 21–22.

MacLennan, Hugh. 1945. *Two Solitudes*. New York: Popular Library.

Malcolm, Noel. 1996. *Bosnia: A Short History*. New York: New York University Press.

———. 1998. *Kosovo: A Short History*. New York: New York University Press.

Mamdani, Mahmood. 2001. *When Victims Become Killers*. Princeton: Princeton University Press.

Mousavizadeh, Nader, ed. 1996. *The Black Book of Bosnia*. New York: Basic Books.

Nickel, James. 1995. "What's Wrong with Ethnic Cleansing?" *Journal of Social Philosophy* 25 (spring): 5–15.

Nyegosh, P. P. 1930. *The Mountain Wreath*. Translated by James W. Wiles. London: George Allen and Unwin.

Riesman, David. 1942. "Democracy and Defamation: Control of Group Libel." *Columbia Law Review* 42.

Simon, Thomas W. 1995. "Group Harm." *Journal of Social Philosophy* (winter): 123–38.

———. 1996. "Defining Genocide." *Wisconsin International Law Review* (fall):243–56.

Smith, Anthony D. 1996. "Nations and Their Past." In *Nations and Nationalism,* vol. 3.

Sofos, Spyros and Brian Jenkins, eds. 1996. *Nation and Identity in Contemporary Europe.* Routledge.

Suhrke, Astri, and Bruce Jones. 2000. "Preventative Diplomacy in Rwanda: Failure to Act or Failure of Actions?" Pp. 238–64 in *Opportunities Missed, Opportunities Seized: Preventive Diplomacy in Post–Cold War World.* ed. Bruce W. Jentleson. Carnegie Commission on Preventing Deadly Conflict. New York: Carnegie Corporation.

Szayna, Thomas S., ed. 1998. *Identifying Potential Ethnic Conflict: Application of a Process Model.* Santa Monica: RAND Arroyo Center.

Tomkin, Elisabeth, Maryon McDonald, and Malcolm Chapman. 1989. *History and Ethnicity.* London: Routledge. Reprinted in John Hutchinson and Anthony Smith, ed. 1996. *Ethnicity.* New York: Oxford University Press, 18–24.

Turnbull, Colin M. 1972. *The Mountain People.* New York: Simon & Schuster.

Ugresic, Dubravka. 1998. *The Culture of Lies: Antipolitical Essays.* University Park: Pennsylvania State University Press.

Vickers, Miranda. 1998. *Between Serb and Albanian: A History of Kosovo.* New York: Columbia University Press.

West, Rebecca. 1941, 1982. *Black Lamb and Grey Falcon: A Journey through Yugoslavia.* New York: Penguin Books.

Wirth, Louis. 1949. "Why the Jewish Community Survives." Pp. ??? in *When People Meet,* ed. Locke and Stern. New York: Hinds, Hayden & Eldredge.

Woodward, Susan L. 2000. "Costly Disinterest: Missed Opportunities for Preventative Diplomacy in Croatia and Bosnia and Herzegovina, 1985–1991." Pp. 133–72 in *Opportunities Missed, Opportunities Seized: Preventive Diplomacy in Post–Cold War World,* ed. Lanham, Md.: Rowman & Littlefield.

Part 3

Interrogating the Logic
of Cultural Politics

Chapter 5

Forjando Patria

Anthropology, Criminology, and the Post-Revolutionary Discourse on Citizenship

Robert Buffington

> . . . it is necessary that the three big groups of our population—indigenous, mestizo, and white—come together, mix, and become confused until they manage to homogenize and unify the racial type, procuring through the application of a sensible eugenics, to cultivate the satisfactory physical gifts and correct the defective ones.
>
> —Manuel Gamio, "Pueblos nuevos"

The failure of the post–revolutionary project of Mexican national integration is the general theme of this chapter. The political, economic, and social causes of this failure—including halfhearted post-revolutionary commitments to education and land reform, the "logic" of dependent capitalist development, and a racist colonial legacy—are relatively well understood. The perceptual and discursive causes, however, are less clear, and yet they lie at the heart of the "Indian problem." Even when the will was there (which it often was not), the very manner in which the Mexican intelligentsia, professional social analysts, and official policy makers constructed the problem guaranteed that any solution would be partial, difficult, and painful. In the introduction to this book, Toffolo comments that mass-based liberation movements often "reenergized" traditional identities (*ECP*, 8). That was certainly the case in Mexico during and after the great revolutionary struggles (1910–1920), as Zapatistas, among others, asserted historical, and often communal, rights to land. The general thrust of post–revolutionary Mexican nationalism, however, favored cultural integration, even as it recognized and sometimes endorsed ethnic difference.

This chapter specifically examines the intersection of anthropological and criminological discourse in the context of post–revolutionary efforts to forge a modern nation-state. Anthropologists such as Manuel Gamio, author

81

of the much-cited *Forjando patria* (Forging the Fatherland), imagined an inclusive national community that revalued indigenous cultures, reincorporated indigenous peoples, and prepared them for the responsibilities of citizenship (Gamio 1960). Criminologists, as professional analysts of society's excluded criminal elements (those legally denied the rights of citizens), clarified and qualified the terms of acceptance. The exclusions built into criminological discourse contributed a disturbing counter-current to anthropological inclusiveness, but mixed message aside, practitioners openly acknowledged and even welcomed the methodological and discursive linkages between the two disciplines. The implications of that linkage, however, were left unimagined or at least unspoken. Covert or not, the criminological subtext of post–revolutionary anthropology contained the proverbial weak link, the fatal flaw that exposed the big lie behind the inclusive rhetoric of *indigenista* anthropologists and, by extension, of revolutionary nationalism itself (Brading 1988b). After all, for indigenous groups, conditional acceptance was nothing new.

ON INTEGRATING INDIANS: A BRIEF SKETCH

Elite concerns about the need to integrate Mexico's indigenous peoples into national life took on a certain immediacy after the 1821 severing of colonial ties with Spain. In his monumental *Historia antigua de México*, Mexican-born Jesuit historian Francisco Javier Clavigero had blamed Spanish colonial practice for the degraded state of the Indian population:

> If their upbringing were carefully supervised, if they were educated in schools by competent teachers, and if they were encouraged by rewards, one would see among the Indians philosophers, mathematicians and theologians who would vie with the most famous of Europe. (Phelan 1960, 765)[1]

And two years before Father Hidalgo's 1810 *Grito de Dolores* initiated the struggle for independence, Prussian scientist Alexander von Humboldt had bluntly informed his international readership that "Mexico is the country of inequality," its indigenous people "a picture of extreme misery," thanks to years of abuse, racial prejudice, and the misguided segregationist policies of the Spanish crown (Humboldt 1966, 184-85). For self-consciously progressive Mexican elites, Independence offered the opportunity to redress these colonial mistakes and transform the fledgling nation into an enlightened modern state (Brading 1991; Schmidt 1978; Bartra 1992).

The nature of that transformation was hotly contested, but in spite of the profound disagreements that plunged Mexico into a half century of political chaos, liberals and conservatives shared a common concern about the Indian problem. Both groups criticized the crown's segregationist policies which, for all their humanitarian intent, had set indigenous groups apart from dominant whites and mestizos and thus exacerbated heterogeneous Mexico's already considerable social tensions. Conservative Lucas Alamán, for example, considered the Indians an "entirely separate nation" that in spite of their colonial privileges "looked at everyone else with hate and distrust." His liberal adversary, Lorenzo de Zavala, proposed the "incorporation of those of indigenous descent into society, under the same laws and civil and political rights," provided they "be obliged to form regular societies or leave the territory of the Republic" (quoted in Chávez Chávez 1988; Brading 1988a). Similarly, a mid-century optimist welcomed the end of the "odious" colonial caste system and declared that "now we have only free Mexicans with no distinctions other than aptitude and merit" (Larrainzar 1852, 232). In modern Mexico, conservative or liberal, Indians would be productive citizens or be damned!

Ironically perhaps, just as citizenship was being thrust upon them, Indians also became important symbols of Mexican separateness from Spain. And although liberals lauded Aztec glories, while conservatives propagated a Hispanic origin myth—Alamán hid Cortés's bones to protect them from liberal desecration—both agreed that contemporary Indians bore faint resemblance to their illustrious ancestors. The 1825 founding of the Museo Nacional Mexicano (Mexican National Museum) to display and preserve national antiquities thus had little to do with recognizing the contributions of contemporary indigenous peoples and everything to do with propagating the symbols of incipient nationalism. More importantly, this incongruous dual construction—suspicious contemporary Indian as reluctant citizen, glorious pre-Conquest Indian as national symbol—which included a threat (of national disintegration) and a promise (of redemption), formed the basis for future approaches to the Indian problem. Proposals and even policies might reflect considerable differences among elites, but most accepted this fundamental construction of the Indian problem.

If nationalists had new plans for the Indians, they were based on long-standing racial prejudices. The Mexican origins of the stereotypical Indian likely began with the inevitable "Othering" engendered by conquest and colonial domination (Todorov 1984). Whatever its roots, by Independence the stereotype was well developed and ubiquitous. Some commentators stressed the Indian's political apathy, primitive economy, and traditionalist culture:

The native is quiet, long-suffering, apathetic when his interests are not involved; but when they are, he is obstreperous, insolent, and enterprising. Monotonous in his customs, he does today what he did yesterday and what he will do tomorrow. The plow and the hoe, these are the objects of his concern. . . . Towards everything, finally,

he is indifferent: fatherland, government, institutions; nothing moves
him as long as it doesn't disturb his repose. (Larrainzar 1852, 234)

In this vision, the Indian is not only disengaged but actively blocks engagement. Generally dull and apathetic, the Indian (like a wild animal) becomes
clever and dangerous when cornered. And this was a sympathetic treatment!
Other commentators went further, accusing Indians of habitual drunkenness
and of being natural sneak thieves, "always and without exceptions"
("Estadística" 1852, 294). Apathetic, alcoholic, backward, resistant (sometimes to the point of violence), and inherently criminal, Indians presented an
imposing obstacle to national consolidation and economic progress.

To make matters even worse, according to Emperor Maximilian's French
scientists, and contrary to appearances in a country where indigenous bearers
carried most everything on their backs, Indians were a weak, degenerate race.
In an 1865 translation for the *Bulletin of the Mexican Geographical and Statistical Society*, a Dr. Jourdanet warned that "although generally healthy and
often long-lived, they are weak and can bring to field work only very modest
forces," a condition he blamed on the degenerative effects of the central
plateau's high altitude and poor living conditions (Jourdanet 1865, 240).
Jourdanet's findings received further endorsement in an 1878 study of the
"Influence of Altitude on the Life and Health of the Inhabitant of Anahuac."
Its author, after a careful study of relative lung capacity and oxygen in the
blood, attempted to merge European science and Mexican prejudice. "The
inhabitant of Anahuac," he advised,

> is less robust than at lower elevations in the country, his constitution
> is generally weak, his muscles little developed and his material work
> relatively minimal. His complexion is pallid and yellowish, his face
> sullen, his air is sad and pensive, his step slow and always with a
> reflection of melancholy vacillation . . . the great majority of the
> population is submerged in an undefinable apathy, takes no part in
> public life, and lives day-to-day without worrying about the future.
> (Belina 1878, 303)

This new twist on the established stereotype not only provided scientific
endorsement for long-standing racist attitudes but undermined hopes that
Indians might someday be productive citizens. Even physical labor, their one
solid historical claim to a place in Mexican society, was less than adequate:
a perpetually exhausted race was hardly the foundation of a dynamic, modern
nation. For elites, enamored of the "productive" capitalist economies of Western Europe and North America, it was an ominous sign.

Grounded in the evolutionary theories of Lamarck and Darwin, via Comte
and Spencer, turn-of-the-century Porfirian positivism roused further fears of

national decline (especially after a disastrous nineteenth century). Even while Porfirian elites gloried at home and abroad in Mexico's distinctive Indian heritage, concern about the current Indian problem grew apace (González Navarro 1988; Powell 1968; Raat 1971; Stabb 1959; Hale 1989, chapter 7). Some social commentators, such as Francisco Bulnes, gave in to blatant racism and despair. "The Indian," he lamented with more art than originality,

> is disinterested, stoic, without enlightenment; depreciates death, life, gold, morality, work, science, sadness and hope. He loves four things seriously: the idols of his old religion, the earth that feeds him, personal liberty, and the alcohol which produces his dismal and dreary deliriums. (Bulnes 1968, 155)

More optimistic analysts, such as Porfirio Díaz's Education Minister, Justo Sierra, sought to "convert the native into a social asset" through the traditional liberal combination of education and immigration. "We need to attract immigrants from Europe so as to obtain a cross with the indigenous race," he suggested, "for only European blood can keep the level of civilization that has produced our nationality from sinking, which would mean regression, not evolution" (Sierra 1895, 368). Both visions reinforced long-standing prejudices, and even Sierra's relatively moderate reading of the Indian problem depreciated the Indians' potential contribution. Given general concerns about national survival in the international struggle for life (especially with a belligerent, expansionist United States on the northern border), these readings deliberately created a sense of impending crisis that boded ill for Mexico's indigenous peoples.

But while the Indian stereotype suffered ever-greater indignities over the course of the nineteenth century, the fortunes of the mestizo gradually improved.[2] In the colonial and early national periods elite observers had commented repeatedly on the volatile mestizo: "easily upset, and once upset, tenacious in his judgments, terrible in his resolutions, and atrocious in his vengeance" (Larrainzar 1852, 234).[3] "It is well-known," another observed, "that a higher level of culture that is not grounded on a moral or religious base increases rather than diminishes crime" ("Estadística" 1852, 294). More politically active than most indigenous peoples and the principal perpetrators of urban crime, mestizos (especially of the lower classes) were a more familiar and immediate threat to elites. Some analysts, such as Porfirian criminologist Julio Guerrero, went so far as to contrast the immoral mestizo and Indian urban poor with the honorable rural Indians, who "never live in sexual promiscuity" (Guerrero 1901, 161). But this was a secondary discussion about the corrupting influence of the city on family values that ignored larger issues of race and citizenship. Most observers agreed that mestizos, for all of their many flaws, contributed far more to Mexican national life than their Indian counterparts.

More than that, as the racial constructions of European social Darwinism collided with Mexican nationalist discourse after mid-century, social commentators began to see the mestizo population as the foundation of a national race. Politicized biological metaphors that stressed the hybrid vigor of mixed races dominated the discourse. Even Ignacio Manuel Altamirano, of indigenous descent, like fellow *puro* liberal Benito Juárez, praised the "homogenization of the conquering and conquered races . . . that should constitute physiologically and politically speaking the great force of the nation" (González Phillips 1988, 104). Another prominent liberal (and positivist), Justo Sierra, rejected European notions of racial purity and praised the "virility" of the "new race" (Sierra 1895, 11).[4] For Sierra, the middle-class mestizo—purified of the "socio-pathogenic microbes" of alcoholism and superstition that bubbled up from the Indian underclass—represented an end to the racial divisions that obstructed Mexico's "social evolution" and thus provided the key to national progress (Sierra 1895, 360). Not surprisingly, this newly constructed progressive mestizo often was contrasted with the weak, degenerate Indian. In his "Memorandum on the causes that have created the current situation of the indigenous race of Mexico . . . ," Francisco Pimentel, a prominent scholar and Second Empire functionary, gave a positive spin to the volatile mestizo stereotype, noting that "it is easier to cure an excessively robust man than it is to revive an exhumed corpse, weakened by endless privations and overwork" (Stabb 1959, 407). Positivist sociologist Andrés Molina Enríquez's "revolutionary" 1909 indictment of Mexican development, *Las grandes problemas nacionales*, echoed Pimentel's assessment. After deploring the moral and physical degradation of Mexico's Indian population, Molina Enríquez praised the energetic "mestizo, who [because he] has always been poor, is vulgar, crude, suspicious, restless and impetuous; but stubborn, faithful, generous and patient" (Molina Enríquez 1981, 110).[5] In the constructions of social analysts such as Altamirano, Pimentel, Sierra, and Molina Enríquez, then, the mestizo symbolized a vigorous, new, autarkical Mexican race that reconciled a divisive racial and cultural heritage. The Indian, like the Spaniard, harkened back to the tainted colonial past.

Homogenization, as Altamirano called it, became the leitmotiv of nineteenth-century nationalist discourse. Pimentel argued that "Indians [should] forget their customs and even their language . . . and form with the whites a homogeneous mass, a true nation" (Castellón Huerta 1988, 199). Even historian Vincente Riva Palacio, who considered Indians more physically evolved than whites, argued that:

> In order for true nationality to exist it is indispensable that its individuals have relatively similar aptitudes, harmonious tendencies, similarly-constituted organisms, that they be subject in general to the same morphologic and functional viscidities, to the same epidemic

dangers and that they not present within themselves anything more than individual anomalies and in their many intellectual manifestations a trait not possessed by the race in general. (Serrano and Rodríguez 1988, 311–12)

Once thought to possess all of the bad traits of both parent races, mestizos now represented the obvious source of the racial and cultural unity that nationalists saw as Mexico's best hope for the future. The mestizo, as Dr. Jourdanet had declared, is "he who progresses"; the Indian (and after Independence, the creole as well) obstructed progress.

ON ANTHROPOLOGISTS AND INDIANS

The long gestation of Mexican anthropology that began with the founding of the National Museum in 1825 was inextricably bound up with the nationalist discourse about Indians. The antiquarian investigation of pre-Conquest indigenous cultures, which romanticized the Indian past as the foundation of Mexican national identity, dominated early "amateur" anthropology. The study of contemporary Indians was left to "undisciplined" social commentators. Ironically, scientists from a Franco–Mexican Commission, organized by the Paris-based Societé d'Anthropologie in the 1860s, were the first self-identified professionals to attempt a systematic investigation of Mexico's indigenous peoples (Serrano Sánchez and López Alonso 1988, 204–205). The untimely demise of Maximilian cut the project short, but not before inspiring Manuel Orozco y Berra's "Geography of the Languages and Ethnographic Map of Mexico in 1864" and Francisco Pimentel's previously mentioned memorandum of the same year (Chávez Chávez 1988, 671). Both works set important precedents, not only in their concern for living Indians, but in their obvious attempt to inform government policies.

The practical need for information, and especially accurate statistics, had been recognized earlier. An 1851 article for the *Bulletin of the Mexican Geographical and Statistical Society* called for a panoply of racial data (under the general rubric of "moral" statistics). A subsequent article in the same journal argued that "without a practical knowledge of the [Mexican] peoples, one cannot calculate their civilization, their morality, their wealth, nor their specific needs" (Larrainzar 1852, 232). The interest in statistics persisted. A 1902 study of "Statistics and Their Function as Bonds of Union between Individuals and Peoples" even suggested making statistics the "Mexican national science" (Esteva Ruiz 1902, 15). Like anthropology, statistics (and these were anthropological statistics) was a fundamentally nationalistic science with compelling ties to government needs. These ties between scientific study and public policy would become even stronger with the professionalization of anthropology during the late nineteenth and early twentieth centuries, the will to knowledge inextricably interwoven with the will to power.

Not surprisingly, the positivist-inspired Porfirian era, with its commitment to "scientific politics," produced Mexico's first generation of professional anthropologists.[6] Physical anthropology, with its compulsive measuring and comparing of racial bodies, quickly carved out a professional space. Its ascendency to disciplinary status was marked by the 1887 establishment of the Physical Anthropology Section at the National Museum, its hiring of Nicolás León as director in 1900, and his 1903 appointment as its first professor of anthropology and ethnology (León 1919, 231-35). León, in turn, would train the next generation of Mexican anthropologists.

North American physical anthropologists working in Mexico, in particular Aleš Hrdlička (León's mentor) and Frederick Starr, played a crucial role in this process, providing legitimacy and direction to the fledgling discipline. Neither was particularly racist by the European standards of Gustav Le Bon and Arthur de Gobineau: they attributed the apparent degeneration of Mexican Indians to environmental and social causes rather than to inherent racial inferiority. Nevertheless, the racial nature of their investigations and those of their Mexican colleagues and protégés carried considerable baggage: degeneration was no less dangerous to national well-being, just because its causes came (at least initially) from outside of the carefully measured body of the anthropological subject. As might be expected, this North American racial agenda and its colonialist subtext resonated powerfully with the social concerns of subsequent Mexican anthropologists.

Mexican anthropology's big break came with the Revolution. Porfirian scientific politics was, more than anything, an ideological construct designed to legitimize an undemocratic regime. In practice, most *científicos* showed little inclination to undertake serious social reform. The victorious revolutionaries, compelled by a populist ideology, had bigger plans, and the activist state that emerged from revolutionary struggle seemed an ideal vehicle for ambitious social scientists.

The auspicious appearance of Manuel Gamio's *Forjando Patria* in the midst of the Revolution thus marked a watershed in Mexican anthropology. "Today," he proclaimed, "it is up to Mexican revolutionaries to seize the hammer and tighten the blacksmith's apron so that from the miraculous anvil a new fatherland will arise from a combination of [Spanish] iron and [Indian] bronze" (Gamio 1960, 6). Not surprisingly, in Gamio's vision of national consolidation, anthropology played the crucial role. "It is axiomatic," he insisted, "that Anthropology in its broadest sense should be fundamental to the discharge of good government" (Gamio 1960, 23). The need for a comprehensive study of Mexico's indigenous peoples, prominent in nineteenth-century anthropological discourse, figured into Gamio's scheme as well:

We not only need to know how many men, women, and children
there are in the Republic, the languages they speak, and how they
control their ethnic groups. We need to know many other things:
geography, geology, meteorology, flora and fauna . . . also language,
religion, industry, art, commerce, folklore, clothing, food, strength,
physical-anthropological type, etc., etc. (Gamio 1960, 50–51)

This comprehensive knowledge, he insisted, would help "us understand our needs,
aspirations, deficiencies and qualities," which would in turn allow "[us] to procure
the betterment of [Mexico's] diverse ethnic groups" (Gamio 1960, 50–51).

According to Gamio, only the potent combination of anthropological
knowledge and revolutionary fervor could span heterogeneous Mexico's vast
cultural divides. In the conclusion to *Forjando Patria*, he outlined a program
for national integration:

*Fusion of races, convergence and fusion of cultural manifestations, lin-
guistic unification and economic balance of social elements* . . . ought to
characterize the Mexican population, so that it constitute and incar-
nate a powerful Fatherland and a coherent and defined nationality.
(Gamio 1960, 325, emphasis in original)

Aside from the nod to "economic balance," the line could have come from
Pimentel or Sierra. However, there were some differences. Unlike Porfirian
commentators such as Francisco Bulnes, Gamio, a disciple of renowned cultural relativist Franz Boas, was repelled by racist European anthropology.
"The Indian has the same aptitudes for progress as the white," he noted,
"being neither superior or inferior." And, he added, with typically liberal
optimism, "with improvements in his food, clothing, education, and enter-
tainments, the Indian will embrace contemporary culture the same as any
other race" (Gamio 1960, 38). Thus although he rejected biologically based
racism, Gamio still privileged a progressive, homogeneous national culture
that could only come from *mestizaje* (race mixture). Mestizo culture, for all
of its "deficiencies" and "deformities," was "the national culture . . . of the
future"; Indian culture (or Spanish culture, for that matter) was not so much
inherently inferior as inappropriate, divisive, and doomed to extinction. Biological differences might persist for a while; cultural unity would first make
them irrelevant and consequently—through increased intermarriage—break
them down altogether. Complete integration seemed just a matter of a few
generations. And the need was pressing. In Gamio's positivist vision, Mexico's
national health, and by extension its survival in the international struggle for
life, required the unity that only a national mestizo culture could bring.

This fundamentally positivist vision of national integration formed the
basis of the post–revolutionary anthropological project, which Gamio, as head

of the newly formed Department of Anthropology (1917) and founder and editor of a popular anthropological journal, *Ethnos* (1920–1925), was well positioned to influence. His 1922 *chef-d'œuvre*, a comprehensive, two-volume study of *The Population of the Valley of Teotihuacán*, which consolidated his international position, brought together all of the threads of Mexican anthropology. As usual, the positivist teleology was transparent.

Gamio's emphasis on applied anthropology in the service of post–revolutionary nation building and his concern about possible "obstacles" took on deeper meaning in the more detailed studies that comprised the two volumes. For example, a study of the indigenous "physical type" noted that most indigenous subjects deviated from the round-headed norm, which indicated some race mixture (a good thing), but that mestizo subjects generally were taller, larger, stronger, and more narrow-headed than their indigenous counterparts (Siliceo Pauer 1922, 165). Another study concluded that although the lack of protein in their diet could account for some deficiencies, "the indigenous people that currently inhabit the valley of Teotihuacán belong to a race in physiological decline" (Izquierdo 1922, 186). Yet another study specified the environmental causes of this decline:

> The lack of cleanliness, the ignorance of the most elemental precepts of hygiene, the abundance of parasites, the poorly-constructed houses, the monotonous diet, the unhealthy water of some of the water holes and wells, the alcoholic abuses and endemic nature of some diseases make the hygienic conditions of the inhabitants not at all favorable. (Siliceo Pauer 1922–1923, 195)

His unsurprising solution: the "socialization and education" of the indigenous population, leading to "spontaneous, progressive, and intense mestizaje" (Siliceo Pauer 1922, 201). Thus even though post–revolutionary anthropologists (like their liberal predecessors) recognized the social, cultural, environmental, and historical causes for Indian "decline," this obstacle to national progress was an accomplished fact that could only be overcome through the redeeming powers of cultural unification and race mixture. The principal message was inclusive, but the conditional nature of inclusion remained a distant, if persistent, murmur.

The 1920 inauguration of *Ethnos*, an anthropology journal directed at the "general public," helped disseminate these ideas among a broader (if still mostly elite) audience of well-informed citizens, fellow intellectuals, and enlightened bureaucrats. Gamio's blend of disciplinary aggrandizement and revolutionary nationalism permeated the journal. By the second issue, he was pushing hard for an anthropologically correct census that would include racial and cultural data. Incomplete data, he argued, "has hindered the development of the population instead of bettering it" (Gamio 1920, 46). In 1923, a new subtitle, "Magazine Dedicated to the Study and Betterment of Mexico's Indigenous Population," further clarified its practical, proselytizing mission.

This mission did not develop in a vacuum. Gamio's 1920 selection as a vice president to the Second International Eugenics Congress in Washington, D. C., recognized his often-stated commitment to "bettering" Mexico's indigenous peoples and preparing them for the "racial fusion . . . cultural generalization and linguistic unification" that would spawn a vigorous, hybrid Mexican race ("El Segundo Congreso" 1920, 128-30; "La segunda época de Ethnos," 1922, 2). In an article on "Nationalism and Internationalism," he noted that Mexico might eventually become part of an international federation (a bureaucratization perhaps of Vasconcelos's "cosmic race"), but that "at this moment, we ought first of all form a nation" (Gamio 1923, 3). A colleague observed that physical anthropology in particular applied "the principles of Eugenics for the racial betterment of populations" and lamented that Mexico still lacked a preliminary study of racial degeneration (Siliceo Pauer 1922–1923, 15, 18).[7] In Mexico's case, international science again served a nationalist cause, even as it continued to reinforce racial thinking in Mexican anthropologists.

The 1925 takeover of *Ethnos* by the Secretariat of Public Education, in the wake of Plutarco Elías Calles's ascension to the presidency, further cemented anthropology's ties to government-directed social reform. The new director, Lucio Mendieta y Núñez, surpassed even Gamio in his bluntness. Inspired perhaps by the new regime's more active (and sometimes brutal) approach to social reform, he declared baldly that the purpose of anthropological study was "to obtain a complete and as exact as possible knowledge of the principal indigenous populations of the Republic, past and present, in order to uncover the causes of their present vices and the scientific means of correcting them" (Mendieta y Núñez 1925, 46). Calles's accelerated land distribution program of the mid-1920s favored the communal *ejido* landholding system. This system both presupposed and sought to foster a cooperative (co-opted), acculturated peasant class integrated into the national economy, and as his response to the Cristero Revolt made clear, Calles brooked no resistance. In this political context, and with the introduction of eugenics and the frank acknowledgment that anthropology's purpose was to uncover and correct vices, officially sanctioned anthropological discourse had crossed the fine line that separated anthropology and criminology. The essentially positive, inclusive thrust of Gamio's message (at least on the surface) had taken on a negative, exclusive tone. His vision had always tacitly assumed the need to change unprogressive attitudes; now that need had become the guiding principle of anthropological knowledge.

ON RECONSTRUCTING THE INDIAN CRIMINAL

The line dividing between anthropology and criminology had never been particularly clear. Both were offshoots of positivist sociology, and both owed a considerable debt to the nineteenth-century evolutionary paradigms of Lamarck and Darwin. Shared methodologies strengthened the bond. Physical anthropology benefitted immensely from the pioneering work of self-described Italian criminal anthropologist Cesare Lombroso, who built an international reputation on his discovery of the hidden physiological "stigmata" (mostly cranial) of criminality. Lombroso's refinement of the methodology of early nineteenth-century phrenologists, which had posited crude links between cranial development and personality, was based on earlier work by French physical anthropologist Paul Broca. Likewise, the internationalization of Parisian police clerk Alfonse Bertillon's elaborate system for measuring criminal bodies (derived from Broca and Lombroso) provided a useful example for physical anthropologists as they sought to standardize their own measuring procedures.[8] This cross-fertilization also provided a considerable amount of interpretive baggage, the most egregious examples being Broca's theories of racial inferiority based on brain structure and Lombroso's theory of "atavism," which linked criminality with the physical traits of "primitive" races. Intentional or not, this racist baggage increased the ideological potential of both anthropology and criminology, because it legitimized long-standing social inequities.

The connections between cultural anthropology and criminology were nearly as strong. French criminologist Gabriel Tarde had insisted, in opposition to Lombroso's biological determinism, that milieu—living conditions, social status, cultural background, health, education, and so on—rather than heredity, was the crucial variable in determining criminality. Most criminologists, including Lombroso himself, responded by creating elaborate causal hierarchies and criminal typologies that factored in both heredity and milieu in varying degrees. And although focused on the criminal subject, both the data and methodology of this more refined criminology borrowed heavily from anthropology, and vice versa.

For late nineteenth-century Mexican criminal anthropologists Francisco Martínez Baca and Manuel Vergara, the disciplinary connection had seemed obvious. In their study of the skulls of indigenous criminals who died in the Puebla penitentiary, they noted that small craniums, less developed occipital (back brain) regions, and "simple" sutures indicated inferiority "according to the observations of Broca" (Martínez Baca and Vergara 1892, 10). This scientific verification of Indian inferiority was hardly surprising. The real problem, they cautioned, was to determine the specific stigmata of Mexican criminality in a country where European atavisms represented the norm. Careful measurement of Indian subjects, then, would provide a baseline "of the physiognomi-

cal features of this race which will allow us to distinguish the anomalies"
(Martínez Baca and Vergara 1892, 98).

In addition to these cranial measurements, they also collected information on each subject's personal, family, and cultural background. Alcoholism, for example, indicated a predisposition to crime, because it lowered
inhibitions and caused both personal and inherited degeneration (Martínez
Baca and Vergara 1892, 33–34). But it was only one factor, and a fairly
obvious one at that. The combined data sets, however, eventually would
allow professional criminologists to identify even the previously hidden
stigmata of the Indian criminal. The potential benefits to the forces of
social order were incalculable. The self-aggrandizing will to knowledge and
power (or at least bureaucratic positions), so evident in Mexican anthropology, was matched by its sister discipline, and the drive to determine physiological and behavioral norms in order to identify deviance supplied a
compelling raison d'être for subsequent anthropological studies. In light of
this disciplinary connection, studies on indigenous peoples by physical and
cultural anthropologists took on a more ominous tone, not altogether suppressed, even in Gamio's heyday.[9] Strongly implicated (as a branch of scientific
politics) in the Porfirian criminalization of the urban lower classes, criminologists kept a low profile in the years that immediately followed the
Revolution. By the late 1920s, as revolutionary populist fervor cooled under
Calles's increasingly dour gaze, they were ready to reclaim their professional
and discursive spaces, and resurgent criminology quickly made its mark on
its sister discipline. A new, popular anthropology journal, *Quetzalcoatl* (1929–
1931), demonstrated the more exclusive, pessimistic orientation of 1930s'
anthropology (González González 1988). Paradoxically, perhaps, the founding
of a broad-based National Revolutionary Party (PNR) in 1929 clearly de-
lineated the parameters of political participation and thus clarified the
requirements for citizenship. This delimitation of boundaries, which highlighted the inclusive/exclusive nature of the social contract, doubtlessly
encouraged a criminological perspective. An article on "The Redemption of
the Indian from a New Perspective," by editor Carlos Basauri, noted the
widespread presence of "various stigmata of degeneration" among Indians,
which he attributed to "precocious sexual unions, defective alimentation,
alcoholism and lack of hygiene." Moreover, these causes were more cultural
than circumstantial. Regarding nutrition, for example, he asserted that "on
many occasions the economic circumstances . . . the scant agricultural production and miserable living conditions impose this diet; but in *most* cases
it is traditional custom and ignorance that cause [Indians] to persist in such
a lamentable system" (Basauri 1929, 8–9, emphasis added). Basauri's social
consciousness, meant to spur reform, also reinforced classic stereotypes,
such as the drunken Indian mother who weaned her children on pulque. And
if the degenerate Indian male resisted criminality—congenital lassitude made

even criminal acts difficult—his biological degeneration still presented an obstacle to national progress.

In a subsequent article on "The Mexican National Type of the Future," Basauri presented the inescapable solution: mestizaje. He argued that although education might raise the Indian's "moral level," the race had already reached the "limit of its biological development." On the other hand, he insisted, "the strongest races, the most beautiful and most talented, are the result of many ethnic combinations." Racial biology aside, this mestizo "psychological and social type" represented (yet again) the national future (Basauri 1930, 6–7). The message echoed Gamio's; the virulent attack on indigenous races and cultures, however, was even more pronounced. Indians might have a secondary place in the new Mexico; their culture, which encouraged degeneration and even criminality, did not.

Once again, foreign anthropologists helped reinforce and legitimize this trend. In 1933, an Italian–Mexican team, which included Carlos Basauri, measured and photographed nearly 2,000 indigenous subjects (Serrano and Mejía Sánchez 1988). The expedition's avowed purpose was to study the evolution of populations and race mixture in Mexico. Their new technique, biotyping, sought to categorize and map human populations according to various physical criteria, including the inevitable cranial and nasal indices. It seemed the perfect solution to the often-lamented but still unsolved problem of defining and delimiting Mexico's racially heterogeneous population. Mexican anthropologist José Gómez Robledo pointed out that "in Mexico, where the number of aboriginal groups . . . passes fifty, biotypology can lead us to create a true ethnic inventory through which we will arrive at the knowledge of the value of the indigenous human material and the most adequate ways and means to manage their assimilation into modern society" (Gómez Robledo et al. 1943, xvi–xvii; Romero 1966, 80).

Even a partial analysis of the results offered no surprises. Expedition leader Corrado Gini noted of the Seri that "if one cannot deny their degenerative flaws, one should nevertheless allow that they are flaws caused by inbreeding, if not defective alimentation, flaws that will probably disappear with mestizaje and better living conditions." Not only would "incorporation" benefit the Seri but it "could only augment that extreme variety and multiple combinations . . . [that] after a rigorous selection, we suspect will result in the [racial] type that will create the future of this beautiful country" (Gini 1935, 133-34).[10] This rigid eugenic approach left little room for a "degenerate" Seri culture that foolishly sought isolation to preserve "the purity of their customs and the individual and moral integrity of their race" (Gini 1935, 119). The latest innovation in anthropological science thus confirmed the widely accepted conclusion that physically degenerate, tradition-bound indigenous peoples (often deliberately) hindered national development.

Biotypology also bolstered the already strong ties between Mexican anthropologists and an increasingly corporatist state. The links between Italian fascism and criminology—renowned criminologist and Lombroso disciple Enrico Ferri wrote a "fascist" penal code—were well known. The push to biotype national populations was part of the same statist agenda in both Italy and Mexico. As we have seen, new Mexican federal penal codes promulgated in 1929 and 1931 promoted increased judicial discretion in the name of "social defense," and increased judicial discretion required the "scientific" data that biotypology promised to provide, as well as the experts (criminologists or anthropologists in this case) to interpret the data accurately (Buffington 2000, chapter 5). With proper information and interpretation, criminologists argued, the criminal justice system could identify and isolate dangerous "born" and career criminals, while "occasional" and accidental criminals were rehabilitated or spared the corrupting prison experience altogether. This statist agenda became even more pronounced after the 1934 ascension of Lázaro Cárdenas to the Mexican presidency. Cárdenas broadened the political base still further, created official sectors for the renamed Mexican Revolutionary Party (PRM), and expanded the education and transportation infrastructures. These efforts purposefully expanded the reach of the state, and thus the pressure to conform to national standards. As the intellectual vanguard of integrationist thought, anthropologists were hardly disinterested observers.

Given its scientific and professional attractions, biotypology retained its fascination for Mexican criminologists and anthropologists. Gini's disciple, Ada D'Aloja, even took up residence in Mexico, teaching biotypology, demographics, and human genetics at the National School of Anthropology and History, the National University, and the University of the Americas, from 1939 until 1976 (Faulhaber 1988). With this kind of impetus, the new techniques expanded quickly in both disciplines. The results, however, were nothing new. Criminologist Anselmo Marino Flores, for example, remeasured a cache of Indian and mestizo skulls collected by Martínez Baca at the Federal Penitentiary for a 1945 article. In it, he blithely admitted that "the different schools of Biotypology . . . are not, in the final analysis, anything but continuers and developers of the ideas of Lombroso," and he went on to distinguish between the cranial types of murders and thieves (Marino Flores 1945, 128, 146–47). A cowritten 1963 article repeated the same procedure, this time using the Puebla skulls from Martínez Baca's and Manuel Vergara's original study! (Marino Flores and Serrano Sánchez 1963). That both works appeared in anthropology journals highlighted the (re)tightening of disciplinary bonds.

Anthropologists also employed this new methodology, both to refurbish old ideas about Indians and to demonstrate their usefulness to government functionaries. A 1945 article lamented the decline of physical anthropology since the death of Nicolás León and called for an extensive anthropometrical study comparing rural Indians to their urban counterparts (Romero 1945). Gómez Robledo, a student of D'Aloja's, was probably the most active promoter of biotypology, authoring or coauthoring biotypical studies of Tarascans, Zapotecs, and Otomís. These studies not only reinforced expectations but also served a practical end. "The biotypical orientation," he observed "is very preoccupied with differentiating racial groups and serves for that reason to opportunistically diagnose the predisposition to illness of the people examined, to know aptitudes and ineptitudes for work, and to suggest teaching methods and education programs (Gomez Robledo et al. 1961, 10; Romero 1966, 81). Thus in the guise of new science, biotypology reinforced long-standing anthropological and criminological traditions, cemented the ties between the two disciplines, and strengthened the already tight bonds that bound these disciplines to an ever-more-powerful, one-party state.

Anthropological studies that focused on indigenous cultures, rather than on bodies, also took on a criminological tone. This was especially true of the ongoing debate about the social dangers of alcoholism, traditionally associated in the Spanish colonial imagination with Indian culture. In 1929, with the moralistic Calles still lurking in the background, President Emilio Portes Gil sponsored a nationwide campaign against alcoholism, which "undermines the physical and moral strength of our men; ends conjugal happiness and destroys with degenerate children all possibility of greatness in the future of the Fatherland" ("La campaña" 1930, 4). His fellow campaigners were more explicit, especially regarding the Indian problem. One cited nineteenth-century French psychiatrist Benedict Morel's theory of progressive "moral insanity"— alcoholism in the first generation, criminality by the third, and racial extinction by the fourth—while noting widespread "drunkenness among our primitive peoples" (Galindo 1930, 24, 42).

In this moralistic context, anthropologists redoubled their attacks on Indian culture. In a 1939 "Essay on Alcoholism among the Indigenous Races of Mexico," the ex-editor of *Ethnos*, Lucio Mendieta y Núñez, underlined the social dangers of this modern plague:

When a great number of persons abandon themselves to the vice of drunkenness to such a degree that they produce organic hereditary degenerations, the evil oversteps the orbit of the individual life to become a social danger that manifests itself in damage to the economy, culture, and the vitality itself of the society in which it occurs. (1939, 77)

Crime was one of those social dangers: "among the indigenous," he noted, "alcoholism provokes the commission of crimes of violence, from simple scuffles to frequent homicides." And custom—"meetings, festivities, religious and magical ideas, the payment of wages with alcohol"— was largely to blame

(Mendieta y Núñez 1939, 78, 89). Many of his recommendations, especially the creation of sports leagues with game days scheduled for Sundays and traditional "fiesta days," thus attempted to break the stranglehold of tradition on indigenous cultures. Most required "the intervention of all the organs of the Federal and State governments." The need for more studies was, of course, a given (ibid., 92–93). At least in Mendieta's case, then, the fine line between anthropological knowledge and public policy had all but disappeared. In case any doubts remained, he followed up these recommendations with an edited "Ethnology of Mexico," which included data on the criminal tendencies of various indigenous groups. Most, unsurprisingly, showed a predisposition to violent crimes involving alcohol (Quiroz Cuaron 1959, 649-53).

As these attacks on Indian alcoholism and Indian culture demonstrate, the criminological subtext, a bit player in earlier Mexican anthropology, had now taken center stage. The appearance of articles reviewing new criminological theories and techniques in journals such as *Quetzalcoatl* made the disciplinary connection explicit (Gómez Robledo 1930; Núñez Chávez 1931). Even Mexican criminologists, who generally left Indian affairs to anthropologists, got in a few digs. A 1939 article on "The Indigenous Races and Social Defense" in *Criminalia*, the professional journal for Mexican criminologists, argued that while judicial discretion might take into account racial and cultural differences, Indians should be subject to the same laws as anyone else. Race, after all, was fundamentally "psychological and cultural," as was Indian "inferiority." In Mexico, the author insisted, "we are all mestizos, and on being mestizos, with a common tradition, with a common mestizo intellectual formation and culture, rests the great future of our country and the solution to ethnic problems." Refusal to assimilate, to adapt mestizo culture, thus transformed the tradition-bound Indian from reluctant citizen to "delinquent as a result of antisocial action" (Loyo 1939, 517–21).

Prominent criminologist Carlos Franco Sodi explained the roots of these antisocial tendencies in an essay on "Indigenous Delinquency." He noted that in his experience as a Mexico City judge and former director of the Federal Penitentiary, Indians rarely understood the reasons for their imprisonment, because they interpreted crime differently than non-Indians, and he provided an illustrative anecdote in which the young men of a village kill a family of witches under orders from the council of elders. Their shock at being tried for a murder they freely admitted and saw as completely justified symbolized the vast chasm that separated them from mainstream Mexican society. Nor was the perverse resilience of Indian traditions lightly overturned: even after their crime was explained and the remorseful men convicted and imprisoned, villagers murdered the last surviving witch. Aside from a lighthearted sense of irony, Franco Sodi's description of the uncomprehending Indian could have come straight from an earlier era:

There he sits, silent and taciturn, just like we see him on the edges of sidewalks or the sides of roads, look fixed on the ground, his face unexpressive and his spirit far away, very far away, from that filthy cell, melancholically remembering perhaps his beloved fields, nostalgically recalling his poor distant hovel and without understanding why some laws and strange men have deprived him of his liberty... and put between him and the luminous horizons which he always contemplates ecstatically, bars so tall and cold and walls so dismal and black.

This persistent stereotype, the apathetic and resistant Indian, Franco Sodi concluded, "bears in his breast the seeds of his own destruction, seeds *that will not disappear* while the Indian and ourselves are distinct, while that one and the man of the city think and feel differently, while one and the other speak diverse languages, and understand family, society, and morality in such opposed ways" (Franco Sodi 1951, 137–38). For criminologists and increasingly for anthropologists, Indianness itself was a tragedy; it also was a crime.

CONCLUSION: *PLUS ÇA CHANGE*...

This chapter has examined the constructions of social commentators, anthropologists, and criminologists—the self-proclaimed experts on the Indian problem. For all of their many differences, the vast majority of these observers shared three basic assumptions: first, Mexico's contemporary indigenous peoples were the tired, tattered, and besotted remnants of a once-great race; second, they represented a substantial obstacle to national progress; third, only racial and cultural mestizaje could unify the nation and remove that obstacle.

In a burst of post–revolutionary optimism, anthropological discourse seemed to favor its indigenous subjects, bestowing its blessings, insights, and prestige on their culture and on their bodies. Its knowledge was the key to the kingdom, to the long-awaited redemption of the long-suffering Indian. But the discipline existed at the sufferance of politicians and bureaucrats, and in serving Caesar, it lost its innocence. Applied anthropology became an ideology in the service of the post–revolutionary state.

By 1930, the exclusionary criminological subtext embedded in the Mexican elite's construction of national integration resurfaced with a vigor: the stubborn, tradition-bound Indian who resisted the responsibilities of citizenship became a criminal. This shift from irresponsible citizen to violent criminal may have been the only real change in the Indian's discursive status: a discursive sleight of hand—from violent mestizo/thieving Indian to violent Indian/thieving mestizo—that symbolized the "evolution" of the mestizo in the elite imagination. In post–revolutionary Mexico, the Indian who could not or would not adapt to the new mestizo national culture was likely to contemplate the future from behind "bars so tall and cold and walls so dismal and black." Mestizaje had undoubtedly forged a dominant—Gramsci would call it "hegemonic"—national culture, but the remaining indigenous peoples faced (and face) considerable pressure to conform. Inclusion could only come with the unconditional surrender of cultural identity which was, after all, what many elites had wanted all along.

As the Mexican case makes clear, cultural pluralism is not a simple matter of respect for cultural difference. The imperatives of modernity—strong nation-state, developed economy, educated citizenry—are at odds with any cultural difference that might subvert national progress, at least as imagined by elite policy makers. In the introduction to this book, Toffolo insists on the need "to delink examinations of cultural pluralism from the evolutionary view of history, its dichotomies of modernity and tradition and individual and community, and its assumptions about the anachronistic nature of ascriptive identities." The failures of the post–revolutionary Mexican experiment in cultural integration are especially instructive here. Anthropologists such as Manuel Gamio espoused a *progressive* biological and cultural eugenics that validated indigenous cultures; they also sought to reorder those cultures in the name of national development. And they certainly never attempted "*an epistemology rooted in a social and cultural definition of the human which can articulate a reconceived vision of the rational*" (*ECP*, 13). Under the circumstances, failure to achieve cultural integration seems inevitable; success might have been still worse.

NOTES

1. Written from exile after the 1767 expulsion of the Jesuit order, Clavigero's work was published in 1780–1781 and widely disseminated in Europe and America (Phelan 1960, 763).

2. The consequences of the cultural hegemony of *mestizaje* for indigenous peoples in Latin America have sparked a flurry of recent scholarly activity. *The Journal of Latin American Anthropology* 2:1 (1996) devotes an entire issue to the problem (see also V. Tilley 1997). Most, if not all, of these scholars note the considerable influence of Mexican intellectuals in the construction and promotion of mestizaje as a nationalist discourse.

3. One important exception was Fray Servando Teresa y Mier, who argued that "all we creoles are mestizos," but even he was careful to accept only "the pure blood of the native lords of the country" (Brading 1991, 595).

4. Not all Europeans favored racial purity. Dr. Jourdanet, for example, repeated the "well-known truths" about "the decadence of the pure races and the progressiveness of the men of mixed blood." The mestizo, he stated (before Sierra), "is [the

group] that progresses." This European endorsement published in a Mexican journal may well have influenced the *científico francophiles* (Jourdanet 1865, 244).

5. Molina Enríquez's position on mestizaje was quite influential (Basave 1992).

6. The phrase is Charles Hale's (Hale 1989, chapter 2).

7. The history of Mexican eugenics has seen two important new studies (Stepans 1991; Stern 1999).

8. Concern about proper technique (crucial to international racial comparisons) eventually led to an "International Convention for the Unification of Craneo- and Cephalo-metric Measurements" in Monaco. The guidelines were translated and published in the *Boletín del Museo Nacional de Arqueología, Historia y Etnología* 2:9 (marzo 1913): 174–83.

9. Nicolas León's brief "History of Physical Anthropology in Mexico" devoted one-third of its pages to the history of criminal anthropometry, including Martínez Baca's and Manuel Vergara's study (León 1919, 231–35).

10. Gini was Gamio's counterpart on the Italian Committee for the Study of Population Problems and a fellow vice president of the Second International Eugenics Congress.

REFERENCES

Bartra, Roger. 1992. *The Cage of Melancholy: Identity and Metamorphosis in the Mexican Character.* Translated by Christopher Hall. New Brunswick: Rutgers University Press.

Basauri, Carlos. 1929. "La redención del indio desde un nuevo punto de vista." *Quetzalcoatl* 1:1 (mayo): 8–9.

———. 1930. "El tipo nacional mexicano del porvenir." *Quetzalcoatl* 2:1 (septiembre): 6–7.

Basave, Agustín. 1992. "El mito del mestizo: el pensamiento nacionalista de Andrés Molina Enríquez." Pp. 221–58 in *El nacionalismo en México,* ed. Cecilia Noriega Elío. México: El Colegio de Michoacán.

Belina, Dr. de. 1878. "Influencia de altura sobre la vida y la salud del habitante de Anahuac." *Boletín de la Sociedad Mexicana de Geografía y Estadística* 4:4–5: 303.

Brading, David A. 1988a. "Liberal Patriotism and the Mexican *Reforma,*" *Journal of Latin American Studies* 20: 27–48.

———. 1988b. "Manuel Gamio and Official Indigenismo in Mexico." *Bulletin of Latin America Research* 7:1: 75–89.

———. 1991. *The First America: The Spanish Monarchy, Creole Patriots, and the Liberal State, 1492–1867.* New York: Cambridge University Press.

Buffington, Robert. 2000. *Criminal and Citizen in Modern Mexico.* Lincoln: University of Nebraska Press.

Bulnes, Francisco. 1968. *Páginas escogidas.* México: Universidad Nacional Autónoma de México.

"La campaña contra el alcoholismo." 1930. *Boletín de la Sociedad Mexicana de Geografía y Estadística* 42:1 (abril): 4–83.

Castellón Huerta, Blas Román. 1988. "Francisco Pimentel." In *La antropología en México,* vol. 9, ed. Carlos García Mora. Colección Biblioteca del INAH.

Chávez Chávez, Jorge. 1988. "El pensimiento indigenista decimonónico." In *La antropología en México,* vol. 3, ed. Carlos García Mora. Colección Biblioteca del INAH.

"Estadística de Yucatán." 1852. *Boletín de la Sociedad Mexicana de Geografía y Estadística* 3: 294.

Esteva Ruiz, Roberto A. 1902. " La estadística y sus funciones como lazo de unión entre los individuos y entre los pueblos." *Boletín de la Sociedad de Geografía y Estadística de la República Mexicana* (quinta época) 1:1:15.

Faulhaber, Johanna. 1988. "Ada D'Aloja." Pp. 21–25 in *La antropología en México,* vol. 9, ed. Carlos García Mora. Colección Biblioteca del INAH.

Franco Sodi, Carlos. 1951. "Delincuencia indígena." In *Don Juan Delincuente y otros ensayos,* ed. Ediciones Bota.

Galindo, Miguel. 1930. "La patria enferma: memoria sobre el alcoholismo." *Boletín de la Sociedad Mexicana de Geografía y Estadística* 42:1 (abril): 24–42.

Gamio, Manuel. 1920. "El censo de la población mexicana desde el punto de vista antropológica." *Ethnos* 1:2 (mayo): 46.

———. 1923. "Nacionalismo e internacionalismo." *Ethnos,* segunda época 1:2 (abril): 3.

———. 1930. "Pueblos nuevos." *Quetzalcoatl* 2:3 (septiembre): 4.

———. 1960. *Forjando Patria.* Editorial Porrúa.

Gini, Corrado. 1935. "Premiers resultats d'une expédition italo-mexicaine parmi les populations indigènes et métisses du Mexique." *Boletín de la Sociedad Mexicana de Geografía y Estadística* 45:3–4 (noviembre-diciembre): 133–34.

Gómez Robledo, José. 1930. "Algunas consideraciones sobre antropología criminal." *Quetzalcoatl* 2:3 (septiembre): 8–10.

Gómez Robledo, José. et al. 1943. *Pescadores y campesinos tarascos.* Secretaría de Educación Pública.

Gómez Robledo, José. et al. 1961. *Estudio biotipológico de los Otomí.* Instituto de Investigaciones Sociales, UNAM.

González González, María Guadalupe. 1988. "Quetzalcoatl." In *La antropología en México,* vol. 8, ed. Carlos García Mora. Colección Biblioteca del INAH.

González Navarro, Moisés. 1988. "Las ideas raciales de los científicos, 1890–1910." *Historia Mexicana* 37:4 (abril-junio): 565–83.

González Phillips, Graciela. 1988. "Ignacio Manuel Altamirano." In *La antropología en México,* vol. 9, ed. Carlos García Mora. Colección de INAH.

Guerrero, Julio. 1901. *La génisis del crimen en México: ensayo de psiquiatría social.* Imprenta de la Vda. de Ch. Bouret.

Hale, Charles Hale. 1989. *The Transformation of Mexican Liberalism in Late Nineteenth-Century Mexico.* Princeton: Princeton University Press.

Humboldt, Alexander von. 1966. *Political Essay on the Kingdom of New Spain,* vol. 1. Translated by John Black. New York: AMS Press.

Izquierdo, José Joaquín. 1922. "Estudio fisiológico del indígena adulto del valle de Teotihuacán." In *La población del valle de Teotihuacán,* ed. Mauel Gamio. Secretaría de Educación Pública.

Jourdanet, Dr. 1865. "De la estadística de México considerada en sus relaciones con los niveles del suelo y con la aclimatación de las diferentes razas humanas que lo habitan." *Boletín de la Sociedad Mexicana de Geografía y Estadística* 11:4: 240–44.

Larrainzar, Manuel. 1852. "Noticia histórica de Soconusco." *Boletín de la Sociedad Mexicana de Geografía y Estadística* 3: 232–34.

León, Nicolás. 1919. "Historia de antropología física en México." *American Journal of Physical Anthropology* 2:3 (July–September): 231–35.

Loyo, Gilberto. 1939. "Las razas indígenas y la defensa social." *Criminalia* 1:1 (septiembre): 517–21.

Marino Flores, Anselmo. 1945. "La criminología y una nueva técnica de craneología constitucionalista." *Revista Mexicana de Estudios Antropológicos* 7:1–3 (enero–diciembre): 128, 146–47.

Marino Flores, Anselmo, and Carlos Serrano Sánchez. 1963. "Craneología y criminología." *Anales del Instituto Nacional de Antropología e Historia* 16: 123–33.

Martínez Baca, Francisco, and Manuel Vergara. 1892. *Estudios de antropología criminal.* Puebla: Imprenta, Litografía y Encuadernación de Benjamin Lara.

Mendieta y Núñez, Lucio. 1925. "Importancia científica y práctica de los estudios etnológicos y ethnográficos." *Ethnos,* tercera época 1:3–4 (marzo y abril): 46.

——— 1939. "Ensayo sobre el Alcoholismo entre las Razas Indígenas de México." *Revista Mexicana de Sociología* 1:3 (julio–agosto): 77, 78, 89, 92–93.

Molina Enríquez, Andrés. 1981. *Las grandes problemas nacionales.* Era.

Núñez Chávez, Francisco. 1931. "Las relaciones de la clínica criminológica con la antropología." *Quetzalcoatl* 3:4 (enero): 10–11.

Phelan, John Leddy. 1960. "Neo-Aztecism in the Eighteenth Century and the Genesis of Mexican Nationalism." Pp. 765+ in *Culture in History: Essays in Honor of Paul Rabin,* ed. Stanley Diamond. New York: Columbia University Press.

Powell, T. G. 1968. "Mexican Intellectuals and the Indian Question, 1876–1911." *Hispanic American Historical Review* 48:1 (February).

Quiroz Cuaron, Alfonso. 1959. "Etnografía de México." *Criminalia* 25:1–12: 649–53.

Raat, William D. 1971. "Los intelectuales, el positivismo y la cuestión indígena." *Historia Mexicana* 20:3 (enero–marzo): 412–23.

Romero, Javier. 1945. "El Departamento de Antropología Física del Museo Nacional." *Anales del Museo Nacional de Arqueología, Historia y Etnografía* 5:3: 201–202.

———. 1966. "De la biotipología a la psicobiología." *Anales del Instituto Nacional de Antropología e Historia* 19: 80.

Schmidt, Henry. 1978. *The Roots of Lo Mexicano: Self and Society in Mexican Thought, 1900–1934*. College Station: Texas A & M Press.

"La segunda época de Ethnos." 1922. *Ethnos*, segunda época 1:1 (enero): 2.

"El Segundo Congreso Internacional de Eugenesia." 1920. *Ethos* 1:5 (agosto): 128–30.

Serrano, Carlos and Martha Eugenia Rodríguez. 1988. "Vincente Riva Palacio." In *La antropología en México*, vol. 11, ed. Carlos García Mora. Colección Biblioteca del INAH.

Serrano, Carlos, and Mercedes Mejía Sánchez. 1988. "Misión italiana para el estudio de la población indígena y mestiza de México." Pp. 102–106, in *La antropología en México*, vol. 8, ed. Carlos García Mora. Colección Biblioteca del INAH.

Serrano Sánchez, Carlos and Sergio López Alonso. 1988. "Los aportes de la antropología física europea." Pp. 203–22 in *La antropología en México*, vol. 5, ed. Carlos García Mora. Colección Biblioteca del INAH.

Sierra, Justo. 1895. "Discurso de clausura pronunciado por el Sr. Lic. D. Justo Sierra en la sesión solemne del 18 de Agosto de 1895, en la Cámara de Diputados." Oficina Tipográfica de la Secretaría de Fomento.

Siliceo Pauer, Paul. 1922. "Tipo físico." Pp. 165+, in *La población del valle de Teotihuacán*, ed. Manuel Gamio. Secretaría de Educación Pública.

———. 1922–1923. "Conocimiento antropológico de la agrupaciones indígenas de México." *Ethnos*, segunda época 1:1 (noviembre 1922—enero 1923): 15–18.

Stabb, Martin S. 1959. "Indigenism and Racism in Mexican Thought: 1857–1911." *Journal of Inter-American Studies* 1:4 (October): 405–23.

Stepans, Nancy. 1991. *The Hour of Eugenics: Race, Gender, and Nation in Latin America*. Ithaca: Cornell University Press.

Stern, Alexandra Minna. 1999. "Mestizophilia, Biotypology, and Eugenics in Post–Revolutionary Mexico: Towards a History of Science and the State, 1920–1960." Working Papers Series No. 4. University of Chicago, Mexican Studies Program.

Tilley, Virginia. 1997. "Indigenous People and the State: Ethnic Meta-Conflict in El Salvador." Ph.D. dissertation, University of Wisconsin at Madison.

Todorov, Tzvetan. 1984. *The Conquest of America: The Question of the Other*. Translated by Richard Howard. New York: Harper Perennial.

Chapter 6

The Shari'a State

The Case of the Islamists in the Sudan

Ismail H. Abdalla

Ever since September 1983, when Lieutenant-General Ja'far Mohammed Nimeiri, the then president, proclaimed the shari'a or Islamic laws by presidential decree, events in Sudan have taken a turn for the worse. The north-south conflict that has plagued it for so many years assumed an openly threatening religious character that had hitherto been hidden under the surface. Abolishing Islamic law became one of the central demands of many opposition groups, including the Sudan Peoples' Liberation Movement (under the leadership of John Garang), the Sudan Communist Party, the trade unions, and other secular elements in the north. Even the two dominant traditional sectarian parties, the Umma of the Ansar (followers of the Mahdi) and the Democratic Unionist Party of the Khatmiyya religious fraternity, objected to these laws, not so much out of conviction that Islam and politics do not mix, but rather because they disliked Nimeiri's obvious opportunism.

In April 1985, Nimeiri's military dictatorship was overthrown by a popular uprising, but the succeeding governments, both military and civilian, failed to strike down Nimeiri's so-called Islamic laws. This failure more than anything else confirmed the worst suspicions of southerners and their liberal and secular-minded allies in the north, that the mainstream northern political parties were either unwilling or unable to face up to the challenge of separating religion from politics, their own rhetoric notwithstanding. When the government of Sadiq al-Mahdi began in mid-1989 to cautiously explore the possibility of ending the civil war and expressed interest in suspending the shari'a laws until a final agreement on the future of the Sudan was reached with the rebels in the south, the army, led by Lieutenant-General Umar Hasan Ahmed al-Bashir, ousted him from power on June 30, 1989. The true nature of the coup d'etat soon became clear, even if its leaders tried hard to conceal it. It was an Islamist move, planned and executed by members of the Muslim Brothers in the army. The newly constituted government of *al-Inghadh al-Watani,* or the National Salvation Revolution (NSR), was committed to preserving Nimeiri's Islamic laws, and indeed, to transforming the entire society into a truly Islamic *ummah,* or community, under God. Its only question was what constitutional framework, within the context of the shari'a, would best facilitate the engineering of an authentic Islamic society. For it, the shari'a has been and will always remain the quickest, most effective instrument of social transformation. The shari'a is perceived by its advocates as both liberating and regenerating. It is liberating because of its advocates' endeavor to break loose simultaneously from bondage to Western ways and from a traditional Islamic discourse bogged down by centuries of conservatism, ineptitude, and derivative scholarship. It is regenerating because of the intent of relinking Muslim society to a perfect era in the past, a golden era whose premise and ideals, as interpreted by contemporary Islamists, would at the same time also be dialectically in harmony with modernity.[1]

This chapter explores the worldview of the Sudanese Islamists that informs their political program. It will define those essential features of the Sudanese Islamic paradigm and situate Sudanese Islamists' discourse within the ideology of contemporary self-conscious political Islam. It also attempts to identify some salient features in the Sudanese Islamists' movement and thought that may enable us to establish some general theoretical formulations useful in understanding similar experiences elsewhere.

For a better understanding of the political paradigm of the Sudanese Islamists, one must focus on the work of their leader, Dr. Hasan Abdallah al-Turabi. Until the 1989 coup, he was the real power behind the military government in Khartoum, and he continues to be its main ideologue. Also, the Muslim Brotherhood, under his leadership, became a powerful political force in Sudanese politics, even before the 1989 military takeover (El-Affendi 1991, 71).[2]

Unlike other recent Muslim intellectuals such as Abu al-'Ala Mawdudi of Pakistan (d. 1979), or Hasan al-Banna (d. 1949) and Sayyid Qutb (executed in 1966) of Egypt, Dr. al-Turabi so far has produced only a limited number of publications about the complex problem of the Islamic state in the twentieth century.[3] Thus researchers are handicapped. However, although these publications are few, when taken together with his public statements on different occasions, they stress the place of shari'a in Muslim communities. Certainly in the beginning, al-Turabi and his movement depended greatly on the ideas of the three aforementioned authors. Like them, al-Turabi prefers to talk only in general terms about the constitutional framework of the envisioned Islamic state, its specific administrative structure, its economy, or the principles guiding its foreign policies. Important issues such as individual liberties and rights, separation of powers, time limits for office holding, or federalism receive only scant attention. When mentioned, they often are subsumed into larger issues such as *shura* (consultation) or *ijtihad* (independent interpretation of the main Islamic sources, the Quran and the *Sunna,* or prophetic traditions). Like the writings of other Islamists, al-Turabi's treatises often show ambiguity, sometimes deliberately so, with regard to the fundamental questions of "democracy," "minorities," or international relations. Like them, al-Turabis stresses a set of dichotomies in his discourse about the Islamic *sahwa* (revival): the divine order versus the secular order, the *shura* as opposed to democracy, the *nizam Islami* (Islamic governance in place of the secular nation-state), the shari'a in opposition to human-made legislation and, finally, the *hakimiyya* (rule of Allah) as a substitute for government of the people by the people (Tibi 1998, 138).

The starting point for all Islamic activists, including al-Turabi, is the centrality of the shari'a in human life, but the shari'a itself is an expression of *tawhid,* or divine unity. Knowledge of the latter, according to al-Turabi, is feasible only by *'ibtila,* a term by which he means God's constant testing of the believer's commitment and endurance in the face of worldly and spiritual challenges (Al-Turabi 1999, 16; Ibrahim 1999, 202). As man lives in a specific geographic and cultural environment, with its own specific 'ibtila (material and spiritual challenges), it follows that his response then is also specific and, hence, nongeneralizable. The individual's reaction to his or her religion in the context of his or her interaction with the environment is *tadayyun* (living in the context of one's faith, or *Din,* with a capital "D") (Al-Turabi 1999, 61). Tadayyun is the application of Din in the life of an individual, in an ever-changing environment of 'ibtila.[4] Because the human and physical environment is dynamic, thus creating new 'ibtila all of the time in an endless, cyclical motion, the tadayyun also must change constantly. Only then can the Din with its *thawabit* (basic and unchanging messages of tawhid, revelation and the eternal and universal fundamentals) remain viable and permanent (Al-Turabi, 1995 62). In other words, for the Din (Islam) to be constant and relevant to humanity at all times, its application, the tadayyun, must be in permanent motion. It was precisely because tadayyun was arrested for many centuries that Muslim societies today are backward and underdeveloped. The fault lies with the Muslims' inability to construct a proper and dynamic tadayyun and not with the Din itself (Al-Turabi 1995, 63).

Just as there are two aspects of Islam, Din and the tadayyun, there also are two sides to Islamic revivalism; *'ihya'*(renewal) and *tatwier* (development that goes beyond simple renewal) (Al-Turabi 20). 'Ihya' involves religious exhortation, reminding people of forgotten Islamic principles by disseminating accurate information about the faith, and by infusing energy and movement into an otherwise despondent, pathetic religious milieu. Tatwier, in contrast, occurs when reformers involve themselves intellectually, psychologically, and practically in matters that are at the heart of tadayyun, thus making Islam rich, exulted, and relevant (Al-Turabi: 1995, 20).[5] Such a revival, with a capital "R," is still within the normal framework of the eternal message of the Din. It only makes explicit what is general, or completes what is limited: it takes advantage of contemporary ideas or means unknown to earlier generations (Al-Turabi 1995, 20).[6] An important dimension of this type of revival is the refutation of judgments made and opinions expressed by early jurists who are unsupported by the Quran or the Sunna, or who are rendered hopelessly irrelevant because of changed circumstances.

Al-Turabi's main argument about the necessity of continued dynamic tadayyun, because of the ever-changing human condition, is essential to the whole contemporary Islamic project of revival. Without such bold postulates on his part, he could not have moved courageously to attempt to dismantle the myth about the end of 'ijtihad, that mental blockade that had discouraged so many Muslim intellectuals from revisiting Islam's classical sources with a critical and an open mind.

That this daring approach is indispensable to the Islamists' project becomes clear when one considers al-Turabi's attitude toward traditional fiqh (Islamic jurisprudence). He has respect neither for the received wisdom of traditional fiqh, nor for those conservative fuqaha', or Muslim jurists, who appropriated the discipline to themselves. They were comfortable in their belief that Islam was a closed, sufficient, total system, and that it was the Muslim society, not Islamic law, that needed to change to conform to the legal pronouncements of the jurists (Esposito 1987, 217). Al-Turabi accused them of servility to secular-minded leadership, and of accepting in practice the separation of religion and politics. He also condemns these jurists, especially the contemporary among them, for being closed-minded, resistant even to new linguistic expressions unfamiliar to them (Al-Turabi 1995, 75), not to mention their total rejection of new interpretations of the fundamental sources, the Quran and the Sunna. As he puts it, extant works on jurisprudence explain everything a believer will ever need to know about worship, but they are hardly helpful on how to drive a car or run a business (Al-Turabi 1995, 96). This is why it is imperative for all Muslims to draw on the essentials of Islam (as preserved in the Quran and the Prophetic traditions, as well as received classical literature), to explicate the natural sciences of modern times for the benefit of society. Only then can a true and comprehensive worship of Allah be attained.

For this state of total immersion in tawhid to occur, each and every Muslim, not just the fuqaha', is called upon to become seriously involved in the process of understanding and reinterpreting the shari'a. This is the only course of action if Muslims are to produce a new and viable corpus of jurisprudence (Al-Turabi 1995, 106). This is nothing short of a Protestant-like approach to the main religious sources. The likelihood that this process of democratizing the fiqh, and thus the shari'a, may lead to irreconcilable interpretations of the sources is summarily dismissed by al-Turabi. He strongly believes that, in the end, shura, or consultation, will ensure that only those interpretations that conform to the true spirit of Islam and to its essential message will prevail (Al-Turabi 1995, 106).

Al-Turabi leads us to believe that a shari'a corpus produced collectively in this popular fashion is still divine, for it is the collective tadayyun—every Muslim living in the context of his or her religion.[7] Such a reformulated law is all encompassing and leaves little room for human agency or imagination outside of the Din. The implementation of this God-given law in Muslim societies through the dynamic tadayyun of the worshiper is seen as the only remedy to all of the ills that currently engulf Islam everywhere. The call for the establishment of shari'a society at this juncture in the history of Muslims is a rejection of the status quo. It is a critique of failed government development projects, of inept and inefficient institutions, and of borrowed ethos and values (Khalid 1986, 239). It also is an assertive response to the hegemonic Western culture, believed to be the main source of these ills, and a rebellion against the power structure in a Muslim world identified with the West. According to these Islamic thinkers, the prescribed constitutional order should be based on the teachings of the Quran and on the example of the Prophet Mohammed and his immediate successors, as interpreted by informed and committed contemporary Muslims. This is because the political order, so produced, would be an "eternal model that Muslims are bound to adopt as a perfect standard for all time" (Al-Turabi 1983, 241). The principle on which this constitutional edifice stands or falls is the doctrine of *tawhid*, the belief in the unity of God and of human life, and in the divine will in whose context everything must be explained (Al-Turabi 1983, 241). In classical Islam, this principle of "oneness" was applied only to God, though Muslim mystics used it to refer to the union between the Creator and the Created (Chittick 1989, 90). In the literature of contemporary Islamists, it also is being applied to a society reconstructed in God's image. The political order thus constituted on the principle of tawhid is total, sacrosanct, and self-perpetuating. Indeed, it is the most important "measure of divine *tawhid* (for it) manifests itself not in the private conscience but in commitment . . . toward the Islamization of the state and society" (Al-Turabi 1983, 242; Moussalli 1999, 179). Such an Islamic polity permits no major or permanent fragmentation or cleavages, social, ethnic, or tribal. Nor does it allow the existence of a political authority that is independent of the divine order (Al-'Awwa 1983, 25; Al-Farouqi 1995, 84). It also embraces all human activities. Precisely because government and society are based on tawhid, they cannot be *secular, national, sovereign, or diverse.*

According to al-Turabi, following al-Banna and al-Mawdudi, the Islamic state (left undefined) cannot be *secular* because worship, understood broadly, is the essence of creation. "(P)ublic life is permeated by the experience of the divine," according to al-Turabi. The sole purpose of the individual and community in this world is not the pursuit of happiness but the worship of God, as stipulated in the Quran and the shari'a, which is derived from it (Al-Turabi 1983, 241). *Secularism* is understood as nonreligiosity, that is, living in terms of this world as opposed to the next. According to this interpretation, where religion is absent, only evil thrives. When that happens, the lot of humanity is nothing but selfishness, misery, and suffering (Qutb 1986, 3; Al-Turabi 1985, 7). Immorality and materialism become supreme.

In its purely geographic sense, nationalism, like secularism, also is untenable. Allegiance is to God and to Him alone, and through Him to all other believers, or the *ummah* (Al-Turabi 1983, 242). Thus loyalty to ethnicity, social groups, or territory is unacceptable in Islam, though the existence of a territorially fixed Islamic state, which is not coextensive with the ummah, is conceded out of expedience (Al-Banna 1965, 359). From the Islamists' perspective, nationalism, particularly in its Arab garb, was a Western imperial conspiracy to break down the last Islamic Caliphate of the Ottomans. Its connection in the Middle East to Christian minorities during the first half of the twentieth century made it even more suspicious, for it was these minority intellectuals who formulated the ideology of Arab nationalism (Hourani 1983, 286; 1991, 309).[8]

Peoples' *sovereignty* is another alien notion that contradicts basic Islamic teachings. *Hakimiyya* (sovereignty) is the sole prerogative of almighty Allah, the supreme legislator.[9] Neither the people nor any organic nation-state constituted by them has sovereignty. Article 4 of the 1998 Constitution of the Sudan, written largely by al-Turabi himself, makes this very explicit: "*hakimiyya* or sovereignty in the state belongs to Allah, the Creator, while the *siyada* (authority) is to the people of the Sudan as Allah's Vicegerent who exercise it as worship to fulfil Allah's trust and for national development, justice, freedom and *shura*." Though they may not have sovereignty, al-Turabi says as ummah Muslims may have a "will," which they exercise because they are Allah's agents on earth for the realization of the tawhid principle (Moussalli 1999, 179).[10] Article 65 intimates that the shari'a and the consensus of the ummah, through referendum or custom, are the only foundation for legislation, provided that such legislation does not contradict any Islamic principle. In other words, people have the authority of interpreting and acting upon the commands of the Sovereign Allah, not the power to initiate these commands or modify them in any way.

Finally, the Islamic state is neither primordial nor ultimately necessary: states come and go, while the ummah endures. The primary institution in Islam, therefore, is not the state but the ummah, whose creation was for the sole purpose of the strict observance of the shari'a.[11] When the principle of *tawhid* is universally observed and shari'a is in place, Muslims need no political structure to guide them or to control their actions (Al-Turabi 1983, 243-44).

Al-Turabi also believes that the principle of tawhid, with its intrinsic qualities of religiosity, universality, and subservience to God alone, is a determinant factor of contingent statehood. Such statehood is to ensure the freedom, equality, and unity among all believers, but freedom is restricted, not absolute. It is the freedom of every Muslim to worship God, and to stand up for justice and equality, not to do what he or she pleases. These guidelines are enshrined in the shari'a, which also rules out usurpation or inheritance as a legitimate means of governance (Al-Turabi 1983, 244). The Islamic state constituted on these principles will, by and large, be a replica of the first Muslim state in Medina, with a freely elected head of state (caliph) and representatives of the ummah. The caliph, or any such office holder, is subject both to shari'a and to the "will of his electors," whose *ijma'* (consensus) is mandatory, if major problems of governance are to be resolved. Islamic government, al-Turabi contends, is "essentially a form of representative democracy." It is, however, not "a direct government of and by the people; it is a government of the shari'a." Thus it is a "popular government, since the shari'a represents the convictions of the people, and therefore, their direct will" (Al-Turabi 1985, 7). Through a *majlis al-Shura* (consultative council or parliament), people may exercise their "will."[12]

Al-Turabi and other Islamic activists firmly believe in the necessary agreement of all members of the ummah, no matter what problem they face and regardless of their degree of competence in Islamic law. As long as they debate the matter in good faith, which as good and God-fearing Muslims they must, they will reach the consensus needed for the smooth and effective running of the Islamic state. Hence, there is no room for dissent or disagreement, except during deliberation that is integral to the process of consensus building (Al-Turabi 1983, 245). Government by consensus is a guarantee against majoritarian dictatorship and makes redundant the multiparty system of government that is "a form of factionalism that can be very oppressive to individual freedom and divisive of the community" (Al-Turabi 1983, 250; Moussalli 1999, 90-93).[13]

While the shari'a is comprehensive and its authority absolute, its application in daily life is left largely to the individual and community, not to the state. Article 18 of the Constitution makes it clear that it is the people, not the government, who are responsible for conducting private and public affairs in the spirit of Islam. Whether planning development projects, making laws, or initiating social or cultural policies, the Sudanese people must ensure that such activities are within the context of the Quran and Sunna and are intended to gain Allah's blessing. Where society can manage on its own, enforcing what is good and forbidding what is wrong, government has no business interfering. Article 35, Section (h), actually makes the enforcement of what is good and the forbidding of what is evil *(al-'amr bil ma'rouf wal nahyu 'an al-munkar)* the specific responsibility of every citizen, not a specialized, law-enforcing agency. Islamic government, al-Turabi argues, is minimal government, as opposed to the modern secular state, which often is large, intrusive, and oppressive. It is precisely because the Islamic state is a minimal system of rule that minorities, while protected, are left to regulate their own private lives, enacting their own internal laws and directing their special system of education (Al-Turabi 1983, 250). Their legal and social autonomy is thus guaranteed. Anytime there is a shari'a regulation that these minorities consider incompatible with their own religion, they have the right to be absolved from its application.

In a more recent publication, al-Turabi explains how the Islamic state would come about. It will materialize peacefully through *da'wa* (Islamic propagation), which starts with the individual. "A pious Muslim," he assures his disciples, "would lead to a pious society, which, in its turn, would produce a pious state" (Al-'Awwa and Al-Turabi 1998, 28). He does not, however, exclude the use of force, if necessary, to attain the desired goal. His contention has always been that despotic or un-Islamic governments must be changed by any means possible, including force. His favorite phrase is *inna Allaha yari'u bil-Sultan mala yaza'u bil-Quran* (Allah may allow the use of force instead of persuasion by the Quran to bring about the desired change). "If the Islamic movement attains power whether peacefully or by force then it adds the force of the state to its means of changing reality" (Al-'Awwa and Al-Turabi 1998, 28).[14] Once in control, the Islamic movement "can either adopt a gradual or radical approach to society's Islamization. . . . Both are legitimate methods" (Al-Turabi 1999, 130).

When the Muslim Brothers took power in the Sudan in June 1989, they began to create what they regarded as the only true Islamic society. The process was endorsed in a constitution ten years later. Like all previous military governments, the Military Command Council of the NSR outlawed all political parties, trade unions, and other associations, censored the media, and controlled the institutions of higher education, while reorienting their curriculum toward the new vision. It also purged the army, judiciary, and civil service of individuals accused of being openly opposed to government policies, or who showed no enthusiasm for the radical changes underway in the country (Collins 1999, 106). To be true to the goals of its Islamic project, new shari'a laws were quickly passed in 1991 which, for the first time in the history of the country, gave the responsibility of enforcing the law to individuals rather than to the regular police. It was these people who went about in towns whipping women who wore un-Islamic garb and harassing or beating men whose public behavior they deemed inappropriate.

To summarize al-Turabi's ideas: the Islamic state is contingent and transitory, because it is the ummah, the community of God, not the state, that is the ultimate design for the universe. The state as an instrument of power exists only insofar as the ummah needs it. It functions as a "democratic" polity run by consensus. The democratic process by which consensus is reached is valued not because it is a good system of effective representation and participation, but because the ummah abhors disunity, shuns disagreement, and yearns for shura. The ummah itself is "sovereign" not by an inalienable natural right to the power possessed by the citizens, but by virtue of the fact that it is an extension of the sovereignty of God and an instrument of His divine plan. The authority of the state is minimal, since the shari'a is autonomous and exists in a parallel space to that of the state itself which, ideally, it should supersede. The exercise of power by any functionary of the state, who must always be a Muslim (especially in positions considered critical for state survival), is legitimate only insofar as that functionary abides by the rules and the regulations already set out in the shari'a. Citizens owe him no allegiance if he transgresses from the Divine law. When rules and regulations dealing with specific situations are absent from the body of the shari'a, the community has the power of enacting them by the painstaking process of ijma', or consensus building, and then only if these new laws do not in any way circumvent or contradict the shari'a.

Furthermore, the Islamic polity is both a *state*, insofar as it must function in the contemporary international system (a system whose rules and norms apply to the geographically defined nation-states), and a *nonstate*, because ideally it must strive to become coterminous with the universal ummah. Al-Turabi also believes that the Sudanese people have a "will" that they can express openly and freely. Because Muslims are the majority of the population, their "will" must prevail. That "will" has always been their desire to govern themselves according to the dictates of the shari'a.

As to how al-Turabi's own movement may attain power, the ends justify the means. Despite his rhetoric to the contrary, al-Turabi firmly believes that the Sudanese understand only one brand of political relationship; a top-down decision-making procedure initiated and executed by an elite leadership. Consciously or not, al-Turabi thus threw away everything he had said about the "will" of the people, the "minimal Islamic government," and the democratization of the shari'a.

HISTORY OF THE DRIVE FOR AN ISLAMIC STATE AND THE SHARI'A

It is useful to stress here that when al-Turabi expressed his ideas about the political structure of the Sudan, first in 1966 and then again in the early 1980s, he and his Muslim Brotherhood movement had already committed themselves openly to the establishment of an Islamic state based on an Islamic constitution (El-Affendi 1991, 57). Also during the same period, they evolved from an elitist pressure group, confined largely to university campuses, to a political party with a specific Islamic agenda. The Brothers played a prominent role in the popular uprising of October 1964, which toppled General Abboud's military government and restored democracy. Then they took advantage of the democratic climate after 1964 to establish the Islamic Charter Front, a coalition of right-of-center political parties and religious sects that began to push for an Islamic constitution and the application of shari'a law (El-Affendi 1991, 85). While they did not succeed in these principal goals, they did triumph over their main rivals, the Communists. Using emotive Islamic symbols, the Brothers put enough political pressure on members of the Sudanese Parliament to amend the Constitution so as to ban the Communist Party, and to expel its elected members from Parliament (El-Affendi 1991, 82; see also Sidahmed 1996, 181). The Communists and liberals challenged the constitutionality of the Parliament's action in court, and after deliberating for a whole year, the Supreme Court decided in their favor, but the conservative government of the time and Parliament refused to budge. They simply ignored the Court's decision (El-Affendi, 83). This victory was beyond the wildest dreams of the Brothers. Unfortunately for them, in May, 1969, when Parliament passed the second reading of a draft constitution that was essentially Islamic, the military intervened and toppled the civilian government. Led by Colonel Ja'far Mohammed Nimeiri, and supported by the Communists who were disenchanted by the conservative and pro-Islam political climate in the country, the new military government set out to curb the influence of the Islamists and to steer the country once more toward secularism (Woodward 1997, 98). This trend continued until Nimeiri faced several serious challenges to his rule, including a 1976 failed military coup planned and carried out by his rivals, the *Umma* party and the *Ikhwan*, or Muslim Brotherhood (Woodward 1997, 90; El-Affendi 1991, 115). It was a wake-up call for Nimeiri, who thereafter accommodated the opposition and included some of their leaders in his government. Al-Turabi was appointed Attorney General. The Ikhwan took full advantage of the opportunity and entrenched themselves in key administrative and financial institutions, to the envy and dismay of the traditional political parties. It was during this period of reconciliation that Nimeiri rediscovered Islam to the applause and encouragement of the Islamists (Khalid 1986, 243–50). The Ikhwan were happy to welcome him as a born-again Muslim and, accordingly, they provided the necessary expertise for rewriting the country's laws to make them conform to the shari'a (Khalid 1986, 250). Falling increasingly under the influence of *tariqas* (religious fraternities), Nimeiri decided, nonetheless, to outmaneuver the Ikhwan in their own game. In September 1983, he proclaimed the shari'a as the law of the land (Sidahmed, 1996, 184). He also bypassed the judiciary and constituted new courts which, to the horror and disgust of Muslims and non-Muslims alike, began to apply some of the most stringent articles in these laws, including amputation.[15] Though Nimeiri's main concern was survival, not crusade, the Ikhwan were gratified that finally there was a Sudanese politician willing to enforce the shari'a. Enforcing Islamic penal codes, they reasoned, was of far greater import for the Islamic project than the slow process of educating the masses to live according to the rules of their religion (Ali 1996, 306). However, the alliance of convenience between Nimeiri and the Ikhwan soon collapsed, whereupon he dismissed them from government posts and imprisoned their leaders, just before he himself was overthrown in the popular uprising of April 1985. Because of Nimeiri's harsh treatment of the Ikhwan during the last months of his regime, they were able to rehabilitate themselves politically by convincing many that they too were victims (Sidahmed 1996, 184). Using the immense financial resources that they had accumulated, as well as their improved party organization, they made impressive gains in the elections that followed and became a formidable force in Parliament.

During the second republic, 1986 to 1989, the Ikhwan once again played the Islamic constitution card and paralyzed several of the coalition governments of which they were a part. When they failed to persuade other partners in government to adopt an Islamic constitution or to militarily solve the problem of southern Sudan, they opted out of the coalition. Once the Ikhwan was in the parliamentary opposition, a consensus began to emerge among the other northern parties in mid-1989 to accommodate the southerners' viewpoint and thus to end the civil war. Rather than conceding to the will of the Sudanese majority, as represented by the main parties, the Ikhwan launched a campaign against all northern political parties working to bring the hostilities to an amicable resolution. They accused northern party leaders of selling out to infidel John Garang, the leader of the rebels (Ali 1991, 93). More importantly, their well-financed, noisy newspapers started a relentless smear campaign against Prime Minister Sadiq al-Mahdi and his allies, accusing them of disloyalty to Islam and the Sudan. At the same time, they portrayed themselves as the only loyal friends and unselfish supporters of the embattled Sudanese Armed Forces. They did this in order to drive a wedge between the army and all other political parties, but when new tactics failed, they worked with committed brethren among the junior officers in the army to stage a bloodless coup in June 1989.[16] Since that time, the Muslim Brothers assiduously established, piece by piece, a legal system and a constitutional structure they believe are wholly Islamic.

CRITICISM OF AL-TURABI'S FORMULATIONS OF THE ISLAMIC STATE

In the beginning, liberal Muslims and leftist intellectuals in the Sudan, as elsewhere, did not take the propaganda of the Islamists seriously. Preoccupied as they were with the struggles over colonialism, and then modernism, they dismissed the revivalist Islamic writings and propaganda as irrational and reactionary. Like modernization theorists everywhere, they believed that time and development on a rational basis were sufficient to curb the influence of the Islamists (Sivan 1957, 160). According to this thesis, identity formation in the postindependence state (itself part of national integration) would naturally be accompanied by the secularization of the political culture.

Only in the last decade or so did Muslim intellectuals and liberals begin to engage the Islamists in a direct dialogue. They armed themselves this time with a thorough knowledge not of Cartesian skepticism, popular among Arab intellectuals in the 1930s, but of Islamic history, Quranic exegesis, and Islamic jurisprudence.[17] If they were to prevail, they figured they must challenge the Islamists in their own court.

Criticism of the formulations by al-Turabi and other Islamic activists about the postcolonial Islamic state came from those of different political persuasions: from the Left, represented by the now-weakened Sudan Communist Party; from southerners, as voiced by the Sudan Peoples Liberation Movement and Army (SPLM/ SPLA); and from nonpartisan liberals in the north. They all agreed that the Islamists' representation of a historic Islamic state that was democratic, egalitarian, universal and nonsecular was utopian. Such a state never existed historically (Khalid 1986, 123; Ali 1991, 96). They argue that inventing history, acceptable though it may be for propaganda purposes, cannot constitute a good basis for building a united Sudan from its heterogeneous elements (Qiliyun 1991, 58). The critics point out, for example, that the companions of the Prophet, who were supposed to have been thoroughly inculcated with high religious values, just barely avoided coming to blows over who should succeed him as caliph, while his dead body was still awaiting burial (Khalid 1986, 154). What is remarkable is that their quarrel was for personal and ethnic reasons, and not for the high ideals of the new religion. When the choice of the first successor to the Prophet was finally made, it occurred as a fait accompli, not through elections. It is, therefore, misleading to say that the noisy and acrimonious meetings that preceded the selection of the first caliph in Islam were democratic, or that the example is profitable to later Muslims. They also argue that al-Turabi is not consistent regarding the relationship between the state and the shari'a. On the one hand, he implies that the state is superfluous, once shari'a is firmly established by the ummah. On the other hand, as the example of the Islamic state he proposes Medina under the Prophet Mohammed where the shari'a *was* the law of the land. Yet neither the Prophet nor his successors disposed of the state or its structures, even though the shari'a was the only political and religious framework they knew. The fact that the Prophet himself established and maintained a state apparatus, a practice that continued after him, indicates that the institution is not superfluous or contingent for the Muslim community. When one considers the behavior of the Islamists in Khartoum, the inconsistency between theory and practice becomes even more clear. After twelve years in power, the Ikhwan have consolidated rather than dismantled the state, much to the detriment of the citizenry. But the biggest problem for these critics is the shari'a itself, the very foundation upon which the proposed Islamic state is supposed to stand. They rightly contend that this body of Islamic laws, with its various schools of thought and long and varied historical experiences, is hopelessly imprecise as a constitutional framework. It also is out of touch with the reality of the contemporary world (Khalid 1986, 259). For one thing, the shari'a is opposed to democracy in principle. This fact is repeatedly stressed by eminent Islamists such as Abu A'la Mawdudi and Taqyi al-Dein al-Nabahani (d. 1977), whose ideas are popular among Islamic activists in many Muslim countries, including the Sudan (Mawdudi 1982, 253; Taji-Farouki 1996, 41). While al-Turabi may leave some room for the practice of "democracy" in the Islamic state, once it has been appropriated and Islamacized,[18] he is definitely not wedded to the democratic system of rule before authentic Islamic government is in place. The term "the will" of the people, to which he frequently makes reference in his communications, is nothing more than a formality intended to assuage the fears of secularists and non-Muslims, for the people's will, as explained earlier, is limited to their ability to find the most appropriate Islamic law that they then can apply to a particular problem facing society. Any attempt to abrogate, circumvent, or amend specific regulations in the shari'a is prohibited. Even then, the mechanism by which such a will can be regularly exercised is not spelled out in any detail (Ali 1991, 198). The shura, or consultation, may arguably provide an avenue for ascertaining people's opinion, but such an opinion, even if it could be determined in a timely manner, is not binding on those in authority. In other words, democracy for Islamists such as al-Turabi means *one man, one vote, one time.* When he and his movement were firmly in control in the Sudan after 1989, he spoke rather of taking the Sudanese people back to unity and to a closer association with God and away from worldly temptations (Al-Turabi 1992, 29). Again, al-Turabi insists on a consensus-building rule and not on a majoritarian system, as the latter may oppress individual freedom. But he immediately contradicts himself when he says that Sudanese Muslims must, by virtue of being the majority, determine the type of government. Another weakness of al-Turabi's plan for the Sudan is his acceptance of the legitimacy of the use of force in order to establish the shari'a and transform Sudanese society. He also fails to resolve the tension in his model between a hegemonic government, such as the one of which he was a part until recently, and a Muslim society applying shari'a law in its own way and because of that remaining essentially outside of the domain of the central political power.

The application of shari'a is problematic in other areas as well. By accepting the legality of slavery, the shari'a flies in the face of international prohibitions against this inhumane institution. No amount of sophisticated argumentation can blur this startling and embarrassing fact (An-Naʿim 1990, 175). Similarly, the shariʿaʾs conception of warfare as a religious obligation, undertaken in the interest of expanding the *dar al-Islam* (the abode of Islam), with its unavoidable consequence of enslaving the vanquished, contravenes all accepted international norms regarding the justifications for war and the treatment of captives (An-Naʿim 1900, 175; Collins 1999, 110). Furthermore, the expressly biased treatment of women under the shariʿa in marriage, inheritance, or leadership is indefensible in the modern world where discrimination because of gender, race, or religion is discouraged (An-Naʿim 1990, 217). More to the point, from the perspective of a multicultural and polynational modern state such as the Sudan, the shariʿaʾs insistence that sovereignty belongs to God alone is divisive and discriminatory (Lesch 1998, 212-13). Those citizens who are not Muslims, or Muslims who prefer to govern themselves by rules of their own making, cannot challenge the shariʿa or hope for a reprieve within that system.[19] This amounts to giving license to those Islamic jurists such as al-Turabi (who claim an exclusive knowledge of, and the prerogative to, interpret God's will) to abuse that prerogative without being held accountable for their deeds (Moussalli 1993, 138; Ali 1991, 200). As leaders, they are accountable only to God by His own rules and regulations, rules and regulations that only they are competent to interpret! Skeptics have every reason to be wary of such a political system, especially since the shariʿa state excludes all non-Muslims from participation in administration and denies them full citizenship rights. No non-Muslim, for example, can ever be the head of an Islamic state or hold a sensitive post in the administration. Al-Turabi made this clear as early as 1964 (Khalid 1986, 267; Mawdudi 1982, 257). It is true that the current government in Khartoum includes ministers who are Christians, but they are only tokens intended more for propaganda than for substance.

Another area of weakness in al-Turabi's formulation, according to the critics, is the unexplained relationship between the ummah, as an Islamic universal body, and the nation-state, which is a legal actor in the international arena. Al-Turabi and his supporters have not successfully resolved the tension between these two incompatible polarities of identity.[20] Al-Turabi and Islamists like him would like to have it both ways; to establish the universal ummah, even while closely identifying themselves and their movements with the contemporary territorial nation-state. At times, they even fight other Muslims to preserve the independence of their own nation-state.[21]

As pointed out earlier, a major problem with al-Turabi's position on government in the Sudan is his unequivocal endorsement of the use of force for the purpose of control, and the reconstruction of society on Islamic principles. His association with the 1989 military coup that overthrew a democratically elected government proved beyond any doubt that he and his movement had nothing but contempt for the democratic process.[22] To them, formal participation in elections and sitting in parliaments were tactical moves, as was their willing collaboration with Nimeiri's military dictatorship a decade earlier. Al-Turabi writes, "if the people of the *Din* [read the Ikhwan] manage to come to power on earth peacefully or *by force* [emphasis added], they would then strive to purify society (a goal they would achieve) with the power of the state." Here he is not alone. Other Islamic activists have held similar ideas, ideas with which al-Turabi was only too familiar. Mawdudi, for example, talked about the "Islamic revolution" by which he meant the Islamists' assumption of power by peaceful or, if necessary, violent means for the purpose of establishing the shari'a and transforming the populace into true Muslims (Enayat 1988, 30). Mawdudi maintains that for the successful establishment of the Islamic state, it is "essential that a particular type of movement should grow up, permeated by the same spirit, the same sort of mass character should be molded, the same kind of communal morality should be developed, the same kind of workers should be trained, and the same type of leadership should emerge" (Mawdudi 1955, 25–26). One could hardly think of a more single-minded totalitarian system than this. Al-Turabi, however, seems to have come to the conclusion that the use of force is legitimate only after Nimeiri's 1969 military takeover in which the Communists and left-of-center elements in the army played a major role. He reasoned, that if these elements who enjoyed no significant following among the Sudanese could use the army to bring down elected governments, the much more popular and powerful Ikhwan had even greater justification to do the same. This explains his own and the Ikhwan's involvement in the 1989 military coup d'etat. All the same, his admission only confirmed his opponents' worst fears. To them, the Brothers' use of force was the only logical conclusion of a long and an extremist reactionary ideology that taught bigotry and fanaticism, starting with al-Banna[23] and Sayyid Qutb[24] of Egypt in the 1940s and 1960s and ending with al-Turabi in the 1990s.

SOME THEORETICAL PROPOSITIONS

Modernization theorists have no difficulty explaining the rise of the Muslim Brothers in the Sudan as a manifestation of a too-rapid or an uneven modernization process. As in the Iranian revolution, the quickened pace of development, with its concomitant heightened social tensions, generated a crisis of legitimacy of political leadership. They argue further that the expanding educational opportunities, limited employment, rapid urbanization, ruralization of cities, faster means of communication, breakdown of extended family structures, insatiable consumption, and emergence of a new parasitic class of mini bourgeoisie all combined to create a sense of frustration and loss of direction among a growing number of young, restless Muslims (Moussalli 1999, 2;

Woodward 1997, 23; Esposito 1987, 153-55). With the embarrassing collapse of the ideologies of liberalism, nationalism, Arabism, and socialism, which looked promising decades earlier, as well as the unexpected disintegration of Communism, Islamism became the only viable alternative. Liberalism collapsed in the Middle East, because liberalism in the West itself was under attack from several corners: religious conservatism, epistemological behaviorism, and moral uncertainty (Moussalli 1999, 2). As the Western liberal thinkers doubted the West's moral superiority, liberal rationality, which had hitherto attracted many Muslim intellectuals, ceased to provide a plausible explanation of political practice. As a consequence, Islamic traditions, ideas, or projects that were once deemed irrational or out of place were reinterpreted to mean only being different, hence, authentic and attractive (Binder 1988, 5). The stress of political Islam on authenticity and purity, and its rejection of imported norms and institutions, resonates well with values and meanings held dear by the bulk of the population in the Sudan and elsewhere in the Middle East.

Other writers believe that there are as many explanations of resurgent Islam as there are political movements that claim it as an ideology. Hrair R. Dekmejian, for instance, attributes the phenomenon to the following causes: the illegitimate political elite and political systems, the dearth of social justice, an excessive dependence on coercion, military vulnerability, and the unruly impact of modernization (Dekmejian 1980, 2). The Egyptian critic, Saad Edein Ibrahim, gives five reasons for the rise of Islamic fundamentalism in his own country, which he classifies into five categories. These are: (1) the *social question*, which debates whether the current Egyptian system provides social justice and opportunity fairly to all citizens; (2) the *economic question*, which doubts government competence in wisely using national resources and promoting development; (3) the *patriotic question*, which is skeptical of the system's ability to preserve Egypt's independence and avoid subservience to foreign powers; (4) the *nationalistic question*, which debates Egypt's role in the greater Arab nation; and finally (5) the *civilization question*, which is critical of the relative balance between Westernization and the preservation of Egypt's own historic tradition (Ibrahim, S., 5-7). While Egypt's situation may not be the same as Sudan's, many of the points raised by Ibrahim are relevant to the Sudan's Islamic revival movement.

Modernization and its accompanying Westernization are only two of the many root causes of Islamic resurgence. There are other equally significant factors. The cause also must be sought in the relentless search for both *authenticity* and *liberation*, especially in the case of the Sudan. Neither of these objectives is new. Through the centuries, Muslim societies from time to time have embraced the concepts of *islah* and *tajdid* to deal with what they consider social or political shortcomings of the ummah. Islah usually is translated as reform, but it is a reform with a strong sense of moral righteousness and a commitment to reshape things for the better. Tajdid, on the other hand, means renewal, the regeneration of society's faith and practice in order to

conform to the true message of Islam. Both concepts presuppose the existence of a rightful and historic moral world whose imitation is or ought to be
desired by contemporary Muslims. The urgency of authenticity and liberation
has to do with the failure of the development programs of the secularists and
the dependence of those in authority in the Middle East on outside powers
for decision making. For authenticity and liberation to become reality, an
ideology to inform and legitimate them has to be worked out. As Stephen
Humphrey observes, any ideology is necessarily linked to a general understanding of the universe that attempts to give answers to fundamental questions. Is the nature of the world, for example, essentially material, spiritual,
or both? Is it created and controlled by chance, impersonal law, or the active
agency of a deity? And what are the implications for humans in each case?
Ideology, to use Humphrey's definition, "is a critique of a given sociopolitical
order that simultaneously describes that order and calls upon its members
either to defend and preserve it, or, failing that, to transform or overthrow it"
(Humphrey 1982, 69). This, in essence, is what the Ikhwan in Khartoum
claim to be doing. *Al-Mashru' al-Hadari,* or the "civilization project," as they
describe their cultural, social, and economic policies, is their attempt to rebuild Sudan and Sudanese society on an old-new basis.

The Islamists' incessant drive for authenticity sets them apart from both
leftist Muslims and liberals, on the one hand, and from the traditional *ulama,*
on the otherhand. They are set apart from the first group because of their
presumed intellectual and ethical subservience to the West, and from the
second because of their postulated, uncritical acceptance of the received Muslim
tradition. Al-Turabi and his Sudanese Muslim Brothers now insist on the
concept of authenticity, almost to the exclusion of other equally important
concerns. Whether it is the educational curricula or institutions, television
programs, alms collection and distribution, or women's dress, the Sudanese
are exhorted, and often obliged, to do things the "Islamic way." They are led
to believe that what they are implored to do is required by their own faith and
is essential for maintaining their own distinctive character and identity. As
Robert Collins puts it, "the search for the Sudanese identity has ended; Hasan
al-Turabi has closed the debate" (Collins 1999, 110). What the Ikhwan in the
Sudan endeavor to accomplish is nothing short of reconstruction, however, it
is the reconstruction of Sudanese society on a model that is yet to be determined, since it involves extraction from a reified past and projection into an
unknown future. It is an arduous task.

The Ikhwan's campaign for liberation is closely related to their search for
authenticity. They believe that they cannot achieve one without the other. To
them, liberty is the ability to be free in their own country, to make their own
decisions, and to bear the consequences of such decisions. They are indignant
that the West failed to respect its own principle of liberty and began to
interfere destructively in Sudanese affairs, so as to abort the only serious
Muslim experiment to live by the teachings of their religion. Total liberation

by the definition of the Ikhwan means the Arabicization of the curricula, the Islamization of the economy and the banking system, self-reliance on home-grown food, and the establishment of Islamically oriented charitable organizations. These are precisely the types of programs underway in the Sudan at the present time. They are meant to deepen and strengthen the movement toward authenticity and to promote the freedom of the Sudanese people.

CONCLUSION

The assertive ideology of the revivalist Islamic movement in the Sudan, led by the Muslim Brothers and the neoreligious nationalism associated with it, cannot be explained by reference to the theories of instrumentalism or primordialism, even when the Brotherhood often behaves as through it is an ethnic group, "combining interest with affective ties." For its Sufi-style strict discipline, its rejection of blood ties as normative, and its commitment to the universal ideal of Islam set it apart from any other social group. There is, however, an element in this organization of what primordialists such as A. L. Epstein and Harold Isaacs would identify as characteristic of ethnic affiliation: "the powerful emotional charge" or the "peculiarly coercive powers." In this case, however, the powerful emotive charge and the coercive power are directed toward a deity, and not toward humans. These spiritual affective bonds are to serve a sacred ideal whose rewards are in Heaven, not in this world.

The constructivist approach is perhaps most appropriate to help us explain the Brotherhood's rapid rise to power in the Sudan. As we have seen, this well-disciplined organization uses discursive narrative to reconstruct a golden past that is now the yardstick against which progress is measured. In the process, the Brotherhood has "manufactured," to use Crawford Young's term (1993, 23), not an ethnic group but a religious community whose impenetrable borderland is the shari'a, and whose territory is shielded and insulated from outside destructive influences by its authenticity and liberation. Sudanese society must be transformed to create the *imagined* community of believers, the ideal ummah, the vicegerent of Allah on earth. In this divine plan, whose instrument is the Muslim Brothers, multiculturalism is accepted, and even promoted, but only within a clear, hierarchical order in which the ummah of Sudanese Muslims is permanently on top.

NOTES

1. While Islamic revival of the Shi'a sect in Iran looks *forward* to the golden age when their hidden Imam reappears for the final realization of the Islamic message, Sunni Muslims often look *backward* to a reified past, a past that is largely outside of

concrete history and defiant of circumstance. However, present-day Islamic activists such as the current rulers of the Sudan go a step further and, unlike early Islamic modernists, stress their freedom to critically engage that golden past, reinterpret it, and relocate it successfully within their respective modern communities.

2. After his return in 1964 from study in France and England, with degrees in law, Dr. al-Turabi became the uncontested leader of the Muslim Brotherhood in the Sudan, in the process replacing formidable leaders such as al-Rashid al-Tahir and Ali Tab-Allah (El-Affendi 1991, 64). It also was during this period that the intellectual and administrative linkages connecting the Sudanese movement to its Egyptian parent Muslim Brotherhood were finally broken (El-Affendi 1991, 145). Because of his long career in politics, but especially as a result of his advocacy on behalf of Islam nationally and internationally, he also is recognized by thousands around the Arab and Muslim worlds as an able, articulate spokesman of the new vision of political Islam.

In 1994, al-Turabi used his position in the Sudanese Islamic establishment to set up the Popular Arab and Islamic Conference, with headquarters in Khartoum, and accordingly he was elected its general secretary. It was his way of bypassing governments and other institutions in the Middle East that he accused of being subservient to the West, indifferent to the plight of Muslims, and outrightly hostile to the kind of movement he led (Ali 1996, 383).

3. For a complete list of al-Turabi's publications, see El-Affendi 1991, 202, and Ibrahim 1999, 221.

4. This distinction between the shari'a and its application is not new. Hasan al-Banna, the founding father of the Muslim Brotherhood in Egypt, already stressed a similar approach in the 1920s (see Esposito 1987, 139). Al-Turabi goes much further, however, and calls for what appears to be the democratization of the very process by which the shari'a is formulated.

5. According to el-Affendi (1991, 170), al-Turabi said in one of his public expositions that "Islam needs to be rethought radically. It is not true, he said, that Islam is eternal and cannot change."

6. These kinds of bold statements, which implied that Islam was an incomplete message in need of additions or amendment, brought the wrath of conservative Muslims who accused al-Turabi of heresy. Among these were several prominent members of the Sudanese Muslim Brotherhood, such as the academician, Ja'far Sheikh Idris, who now lives in the United States.

7. Al-Turabi has built his notion of a "democratically" formulated shari'a on the Islamic principle of 'ijma', or consensus, even if he does not say so. This principle was established by the very classical Muslim jurists he condemns, which is why writers such as Ahmad S. Moussalli argue that al-Turabi is, after all, a "traditionalist." Like all classical jurists, Moussalli maintains, al-Turabi accepts the classical formulation that the shari'a could only be derived from the four main sources: the Quran, the Sunna, the *Qiyas*, or analogy, and the `ijma'. (Moussalli 1993, 138).

8. Islamists might have found some room for accommodating Arab nationalism had it not been for the catastrophe of the Arab defeat of 1967, which demonstrated clearly the bankruptcy of Arabism in all of its forms (Sivan 1957, 131).

9. The concept of *hakimiyya* was central to Mawdudi's discourse, and to a lesser extent to that of al-Banna (Binder 1988, 175-77). Al-Turabi, in contrast, speaks about it only in very general terms. On the other hand, Fazlur Rahman accused Mawdudi and other Islamists of confusing religio-moral and political issues. He argues that sovereignty, in the sense of coercive force, belongs only to the people, not to God (Rahman 1982, 264).

10. Al-Turabi seems to stress either the "minimal" or the "absolute" Islamic state, depending on whether or not he himself is in power. When he and his movement were partners of the military dictatorship of President Nimeiri, as they now are with General al-Bashir, al-Turabi emphasized in his discourse the central role of government in enforcing the shari'a and transforming the Sudanese people into a wholly Islamic society (see Collins 1999, 110).

11. In 1925, the Egyptian Muslim critic, Ali Abdel Raziq, argued vehemently against the idea that an Islamic state, or *khilafa*, was necessary or a religious obligation, an opinion that brought upon him the wrath of many conservative Azharite jurists (see Raziq 1999, 73).

12. In his most recent publications, al-Turabi is convinced that *shura* and democracy are compatible to the extent that Muslims appropriate and Islamacize the latter. The appropriated democracy would then be for the sole purpose of serving Allah.

13. It was perhaps because of the Muslim Brotherhood's distinct distrust of political pluralism and its dislike of dissent that Article 26, Section 2, of the 1998 Constitution speaks only of one political organization, the so-called political *tawali* (association). Even the word *hizb* (party) is avoided, as it implies fragmentation and disunity. Again, Article 6 of the same constitution explicitly requires the government to ensure national unity by outlawing the emergence of associations based on ethnicity, faith, or partisan affiliation.

14. Al-Turabi has admitted recently that he sent General al-Bashir to the Palace while he went to prison after the Brotherhood's military takeover in June 1989 to conceal his involvement in the coup (see *Majallat al-Wasat* 2000).

15. According to Mansur Khalid, al-Turabi not only welcomed the new Islamic laws but also approved of the state of emergency declared by President Nimeiri in order to clamp down on opposition to these laws. Al-Turabi and his followers even offered Nimeiri their *bay'a* (oath of allegiance) as an Imam or a religious leader. (see Khalid 1986, 280-81).

16. The Muslim Brotherhood in the mid-1980s began to infiltrate the Sudan Armed Forces by various means, especially education, and it succeeded in indoctrinating many young officers who were then recruited into the Ikhwan movement (see Kok 1996, 42).

17. For a good commentary on this issue, see Tibi (1998, chapter 9).

18. Al-Turabi is of the opinion that Muslims should appropriate concepts such as "democracy" and "revolution," Islamicize them by adapting them to the worship of Allah, and then apply them in Muslim societies (see Hasan Abdallah Al-Turabi (1985). "al-Shura wal Demoqratiyya," in Al-Mustaqbal al-'Arabi. 75:7: 9).

19. Recently the Tunisian Islamist al-Ghannushi made bold new reinterpretations of Islamic dogma to allow for equality among all citizens of an Islamic state,

regardless of their religious affiliations. All along this has been the message of the Republican Brothers of the Sudan, whose leader, Mahmud Muhammad Taha, was executed by President Nimeiri for his liberal views about Islam.

20. Nor does al-Turabi explain how the Islamic state, which functions in accordance with the shari'a, solves the inevitable conflict over international loans. As it happened, after outlawing *riba*, or interest, on loans, the Ikhwan-led government of Khartoum found it necessary to accept the sinful practice and to continue to pay interest on all of its international debts, the objections of the shari'a-minded notwithstanding.

21. This was the situation in which the Ikhwan in Khartoum found themselves in 1994, when both Egypt and the Sudan claimed the northeastern borderland of Halaib and just barely avoided a bloody confrontation. The Ikhwan government tried but failed to mobilize the Sudanese behind a jihad against fellow Egyptian Muslims, but when the Sudanese Muslims were called upon to defend the territorial integrity of their country, whether in the northeast or in the south, the response was great. Nationalism, with which the Ikhwan reluctantly has identified itself seems to have been a more effective instrument of mobilization than the Islamic ideology to which they are committed. Ironically, the Islamist government in Khartoum lodged an official complaint against Egypt with the United Nations, the very institution it had previously condemned as a tool of Western imperialism, headed by the United States!

22. In this the Ikhwan of the Sudan are no different from other Islamists in the Middle East. Ali Bilhaj, a prominent Algerian Muslim leader, declares his indifference to the democratic process when he writes, "as for us we the people of the Sunna and the Community (of Muslims) truth is not measured by how many votes (a candidate gets). . . . nor by majority, even a Muslim majority" (see Bilhaj 1990, 10).

23. Al-Banna once wrote, "our call is to return to true Islam, which is a belief and [an] application, a home and a nationality, a religion and state, a spirit and body, and a Quran and a *sword*" (emphasis added, Al-Banna 1965, 45).

24. The slogan of the Egyptian Brothers in the 1950s, under the leadership of Sayyid Qutb, was this: "God is our highest end. The Prophet is our leader, the Quran is our law, jihad is our means, and death for the cause of Allah is our highest ambition" (Dessouki 1982, 18).

REFERENCES

Al-'Awwa, Mohammed Salim. 1983. *Fi al-Nizam al-Islami*. Cairo: al-Maktab al-Masri al-Hadith.

Al-'Awwa , Salim, and Hasan al-Turabi. 1998. *Min Ma'alim al-Nizam al-Islami* (Principles of Islamic Political System). Khartoum: Jama'at al-Fikr wal-Da'wa al-Islamiya.

Al-Banna, Hasan. 1965. "Mushkilatuna fil Daw'i al-Nizam al-Islami" (Our Problem in Light of the Islamic Project). *Majmu'at Rasa'il al-Imam al-Shahid Hasan al-Banna*. Beirut: Dar al-Andalus.

Al-Farouqi, Suha. 1995. "Nizariyat al-Dawla al-Islamiya." 5:1:83–98. *Qira'at Siyasiya.*

Ali, Haydar I. 1991. *Azmat al-Islam al-Siyasi* (Crisis of Political Islam). Rabat: Dar Qurtuba.

———. 1996. *Al-Tayyarat al-Islamiya wa Qadiyyat al-Demoqratiyya.* Cairo: Sudanese Studies Center.

Al-Turabi, Hasan A. 1983. "The Islamic State." Pp. 228–44 in *Voices of Resurgent Islam.* Edited by J. Esposito. New York: Oxford University Press.

———. 1985. "Al-Shura wal Dimoqratia: Ishkaalat al-Mustalah wal Mafhum" (The Shura and Democracy: Problems of Concept.) In *Al-Mustaqbal al-'Arabi* 75.

———. 1992. "A Dialogue with Dr. Hasan al-Turabi." *Qira'at Siyasiya* 3.

———. 1995. *Qadaya al-Tagdied: Nahwa Manhagin 'Usuli,* Ma'had al-Buhouth, Khartoum.

———. 1999. *Al-Haraka al-Islamiyya fi al-Sudan: AI-Tatawwur, al-Kasb wal Manhaj* (Islamic Movement in the Sudan: Development, Gains, and Ideology). 2d ed. Rabat: Furqan Publications.

An-Na'im, Abdullahi A. 1990. *Toward an Islamic Reformation: Civil Liberties, Human Rights and International Law.* Syracuse: Syracuse University Press.

Binder, Leonard. 1988. *Islamic Liberalism: A Critique of Development Ideologies.* Chicago: University of Chicago Press.

Chittick, William C. 1989. *Ibn al 'Arabi's Metaphysics of Imagination: The Sufi Path of Knowledge.* Albany: State University of New York Press.

Collins, Robert O. 1999. "Africans, Arabs and Islamists: From the Conference Tables to the Battlefields in the Sudan." *African Studies Review* 42:2: 105–24.

Commins, David. 1994. "Hasan al-Banna 1906–1949." *Pioneers of Islamic Revival.* Edited by Ali Rahnema. London: Zed Books.

Dekmejian, Hrair R. 1980. "The Arab Anatomy of Islamic Revival: Legitimacy Crisis, Ethnic Conflict and the Search for Islamic Alternatives." *Middle East Journal* 34.

Dessouki, Ali H. 1982. "The Islamic Resurgence: Sources, Dynamics and Implementations." *Islamic Resurgence in the Arab World.* Edited by Ali H. Dessouki. New York: Praeger.

El-Affendi, Abdelwahab. 1991. *Turabi's Revolution: Islam and Power in the Sudan.* London: Grey Seal Books.

Enayat, Hamid. 1988. *Modern Islamic Politics.* Austin: University of Texas Press.

Esposito, John L. 1987. *Islam and Politics.* Syracuse: Syracuse University Press.

Esposito, John L., and J. Donahue, eds. 1982. *Islam in Transition.* London: Oxford University Press.

Hourani, Albert. 1983. *Arabic Thought in the Liberal Age.* Cambridge: Cambridge University Press.

———. 1991. *History of the Arabs.* New York: Warner Books.

Humphrey, R. Stephen. 1982. "The Contemporary Resurgence in the Context of Modern Islam." *Islamic Resurgence in the Arab World*. Edited by Ali H. Dessouki. New York: Praeger.

Ibrahim, Abdullahi Ali. 1999. "A Theology of Modernity: Al-Turabi and Islamic Renewal in the Sudan." *Africa Today* 46: 3\4: 195–220.

Ibrahim, Saad E. No Date. *Misr Turaji' Nafsaha*. Cairo: Dar al-Hilal.

Khalid, Mansur. 1986. *al-Fagr al-Kadhib, Nimeiri wa tahrif al-shari'a, The False Dawn: Nimeiri and the Mis-interpretation of the Shari'a*. Cairo: Dar al-Hilal.

Kok, Peter N. 1996. *Governance and Conflict in the Sudan, 1985-1995: Evaluation and Documentation*. Hamburg: Deutsches Orient-Institut.

Lesch, Ann M. 1998. *Sudan: Contested National Identities*. Bloomington: Indiana University Press.

Maududi, A. A. 1955. *The Process of Islamic Revolution*.

Mawdudi, Abu A'la. 1982?. "Political Theory of Islam." In *Islam in Transition*, ed. J. Donahue and J. Esposito. London: Oxford University Press.

Moussalli, Ahmad S. 1993. *Qira'at Nazariyyat Siyasiyya fil al-khitab al-Islami al-'Usuli*. Beirut.

———. 1999. *Moderate and Radical Islamic Fundamentalism: The Quest for Modernity, Legitimacy and the Islamic State*. Gainesville: University of Florida Press.

Qiliyun, Burhan, 1991. *Naqd al-Siyasa: Al-Din wal-Dawla* (Critique of Politics: Religion and the State) Beirut.

Qutb, Muhammad. 1986. *Islam: The Misunderstood Religion*. Translated by Aziz Bilyameena. Lahore: Islamic Publications.

Qutb, Sayyid. 1983. *Ma'alim fil Tariq*. 7th ed. Beirut: Dar al-Shuruq.

Rahman, Fazlur. 1982. "The Islamic Concept of State." *Islam in Transition*. Edited by J. Donahue and J. Esposito. London: Oxford University Press.

Raziq., Ali Abdel. 1999. *Al-Islam wa 'Ususl al-Hukm* (reprint, Islam and the Principles of Government). Tunis.

Roy, Oliver. 1994. *The Failure of Political Islam*. Translated by Carol Volk. Cambridge: Harvard University Press.

Sidahmed, Abdel Salam. *Politics of Islam in Contemporary Sudan*.

———. 1996. "Sudan: Ideology and Pragmatism." Pp. 179–98 in *Islamic Fundamentalism*, ed. Abdel Salam Sidahmed and Anoushiravan Ehteshami. Boulder: Westview Press.

Sivan, E. 1957. *Radical Islam: Medieval Theology and Modern Politics*. New Haven: Yale University Press.

Taji-Farouki, Suha. 1996. "Islamic State: Theories and Contemporary Realities." Pp. 35–50 in *Islamic Fundamentalism*. Edited by Abdel Salam Sidahmed and Anoushiravan Ehteshami. Boulder: Westview Press.

Tibi, Bassam. 1998. "Democracy and Democratization in Islam." *The Challenge of Fundamentalism: Political Islam and the New World Order.* Berkeley: University of California Press.

Warburg, Gabriel R. 1991. "The Sharia in the Sudan: Implementation and Percussions." *Sudan: State and Society in Crisis.* Edited by John Voll. Bloomington: Indiana University Press.

Woodward, Peter. 1997. "Sudan: Islamic Radicals in Power." In *Political Islam: Revolution, Radicalism or Reform*, ed. John Esposito. Boulder: Lynne Rienner.

Young, C., ed. 1993. *The Rise of Cultural Pluralism: The Nation State at Bay?* Madison: University of Wisconsin Press.

List of Newspapers Consulted

Al-Duds

Al-Munghidh

Al-Sharq al'Awsat

Majallat al-Wasat

Chapter 7

Mahatma Gandhi on Indian Self-Rule

An Instrumentalist, an Ethno-Symbolic, or a Psychological Discourse of Nationalism?[1]

Manfred B. Steger

The rising fortunes of "nationalism studies" became apparent in 1983 with Ernest Gellner's reformulation of the relationship between industrialization, cultural homogeneity, and nationalism (1983, 1994), Benedict Anderson's characterization of the nation as an "imagined political community" (1991), and Eric Hobsbawm's critique of the divisive "inventions" of ethno-linguistic nationalisms (Hobsbawm and Ranger 1983; Hobsbawm 1990). For the last several years, proponents and detractors of these new perspectives have crossed swords, in the process extending the discussion on nationalism to issues of gender, sexuality, postcolonialism, group rights, citizenship, multiculturalism, and political violence. Much energy has been expended in the search for more precise definitions, typologies, and classifications of core concepts such as "nation," "national identity," and "ethnicity" (Hall 1993, 1-28; Connor 1994). While this quest for analytical clarity has created various schools of analysis whose members subscribe to disparate modes of theoretical discourse, there remain nonetheless serious doubts whether any unitary theory of nationalism or ethnicity has succeeded in capturing the complex and ambiguous phenomenon of nationalism (Young 1993, 21–23).

Craig Calhoun, for example, readily concedes that nationalism and its corollary terms "have proved notoriously hard concepts to define," because

The initial draft of this chapter was presented in "Nation, State, and Cultural Pluralism," a 1997 NEH Summer Seminar at the University of Wisconsin-Madison. My thanks go to the director, Crawford Young, as well as to Cris Toffolo and the other participants in that seminar for their helpful comments and suggestions. I also want to acknowledge the support I received from Illinois State University in the form of a 1997 University Research Grant.

"nationalisms are extremely varied phenomena," and "any definition will legitimate some claims and delegitimate others" (1993, 215–16). John Dunn seconds this view, adding that, "[This] unsteady mixture [of nation and state] has proved unsuitable for clear analytical thought. But its analytical debility has been no bar to ideological or practical potency" (1995, 3).

To be sure, I am not suggesting that we abandon empirically sustainable research programs for the study of nationalism, nor do I want to disavow the importance of conceptual distinctions made for heuristic purposes. However we do move beyond stale disputes over definitions toward a better understanding of the potency of nationalism and its implications for modern politics.

In this chapter, I argue that instrumentalist, ethno-symbolic, and psychological approaches to nationalism should not be considered mutually exclusive perspectives. The quest for a better understanding of the many sources of nationalism's "explosive energy and awful power" requires that these approaches be employed in a complementary fashion. Assuming that prominent nationalist leaders play a vital role in this process, I develop my complementary perspective as a micro-level analysis of text(s) and context(s)—the use of material resources, cultural narratives, symbols, moral ideals, and religious beliefs—through which individual nationalist authenticators define themselves, their constituents, and their longing for self-rule. Focusing on Mahatma Gandhi's influential views on *swaraj* (self-rule; independence), Indian civilization, and *ahimsa* (nonviolence), as formulated in his seminal work *Hind Swaraj* (Indian Home-Rule), this chapter seeks to identify and account for various instrumentalist, ethno-symbolic, and psychological aspects that give his nationalist discourse its unique *gestalt* and power.

Pointing to Gandhi's seemingly universalist and humanistic discourse of moral individuation, several writers have erroneously suggested that it was perhaps not a nationalism at all, at least not in the Western sense of the term (Parekh 1995, 39–41; 1989; Nandy 1994, 3). Yet Gandhi himself, distinguishing between *violent* and *nonviolent* forms of nationalism, repeatedly acknowledged that, "Non-violent nationalism is a necessary condition of corporate or civilized life" (Gandhi 1958–1994, 25:369). Indeed, many prominent Gandhi scholars have emphasized the impact of his ideas on the construction and evolution of India as an independent nation-state. Ainslie Embree's observation emphasizes this point: "[O]ne dares to venture the opinion that no other leader in history in his own lifetime has done so much to make a people into a nation" (1989, 172).

Gandhi's vision of nonviolent nationalism represents an especially challenging case for existing theories of nationalism, for a number of reasons. First, his insistence on achieving swaraj, through *satyagraha* (truth-force) based on the moral ideals of self-control, ahimsa, and *satya* (truth; being), highlights the central role of value-rationality and noninstrumental social action. It thus seems to contradict instrumentalist explanations of nationalism. Second, his

unwillingness to share the historicism of many contemporary Indian nationalists appears to undermine Anthony Smith's ethno-symbolic reading of nationalists as archaeologists who rediscover and reinterpret the communal past
in order to regenerate the community (Smith 1995, 1996a, 1996b). Third, his
"saintly" moral qualities of selflessness and simplicity seem to run counter to
the pivotal role of vanity and status seeking, which Greenfeld assigns to
nationalist authenticators.[1] Finally, a consideration of Gandhi's nationalist
discourse shifts the debate on nationalism from familiar Western to the frequently neglected non-Western colonial soil. Thus this chapter engages in
what Fred Dallmayr has called the process of "comparative political theorizing in the global village"—an inquiry aimed at cross-cultural learning through
mutual interrogation, contestation, and engagement (1997, 421-27).

THE SOUTH AFRICAN CONTEXT

Confronted by Mohandas Karamchand Gandhi's full-blown nationalist discourse in his 1909 dialogue *Hind Swaraj*, one easily forgets its origins as a
relatively modest plea for civil and economic rights on behalf of the South
African Indian commercial elite. Indeed, the failure to connect one's textual
analysis to the political and socioeconomic conditions of *fin-de-siècle* South
Africa might result in downplaying the importance of the material and instrumental forces of modernity in the conception and construction of Gandhi's
Indian nationalism. Moreover, by focusing too narrowly on the text, one
might pay insufficient attention to the location and significance of Gandhi's
nationalist writings within a long literary history of cultural interaction between nineteenth-century Western discourses of nationalism and those of
Hindu and Muslim religious communities in India. Hence, before embarking
on the necessary textual interpretation of his mature work on Indian self-rule,
first I will consider some of these contextual matters.

Gandhi's gradual transformation from a shy Bombay attorney to the
outspoken opponent of South Africa's political system of racial discrimination
has been duly noted by his principal biographers (Rolland 1924; Fischer
1951; Nanda 1958; Tendulkar 1960-1963; Payne 1969; Brown 1989; Greenfeld
1993; Dalton 1993). Yet most of these accounts pack his formative years—
from 1893 to 1914 in Natal and the Transvaal—into relatively short chapters,
allotting most of the discussion to his later activities as a leader of the Indian
National Congress. Such superficial treatments of the South African context
are quite surprising in the face of widespread scholarly acknowledgment that
Gandhi, "having laid down the foundations of his thought during the pioneering days of his campaigns in South Africa," returned to India as "a
mature man of forty-five who had done his essential thinking on morals and
politics" (Iyer 1973, 9-10; 1986, 2).

A few leading Gandhi scholars have only fairly recently embarked on the critical task of exploring the many ways by which "South Africa made the Indian Gandhi" (Brown 1996, 22; Huttenback 1971; R. Gandhi 1994; Du Toit 1996, 643-60; Hunt 1989, 61-81; Switzer 1986, 122-28; Swan 1985). In particular, they have sought to complement Gandhi's romanticized account of his political engagement with an examination of the economic stratification of his South African constituents—the political agenda of the Indian commercial elites, the relationships among the various socioeconomic classes, and the interactions between South African Indians, other non-European immigrants, and Black Africans.

Gandhi's arrival in the Natal province coincided with the rapid transformation of South Africa's pastoral and agricultural economy into a modern capitalist economy mostly based on mining (Singh 1996, 82-101). These new economic realities attracted immigrants with very different socioeconomic backgrounds. Gandhi never encountered a monolithic "Indian community," nor did he ever succeed in forging the existing plurality of highly stratified communities into one political community. Deep social, economic, and cultural cleavages separated old commercial elites, chiefly made up of Gujarat Muslims who had emigrated to South Africa at their own expense, from a vast underclass of mostly low-caste Hindus who subsisted as indentured laborers and servants (Swan 1985, xv, 1–28). A new generation of South African-born professionals—teachers, bookkeepers, lawyers, civil servants, clerks, and petty entrepreneurs—did not materialize as an objectively definable group with distinct political and economic interests until around 1906. Hence, Gandhi's relatively rare status as a middle-class, educated lawyer from the merchant caste made it rather easy for him to attach himself socially, professionally, and emotionally to the commercial elites.

The activities of these elites could hardly be considered apolitical. By the time Gandhi became involved in South African politics in 1894, Natal merchants had already established viable political organizations. They were fully aware that their business interests were threatened by a new wave of racially discriminatory measures and pending anti-immigration bills originating in the rising tide of economically motivated hatred against all "Colored" in the Orange Free State and the Transvaal, and quickly spreading to Natal. It appears that Indian merchants in Natal, driven by the urgent need for a full-time political organizer with an appropriate professional background, actively recruited Gandhi. "Gandhi was perfectly suited to the merchants' needs from the point of view of linguistic and legal qualifications, as well as ideological compatibility. As their hired representative he ensured the continuity of merchant political philosophy and practice between 1891 and 1906 (Swan 1985, 38)." This is not to say that Gandhi was unconcerned with the plight of the underclass or did not undertake legal and political representations on its behalf. Yet it must be emphasized that his main political strategy of polite constitutional protest remained for a long time connected to the commercial interests of the merchants. This also is true of his well-known institutional achievements: the Natal Indian Congress (1894), the newspaper *Indian Opinion* (1903), and the communal settlement at Phoenix, near Durban (1904). Only when discriminatory legislation directed toward "Indians" in general thwarted the interests of the commercial elites did Gandhi attempt to form short-lived alliances with parts of the underclass. Even at the height of his Transvaal struggle between 1908 and 1914, when his increasingly radical language of moral individuation, self-sacrifice, and romanticization of the peasantry began to alienate growing numbers of merchants, Gandhi continued to appeal to the merchants' patriotic feelings and purses by stressing the nationalist character of the satyagraha campaigns: "Money too will be needed for such an agitation; for this regular provision should be made. If every Indian does his duty and performs the community's task in the same spirit that he does his own, it will not be surprising to see India being forged into a nation in South Africa" (Gandhi 1958–1994, 9:202). By 1913, it was clear that Gandhi had to compensate for his decreasing support by the commercial elite by broadening his mobilization efforts in the direction of the upwardly mobile strata of the lower classes and castes; still, he held fast to his cherished identity as a "humble interpreter between the two [British and "Indian"] communities," preaching social harmony under the slogan of "Indian unity" (Gandhi 1958–1994, 2:163; Brock 1983, 90). To safeguard his dwindling material foundation, Gandhi accepted ethical compromises such as minimizing the central idea of self-sacrifice by telling potential satyagrahis that possible jail sentences would be brief, and that their engagement would not endanger their private property, resident permits, and businesses (Swan 1985, 243–45; 272–73).

At no time, however, did his coalition-building processes include lasting alliances with the South African Chinese and other Asian immigrant populations, not to speak of trying to rally Black South Africans behind the fight against racial discrimination (Harris 1996, 89; Switzer 1986, 123-27). Gandhi's consistent use of exclusionary language against the "underdeveloped Kaffir" was intended to preserve Colored Indians as a distinct pressure group, thus preventing the sharing of achieved material benefits with Black Africans. Hence, Gandhi's politically effective objection to the official use of the category "Colored" as including both Indians and Blacks can only be fully explained with the help of instrumentalist models of nationalism and ethnicity that stress the maximization of material benefits through strong social mechanisms of inclusion and exclusion (Bates 1983; Hechter 1986, 264-79).

In speeches to his Indian audiences as well as in petitions to the British authorities, Gandhi pointed out that "both the English and the Indians spring from a common stock, called the Indo-Aryan." And he protested the "degradation sought to be inflicted upon us by the Europeans, who desire to degrade us to the level of the raw Kaffir whose occupation is hunting, and whose sole ambition is to collect a certain number of cattle to buy a wife with and, then, pass his life in indolence and nakedness" (1958–1994, 2:74, 105; 1:149). A few months before he wrote *Hind Swaraj*, Gandhi observed "with regret" that Indian prisoners were "happy to sleep in the same room as Kaffirs." "This is a matter of shame to us," he concluded, since "we cannot ignore the fact that there is no common ground between them and us in the daily affairs of life" (1958–1994, 9:149).

While these vivid examples of Gandhi's exclusiveness are not sufficient to establish his complicity in racism or proto-apartheid policies, they are nonetheless clear indicators of the workings of powerful material imperatives. By now it should be obvious that it would be a mistake to examine Gandhi's nationalist discourse without the utilization of some instrumentalist insights. The political and economic interests of Gandhi's South African constituencies were undoubtedly served by his activation of Indian patriotism within the framework of developing capitalism in South Africa. While instrumentalist approaches cannot account for the full power of Gandhi's ideas, it must nonetheless be acknowledged that *Hind Swaraj*, his nationalist manifesto, could not have been written without his deep involvement in the calculating activities of self-interested social groups seeking to extend their political power.

SELF-RULE AND THE CRITIQUE OF MODERN CIVILIZATION

Returning to South Africa from a futile political mission in London on behalf of the Transvaal Indians in November 1909, Gandhi wrote *Hind Swaraj* on board the *Kildonan Castle* in only ten days. Divided into twenty chapters, the book is a dialogue between two fictional characters: a newspaper editor (representing Gandhi's point of view) and a radical reader whose political position sometimes resembles that of V. D. Savarkar and Madan Lal Dhingra— two revolutionary Indian nationalists responsible for the 1909 assassination of Sir William Curzon-Wyllie, the political secretary of the Secretary of State for India. As Anthony J. Parel (Gandhi 1997, xiv) has pointed out, *Hind Swaraj* is addressed to a mixed audience, ranging from ordinary Indians inhabiting the subcontinent, to expatriate Indians greatly attracted to political violence, extremists and moderates of the Indian National Congress, South African Indians, and "the English."

Already in his 1910 preface to the English translation, Gandhi announces his eagerness "to serve his country" as the main motive for writing the book. Connecting "the defense of the Motherland" to a necessary process of "finding out the truth about civilization," he offers a theoretical alternative to the "suicidal policies" of Indian nationalists who have mistakenly adopted "modern civilization and modern methods of violence to drive out the English"

(Gandhi 1997, 7–11). Deeply influenced by Edward Carpenter's arguments against modern civilization in *Civilization: Its Cause and Cure*, Gandhi suggests that only by "revert[ing] to their own glorious civilization" would Indians find their true national identity and thus the moral strength and cultural resources necessary for a successful resistance to the British occupiers. Inverting British orientalist stereotypes, Gandhi rediscovers true "Indianness" as the culturally regenerative and deeply political process of resurrecting the principles and values of an "Ancient [Indian] Civilization, which is the Kingdom of God." The full restoration of this imagined civilization and its values would leave the colonizers with only two choices: either they would allow themselves to be "Indianized," or they would "find their occupation in India gone" (Gandhi 1997, 7). Thus *Hind Swaraj* contains a passionate exhortation to all Indian patriots to return to the moral and spiritual essence of their civilization and to abandon all Western forms of nationalism that bear the marks of a modernity whose uncritical acceptance would simply result in the establishment of an independent India as just another "Englistan" (Gandhi 1997, 28).

Like Plato, whose *Apology of Socrates* is included as an "authoritative source" in the appendix of *Hind Swaraj*, Gandhi chooses health and sickness as the guiding metaphors of his dialogue. The editor (Gandhi) soon emerges as the virtuous "doctor," skillfully diagnosing the misguided vision of violent Indian nationalists as the deplorable symptom of the underlying "disease of modern civilization" spread to India by the British. In a passionate narrative whose accusatory power rivals even the most memorable lines of Marx's and Engels' *Communist Manifesto*, the editor proceeds to describe the condition of modern civilization as one of "attachment to brute force" and enslavement to sensual pleasures, ever-growing appetites, luxury, and *adharma* (irreligion). Embracing chiefly "bodily welfare" as the object of life, modern civilization in its British variety has gnawed away at the health of the old Indian civilization, which once provided the social and moral foundations of an ancient united and "naturally undivided" Indian nation. But with the arrival of the Europeans, the railway has appeared as a "carrier of plague germs"; modern lawyers are teaching immorality by selfishly advancing conflicts instead of helping to resolve them; and the modern medical professions and their supporting technologies and institutions represent the results of people's physical indulgence and sin. To add insult to injury, the British have deliberately set Hindus against Muslims, thus destroying the cultural and religious pluralism characteristic of pre-modern India (Gandhi 1997, 31–63).

Further developing his binary opposition of a nation's "health" and "sickness" in chapters on British political institutions, education, and technology, the editor consistently arrives at the same conclusion: in a colonized nation beset by the disabling disease of a modern, alien civilization, only the correct diagnosis holds out a faint promise of cure. What, then, is the root of this sickness? Appropriately, the editor responds to this question in a long passage that criticizes the alleged progress of Western medicine: "We may pretend to be civilized, call religious prohibitions a superstition and wantonly indulge in what we like. The fact remains that the doctors induce us to indulge, and the result is that we have become deprived of self-control and have become effeminate. In these circumstances, we are unfit to serve the country" (Gandhi 1997, 64). Driven by appetites and desires generated by modern civilization, Indians have lost their traditional connection to spirituality, *ahimsa*, and tolerance—values that are indispensable for moral self-rule. Morally weak and ethnically divided, modern Indians are no longer capable of drawing strength from their cultural diversity—even though "Hindus and Mahomedans own the same ancestors, and the same blood runs through their veins" (Gandhi 1997, 53). Having fallen prey to the materialism of modern civilization, these "half-Anglicized Indians" should therefore no longer be considered "good specimens of the real Indian nation" (Gandhi 1997, 115).

Thus the individual's dedication to traditional Indian religious and moral tenets becomes the key to sound nation building: "In order to restore India to its pristine conditions we have to return to it [religious education]. In our own civilization, there will naturally be progress, retrogression, reforms and reactions; but one effort is required, and that is to drive out Western civilization. All else will follow" (Gandhi 1997, 106). Infusing his nationalist message with a good dose of inverted orientalism, Gandhi presents the alleged values of Indian civilization as universal norms applicable even to the Europeans—provided that they forsake the core principles of their own civilization.[2]

In typical Platonic fashion, Gandhi links politics to the more primary problem of moral self-rule. Indeed, his nationalist discourse assumes the character of a moral-political enterprise strikingly similar to that of the *Republic*: the political restoration of the community must go hand in hand with the moral reordering of the collective psyche. One by one, each individual soul must be turned away from the enticing shadows of modern civilization and reoriented toward the ancient ideals of community, equality, physical health, and spiritual Truth. It is therefore not surprising that the editor refers to "doing one's duty (*dharma*)" as the only appropriate educational path leading to both individual and national self-rule: "Civilization is that mode of conduct which points out to man the path of duty. Performance of duty and observance of morality are convertible terms. To observe morality is to attain mastery over our mind and passions. So doing, we know ourselves" (Gandhi 1997, 67). The message is clear: if Indians want to assume control over their nation's future, they must rediscover the true essential qualities that make up "genuine Indianness," according to Gandhi—the spiritual athleticism of venerable ancestors who mastered their passions and appetites, controlled their physical desires, and disciplined their bodies. Once again, Gandhi's narrative is deeply embedded in his orientalist belief in India as a "land which is the source of religions" (Gandhi 1997, 115).

Here, then, are the seeds of Gandhi's own personal transformation that culminates in his proud proclamation that "ancient Indian civilization represents the best that the world has ever seen" (1997, 7). Inverted orientalist concepts provide him with an alternative viewpoint and an activist understanding of nationalism as both a politically emancipatory movement and a spiritual revolution carried on by Indian truth seekers against the fatal defects of modernity. While he rejects the violent nationalism espoused by Tilak, Aurobindo, Krishnavarma, and V. D. Savarkar, as constituting a mere imitation of behavior based on Western forms of nationalism and imperialism, Gandhi nonetheless remains within the parameters of a modern Hindu nationalist discourse that essentialized spirituality, arguing that the ancient Indian wisdom of *ahimsa* pointed the way to the startling possibility of an authentically Indian "nonviolent nationalism." A good part of the unique power of Gandhi's own version lies in its effective employment of a vernacular mode of moral discourse accessible to ordinary people and deeply rooted in an idealized image of Indian civilization (Parekh 1989, 79).

By embracing Indian spirituality as the defining feature and the indispensable precondition of genuine nationhood and political self-rule, Gandhi also seeks to emphasize the "old Indian values" of tolerance and pluralism at the expense of highly problematic ethnic, communalist, and sectarian forms of identity. As long as the national struggle was directed against external forms of imperial domination, Gandhi's emphasis on the cultural unity of India, based on the existence of a common spirituality, proved to be a highly effective weapon, capable of mobilizing South African Indians and, later, millions of Indian peasants, for whom the combination of anti-industrialism, demands for land reform, religiosity, and anti-colonialism represented a particularly potent formula. Moreover, the transparency of Gandhi's political style and his "saintly" personality signified for large segments of the population an emotional return to their traditional moral virtues of self-control, self-suffering, and courage. Gandhi and his message served them, ministered to their needs, and righted their wrongs, thus producing the popular belief that he was endowed with extraordinary powers ("charisma") to compel his environment (Rudolph and Rudolph 1983).

Thus one ought to acknowledge the importance of psychological perspectives of nationalism in explaining its mobilizing power. To be sure, Gandhi's nationalist discourse clearly evokes mass sentiments of identification with the Indian nation and thus caters to the psychological need of his constituencies to define themselves in opposition to the non-Indian Other. Still, it is dangerous to reduce explanations of nationalism's power to primordialist-psychological narratives, contending that nationalist sentiments and attachments derive from enduring and unalterable features of human psychology. Without falling into the trap of essentialism, scholars of nationalism must face a set of useful questions about the moral psychology of nationalism that deals with the ways in which nationalist leaders draw upon and contribute to a discourse of belonging that penetrates deeply into the human psyche (McKim and McMahan 1997; Tyrrell 1996, 247–48).

Both psychologists and psychoanalysts have offered critical insights into the relationship between Gandhi's employment of certain political techniques, such as fasting and nonviolent noncooperation, and significant experiences in his childhood (Erikson 1969; Adelman 1980, 543-61; Buck 1984, 131-41; Nichtern 1985, 17-23; Kakar 1990, 85-128). Some of these psychological observations have centered on the connection between Gandhi's critique of Western civilization and his conscious display of apparent forms of irrationality, which his antagonists labeled as eccentric, mad, and childish. As Ashis Nandy (1987, 132, 159) emphasizes, Gandhi's radical willingness to appear to the Western world as "irresponsible, effeminate, immature, and insane" served as a powerful defense—both in the psychoanalytic and political sense—against the near total hegemony of modern scientific rationality. Using his external appearance to communicate to the masses the living greatness of an imagined ancient Indian civilization, Gandhi endowed his message with an easily comprehensible, sentimental charge that led many of his followers to adopt an ideologized position toward "Gandhian" national symbols, such as the spinning wheel, homespun cotton cloth (khadi), and the "Gandhi cap" (Bean 1989, 355-76; Tyrrell, 233–50). In the minds of many ordinary Indians, their Motherland ceased to be a remote abstraction not worth suffering for, because it could be known, defended, and worshipped in its concrete spirituality as the "Mahatma," the Great Indian Soul.

Thus Gandhi's nationalist discourse also contains an emancipatory political potential: while accepting the orientalist image of India as the "wonderland of wisdom," he nonetheless refuses to go along with a rigid essentialism that equates spirituality to "other-worldliness." As Joseph S. Alter notes, Gandhi's notion of swaraj should not be seen as a merely spiritual project of only derivative political value. Since he considered good physical health a necessary condition for self-rule, he connected spirituality to the rational, biomoral logic "of what might be called a sociology of individual increments, and elemental configurations, in which the geopolitical state of the nation gets reimagined one patient at a time" (Alter 1996, 314).

Hence, Gandhi's lifelong experiments with a vegetarian diet, fasting, public health and hygiene, pranayama (mechanics of breathing fresh air), hydrotherapy, naturopathy, walking, and, most importantly, brahmacharya (sexual abstinence) were not just the religious whims of a Hindu ascetic whose gaze was fixed on transcendental Truths. These exercises, in fact, represent the crucial microphysics of self-discipline required for all of those political reformers who, having abandoned the lures of modern civilization, are working for independence on a national scale in accordance with the principles of India's ancient civilization. As Alter (1996, 305) puts it, "Gandhi was interested in the success of his own experiments primarily to the extent that others might learn from them and subscribe to a regimen of self-discipline. He wanted to engage young Indians on a level that would lead to self-control rather than mandate institutional reform through policy. He wanted to persuade people to change their way of life in order to rebuild India."

But in order to entice people to exert strict moral self-rule for the sake of their *patria*, nationalist leaders need to draw on more than just personal charisma and material support. Much of the power of Gandhi's nationalist discourse depended on securing the emotional support of the masses through the mobilization of potent cultural meanings encoded in religious myths, historical narratives of heroic self-sacrifice, and epic tales of moral strength. Along with a number of other prominent India scholars, Partha Chatterjee (1995, 94) has insisted that Gandhi quite emphatically rejects the historicism of Bankimchandra Chattophadhyay, B. G. Tilak, and other Western-influenced nationalist reformers of his time by emphasizing that truth lay outside of history. While this might be true with respect to certain aspects of Gandhi's ontological reflections on human nature, a close analysis of *Hind Swaraj* reveals that he consciously activated what Anthony D. Smith calls "deep ethno-symbolic resources" in the form of shared memories of a "golden age," and religiously motivated sentiments of belonging to ancestral homelands and sacred territories.

This imagined history of ancient India and its significance for moral self-rule lies at the heart of the editor's assertion that India's cultural resources are intrinsically rich enough to inspire moral heroes to "set a limit to our indulgences" (Gandhi 1997, 67–68). Over long stretches of the text, Gandhi conjures up the idealized vision of India as comprised of ancient, agricultural communities whose members lived fulfilling lives without the support of advanced machinery, complex monetary systems, and alienating political institutions. The ancients kept their villages rather small, crimes were rare, and religious practices were more important than excessive money making. Even when the skeptical reader raises problematic issues commonly associated with ancient cultural practices, such as child marriage, temple prostitution, animal sacrifice, and polygamy, the editor refuses to abandon his imagined past: "The defects that you have shown are defects. Nobody mistakes them for ancient civilization. They remain in spite of it. Attempts have always been made, and will be made, to remove them" (Gandhi 1997, 71).

Thus Gandhi employs an idealized historical narrative of a golden age to persuade his contemporaries that Indians once enjoyed true home rule: "The tendency of Indian civilization is to elevate the moral being, that of Western civilization is to propagate immorality. The latter is godless, the former is based on a belief in God. So understanding and so believing, it behooves every lover of India to cling to the old Indian civilization even as a child clings to its mother's breast" (Gandhi 1997, 69-71). It is hard to believe that Gandhi was not aware of a number of serious factual shortcomings contained in his idealized interpretation. But it seems that, for educational purposes, he prefers to present his readers with a Platonic "noble lie"—one that portrays his nation's history as a story of social harmony and the workings of truth-force rather than a record of disunity, human cruelty, and frequent warfare.

In accordance with this idealized narrative, the editor finally introduces the satyagrahi (adherent to truth-force) as the modern equivalent of the ethical heroes of the golden age. Their "manhood" rests on the performance of moral duty, "control over the mind," and the courage to use only non-violent means and "soul-force" against the "brute force" of the oppressor—even at the risk of losing their lives: "That nation is great which rests its head upon death as its pillow. Those who defy death are free from all fear" (Gandhi 1997, 94–95). Insisting that the use of violence is "not natural to India," Gandhi introduces unspecified historical examples where the practice of satyagraha forced unnamed tyrannical princes to realize the inferiority of power based on violence. *Satya* employed as soul-force by ordinary subjects forced those princes to "apologize to the people" and "reverse their unjust orders," proving that "real home rule is possible only where *satyagraha* is the guiding force of the people. Any other rule is foreign rule" (Gandhi 1997, 95–96; 112).

At this point, Gandhi's theoretical alternative to Savarkar's violent swaraj becomes fully apparent in the vision of a nonviolent nationalism, carried forth by satyagrahis who overcome their fear and violence as a result of realizing self-rule in both a political and a psychological sense: "[I]t seems to me that those who want to become passive resisters for the service of the country have to observe perfect chastity, adopt poverty, follow truth, and cultivate fearlessness" (Gandhi 1997, 96). According to Gandhi, any nationalism consistent with Indian civilization must be based on the moral self-rule of the individual and practiced as "passive resistance" (Gandhi later substitutes *satyagraha* for this term) against the colonizer. "Passive resistance is a method of securing rights by personal suffering; it is the reverse of resistance by arms. When I refuse to do a thing that is repugnant to my conscience, I use soul-force. . . . It involves sacrifice of self" (Gandhi 1997, 90). To be sure, such a project stands and falls with the proper education of the young who must cultivate these ancient Indian virtues: "Our ancient school system is enough. Character-building has the first place in it, and that is primary education. A building erected on that foundation will last" (Gandhi 1997, 102–3).

Like Socrates in his vision of the Just City, Gandhi sought to establish a just and an independent India as a pluralistic community of communities, guided by moral doctors who mend souls and lead the nation to political freedom. "Real home-rule is self-rule or self-control," the editor concludes, and the way to it is the practice of satyagraha and self-suffering (Gandhi 1997, 118).

Looking at India today, however, one cannot help but be struck by the contrast between the Mahatma's vision of a morally regenerated, nonviolent nation and the stark reality of large nation-states plagued by communal violence and religious strife. In the decades following Gandhi's death in 1948, the furies of Indian communalism have threatened to tear Indian society apart. In December 1992, for example, extreme Hindu nationalists belonging to organizations such as the Rashtriya Swayamsevak Sangh and the National Volunteer Corps engaged in the shameful destruction of the Babri mosque in Ayodhya, which led to months of retaliatory violence throughout the country perpetrated by both Hindus and Muslims. More recently, the systematic terrorization of India's Muslim population through pogroms orchestrated by Hindu nationalists has been complemented by similar acts of violence directed against the country's small Christian minority. In 1997, it appeared that the fiftieth anniversary of India's independence offered a short window of opportunity for collective reflection and national reconciliation. Yet in spite of the almost ritualistic invocation of Mahatma Gandhi's name and memory, the festivities passed without producing any significant changes in people's communal sentiments.

The lasting popular appeal of Indian political parties committed to Hindu nationalism is especially evident after the decisive 1999 election victory of Prime Minister Atal Bihari Vajpayee's right-wing Bharatiya Janata Party. In addition to the existing intra-Indian communal tensions, the policies of the last few years have produced a further deterioration of the neighborly relations between India and Pakistan, to the point where the conflict over disputed territories in Kashmir has raised the specter of nuclear war on the subcontinent.

Certainly Gandhi would shudder at these unfortunate developments in contemporary South Asia, wondering what, if anything at all, remained of his efforts to create a unifying framework of a nonviolent, moral Indian nation by balancing governmental needs for national solidarity and social cohesion with the celebration of cultural, religious, and communal differences. How would he explain the stubborn persistence of ethnic and religious violence? Would he view his own nationalist project differently in light of current events? As I suggested elsewhere, any comprehensive assessment of Gandhi's nationalist thought must contain questions about the extent to which his own theoretical and practical contributions to the phenomenon of nationalism conflicted with his commitment to a philosophy of nonviolence and its implied imperatives of moral universalism (Steger 2000).

CONCLUSION: TOWARD A COMPARATIVE POLITICAL THEORY

In order to move beyond disputes over definitions toward a better understanding (*verstehen*) of the complex gestalt of various nationalisms, it is important that the most promising theoretical perspectives be employed in complementary fashion. Offering a micro-level approach to the study of nationalist thought, I have argued that Gandhi's views on Indian home rule are the product of a historically specific, highly interdependent network of instrumentalist, ethno-symbolic, and psychological forces that both constrain and enable nationalist appeals to "self-rule" and "national community." Yet two theoretical problems persist and must be explored in greater detail in future studies of nationalist ideas.

First, by offering a more eclectic approach to the study of nationalist thought, one does not escape the difficulty of assessing the relative weight of instrumentalist, psychological, ethno-symbolist, and other promising explanatory models. This necessary process of assigning more or less significance to any one narrative might be developed further from within a hermeneutical framework that explores the prominent features of various nationalist imaginings as well as their political, social, and intellectual contexts. Any comprehensive study that seeks to account for the power of nationalist discourses must examine the structural framework of existing material and ideal interests, symbolically and politically effective processes of authentication and personification through charismatic leaders, and the ways by which their messages convey emotionally charged images of national identity, solidarity, collective destiny, and "otherness."

Second, in order to both assess the significance of each methodological approach and compare the distinguishing features of different nationalist discourses, we need to generate more micro-level case studies of how nationalist authenticators and their narratives emerge and develop in different cultural and historical settings. As several scholars have pointed out, one of the paradoxes of the recent resurgence of interest in nationalism is that too little attention has been devoted to what nationalists actually thought (Haddock 1999, 313). A comprehensive research program can best be pursued within the framework of a comparative political theory that complements, connects, and unsettles the traditional fields of political theory and comparative politics (Dallmayr 1997, 421–27).

Comparative political theory transgresses the traditional canon of (Western) political thought by encouraging the development of new cross-cultural approaches; it deviates from dominant methodologies in comparative politics, in that it is neither empirical-descriptive in character nor governed by stylized or moral modes of analysis. Rather, it is a fundamentally critical-hermeneutical enterprise. Drawing on narratives emerging from different cultural zones, comparative political theory is likely to challenge academic accounts that present political theory as a rather coherent, or even monolithic, edifice, while pointing to the coexistence of contradictory aspects within and among various cultural and ideological constellations.

Comparative political theory also counteracts the unwillingness of many researchers to escape the narrow parameters of their Western philosophical heritage. A more careful exploration of non-Western models facilitates new, radical politics of transforming identity, culture, and society. As Cris Toffolo emphasizes in the introduction to this book, human emancipation depends on developing new epistemological approaches that are engaged and contextualized, and whose research questions are fueled by a committed stance. Thus my analysis of Gandhi's nationalist discourse serves a dual emancipatory purpose: it explores new ways of understanding the "explosive energy and awful power" of nationalism and also emphasizes the importance of moving beyond conventional philosophical framework.

NOTES

1. Explaining the power of nationalism as the complex interaction of structural and psychological factors, such as pride, self-respect, vanity, and the desire for status, Liah Greenfeld attempts to show how "political, and even economic, realities of the modern world were to a significant extent shaped by nationalism born of preoccupation with status" (1992, 488; 1993, 47-62; 1996, 169-91). Unfortunately Greenfeld's imputation of aggressive expressions of *ressentiment* to "collectivistic nationalisms" of the German and Russian kind (echoes of earlier binary oppositions of "good" versus "bad" and "Western" versus "Eastern" forms of nationalism) mars her analysis, as does her astonishing silence on the role of European imperialism and colonialism in the development of nationalism.

2. For a detailed analysis of the tensions and contradictions involved in Gandhi's attempt to reconcile the universalist message of his nonviolent philosophy with his nationalist quest for political power, see Steger (2000).

REFERENCES

Adelman, Howard. 1980. "Hitler and Gandhi: The Will As Spirit and As Flesh." *Psychoanalytic Review* 67:4 (winter): 543–61.

Alter, Joseph S. 1996. "Gandhi's Body, Gandhi's Truth: Nonviolence and the Biomoral Imperative of Public Health." *Journal of Asian Studies* 55:2 (May): 301–22.

Anderson, Benedict. 1991 (1983). *Imagined Communities.* 2d ed. London: Verso.

Bates, Robert. 1983. "Modernization, Ethnic Competition and the Rationality of Politics in Contemporary Africa." Pp. 152–71 in *State Versus Ethnic Claims: African Policy Dilemmas,* ed. Donald Rothchild and Victor Olorunsola. Boulder: Westview Press.

Bean, Susan S. 1989. "Gandhi and *Khadi*, the Fabric of Independence." Pp. 355–76 in *Cloth and Human Experience*, ed. Annette B. Weiner and Jane Schneider. Washington: Smithsonian Institution Press.

Brock, Peter. 1983. *The Mahatma and Mother India: Essays on Gandhi's Non-Violence and Nationalism.* Ahmedabad: Navajivan Publishing House.

Brown, Judith M. 1989. *Gandhi: Prisoner of Hope.* New Haven: Yale University Press.

———. 1996. "The Making of a Critical Outsider." Pp. 21–34 in *Gandhi and South Africa: Principles and Politics*, ed. Judith M. Brown and Martin Prozesky. New York: St. Martin's Press.

Buck, Lucien A. 1984. "Nonviolence and Satyagraha in Attenborough's *Gandhi*." *Journal of Humanistic Psychology* 24:3: 131–41.

Calhoun, Craig. 1993. "Nationalism and Ethnicity." *Annual Review of Sociology* 19: 211–39.

Chatterjee, Partha. 1995. *Nationalist Thought and the Colonial World: A Derivative Discourse?* Minneapolis: University of Minnesota Press.

Connor, Walker. 1994. *Ethnonationalism: The Quest for Understanding.* Princeton: Princeton University Press.

Dallmayr, Fred. 1997. "Introduction: Toward a Comparative Political Theory." *The Review of Politics* 59:3 (summer): 421–27.

Dalton, Dennis. 1993. *Mahatma Gandhi: Nonviolent Power in Action.* New York: Columbia University Press.

Du Toit, Brian M. 1996. "The Mahatma Gandhi and South Africa." *The Journal of Modern African Studies* 34:4: 643–60.

Dunn, John, ed. 1995. *Contemporary Crisis of the Nation State?* Oxford: Blackwell.

Eller, Jack David, and Reed M. Coughlan. 1993. "The Poverty of Primordialism: The Mystification of Ethnic Attachments." *Ethnic and Racial Studies* 16:2 (April): 183–201.

Embree, Ainslee T. 1989. "Gandhi's Role in Shaping an Indian Identity." Pp. 162–72 in *Imagining India: Essays in Indian History*, ed. Mark Juergensmeyer. Delhi: Oxford University Press.

Erikson, Erik. 1969. *Gandhi's Truth: On the Origins of Militant Nonviolence.* New York: W. W. Norton.

Fischer, Louis. 1951. *The Life of Mahatma Gandhi.* London: Jonathan Cape.

Gandhi, Mohandas K. 1958–1994. *The Collected Works of Mahatma Gandhi.* 100 vols. New Delhi: Publications Division, Ministry of Information and Broadcasting, Government of India.

———. 1997. *Hind Swaraj and Other Writings.* Edited by Anthony J. Parel. Cambridge: Cambridge University Press.

Gandhi, Rajmohan. 1994. "The Origin and Growth of Satyagraha—Gandhi's Reaction to the Conditions of Indians in South Africa." Pp. 122–44 in *Gandhi and South Africa*, ed. Shanti Sadiq Ali. Delhi: Hind Pocket Books.

Gellner, Ernest. 1983. *Nations and Nationalism*. Ithaca: Cornell University Press.

———. 1994. *Encounters with Nationalism*. London: Blackwell.

Green, Martin. 1993. *Gandhi: Voice of a New Age Revolution*. New York: Continuum.

Greenfeld, Liah. 1992. *Nationalism: Five Roads to Modernity*. Cambridge: Harvard University Press.

———. 1993. "Transcending the Nation's Worth." *Daedalus* 122:3 (summer): 47–62.

———. 1996. "The Modern Religion?" *Critical Review* 10:2 (spring): 169–91.

Haddock, Bruce. 1999. "State and Nation in Mazzini's Political Thought." *History of Political Thought* 20:2 (summer): 313–36.

Hall, John A. 1993. "Nationalisms: Classified and Explained." *Daedalus* 122:3 (summer): 1–28.

Harris, Karen L. 1996. "Gandhi, the Chinese, and Passive Resistance." Pp. 69–94 in *Gandhi and South Africa: Principles and Politics*, ed. Judith M. Brown and Martin Prozesky. New York: St. Martin's Press.

Hechter, Michael. 1986. "Rational Choice Theory and the Study of Race and Ethnic Relations." Pp. 264–79 in *Theories of Ethnic and Race Relations*, ed. John Rex and David Mason. Cambridge: Cambridge University Press.

———. 1995. "Explaining Nationalist Violence." *Nations and Nationalism* 1:1: 53–68.

Hobsbawm, Eric J. 1990. *Nations and Nationalism Since 1780: Programme, Myth, Reality*. Cambridge: Cambridge University Press.

Hobsbawm, Eric J., and Terence Ranger, eds. 1983. *The Invention of Tradition*. Cambridge: Cambridge University Press.

Hunt, James D. 1989. "Gandhi in South Africa." Pp. 61–81 in *Gandhi's Significance for Today*, ed. John Hick and Lamont C. Hempel. New York: St. Martin's Press.

Huttenback, Robert A. 1971. *Gandhi in South Africa: British Imperialism and the Indian Question 1860–1914*. Ithaca: Cornell University Press.

Iyer, Raghavan N. 1973. *The Moral and Political Thought of Mahatma Gandhi*. New York: Oxford University Press.

———. 1986. "Introduction." *The Moral and Political Writings of Mahatma Gandhi*, vol. 1. Oxford: Clarendon.

Kakar, Sudhir. 1990. *Intimate Relations: Exploring Indian Sexuality*. Chicago: University of Chicago Press.

McKim, Robert, and Jeff McMahan, eds. 1997. *The Morality of Nationalism*. New York: Oxford University Press.

Nanda, B. R. 1958. *Mahatma Gandhi: A Biography*. London: Allen and Unwin.

Nandy, Ashis. 1987. *Traditions, Tyranny and Utopias: Essays in the Politics of Awareness*. Delhi: Oxford University Press.

———. 1994. *The Illegitimacy of Nationalism: Rabindranath Tagore and the Politics of Self*. Delhi: Oxford University Press.

Nichtern, S. 1985. "Gandhi—His Adolescent Conflict of Mind and Body." *Adolescent Psychiatry* 12: 17–23.

Parekh, Bhikhu. 1989. *Colonialism, Tradition and Reform*. Delhi: Sage.

————. 1995. "Ethnocentricity of the Nationalist Discourse." *Nations and Nationalism* 1:1: 39–41.

Payne, Robert. 1969. *The Life and Death of Mahatma Gandhi*. London: Bodley Head.

Rolland, Romain. 1924. *Mahatma Gandhi: The Man Who Became One with the Universal Being*. London: Allen and Unwin.

Rudolph, Susanne, and Lloyd Rudolph. 1983. *Gandhi: The Traditional Roots of Charisma*. Chicago: University of Chicago Press.

Singh, Daleep. 1996. "The Socio-Economic Conditions in South Africa 1652–1893." Pp. 82–101 in *Gandhi and South Africa: Principles and Politics*, ed. Judith M. Brown and Martin Prozesky. New York: St. Martin's Press.

Smith, Anthony D. 1995. "Gastronomy or Geology? The Role of Nationalism in the Reconstruction of Nations." *Nations and Nationalism* 1:1: 3–23.

————. 1996a. "Memory and Modernity: Reflections on Ernest Gellner's Theory of Nationalism." *Nations and Nationalism* 2:3: 371–88.

————. 1996b. "The Resurgence of Nationalism? Myth and Memory in the Renewal of Nations." *British Journal of Sociology* 47:4 (December): 575–98.

Steger, Manfred B. 1991. "Politician and Saint: Mahatma Gandhi's Ethical Socialism." *The Wittenberg Review* 1: 67–86.

————. 1993. "Mahatma Gandhi and the Anarchist Legacy of Henry David Thoreau." *Southern Humanities Review* 27:3: 201–15.

————. 2000. *Gandhi's Dilemma: Nonviolent Principles and Nationalist Power*. New York: St. Martin's Press.

Swan, Maureen. 1985. *Gandhi: The South African Experience*. Johannesburg: Ravan Press.

Switzer, Les Switzer. 1986. "Gandhi in South Africa: The Ambiguities of Satyagraha." *The Journal of Ethnic Studies* 14:1 (spring): 122–28.

Tendulkar, D. G. 1960–1963. *Mahatma: Life of Mohandas Karamchand Gandhi*. 8 vols. New Delhi: Government of India.

Tyrell, Martin. 1996. "Nation-States and States of Mind: Nationalism as Psychology." *Critical Review* 10:2 (spring): 233–50.

Young, Crawford. 1993. "The Dialectics of Cultural Pluralism: Concept and Reality." Pp. 3–35 in *The Rising Tide of Cultural Pluralism: The Nation-State at Bay?*, ed. Crawford Young. Madison: University of Wisconsin Press.

Chapter 8

Here We Do Not Speak Bhojpuri

A Semantics of Opposition

Beth Simon

The 1951 Commissioner's *Report on the Linguistic Minorities of India* opens with the following quote from the Hindu scriptural commentary, the *Chandogya Upanishad*:

> *If there had been no Speech neither virtue nor vice could be known, neither the true nor the false, neither the good, nor the bad, neither the pleasant nor the unpleasant. Speech alone makes known all this. Meditate upon Speech.* (7-2-1)

Opening the first post–Independence accounting of India's linguistic minorities with this scripture is an indication of how public the construction of India is as a paradigm of plurality as unity. Many languages are spoken in India, but the directive is to meditate not upon linguistic difference but upon Speech. India is a pluralistic nation, with two national languages (indigenous Hindi and colonial-imposed English) and constitutional recognition of thirteen modern languages, as well as Sanskrit and Urdu. This epigrammatic banner on a language report, which was a basis for allocating funds and services, is a reminder that India's linguistic pluralism is a primary cultural idiom.

In this chapter I examine the relationship between the propagation of political ideologies and individual construction of social identity by analyzing a set of speech events that occurred between 1981 and 1983 in Banaras

This chapter originally was presented during a 1997 National Endowment for the Humanities (NEH) summer seminar, "Nation, State, and Cultural Pluralism," directed by Professor M. Crawford Young. I am grateful for NEH support, and for the comments and advice of Professor Young and seminar participants. The original research on which this chapter was conducted between 1981 and 1984 and was funded by grants from the National Science Foundation (NSF) and the American Institute for Indian Studies (AIIS). I am grateful to the NSF and the AIIS for their financial and administrative support. All problems, failures, and mistakes are entirely my own.

(Varanasi), a city on the eastern side of Uttar Pradesh. Banaras, the oldest continuously inhabited city in India, with a population mix of Hindus and Muslims, with small numbers of Christians and neo-Buddhists, is bilingual. In post–Independence India, where two primary identity markers are language and religion, religious identity is symbolically yoked to specific languages. Hindi is the daughter of Sanskrit, the sacred language of Hinduism. Urdu, which is very close to Hindi linguistically, developed in the area around Delhi, the national capitol, during the period of Muslim invasions and Mughal control. It is identified with Islam. As Ellen Christensen's chapter in this book so clearly highlights, one of the defining components of post–Partition political discourse of the Hindu right has been the separating out of Muslim identity from Indian, and in the political arena of the 1980s, the term *Hindu* is the ground against which *Muslim* stands as figure. As contrastive identities, each implicates the other by opposing it. For nonelite Indians, Hindi and Urdu, are emblematic of this Hindu–Muslim opposition.

The language status of Hindi is complicated. Officially, the label *Hindi* is applied to all designated dialects of Hindi, that is, those Indo-Aryan speech varieties within the Hindi Regional Language Area that have constitutional recognition. In this sense, Hindi is a governmental label subsuming varieties from Rajasthan to the western border of Bengal. Among those subsumed varieties is Bhojpuri. Although Banaras lies at the eastern end of the Hindi language area, the mother tongue of Banaras-born residents is a western Bhojpuri known locally as Banarsi Boli (Banaras style speech). The long-term presence of both Hindi and Bhojpuri has resulted in stable bilingualism. Banarsis maintain their mother tongue, Bhojpuri, yet they have a strong sense of themselves as Hindi speakers as well. When asked, Banaras residents account for language choices in terms of style, semiotic, pragmatic, and social concerns.

Although Banaras, City of Light (Eck 1982), is promoted as the city of Hindus, a Muslim presence was established in the eighth century, and in the twentieth century it accounts for 30 to 39 percent of the city's population (see the *Census of India* for specific decades). In the public life of urban Banaras, Hindu and Muslim identities reflect the intersecting history and shared historicity. Daily social relations, however, are informed by the widening political cleavages brought forward from the period immediately following Independence and by more recent technological and economic changes. In this, Banaras is typical of the urban India of the 1980s, a milieu in which religious affiliation is an indicator of overarching ideologies. In this sense, language is coreferential with political and religious labels,[1] and the speech events in which discussions about language occur establish social distance and potential conflict. Thus the pluricentric, multilingual city of Banaras offers a useful site for examining how political ideologies actually play out on the ground. Situated language use and talk about language is iconic of identity and constitutive of ideology.

I offer as case studies, three conversations drawn from over forty that I recorded during a year and a half of fieldwork in Banaras. These cases are neither disconnected nor unusual. They are, rather, typical of the daily exercise of ideology and identity construction. Case studies are invaluable for showing how superposed discourses are actively localized by the speakers themselves: how they are creative, constructive acts. These conversations occurred during a period of increasing visibility and successful activity by fundamentalist Hindu political parties. Analysis reveals the bidirectional connections between real-time speech events and contemporary ideologies of identity and opposition. These connections are dynamic and potentially innovative and are open to structured, theoretical analysis. Because situated speech acts are normative and constructive, they are influential beyond the scope of the immediate social event.

The conversations were unplanned, although in the first instance I was participating in a planned gathering. During each conversation, participants utilize what I call a *semantics of opposition*. By this I mean participants perform culturally resonant sets of rejections. They refuse or negate recognized, marked identities as part of their process of establishing and asserting other identities. In speaking, participants act on existing semantic categories of culturally resonant identities. This approach allows a new type of interrogation of forces driving larger social patterns of Indian life. I hope to provide insight into a set of theoretical questions concerning the relationships between political ideologies, the formation of social identity, and the demarcation of social group borders. How does culturally resonant discourse create intragroup cohesion? How does it demarcate social borders? How does it symbolize group distinctions and establish territory? Searle-Chatterjee (1993) claims that in India, religious identities are prioritized over other cultural identities. What is clear is that from the late 1970s to the present, religious labels have functioned as signposts demarcating important social borders. In Banaras, people talk about the language labels that flag *Banarsis* versus *nonBanarsis*, and *Hindu* versus *Muslim*. And while talking about definitions, they enact them. By conversation, social identity is reiterated, social borders are (re)established, and social cleavages are articulated and justified. In talk, individuals participate in the ongoing Indian dialectic between national, intermediate, and localized categories of social division. They enact, modify, reject, and respond to preconstituted selves, and it is this set of acts that is constitutive of identity.

In each of the following conversations, speakers perform two actions: they establish a social *I* that is either Hindu or Muslim, and in doing so, they establish an opposing social *Other*. They do this by drawing on a set of shared cultural idioms, referencing religious and territorial boundaries through myths of origin, location, and liberation. In these conversations, speakers make links between the language labels *Hindi, Bhojpuri,* and *Urdu*. In Banaras and throughout India, language is highly salient. Social identity, group cohesiveness, and intergroup conflict, as well as intergroup distinctions, are dependent in important ways on agreement regarding language at several levels. Negotiating the meanings of *Hindi* as a language as opposed to *Bhojpuri* or *Urdu*, and thus *Hindu* as opposed to *Muslim*, is the psychosocial ground for a matrix of identities ranging from national to local.

CONVERSATION 1: HERE WE DO NOT SPEAK BHOJPURI

In this first conversation, the primary speaker, a conservative Hindu Brahmin, constructs a set of salient dichotomies (Us versus Them, Hindi versus non-Hindi, Insider versus Outsider) by questioning not only what it is one speaks but what it is one *understands*. The speaker offers propositions about our location in Banaras and who we are in terms of that location. By analyzing this specific, located speech event, we develop a picture of how participants deploy linguistic possibilities to reaffirm social solidarity and demarcate salient sociopolitical borders.

The conversation was recorded at the home of the primary participant, a man characterized as a *pakka* Banarsi: a traditional Brahmin, a religious devotee. He was a Bhojpuri–Hindi bilingual whose family had lived in Banaras for generations. I was invited to his home "for tea and a chat," but when I arrived, I found the front room full of Vishvanath Jyotishi's relatives and neighbors, Hindus whose religious and ritual lives are enacted in the daily round of bathing, cooking, eating, paying bills, raising children, and attending local entertainment. Vishvanath Jyotishi was seated on a cushion at one end of the room, and beside him was another cushion for me. The others were seated on the floor, with a small space between them and us.

Vishvanath Jyotishi asked me to begin, and I posed my usual question. In Hindi, I asked, "How long have you lived in Banaras?" He responded in Hindi, saying his paternal great-grandfather left his village in Rajasthan for Banaras, because it is the site where religious people should live and die. The audience makes sounds of agreement. He then says he is ready for another question. In Hindi, I asked, "What changes have you observed in Banaras?" In Hindi, he said, "Earlier, people died from diseases like malaria and magic, but these have been cured. Lately, people die from new diseases: cancer, car accidents, and so on. But over all, people still die. In that there has been very little change." He then proceeded to talk about death, morality, and liberation, tying everything to life in Banaras. He began praising Banaras. Banaras is the "City of Light," the "Great Cremation Ground," the "True Lingam." He recited verses from the *Kashi Khanda* (the mahatmya that establishes the importance of Banaras) as well as from other texts with scriptural aura. His recitations established an authoritative basis for claiming Banaras as the morally ideal place to live, while simultaneously reinforcing the decision of each individual in the room to actually live there.[2]

Vishvanath Jyotishi then described the mythic geography of the city, exhorted me to attend the performances of the Ram Lila, and told a story about Lord Shankar, the great God Shiva, who walks the streets of Kashi. Whenever Lord Shankar finds a dying animal, he whispers a mantra into the animal's right ear. Although Vishvanath Jyotishi was facing his neighbors, this group already knew the story well; most of them learned it from him. Therefore, they functioned as a chorus, redirecting the story toward me. When Vishvanath Jyotishi reached the punch line—Shiva is outside right now, Banaras is Shiva's own city, dying in Shiva's city liberates even a donkey from the implacable cycle of rebirth—everyone in the room sighed.

As a Brahmin, a holder (*dwara*) of sacred texts[3], instruction through recitation is one of Vishvanath Jyotishi's "modes of talking" (Kress 1985, 28), a function or skill based in his ritual occupation. Vishvanath Jyotishi provides exegesis as he recites, one of his occupational obligations, which in turn validates client expectations for that occupation. Vishvanath Jyotishi is a teacher-guide (*guru*) for many in the room, and this justifies his positioning himself as a guru in relation to me during this interaction. His recitations mirror similar gatherings, and they remind his audience of the purpose of the texts, the religious significance, and the moral obligation. As an outsider to this complex of relations, these references do not resonate for me, but Vishvanath Jyotishi's performance and the audience's response are themselves a demonstration of the relation and the circumstances of the relation.

Finally, Vishvanath Jyotishi asked whether this was enough. In Hindi, he queried, "Is anything left unanswered?" I noticed that he had spoken Hindi exclusively, so I asked about this language choice. In Hindi, I said, "This morning, you've spoken only Hindi. Why not Banarsi Boli? Is it because I'm speaking Hindi?"

The room was suddenly very quiet. Everyone leaned toward us. In Hindi, Vishvanath Jyotishi asked what I meant by Banarsi Boli.

	Hindi	English
Simon	Banaras kii Bhojpurii.	*The Bhojpuri of Banaras.*
V. J.	Banaras kii Bhojpurii! Kya hai?	*The Bhojpuri of Banaras! What is that?*
Simon	Banaras kii bhasha, hai naa~?	*The language of Banaras, isn't it?*

	Bhojpuri	English
V.J.	bhojpurii biharii bhasha hau.	*Bhojpuri is the language of Bihar.*
	ihaa~ ham log bhojpuri bolat naahii.	*Here, we don't speak Bhojpuri.*
	ihaa~ ham log u boojhat bhi naahii.	*Here, we don't even understand it.*

Vishvanath Jyotishi's code switch is significant, one that appears triggered by Banarsi Boli. He does not question the language label. What he does is switch from Hindi *to* Banarsi Boli, which he explicitly labels Bhojpuri, and then he locates the meaning of Banarsi Boli and Bhojpuri on the other side of a salient sociogeographic border.

If language is fundamental to group identity, and I am arguing that it is, then this code switch, one of only two during the two-hour conversation, reinforces the social implications of unilateral language choice. Vishvanath Jyotishi's code switch in the context of the previous two hours of talk about how to be Hindu in Banaras suggests that for this group, Hindi, Hindu, and Banaras map the same territory. Vishvanath Jyotishi utilizes "discourse presuppositions" (Giv'on 1979, 64), relying on a presupposed shared background to substitute *ihaa~* (here) for various places, each with associations that oppose a known series of "someplace elses." Vishvanath Jyotishi's *here* and *we* specify referents and reassert social boundaries of exclusivity and difference. He invites the group to remember and agree, and he encourages me to understand and accept, a complex referent for *ihaa~* within the morning's situated universe of discourse.

Everyone present knows what *Banaras* means and what *Bihar* does not mean. The meanings of "Banaras" can be found in known mahatmya, in history textbooks, and in contemporary political writings. In contrast, no scriptures extol Bihar, and no deity claims it. It appears in newspaper articles on crime and political corruption. There is a political border between Bihar and "here." Here is a sacred city protected by all major Hindu guardians. It is Lord Shiva's City, where dying within the parameters is a sure source of liberation from the cycle of birth and death. And the language of the various scriptures and revered texts describing all of the qualities of sacred Banaras is Sanskrit, the Mother of language, and Hindi, Sanskrit's daughter. "Here" is Asi neighborhood, one of the oldest and best documented within sacred Banaras. "Here" is the geopolitical center of the Hindi National Language Movement, which seeks to establish a *shuud* (pure) Hindi divested of all Perso-Arabic influence, that is, a Hindi consciously developed to be as unlike Urdu as possible. At the center of this circle of "here" is this room, the home of Vishvanath Jyotishi, the place where "we" are gathered.

Vishvanath Jyotishi's deictic "here" locates his discourse within this shared matrix of experience and ideology, and thus he can invoke scripture, mythologized history, and contemporary ideologies. The morning's discourse can be reduced to:

Because we are Hindus, we live in Banaras.
Because we are Banarsi Hindus, we speak Hindi.

"Here" is Vishvanath Jyotishi Sharma's front room, the heart for the entire body of meanings of "Banaras." He makes palpable what is transparent as air

to everyone present, that here is embedded at the center of a series of con-
centric ritual, social, and political rings. His Bhojpuri denial of Bhojpuri
within a gathering of Banarsi Bhojpuri speakers proves that "here" is the
location where only Hindi is spoken, where only Hindi is understood.

CONVERSATION 2: PAKKA BANARSIS ARE MILKMEN AND THIEVES

This second conversation pairs with the first as a demonstration of the
dynamic tension of the language-based construction of Indian identities.
Set against the preceding speech event, in which self-consciously identified
Hindus play with language labels to construct themselves as Hindi speakers,
this second conversation is particularly interesting. In it, a negative construction of Muslim identity by a Hindu-dominated national discourse is
presented in terms of this specific, Banaras location. In this conversation,
the Muslim speaker deconstructs the notion of the Hindu male as normative of Banarasi or Indian identity. The speaker, a Banaras-born Muslim
tailor, draws on the same linguistic strategies as in the earlier conversation
to construct another Banarsi identity. He constructs his own identity by
negation, calling on shared social, political, and mythical icons to deconstruct
a cultural idiom and thus the very iconicity itself. His speech makes clear,
as no generalized analysis of elites can, how symbiotic the opposition of
Hindu-Muslim is.

During my fieldwork, I passed the shop of this Muslim tailor almost
every day. At first, we just exchanged greetings, then social information, and
finally he began asking about my research. Occasionally he would send for
tea, and we would have a longer conversation. We spoke what I thought of
as simple Hindi-Urdu.

One morning, at the beginning of Chaitra, March–April, the "Hot Season," when those who can leave Banaras, the tailor asked when I would leave,
and he said he had thought that I was in Banaras to record the Banaras style
of language. He remarked, as if to no one in particular, that his family had
lived in Banaras for several generations. I said I had not known. He said, "You
didn't ask." He sent his assistant for tea, and after we began to sip, he said,
"You haven't asked to record me. Are you not recording Muslims?"

He was right; I had not included him. In fact, I had few recordings
of Banaras Muslims, and I had not thought how not seeking Muslim
participants meant that my recordings were primarily of Hindus. To the
tailor, I said I had not thought of him as a *pakka Banarsi*. In Banaras, the
designation *Banarsi* means someone or something *of* Banaras and references multiple connections of social identity and the ramifications of those
connections.

The tailor then said the following:

Pakka Banarsi nahii~.	*I'm not a real Banarsi.*
Musilman.	*(I'm a) Muslim.*
Pakka Banarsi dudhwalle<u>yaa</u>	*Real Banarsis are milkmen (yaa = emphatic form)*
aur chorwalle<u>yaa</u>	*and thieves (yaa = emphatic form)*

The adjective *pakka* means complete, permanent, definite, structurally sound, and exactly right. Depending on the context, the meanings of pakka range from "real," "true," "finished," and "confirmed" to "lasting," "strong," and "solid" to "ripe" and finally to "cooked." A pakka building is made of brick or concrete, not mud; it does not fall down or wash away. A pakka agreement is signed, settled. A pakka dish is cooked or seasoned perfectly. The semantics of pakka functions at crucial and intersecting levels of Banarsi life, marking states of completion, perfection, and truth.

The composite phrase, *pakka Banarsi*, yokes the polysemous *pakka* to another cultural idiom, being *Banarsi*, one who embodies the cultural character of life in Banaras. This common phrase, *pakka Banarsi*, is associated with the ritual meanings in Hinduism of cows and dairy products. Muslims keep cows, eat curd, and so on, but the cow is central to Hindu ritual purity and, hence, Hindu identity. The products of the cow (milk, dung, etc.) are sacred, pure, and cleansing. They are a defining part of the Hindu ritual universe. In practice, however, commercial milkmen are viewed with suspicion. They are believed to rig their scales and water the milk. The Muslim tailor, a hard-working man who speaks the local language, rejects an identity as a pakka Banarsi. The tailor uses the surface topic, Banarsi speech and my recording it, to frame his set of negative assertions by first presenting himself as an appropriate subject of my research and then addressing his appropriateness by denying identity as a pakka "real" Banarsi. The tailor personalizes this politicized discourse. He locates the conversation within the Hindu–Muslim opposition and then erases himself by substituting an ironic definition of pakka Banarsi, baiting me with my culpability in formulating the definition. He works against the unquestioned assumptions of the idiom, reversing them, making visible what had been invisible, and dynamic what had been passive. The result is a pair of opposing identities both represented by pakka Banarsi. This set of negations interrogates the notion of Hindu as normative and at the same time offers a hybridized identity as ethically superior.

On the surface, his assertion, "I'm not a real Banarsi. I'm a Muslim," is understood as a claim that Hindus make: Muslim is not Banarsi, not Indian. At the same time, his negation is the following multibarbed insult:

I'm not a real Banarsi, I'm a Muslim.
Real Banarsis are milkmen, and milkmen are thieves.
Since real Banarsis are milkmen, real Banarsis are thieves.
Since real Banarsis are Hindus, Hindus are thieves.
I'm not a Hindu, I'm not a thief, therefore, I'm not a real Banarsi.

The tailor's assertions are not an expression of an age-old irresolvable or generalized animosity. Rather, the tailor uses assumptions about language and shared cultural idioms to formulate contemporary, specific conflicts with contemporary known causes. First, the economic health of Banaras is closely tied to its existence as a Hindu ritual and pilgrimage center, and the local Muslim population contributes substantially to that health. Second, in the 1971 Census, the first that officially recorded Urdu language claims separately from Hindi, the number of monolingual Urdu speakers in Banaras increased by 200 percent. Such an increase was seen as strong evidence that the central government had obscured Muslim presence in earlier decades. Third, in the early-to-mid-1980s, Uttar Pradesh political debates crystalized around the recognition of Urdu as an official language (Sonntag 1996). Fourth, rural Hindus had moved to Banaras and taken up silk weaving in competition with the resident Muslims, for whom this was a traditional occupation. Fifth, between 1981 and 1984, gangs of unemployed, politically active young men used the occasion of the various Muslim and Hindu festivals to attack and seriously injure each other.

The Muslim tailor uses *Banarsi* to implicate *Hindu* and *Muslim* as differentiated social identities. In doing so, he is voicing contemporary disputes in specific cultural idioms that symbolize religion and territory—something that is neither ethnicity nor nationality but resonates with both. By exploiting Banarsi idioms shared by both Muslims and Hindus, he reifies the conflict in the very terms in which the conflict is expressed. The tailor generates the social cleavages that separate the imagined communities of Banaras. His statements suggest that others (including myself) separate the speech of Banaras and the speech of the Muslims of Banaras. His ironic set of negations allows the Muslim tailor to exploit the social implications of a multilingual speech community to foreground oppositions.

CONVERSATION 3: YOU UNDERSTAND, BROTHER?
HE WAS A MUSLIM

In this third conversation, all of the preceding elements come into play. Social identities are constructed within the speech event by asserting a set of culturally shared oppositions. In this speech event, the crucial, dynamic link between language and identity is revealed by the speaker code switching between languages marked for social identity. His exploitation of two languages within a shared repertoire works as an assertion of the groups *We—Hindu—Here / They—Muslim—There*.

One morning, a week before a Hindu holiday season, several men were gathered on a corner in a residential neighborhood. All but one were high-caste, educated, and fluent in Hindi and Bhojpuri. The one low-caste partici-pant was their laundryman, nonliterate but functionally bilingual. These men met at this corner for a half-hour conversation at least once a week. Except for one part of the conversation, discussed below, the entire speech event occurs in Bhojpuri. The laundryman's topic is the vicissitudes of his business. The affordability of easy-care, polyester-blend fabrics has meant financial loss for the laundryman. People are washing their own clothes. The laundryman, formerly a given part of daily life, was now less necessary. The laundryman says: "Nowadays we're in great demand during festival season. Everyone gets new clothes. They want their clothes pressed, and we have a lot of work. I'm busy right now, but later, well, understand. I don't know. Will there be work later? Well, brother, I don't know."

The laundryman then tells a story. Ten years earlier he had gone to Delhi where, he notes, everyone is a stranger. One lives and works without the benefit of family. In Bhojpuri, the laundryman says: "I worked for a Muslim employer. You know, he was a Muslim. A Muslim, in a Muslim neighbor-hood. He paid me 300 rupees, this employer. A Muslim. You understand, Brother? A Muslim."

The laundryman uses the label "Muslim" six times while discussing his personal economic survival. The number of repetitions indicates the saliency of the label in this personal context. He says he worked an eight-hour day with a break at midday during which he worked another job. He says he earned more money in Delhi than in Banaras, and that he had fewer expenses. The listeners make encouraging noises. Then the laundry-man complicates the issue. He mentions his children:

"Here [Banaras] I set up in that park across the way. I send my little girls around [to pick up and drop off clothes]. They don't go to school. They can't read. We're not literate people, you know." His voice becomes louder. One of the listeners interjects, asking why, if Delhi was so satis-factory, he had not remained there. He asks, "Wasn't there any more work in Delhi?" This question appears to trigger the laundryman's shift from storytelling to enactment. The laundryman says, "There was work, but I got a letter." He says his family asked him to return. Introduction of the letter is significant to the laundryman's narrative. His family paid some-one to write. The laundryman paid someone to read. Hiring professionals indicates a situation dire enough that the laundryman's return is not be-cause of a personal failure. The men will recognize the significance of this and fully appreciate the laundryman's next statement, which is addressed to the entire group. He says, "I returned to Banaras. To here. I have a household, you understand. I have children."

At this point the laundryman changes genres, moving from complaint to dramatic performance. He switches from direct address to enacted dialogue, performing a final conversation between himself and his employer in Delhi. He takes both roles, that of Banarsi Hindu and of Delhi Muslim. The laundryman has the employer plead in Hindi: "Don't go, (jaa na)," and "Who will do the work here? (kyon kaam ihaa kar)," and again, "Don't go. There is work here." To each plea, the laundryman responds in Bhojpuri, saying "I told him firmly. I will go," and "I said very staunchly, 'I will go.' " With these statements, he returns to direct address, saying he had received a letter from his former employer asking him to come back.

In his drama, the laundryman code switches between Bhojpuri and a performed Hindi. The Delhi employer's few lines are simple and repetitive. The laundryman uses verb stems, and his "here" (ihaa) is Bhojpuri, but he needs only rudimentary Hindi to sketch a Hindi-speaking Delhi Muslim.

The question is, what does the laundryman accomplish? He is able to remind the younger men of their long-standing relationship. He notes his financial responsibilities. As an Indian husband and father in a group of Indian husbands and fathers, there is no need to detail his extended family. He foregrounds the poverty facing his children by juxtaposing the economics of laundry with his children's illiteracy. This should prod his listeners into acknowledging that theirs is a social relationship with moral obligations. No one challenges the story of the good life in Delhi. No one challenges the premise that when push came to shove, the laundryman took the high road. No one complains of hearing this for the umpteenth time. Code switching from real-world speech to an enacted Bhojpuri and Hindi relies on shared cultural idioms to transform the event from conversation to drama, a drama in which the Good and the Right are represented not by the speech of Banaras, by the Hindu Us, but by the speech of Delhi, the Muslim Other. In the story, it is *outside* the community, amid strangers, on the other side of the territorial line that the laundryman is treated as he should have been at home. Representing the Delhi episode in spoken Hindi constructs social identities associated with morality and cultural territory.

The laundryman plays on cultural knowledge, specifically that in Banaras a monolingual Hindi speaker is not a *Banarsi*. Therefore, his Hindi speaker must be an outsider, without social, traditional, or family ties to the laundryman, and it is the outsider who offers a generous arrangement. This is the pivot upon which the laundryman turns the moral of his story. He establishes moral superiority by code switching, making his audience watch while he reenacts his choosing family over personal independence, group over individual, Banaras over Delhi, Hindu over Muslim. He does this when he performs the Other (Muslim, Delhi) as a Hindi speaker and Himself (Hindu,

Banaras) as a Bhojpuri speaker. The laundryman allows the social meanings of each language to speak for him. In a multilingual speech community, social fluency in more than one language multiplies the possibilities and levels of inference. In the laundryman's performance, the act of code switching allows him to "suggest inferences without actually putting (himself) on record" (Gumperz and Gumperz 1982: 98). Here, as in the three preceding conversations, the social implications of a pluralistic speech repertoire are exploited to foreground the symbolic meanings signaled by the languages in that repertoire.

CONCLUSION

The participants in the aformentioned speech events differ significantly in the socially salient categories of Indian identity: religious affiliation, caste, age, level of education, and occupation, yet in each case they engage in the construction of social identities by performing similar acts. They question, deconstruct, contest, and subvert shared labels of language and religion. Static social variables cannot explain such important and dynamic similarities in these speech acts, nor for that matter can descriptions of institutionalized discourses. Rather, we must look at the intersection where individuals act on ideologies. In these cases we find participants turning to language for the ground of social identity. For Banarsi Hindus and Muslims, the labels *Hindi*, *Urdu*, and *Bhojpuri* coexist in a complex, multivalent relationship, functioning as idioms and icons. Speakers use them to signal identity positions, that is, speakers choose languages, and choose to talk about language, as ways of constructing, moment by moment, in real time, accepted and rejected identities that implicate accepted and rejected imagined communities. Together, speech events are constellations that reveal and compose larger social discourses and the mechanisms by which they operate.

NOTES

1. Brass (1997, 36) writes, "[T]he origins of contemporary Hindu-Muslim communalism . . . and violence in India as a whole lie largely within this state [= Uttar Pradesh]. . . . The language issue became a surrogate for elite competition between the older, privileged Muslim classes and the rising Hindu middle classes." Brass considers Uttar Pradesh to be where the most Hindu resentment against Muslims over partition of the country occurred. "That resentment took concrete form . . . through the adoption of discriminatory policies against Muslims, notably their virtual elimination . . . from the state police forces . . . and the failure to provide in the public schools adequate opportunities for Muslims to be educated through the medium of Urdu" (ibid., 37).

2. One mahatmya, the *Kashi Kedara Mahatmya*, glorifies the southern sector of Banaras in particular. This sector includes Asi neighborhood.

3. Brahmins are said to "hold" the Vedas, the original sacred Hindu scriptures, by memorizing, reciting, and transmitting sacred texts to the next generation. Vishvanath Jyotishi, a ritual expert, recites from a variety of texts, including scriptural commentaries and devotional poetry.

REFERENCES

Anderson, Benedict. 1983. *Imagined Communities: Reflections on the Origin and Spread of Nationalism.* London: Verso.

Bakhtin, M. M. 1990. "Discourse in the Novel." Pp. 259–422 in *The Dialogic Imagination: Four Essays,* edited by Michael Holmes. Austin: University of Texas Press.

Brass, Paul R. 1997. *Theft of an Idol: Text and Context in the Representation of Collective Violence.* Princeton: Princeton University Press.

Census of India. 1981a. Series 22. *Uttar Pradesh, Part-XII, Census Atlas.* Lucknow: Directorate of Census Operations.

———. 1981b. Series 22. *Uttar Pradesh: A Portrait of Population.* Edited by Chandan Ghopal. Lucknow: Directorate of Census Operations.

———. 1991. Series 25. *Uttar Pradesh. Paper 1 of 1991, Provisional Population* Totals: Census Operations.

———. 1992. Series 1. *India. Paper 2 of 1992, Final Population Totals: Brief Analysis of Primary Census Abstract.* New Delhi: Ministry of Home Affairs, Census Operation.

Chatterjee, Partha. 1993. *The Nation and Its Fragments: Colonial and Postcolonial Histories.* Princeton: Princeton University Press.

Das Gupta, Jyotirindra. 1970. *Language Conflict and National Development: Group Politics and National Language Policy in India.* Berkeley: University of California Press.

Duranti, Alessandro, and Charles Goodwin, eds. 1992. *Rethinking Context: Language as an Interactive Phenomenon.* Boston: Cambridge University Press.

Eck, Diana L. 1982. *Banaras, City of Light.* New York: Alfred A. Knopf.

Fasold, Ralph. 1984. *The Sociolinguistics of Society.* Oxford: Blackwell.

Fowler, Roger. 1985. "Power." Pp. 61–82 in *Handbook of Discourse Analysis: Volume 4, Discourse Analysis in Society.* Edited by Teun A. Van Dijk. London Academic Press.

Giv'on, Talmy. 1979. *On Understanding Grammar.* New York: Academic Press.

Green, Keith. 1995. "Deixis: A Revaluation of Concepts and Categories." Pp. 11–25 in *New Essays in Deixis: Discourse, Narrative, Literature,* ed. Keith Green. Amsterdam and Atlanta: Rodopi.

Grierson, George A. 1904. *Linguistic Survey of India: Indo-Aryan Family, Mediate Group,* vol. 6. Calcutta: Office of the Superintendent of Government Printing, 248–70.

Gumperz, John. (1971). "Hindi-Panjabi Code Switching in Delhi." Pp. 205–19 in *Language in Social Groups*. Stanford: Stanford University Press.

Gumperz, John, and Jenny Cook Gumperz. 1982. "Introduction: Language and the Communication of Social Identity." Pp. 1–21 in *Language and Social* Identity, ed. John Gumperz. Cambridge: Cambridge University Press.

Hanks, William F. 1992. "The Indexical Ground of Deictic Reference." Pp. 43–76 in *Rethinking Context: Language as an Interactive Phenomenon*, ed. Alessandro Duranti and Charles Goodwin. Boston: Cambridge University Press.

Heller, Monica, ed. 1988. "Strategic Ambiguity: Code-Switching in the Management of Conflict." *Codeswitching: Anthropological and Sociolinguistic Perspectives*, ed. Monica Heller. New York: Mouton.

Hertel, Bradley R., and Cynthia Ann Humes, eds. 1993. *Living Banaras: Hindu Religion in Cultural Context*. Albany: State University of New York Press.

Imperial Gazetteer of India. 1908. Varanasi, vol. 7. Oxford: Clarendon Press.

Jones, Peter E. 1995. "Philosophical and Theoretical Issues in the Study of Deixis: A Critique of the Standard Account." Pp. 27–48 in *New Essays in Deixis: Discourse, Narrative, Literature*, ed. Keith Green. Amsterdam and Atlanta: Rodopi.

King, Christopher R. 1989. "Forging a New Linguistic Identity: The Hindi Movement in Banaras, 1868–1914." Pp. 170–202 in *Culture and Power in Banaras: Community, Performance, and Environment, 1800–1980*, edited by Sandra B. Freitag. Berkeley: University of California Press.

Kress, Gunther. 1985. "Ideological Structures in Discourse." Pp. 27–42 in *Handbook of Discourse Analysis (vol. 4): Discourse Analysis in Society*, ed. Teun. A. Van Dijk. London: Academic Press.

Laitin, David D. 1992. *Language Repertoires and State Construction in Africa*. New York: Cambridge University Press.

Mukerjee, Malay R. 1996. Personal e-mail communication.

Pattanayak, Debiprasanna. 1983. "India, a Multilingual Sub-continent." *The Courier* (UNESCO). Paris 36 (July): 19–21.

———. 1981. *Multilingualism and Mother-Tongue Education*. Delhi and New York: Oxford University Press.

Perkins, Revere D. 1992. *Deixis, Grammar, and Culture*. Philadelphia: John Benjamins Publishing.

Report of the Official Language Commission, 1956. 1957. Government of India. New Delhi: Government of India Press.

Scotton, Carol Myers. 1978. "Language in East Africa: Linguistic Patterns and Political Ideologies." Pp. 719–59 in *Advances in the Study of Societal Multilingualism*, ed. Joshua Fishman. The Hague: Mouton.

Searle-Chatterjee, Mary. 1993. "Religious Division and the Mythology of the Past." Pp. 145–58 in *Living Banaras: Hindu Religion in Cultural Context*, ed. Bradley R. Hertel and Cynthia Ann Humes. Albany: State University of New York Press.

———. 1994. "Caste, Religion and Other Identities." Pp. 147–68 in *Contextualising Caste: post-Dumontian Aproaches* edited by Mary Searle-Chatterjee and Usurla Sharma. Oxford, UK: Blackwell Publishers (Monograph Series of the Sociological Review).

Shukla, Shaligram. 1981. *Bhojpuri Grammar*. Washington, D. C.: Georgetown University Press.

Simha, Shukadeva. 1967. *Bhojpurii aur Hindii* (Bhojpuri and Hindi, in Hindi). Muzaffarpur: Bhaavanaa Prakaashan.

Simon, Beth Lee. 1993. "Language Choice, Religion, and Identity in the Banarsi Community." Pp. 245–68 in *Living Banaras: Hindu Religion in Cultural Context*, ed. Bradley R. Hertel and Cynthia Ann Humes. Albany: State University of New York Press.

———. 1995. "A Fish Story." *Indiana Review* 18: 75–79.

———. 1996a. "Gender, Language and Literacy in Banaras, India." *Gender and Belief Systems*. Berkeley: University of California Press, 679–87.

———. 1996b. "Sweeper Women." *Iowa Review* 26:3: 93–102.

Sonntag, Selma K. 1996. "The Political Saliency of Language in Bihar and Uttar Pradesh." *Journal of Commonwealth and Comparative Politics* 34: 1–18.

Tiwari, Udai Narain. 1960. *The Origin and Development of Bhojpuri*. Calcutta: The Asiatic Society.

The Twenty-Seventh Report of the Commissioner for Linguistic Minorities in India (for the period July 1986–June 1987). 1988. Allahabad: Office of the Commissioner for Linguistic Minorities in India.

Young, M. Crawford. 1976. *The Politics of Cultural Pluralism*. Madison: University of Wisconsin Press.

Chapter 9

Reclaiming Sacred Hindu Space at Ayodhya

The Hindu Right and the Politics of Cultural Symbolism in Contemporary India

Ellen Christensen

INTRODUCTION

In 1983, the Hindu Right launched a plan to build a temple to the god Rama in the northern Indian town of Ayodhya. The project, initiated by the Hindu nationalist VHP (*Vishwa Hindu Parishad*), was an attempt to liberate the alleged site of Rama's birth. The scheme was supported by other Hindu nationalist organizations, including the VHP's affiliate, the RSS (*Rashtriya Swayamsevak Sangh*), and the BJP (*Bharatiya Janata Party*). Construction of the Rama temple was controversial, as it required the destruction of a sixteenth-century mosque on the site. The temple campaign ended with the 1992 destruction of the mosque, sparking communal violence and rioting across northern India and parts of Pakistan. This chapter presents a concise history of the project, suggesting how the Hindu Right utilized the cultural symbolism of the scheme to help construct an image of Hindu identity under siege, which it mobilized to buttress the BJP's ambitious political agendas.

I use the events at Ayodhya as a case study to address the central theoretical issue of this book, the emancipation of cultural pluralism. As Cris Toffolo points out in the introduction, emancipating the concept of cultural pluralism involves reevaluating the place of ethnicity and identity politics in

I am grateful to the participants in Crawford Young's National Endowment for the Humanities Summer Seminar (summer 1997), "Nation, State and Cultural Pluralism," for their interest in my study of the Ayodhya controversy. I would like to thank Professor John R. McLane, Department of History, Northwestern University, for his lively criticism of the work, and my husband, Brian, for his patience with the project.

relation to a definition of modernity. Modernization theory poses ethnicity and identity politics as traditional and anachronistic, the opposite of rationality and modernity. In architectural history, many scholars are questioning the explanatory power of this paradigm and adopting alternatives. In breaking down the opposition of the traditional versus the modern, and looking again at the nature of modernity, ethnicity and identity, politics gain center stage as "the central theoretical and institutional issues of our times"(*ECP,* 12). An analysis of the cultural symbolism of the Ayodhya controversy suggests the power of identity politics in contemporary India.

My work on the cultural symbolism of the Ayodhya campaign is a contribution to the broader project of investigating not only why, but also how, since the Emergency in the 1970s, Hindu nationalism has garnered popular support and political clout after decades of relative failure on both fronts. While the excellent literature on the contemporary efflorescence of the Hindu Right is growing rapidly, few works focus on analyzing the cultural symbolism of the movement. Social scientists Peter Van der Veer, Tapan Basu, Sumit Sarkar, and Partha Ghosh, for example, have produced compelling works on aspects of this broad subject (Van der Veer 1987, 1994; Basu et al. 1993; Ghosh 1999). I suggest that further research on the cultural symbolism of the Hindu Right is crucial in broadening one's understanding of this complex and controversial movement.

This chapter draws on symbolic action theory and on work in cultural anthropology and psychology to investigate the nature of the symbolic (Cohen 1974; Sperber 1975; Brass 1990, 1991). As Manfred Steger argues in chapter 7 of this book, the explosive and tenacious power of identity politics is difficult to explain through purist theoretical approaches (*ECP,* 130). In this chapter I draw on constructivist, instrumentalist, symbolic, and psychological elements in order to understand aspects of the Rama temple campaign. Here symbols are not merely a question of ritual, or of spatial or architectural form, but a process inseparable from the wider social relations between politicians, religious leaders, and diverse audiences. Cultural symbols can function politically; as such, they can be utilized to help construct national identities. Following the constructivist view of nationalism, I assume that national identities are not given; rather, they are social and political fabrications (Anderson 1991). According to this view, power is not an institution or a force held by certain people; it is a product of the relationships between individuals, social groups and institutions. Manipulating symbols is one of the central ways that social groups negotiate identity formation and compete with other groups for power and advantage. Devising complex symbolic systems may be less expensive and more easily justified as natural than enforcing concepts or policies with physical force. Symbolism can be altered relatively easily to accommodate shifting political situations, and it can be internalized, persuading others to embrace the values and beliefs of a particular group.

THE VHP AND THE AYODHYA TEMPLE CAMPAIGN

The temple campaign was the brainchild of the VHP. As such, it was a reflection of its ideology, which stressed that Hinduism was in danger of being engulfed by secular and foreign nationalisms. The VHP asserted that in 1528 Babur, the first Mughal emperor deliberately destroyed a Hindu temple on the site of the god Rama's birth in the northern Indian town of Ayodhya and constructed a mosque, the Babri Masjid, on the spot (Chandran n.d.; Gopal 1991; Engineer 1992). Throughout the Rama temple campaign, the VHP sought to liberate the site from Muslim and secular national control in a violent manner, and to restore the sacred Hindu nature of the spot. The focus of the Rama temple scheme was not on architectural form per se. Rather, it was on the processes of restoring a sacred Hindu architectural space, imbuing it with religious, cultural, and political significance. Thus the highlights of the temple campaign were the ritualistic activities that the Hindu Right staged to reconvert the site from a government-protected Muslim sacred space to a Hindu sacred space. During the temple campaign, the VHP and the BJP drew on a mixture of traditional Hindu and newly created rites to draw broad popular interest in Hindu nationalist ideology. In turn, these rites were related to the planned construction of a traditional northern Hindu temple in Ayodhya, dedicated to Rama, an incarnation of Vishnu. The Hindu Right's campaign to build the Rama temple at Ayodhya was deeply concerned with the relationship between ethnicity, identity politics, and nationalism. The temple campaign was linked to an ideology expressing desire for a strong central government controlled by the Hindu majority, increased respect for Hindu cultural products, as crucial representations or symbols of national vitality, and adherence to a "siege" mentality, stressing that Hinduism is in danger.

The VHP, a relatively new organization, and its ideology are part of an Indian tradition with strong roots in nineteenth-century thought. The VHP is one of many groups that grew out of the RSS, the parent organization founded in 1925 to promote a militant version of Hindu identity in cultural, religious, and political life. In 1964, 150 religious leaders were invited to Sandeepany Sadhanalaya, the center of a Hindu missionary movement, headed by Swami Chinmayananda. Here the leaders of the VHP agreed to consolidate and strengthen Hindu society. What they and other Hindu nationalist groups share is the idea that India must be a Hindu nation, *Bharatiya*, at once a geographic region and a cultural realm with deep-rooted traditions. Members subscribe to many of the ideas of Hindu nationalist V. D. Savarkar, who argued that underneath the diversity of Hinduism lies an essential cultural unity, that constitutes the nation's essential character. According to Savarkar, India is in a wounded condition, as it had succumbed to foreign domination by the Mughals and the British. According to the VHP, this wounded condition was exacerbated by a long list of events, including Partition in 1947, the actions of the Muslim

League, the growth of Islamic fundamentalism, ongoing issues related to Kashmir and Pakistan, and government policies favoring minority groups. The VHP stressed that cultural regeneration is vital in order to strengthen and unite Hindus in one nation.

Much of the ideology of the contemporary Hindu Right rests on an orientalist inversion of Western values: emphasis on spirituality and self-realization counter materialism and consumerism, while an orientation toward the self is countered by an emphasis on the nation as a collective. Orientalist discourse understood Indians in general as being effeminate, weak, passive, and essentially spiritual. To counter such notions, members of the RSS, for example, use stern physical discipline to attain a deep spirituality. The RSS considers the development of physical strength, militancy, and warlike aggression crucial. Proper training ensures that Hindu men, and increasingly women, can defend the Hindu nation. The VHP stresses the importance of the nation, corporate body, family, and village above the individual as a means of attaining national perfection (Fox 1989; Sinha 1996).

With the help of the RSS, the VHP maintains an action plan for cultural rejuvenation of the Hindu nation. The temple campaign was an important extension of that plan. Originally the plan focused on cultural, social, and political projects, such as: uplifting tribals and *harijans* (untouchables); limiting the state's involvement in social welfare programs; emphasizing decentralization and private initiative; working to ban Christian and Muslim proselytization; promoting Sanskrit as a uniform language; backing political candidates who support Hindu interests; supporting Hindu cultural interests, including traditions such as *sati* (widow burning); and arguing for the adoption of a common legal code for all groups in India. Other concerns included organizing self-defense groups and initiating educational projects, such as teaching the Hindu epics, the *Mahabarata* and the *Ramayana*. The VHP constructed hospitals, schools, and hostels in Bihar. In Vennputhur, a *harijan* village near Thanjavur, the VHP constructed a temple. In 1981, mass religious conversions conducted at Meenakshipuram prompted the VHP to launch a drive that culminated in the reconversion of thousands of Muslims back to Hinduism. As part of the action plan, and perhaps in response to the events at Meenakshipuram, in 1983 the VHP staged a series of mass rituals that it claimed were necessary for national integration. These rituals, and those that later focused on Ayodhya, stressed that liberating sacred Hindu spaces across the Indian subcontinent from Muslim and secular, national control was crucial for cultural rejuvenation ("Road to Revival," *India Today* (November 30, 1983) 82–4; Van der Veer 1987; Jaffrelot 1996).

THE *EKATMATAYAJNA* (SACRIFICE FOR UNITY)

The VHP's Sacrifice for Unity campaign stressed the metaphorical and physical mapping of the body of Mother India and emphasized the connection between the Hindu nation, divine Hindu places, and sacred rivers. Many of the rites staged by the VHP made reference to ritual activities such as circumambulation, a key part of Hindu devotionalism, and to pilgrimage. In Hinduism, pilgrimage is a journey consisting of many stages through which the devotee acquires merit. A key feature of pilgrimage is to travel to sacred Hindu sites. The pilgrimage often is visualized as a progression upward through many states of consciousness (Fuller 1992).

The sacrifice consisted of three main *yatras* (marches or pilgrimages in procession) crisscrossing the country. These emphasized the message: Hinduism in danger. The first proceeded from the Pashupatinath Temple at Kathmandu to Rameswaram in Tamil Nadu; the second began in Gangasagar in coastal West Bengal and ended at the Somnath temple in Gujarat; and the third commenced at Hardwar, a pilgrim town in the Himalayan foothills, and ended at Kanyakumari, the southernmost tip of India, where three oceans meet. Eighty-nine shorter marches joined the three main ones; collectively, the processions ranged over 50,000 miles. According to the VHP, the goal of the rite was the identification of one soul: *Bharat* that is Hindu, Hinduism that is *Bharat*.

Peter Van der Veer describes the symbolism of the rituals, which emphasized water and Mother India. Water drawn from Gangotri, the Himalayan cradle of the Ganga, was stored in eight-foot-high brass vessels mounted atop trucks. Water carried atop a smaller truck, drawn from all of the main rivers of northern India, was distributed at each stop in exchange for local water. Further, volunteers distributed images of *Bharat Mata* (Mother India). Thousands of portraits of Mother India, depicted as a goddess astride a lion, were printed in four colors and were sold for 50 paise apiece. Although technically *Bharat Mata* is a new goddess within the Hindu pantheon, in promoting this image, the VHP drew on a long tradition of Hindu mother goddesses. In order to complete the mapping of the body of the Hindu nation, the waters from all of the stops were taken to two destinations: Rameswaram and Somnath. Somnath was chosen to evoke the memory of the Islamic destruction of Hindu temples throughout northern India. Members of the VHP believed that the rite brought about national unity, a national spiritual revolution in which the devotee's personal merit, acquired through pilgrimage, was successfully sublimated into social and national merit.

LIBERATING SACRED HINDU SPACE AT AYODHYA

In May 1983, the VHP began to focus its mapping activities and sent a demand to the central government for the liberation of sacred Hindu sites at Kasi, Ayodhya and Mathura. This document reached the Uttar Pradesh (U.P.) government in July 1983. The VHP requested that the government give up its "blatant policy of appeasing Muslims, even throwing open mosques which are inside the protected monuments for *namaz* (worship)." It asked for equality of treatment and the restoration of the traditional Hindu places of worship, noted above. These requests were issued, in all probability, in reaction to Muslim attempts to negotiate with the central government to obtain entrance to protected mosques (Verma 1985, 205).

In October 1983, Muslim groups approached Prime Minister Indira Gandhi with the Mushawarat Memorandum on Protected Mosques. It requested the lifting of restrictions on Muslims offering prayers in mosques, which had been declared national or protected monuments under the Ancient Monuments and Archaeological Sites and Remains Act of 1958. Pointing out that the act itself contained no provision under which such restrictions could be imposed, the memorandum emphasized that a mosque did not cease to be a mosque by a declaration under the Acts and requested that the daily attendants at each site should be Muslim, and that the government should restore all protected mosques to the Muslim community and allocate resources for their protection and repair. According to *Muslim India*, Indira Gandhi and members of her government agreed in principle to the idea of *namaz* in all protected mosques. The All India Muslim *Majlis-e Mughawarat* held talks with the government in March 1984 to discuss the problem (Verma 1985, 205).

By July 1984, the *Dharma* Sansad of the VHP had drawn up a list of sacred Hindu sites that it believed required liberation from Muslim and secular, national control. The list included the *Rama Janmabhoomi* at Ayodhya, the *Krishna Janmastan* at Mathura, and the Vishwanath Temple at Varanasi (Kasi). All three sites are located in U.P., a center of ancient Hindu culture and the heartland of Muslim India. The Vishwanath temple at Varanasi, the holiest of Hindu cities, shares its premises with a mosque built during the rule of Mughal Emperor Aurangzeb. The temple and the mosque have a common entrance, and pilgrims respect both shrines. At Mathura, birthplace of the god Krishna, a mosque built during the rule of Aurangzeb shares a common wall with a Hindu temple. At Ayodhya, the birthplace of the god Rama, a mosque constructed in 1528 under Babur, the first Mughal emperor, stands on the alleged site of a Hindu temple dedicated to Rama (Verma 1985, 205).

The Babri Masjid, located in the Faizabad District on the banks of the Ghaghara River, was a single-aisled, three-bay mosque surmounted by three prominent domes. The stucco-covered structure featured carved black stone columns from a pre-twelfth-century Hindu temple embedded into both sides of the central porch. Architectural historian Catherine Asher surmises that the rare Muslim reuse of older Hindu architectural elements on the façade of the mosque suggests that the patron was making a statement concerning Muslim superiority over Hindu populations (Asher 1992). Indeed, the mosque had been the focus of litigation for both the Hindu and Muslim communities since 1949. In December 1949, an idol of Rama appeared mysteriously in the structure, an event that sparked communal rioting. Leaders of both communities began litigation to obtain the right of entrance to the mosque. The space inside the structure was, according to the Muslim community, desecrated, however, the idol remained in the locked structure, and police guarded the building. The *Ram Janmabhumi Seva Samiti* obtained permission to worship the idol once a year, from December 22 to December 23. Further, the committee organized uninterrupted devotional singing in front of the mosque as long as Rama's birthplace was not liberated (Van der Veer 1987). Given the highly charged religious situation at Ayodhya, it is not surprising that the VHP chose to focus on liberating the alleged site of Rama's birth.

RAM JANMABHUMI MUKTI YAJNA (A SACRIFICE TO LIBERATE THE SPOT ON WHICH RAM WAS BORN)

In July 1984, the VHP adopted strident measures to liberate the site, forming the *Ram Janmabhumi Mukti Yajna Samiti*. The ritual that it planned took the form of a *rath-yatra* (temple procession), in which the deity is paraded through the streets in a chariot. The motorized "chariot" carried large statues of Rama and Sita under a banner proclaiming "Hail Mother India." The procession began late in September 1984 in Sitamarhi, the birthplace of Sita, and passed through towns in Bihar on its way to Ayodhya. The procession arrived in Ayodhya in early October. Upon arrival, VHP officials erected a platform on a stretch of land near the river Sarayu. A large painting representing a fight between Muslims with swords and unarmed *sadhus* (Hindu holy men) hung facing the audience. Focusing on the idea that Hindus no longer had access to their sacred sites, VHP leaders asked the audience to give their votes only to those political parties that promised to give Hindus back their sacred places. Peter Van der Veer points out that these speeches were timed to shape the outcome of elections, however, the liberation movement became an anachronism after Sikh extremists assassinated Indira Gandhi. The country, galvanized by the assassination, focused on Rajiv Gandhi as a symbol of Indians against Sikhs. As the son of the slain Mother of the Country, he gained political power and temporarily strengthened Congress I. The VHP's plan to proceed with a *rath-yatra* to Lucknow to present a petition to the Chief Minister of Uttar Pradesh, and then to New Delhi to petition the national government, was suspended temporarily. Although the rath-yatra did reach New Delhi eventually, the momentum of the VHP's program was lost (Van der Veer 1987; "Road to Revival," *India Today* (November 30, 1983) 82–4).

TALA KHOLO (OPEN THE LOCK) CAMPAIGN

Undaunted, the VHP continued to press for the liberation of the Ayodhya site, however, in 1985, it did abandon the image of Mother India in connection with the Ayodhya project, perhaps because it conflicted with the images associated with Indira and Rajiv Gandhi. The organization composed a *Ram-Janaki Rath Yatra*. In six marches, images of Rama behind a padlocked gate toured Uttar Pradesh for 108 days. In each procession, the slogan "Hinduism in danger" was presented to audiences, along with the image, stressing the message that God was imprisoned and had to be liberated. The VHP's *Tala Kholo* (open the lock) campaign aimed at raising 25 million rupees to construct a Hindu temple on the site of the Babri Masjid. The VHP raised a volunteer youth corps, the Bajrang Dal, to assist with the project. The Bajrang Dal, organized around the ideal of the monkey god Hanuman (Rama's devoted servant), adopted the slogan, "Rest not before Rama's work is done" ("Hindu Militant Revivalism," *India Today* (May 31, 1986) 76–85).

In shifting from images of Mother India to those of Rama, the VHP drew on one of the central epics of Hinduism, the *Ramayana*. Rama, an incarnation of Vishnu, is one of the most popular gods of Hinduism, especially in devotionalist religion. The *Ramayana* is well known throughout India. The story is widely available in written form and was the basis for a popular film and a television miniseries. During Ram Lilas, popular folk dramas, whole villages act out the story of Rama and Sita. The *Ramayana* exemplifies underlying central themes and attitudes toward Hinduism as a means of structuring life in India. As such, it is used as a pattern of explanation and motivation to regulate social action.

Rama is the ideal leader, king, and husband, while Sita is the model Hindu woman. She is the ideal devotee and intermediary, although she lacks power, identity, and a will of her own. In the image of Sita, wifely devotion becomes a metaphor for ideal devotion to God. The monkey god Hanuman is Rama's devoted aid. Together, Rama, Sita, and Hanuman personify the idea of devotion as love between master and servant. Rama and Sita are the world's father and mother and, according to popular belief, the sight of them has redemptive power (Fuller 1992; Richman 1991). The VHP's image of a stern Rama brandishing bow and arrow behind a padlocked gate emphasized the militant aspect of his role as an ideal *kshatriya* (warrior) ready to fight the enemies of the Hindu nation.

The VHP's campaign to unlock the Babri Masjid culminated in legal action that opened the structure for Hindu worship. In December 1985, four retired members of the U. P. government called on the Chief Minister and convinced him that locking the mosque was illegal. By February 1986, the structure was open to the Hindu community. The push for the acquisition of land surrounding the building, the demolition of the mosque, and the construction of the Hindu temple in its place had begun in earnest.

While the Hindu community celebrated the opening of the mosque, the Muslim community condemned the action and demanded the restoration of the structure. Arguing that the space rather than the structure of the mosque is sacred, it stressed that if the space is desecrated, then the mosque is in danger. The All India Muslim *Majlis-e Mushawarat* organized a day of protest and formed the Central Action Committee, dedicated to the restoration of the Babri Masjid. In June 1986, the Babri Masjid Action Committee (BMAC) launched a program of peaceful agitation to restore the mosque and submitted a memorandum to the Prime Minister, suggesting the construction of a wall separating the sacred space of the mosque and that of the Ram idol. The committee stressed that this solution would "be in line with the principles of social harmony, co-existence of plurality and unity in diversity which characterizes the spirit of our nation's life and culture." In July 1987, after the BMAC had staged a peaceful agitation, a mass rally, and a conference on the subject of Ayodhya in New Delhi, the central government offered to negotiate directly with it. In November 1987, the central government came to the conclusion that negotiations had yielded no tangible results, and it agreed to establish a special bench for expeditious determination of the title to the land and the structure. The special bench included a chief justice of the Allahabad High Court and two other judges. In 1989, the VHP and the BMAC agreed to abide by a high court decision to maintain the status quo at Ayodhya, to not change the property, and to protect and ensure communal harmony in the town (Gopal 1991; Engineer 1992).

SHILA PUJA AND SHILA YATRA

Despite the high court decision, the VHP continued plans to construct the Rama temple. In early 1989, it devised a building schedule for the temple, with *shilanyas* (laying of foundation stones) projected for November of that year. The floor plan of the structure was designed to encompass the disputed site. In July 1989, members of the Bajrang Dal met in Ayodhya and pledged to lay down their lives for the completion of the Rama temple.

Throughout the Ayodhya temple campaign, the Hindu Right followed many of the traditional rules for identifying a Hindu sacred space. Theoretically, the design and construction of Hindu temples are determined by the *vastushastras*, part of the *shastras*, comprising a portion of the literature of Hinduism. The shastras indicate not only the means of obtaining the correct form for a temple but also the correct rites of consecration, from the placing of the foundation deposit prior to the commencement of building to the anchoring of stone elements crowning the *shikhara* (a tower superstructure). In general, the Hindu temple is a representation of the cosmos. In the temple the deity occupies the central sanctuary chamber, the *garbhagriha*, symbolic of a cave or womblike chamber. The shikhara indicates the position of the central sanctuary and is symbolic of Mount Meru, the mountain home of the gods and the center of the universe. Brahmins carry out the rites of consecration. The site of the temple is selected and ritually purified. The ground plan is laid out, which is of great import as the plan functions as a sacred geometric diagram, or *mandala*, of the essential structure of the universe. The temple itself is designed as a home for the deity and is constructed to bring about contact between man and the gods, as it is here that the gods appear to humans (Michell 1977; Blurton 1993). In Hinduism, it is through rituals and ceremonies that the temple functions as a place of transcendence from the world of illusion to that of knowledge and truth. The temple itself is a *tirtha*, a place of transit or a crossing from the profane to the sacred. As a sacred site, it is a place where the gods dwell or might reveal themselves. When a temple is constructed and completed, the sacredness of the site is revealed, and the distinction between the illusory world and the divine disappears (Michell 1977).

In September, the VHP began to focus on yet another set of rituals connected to the construction of the temple: *shila puja* (brick worship) and *shila yatra* (brick march). In this ritual, invented specifically for the occasion, Rama bricks were worshiped in all Indian villages with over 2,000 inhabitants, and in Indian communities abroad. Subsequently, the bricks were transported in procession to Ayodhya and were stored in temples. Members of the VHP stated that these ceremonies ensured "a kind of Hindu mobilization which would otherwise have been impossible." Although Muslim leaders petitioned the central government to ban shila puja and shila yatra, pointing out that the rituals provoked communal tensions and violence, the government would not agree to the ban. Although the Bihar government eventually banned all religious processions, the shilanyas ceremony was performed on November 9, as scheduled, with ceremonies conducted under the protection of the BJP-led central government on land east of the mosque on the site of an ancient Muslim graveyard. Although construction of the temple was scheduled to begin in February 1990, the VHP leadership postponed the date several times in order to give V. P. Singh's national front government an opportunity to work out an alternative solution to the problem of sacred space at Ayodhya (Gopal 1991; Engineer 1992).

L. K. ADVANI'S *RATH-YATRA*

As the VHP postponed the date to commence construction of the Rama temple, a series of rituals staged by L. K. Advani, leader of the BJP, brought the issue of the temple to national prominence. In an attempt to generate publicity for the BJP and to sway voters to back their candidates, in September 1990, Advani set off on a 10,000-kilometer rath-yatra. The march began at the Somnath temple in Gujarat and led to the Babri Masjid in Ayodhya. Advani traveled in an air-conditioned DCM Toyota van decorated to look like the chariot that held Arjuna in the *Mahabharata* television serial. The van sported the flags of the BJP and the VHP, and a lotus cutout adorned the front of the vehicle. Under a canopy, audiences found a cutout of OM, the sacred syllable, a huge portrait of Advani, and slogans such as "March on for the glory of the temple and the pride of *Hindutva.*"

In interviews with the press, Advani suggested that Indianness, that is, Hinduism, was in danger. Stressing that since Indian independence under Jawaharlal Nehru's leadership, the Indianness of the nation had been deliberately neglected, Advani claimed that "the movement for restoring Ram, revered as '*maryada purushottam*' (quintessential man) to full glory, is simply a manifestation of this new awareness." Pointing out that the controversial Mandal Report published by V. P. Singh's government had galvanized the Hindu community, he stressed that building the Ayodhya temple was "our answer to Mandal." The Mandal Report outlined a system of reservations for lower castes and untouchables, a scheme that the BJP opposed. Advani insisted that reverence for Ram was a national unifying factor, and that the rath-yatra was a symbol of *Ram bhakti* (devotion to Ram). Advani stressed that Ram should be respected by every Indian as a national hero, if not as an *avatar* (incarnation) of Vishnu. Muslims, he argued, should be proud to accept Ram as "a great son of the soil" (*India Today* 1990). Advani's remarks provoked angry responses in many quarters, and the rath-yatra resulted in communal violence and rioting across northern India. Some of the worst violence occurred in Ayodhya: in an attempt to prevent *kar sevaks* (literally, "those who do service through work") from besieging Ayodhya, the police fired on crowds of devotees, killing many people. Advani was arrested, and the rath-yatra was suspended. However, it resumed in November 1990 and reached Ayodhya in early December ("Advani," *India Today* (February 28, 1990) 144–46; Van der Veer 1994).

Advani believed that the publicity surrounding the rath-yatra had generated a distinct political identity for the Hindu community and suggested that the BJP was simply voicing the feelings of the vast majority on the national issue of the Rama temple. Indeed, one result of the rath-yatra was to bring the Rama temple project to national attention. Through Advani, the image of a militant Rama was associated strongly with cultural issues concerning access to sacred Hindu sites, and in turn to issues of Hindu leadership, political representation, and power at the local and national levels. Although the BJP garnered publicity from the rath-yatra and continued to support the temple project in theory, by 1991, its most prominent leaders, including Advani, had moved on to champion other issues, leaving the VHP and the Bajrang Dal to proceed with their plans ("Bharatiya Janata Party," *India Today* (November 15, 1990) 19–21).

LAND ACQUISITION AND THE DESTRUCTION
OF THE BABRI MASJID

The BMAC continued to call for a ban on the VHP and its militant wing, the Bajrang Dal, as well as other groups. Arguing that the site of a mosque is sacred, the committee pointed out to the courts that the mosque could not be demolished, nor could it be removed to another site. The BJP-led state government ignored these requests. In October, the state government began acquiring 2.7 acres of land, including the site of the mosque itself and three plots surrounding the disputed area. The government explained that the land had been acquired to provide amenities to pilgrims and tourists. Further, it demolished two small Hindu shrines on the site. The VHP hoped that the land would be transferred to the organization, however, the transfer was not forthcoming.

By October 1991, the VHP had begun to dig a trench close to the area previously occupied by the two small Hindu shrines, and it claimed that construction of the Rama temple had begun. During the remainder of 1991 and a portion of 1992, the VHP continued to engage in talks with the government and the BMAC concerning the fate of the disputed site. Then the Bajrang Dal staged a violent incident at Ayodhya: in late October, kar sevaks hoisted a small saffron flag on one of the domes, while damaging portions of the outer wall of the shrine. Three hundred kar sevaks were arrested after the incident. Negotiations and talks continued until November 1992, when they were postponed indefinitely ("BJP," *India Today* (April 4, 1991) 22; *Muslim India* 1990-1992).

On December 6, 1992, kar sevaks destroyed the mosque, sparking communal violence and rioting across northern India and Pakistan. Blurry photographs of kar sevaks atop the Babri Masjid accompanied graphic newspaper reports suggesting that the demolition of the structure was proof that the Hindu Right constitutes a significant threat to stable, secular government in India. *The Times of India* noted that the BJP-led state government in Uttar Pradesh supported the destruction of the structure, reporting that "thousands of frenzied *kar sevaks* stormed into it [the mosque] and started dismantling the structure with hammers and rods with the state security forces . . . remaining a mute witness" ("Kar Sevaks Demolish Babri Masjid," *The Times of India* (December 7, 1992); Van der Veer 1994).

The immediate result of the destruction of the mosque was that the BJP-led state government was disbanded, and Hindu rightist organizations, including the VHP and the RSS, were banned. The former site of the Babri Masjid is now slated to become home to an all-India national shrine, dedicated to demonstrating that the modern, secular Indian state can withstand the challenges of cultural pluralism ("Kar Sevaks Demolish Babri Masjid," *The Times of India* (December 7, 1992); Van der Veer 1994).

CONCLUSION

Despite the VHP's and the BJP's defeat at Ayodhya, the controversy helped the Hindu Right gain publicity and a reputation for violent action on behalf of the Hindu majority. As the drive to build the Rama temple at Ayodhya was inextricably linked to the VHP's action plan for cultural rejuvenation of the Hindu nation, the scheme must be viewed not only as a powerful means of mapping and reclaiming sacred Hindu spaces, but as a cultural symbol buttressing a conception of Hindu identity deeply embedded in Hindu nationalist ideology.

In the years following the Ayodhya campaign the BJP has distanced itself from this volatile issue. The BJP has acquired considerable access to political power at the local and national levels. Presently it heads the multiparty government in New Delhi. The VHP never gave up the temple campaign. According to *The New York Times*, artisans in north Indian workshops have spent years chiseling pillars for the structure. In early 2002 Hindu-Muslim rioting in the north Indian state of Gujarat appeared to be related to the campaign. In March the VHP announced that temple construction would begin despite court orders and the reluctance of the BJP-led national coalition government in New Delhi to endorse the project. In a weak attempt to defuse the situation, the central government entered into negotiations with Hindu and Muslim groups to resolve the issue (Dugger 2002, 3) *The campaign, whether or not the central government endorses it, encourages people across India to embrace the militant message of the Hindu right.* The Rama temple scheme continues to test whether the modern Indian state can withstand the challenges of cultural pluralism.

In this essay I have stressed that the rise of the Hindu right since the 1970s cannot be explained solely in terms of social, economic and political factors. The skill of organizations such as the VHP and the BJP in creating and manipulating complex symbolic systems is another crucial factor that must be explored in order to understand this complex and controversial nationalist movement. Clearly, the Ayodhya campaign alone did not bring the BJP to power in the 1980s and 90s. However, as I have attempted to show through a concise history of the Rama temple scheme, a broader understanding of the cultural symbolism of the Hindu Right can help us understand one of the ways that the movement generated and mobilized concepts of Hindu national identity in the struggle for political power in contemporary India.

REFERENCES

Anon. "Advani." 1990. *India Today* (February 28) 144–46.

Anon. "Bajrang Dal." 1991. *India Today* (November 30) 18–19.

Anon. "BJP." 1991. *India Today* (April 4) 22.

Anon. "Kar Sevaks Demolish Babri Masjid." 1992. *The Times of India.* (December 7) 1.

Anon. "Road to Revival." 1983. *India Today* (November 30) 82–84.

Anderson, Benedict. 1983. *Imagined Communities: Reflections on the Origin and Spread of Nationalism.* London: Verso.

Anderson, Walter, and Shridar Damle. 1987. *The Brotherhood in Saffron: The Rashtriya Swayamsevak Sangh and Hindu Revivalism.* Boulder: Westview Press.

Asher, Catherine. 1992. *The New Cambridge History of India: Architecture of Mughal India.* Cambridge: Cambridge University Press.

Awasthi, Dilip. 1990. "State of Chaos," *India Today* (November 30) 13–25.

Badhwar, Inderjit. 1986. "Hindus Militant Revivalism," *India Today* (May 31) 76–85.

Bakker, Hans. 1986. *Ayodhya.* Groningen: Egbert Forsten.

Basu, Tapan et al., eds. 1993. *Khaki Shorts and Saffron Flags: A Critique of the Hindu Right.* Orient Longmans.

Blurton, T. Richard. 1993. *Hindu Art.* Cambridge: Harvard University Press.

Boesch, Ernest. 1991. *Symbolic Action Theory and Cultural Psychology.* Berlin: Springer-Verlag.

Brass, Paul. 1990. *The Politics of India Since Independence.* Cambridge: Cambridge University Press.

————. 1991. *Ethnicity and Nationalism: Theory and Comparison.* New Delhi: Sage.

Chandran, E. n.d. *Ram Janm Bhoomi.* New Delhi: Cosmos Bookhive.

Cohen, Abner. 1974. *Two-Dimensional Man: An Essay on the Anthropology of Power and Symbolism in Complex Society.* Berkeley: University of California Press.

Davis, Richard. 1997. *Lives of Indian Images.* Princeton: Princeton University Press.

Dugger, Celia W. 2002. "Gandhi's Dream and India's Latest Nightmare," *The New York Times* (March 10) 3.

Engineer, Ashgar. 1992. *Politics of Confrontation: The Babri-Masjid Ramjanmabhoomi Controversy Run-Riot.* Delhi: Ajanta.

Fox, Richard. 1989. *Gandhian Utopia: Experiments with Culture.* Boston: Beacon Press.

Fuller, C. J. 1992. *The Camphor Flame: Popular Hinduism and Society in India.* Princeton: Princeton University Press.

Ghosh, Partha. 1999. *The BJP and the Evolution of Hindu Nationalism.* Delhi: Manohar Publications.

Gopal, Sarvepalli. 1991. *Anatomy of a Confrontation: The Babri Masjid-Ram Janmabumi Issue.* New York: Penguin Books.

Jaffrelot, C. 1996. *The Hindu Nationalist Movement and Indian Politics 1925 to the 1990s.* London: C. Hurst and Company Ltd.

Michell, George. 1977. *The Hindu Temple: An Introduction to Its Meaning and Forms.* Chicago: University of Chicago Press.

Richman, Paula, ed. 1991. *Many Ramayanas: The Diversity of a Narrative Tradition in South Asia.* Berkeley: University of California Press.

Sinha, Mrinalin. 1996. *Colonial Masculinity: The "Manly Englishman" and the "Effeminate Bengali" in the Late Nineteenth Century.* Manchester: Manchester University Press.

Sperber, Dan. 1975. *Rethinking Symbolism.* Cambridge: Cambridge University Press.

Spitz, Douglas. 1993. "Cultural Pluralism, Revivalism, and Modernity in South Asia: The Rashtriya Swayamsevak Sangh." Pp. 242–64 in *The Rising Tide of Cultural Pluralism*, ed. Crawford Young. Madison: University of Wisconsin Press.

Van der Veer, Peter. 1987. "God Must be Liberated! A Hindu Liberation Movement in Ayodhya." *Modern Asian Studies* 21: 283-301.

———. 1988. *Gods on Earth: The Management of Religious Experience and Identity in a North Indian Pilgrimage Centre.* London: Athlone Press.

———. 1994. *Religious Nationalism: Hindus and Muslims in India.* Berkeley: University of California Press.

Verma, Ganeshi Lal. 1985. "RSS Plan for Conversion of Ancient Mosques in U.P. into Temples," *The Organiser* (March 31), reprinted in *Muslim India* (May 1985) 205.

Young, Crawford, ed. 1993. *The Rising Tide of Cultural Pluralism: The Nation State at Bay?* Madison: University of Wisconsin Press.

Part 4

Transforming the
Institutional Framework

Chapter 10

Self-Government in the Darjeeling Hills of India

Selma K. Sonntag

India's cohesion and endurance as a nation-state, despite its immense diversity, have baffled many scholars. Its demise has been repeatedly forecast. Harrison (1960) predicted that India's primordial fissiparous tendencies would tear the country apart. Others have defined India as nothing more than a colonial construct (Edney 1999).

The historical interface between India's cultural diversity and its construction as a modern nation-state is strewn with institutional and administrative experimentation and variation. The colonial state, in addition to common administrative units (provinces and presidencies), included such oddities as princely fiefdoms and "excluded" and "partially excluded" areas. Upon independence, India grappled with this inherited institutional maze, finally settling on linguistic federalism. Nonetheless, Jawaharlal Nehru, India's first prime minister, hesitated in adopting the principle of linguistic states for fear of unleashing divisive tendencies. King (1997) has argued that Nehru's "muddling through" the language issue served India well. It provided time for national cohesion to adhere to the body politic.

When, in 1955, India finally passed the (linguistic) Reorganization of States Act, implementation was neither swift nor uniform, for language is only one marker of diversity in India, and the state languages of India's federal system are only a handful of the more than 1,500 reported mother tongues in the censuses. Multilingualism still prevails within the linguistic states, and other markers such as region, caste, religion, and ethnicity complicate India's accommodation to cultural pluralism. This accommodation has varied, both institutionally and administratively. Kashmir, for example, obtained special administrative status upon accession to India. The state of Punjab, in which Sikhs form a (bare) majority, was not instituted until the mid-1960s. The Portuguese enclave of Goa did not obtain statehood until the late 1980s.

The institutional accommodation of cultural pluralism in northeast India has been particularly tricky. Shortly after India's independence, isolated indigenous groups, living in the "excluded" frontier areas of the British Raj, were granted self-government rights. The Sixth Schedule of the Indian Constitution limited "autonomous councils" to tribals living on the southern flank of the Brahmaputra River in the Assam region. In the early 1970s, the entire northeast was "reorganized," with new states being created out of the old Assam. The institutional layer of autonomous councils continued, albeit in a somewhat changed format, with new councils proposed for mobilized groups such as the Bodo.

Institutional and administrative variation seems to be the hallmark of India's accommodation of cultural pluralism. Is this variation the answer to those baffled by India's cohesion and endurance? Did India somehow "get it right" in accommodating cultural pluralism? Surely there are shortcomings in the Indian "model" of accommodating cultural pluralism, evident in the present violence in Kashmir and in the northeast, and in the Punjab in the 1980s. I will argue that India does not present any coherent model of successful accommodation of cultural pluralism. There is no "exportable" theoretical formula that can be derived from India's experience. Rather, India's success, if we wish to define its endurance as such, is the result of "muddling through," of ad hoc, piecemeal, case-by-case accommodation to crises (Prakash 1999, 461). Of course, we may wish to conclude that "muddling through" in and of itself is a model, a desirable approach to accommodating cultural pluralism. Perhaps muddling through is a process that results from the adoption of larger, abstract principles of statehood and governance. I will suggest later that India's "muddling through" approach to accommodating cultural pluralism appears to be constrained by recognizable principles of liberalism, federalism, and democracy. In an attempt to evaluate whether India's accommodation of cultural pluralism is indeed a promising and an emancipatory practice, I dissect a recent case of such accommodation.

In 1988, the Darjeeling Gorkha Hill Council (DGHC) was established in the Nepali-speaking area around Darjeeling in the northern portion of the state of West Bengal. This was the first time that self-government in the form of an autonomous council was granted outside of the northeast (i.e., outside of the purview of the Sixth Schedule of the Indian Constitution). This was also the first time that self-government was granted *not* to an indigenous tribal group threatening secession, as had been the case under the original Sixth Schedule, but to an immigrant group demanding integration. Granting self-government was a response to the demands made by the Gorkha National Liberation Front (GNLF). Yet the GNLF's demands did not reflect a desire to separate from India. On the contrary, they reflected a desire for further integration into the Indian nation-state.

The GNLF made two principal demands. Foremost, GNLF's members and followers wanted clarification of their citizenship status—they wanted to be recognized unequivocally as citizens of India (Sarbadhikari 1991, 65; Datta

1993, 150). Second, they demanded that their language be recognized as a national language of India. Both of these were demands for recognition as Indians, through the state granting citizenship and acknowledging their language as Indian. These were integrationist demands. Even the GNLF's periodic demand for statehood was integrationist: the GNLF wanted the Darjeeling hills on par with other states within the Indian federal union.

What led the Indian state to accommodate these integrationist demands with self-government? This accommodation was new: autonomous councils had not been used outside of the northeast, and there they had been used only for tribals threatening secession. I argue here that this innovation was neither planned nor strategic; it resulted from a "muddling through" by the state in response to the GNLF's (frequently violent) agitation for its demands. The muddling through was constrained by India's liberal democratic federalism. Each of these principles (i.e., liberalism, democracy, and federalism) determined the parameters of the muddling but did not preordain the outcome. Nor should we assume that the outcome is necessarily the best or most desirable accommodation. I only wish to suggest that India may occasionally "get it right" by virtue of its capacity for institutional and administrative variation, the range of which is constrained by federal, liberal, and democratic principles and practices.

LIBERALISM

I am using the term *liberalism* here in the political rather than the economic sense. Hence, liberalism refers to the political philosophy espoused by Nehru and his like-minded contemporaries. It also is the political philosophy endorsed by the Canadian political theorist, Will Kymlicka (1995), who argues that liberalism acknowledges and recognizes minority rights. For "national minorities," this assumes self-government rights. National minorities are distinct from ethnic immigrants (who individually and voluntarily change national identity), in that their historic land has been incorporated into the nation-state. Not only are national minorities geographically concentrated, but they also are culturally distinct. It is for this reason that self-government is needed: self-government preserves the national minority's culture, which provides a meaningful context in which minority individuals can exercise personal autonomy and choice. A liberal state should and usually does, according to Kymlicka, grant self-government to national minorities.

A Kymlickian liberal justification for self-government was evident in the Constituent Assembly debates on the Sixth Schedule, which were "guided by... the necessity to maintain the distinct customs, socio-economic and political culture of the tribal people of the region and to ensure autonomy of the tribal people and to preserve their identities" (Gassah 1997, 3). This idea contrasts with the arguments of those who wanted to assimilate tribals in the northeast into the Indian political and cultural mainstream. The assimilationists worried that self-government would disrupt administrative integrity and national cohesion (Sonntag 1999). The Nehruvian liberals, however, carried the day. The liberal consensus forged by Nehru and others (such as B. R. Ambedkar, the "untouchable" who drafted the Indian Constitution) was instrumental in granting self-government to tribals in the northeast whose homelands were now part of the Indian State.

There is, then, a liberal argument to be made for granting self-government to indigenous tribals of the northeast. The Sixth Schedule was a liberal-derived institutional experiment embarked upon when India was reconstituting itself as an independent modern nation-state. But what about Darjeeling? The Kymlickian argument for self-government does not work as well in this case (Sonntag 1998). The Nepali speakers in Darjeeling are not a "national minority" in Kymlicka's sense; many "voluntarily" immigrated to the area during the colonial period to work in the tea gardens. More importantly, the GNLF was agitating for what Kymlicka calls "polyethnic rights" rather than self-government rights. Polyethnic rights are granted by liberal states to ethnic immigrants to "promote integration into the larger [multicultural] society" by recognizing and supporting certain cultural practices, such as using a particular language in schools through bilingual education or practicing a particular religion (Kymlicka 1995, 31). The GNLF's demand for clarification of the citizenship status of Nepali speakers in Darjeeling and its demand for recognition of their language as a national language of India are quintessential liberal demands for polyethnic rights. Unlike the tribals in the northeast, who emphatically stated that they were *not* Indians (Ghurye 1963, 319), the GNLF repeatedly claimed loyalty to India (Magar 1994, 179, 189). Their main complaint was that although they *were* Indians, the Indian government did not duly recognize them as such and instead regarded them as foreigners from Nepal (Timsina 1992, 41).

Why, then, were they granted self-government, while their "polyethnic" (i.e., integrationist) demands were virtually ignored (see Subba 1992, 166)? Liberalism provided two enabling circumstances. First, the cultural and historical peculiarities of the Nepali speakers in Darjeeling are difficult to categorize. In many regards, this group fits neatly into the Kymlickian liberal category of ethnic immigrants, thereby not qualifying for self-government. Various Tibeto-Burman and Indo-Aryan groups originating in Nepal had migrated to the Darjeeling area, particularly during the colonial period, in search of employment. They soon overwhelmed autochtonous Tibeto-Burman groups such as the Lepchas. They also constructed a pan-ethnic identity, marked by their use of Nepali, an Indo-Aryan language, as their lingua franca. In other respects, however, their situation seemed congruent with that of a national minority. Darjeeling and surrounding areas changed hands repeatedly during early colonial intrusion, with various parcels "gifted" to the British, won in military campaigns, or acceded to colonial authorities through intrigue (Subba 1992, 29–37). The end result was that by the late nineteenth century, the area was incorporated into the British Raj as "partially excluded." Its cultural distinctiveness was preserved.

The second and more important reason their demands were met, however, is likely that self-government was already on the institutional "radar screen." Anand Pathak, a member of Parliament (MP) from the Darjeeling area, had introduced a bill in 1985 providing for self-government in Darjeeling, invoking the Sixth Schedule as a model (Lok Sabha Debates 1985, 353). In promoting his self-government bill, Pathak commented on the Darjeeling inhabitants' "distinct language, distinct culture, distinct habit, manner and aptitude and other peculiarities which are distinguished from the people of West Bengal as well as the rest of the country" (ibid.). He continued, suggesting that "[t]he real intention of this Bill is to allow the Nepali culture, Nepali language and their way of life to develop in their own way" (ibid., 385–86). Pathak's bill failed, but the perception of the Darjeeling folk as a national minority continued. In his speech to the West Bengal State Assembly in September 1988, on the enabling legislation for the Darjeeling Gorkha Hill Council, Chief Minister Jyoti Basu ended by commenting, "This is a new experiment in satisfying the aspirations of an easily identifiable group of people concentrated in a compact area without tearing apart the basic fabric of the State" (Government of West Bengal 1988, 34).

FEDERALISM

The DGHC was the result of a tripartite accord between the central government, the West Bengal state government, and the GNLF. Unlike Pathak's earlier bill proposing a constitutional amendment, the accord was enacted through legislation passed by the West Bengal State Legislative Assembly. This was "a new experiment outside the NorthEastern region" and the constitutional purview of the Sixth Schedule, in that it was "an autonomous development council for a non-[tribal] area within the authority of the State Legislature" (Samanta 1996, 147).

Experimentation with new institutional and administrative forms is facilitated by India's experience with federalism. As noted earlier, India's first post–independence leaders were nervous about adopting federalism. Although "federalism . . . might protect historically constituted cultural-territorial identities" (Baruah 1999, 11), it is "also potentially dangerous . . . in multinational polities" (Stepan 1997, 18), precisely because of the fissiparous tendencies that Nehru worried about. The legacy of this experience is that the "[d]emand for separate states is seldom appreciated as a healthy symptom of the marginalised ethnic groups' desire to be integrated into the Indian mainstream" (Subba 1992, 99). In the Darjeeling case, statehood within the Indian Union had been a demand for some time. The Nepali speakers of Darjeeling had made entreaties to the Dar Commission (and its colonial predecessor, the Simon Commission), which was responsible for recommending the linguistic reorganization of states. However, Nepali was not deemed a major language of India, and serious discussion of separate statehood was not entertained.

In the mid-1980s, at the time of the GNLF-led agitation, self-government was perceived by the state as less threatening than statehood. The West Bengal state government unequivocally announced that "the logic behind the demand for regional autonomy should not be confused with the demand for statehood. While the former is intended to forge national unity, by recognising the cultural and ethnic diversity of the population . . . the latter, in this particular case, is an argument for strengthening the forces of national disunity" (Government of West Bengal 1986, 26).

The fear that constitutionally sanctioned autonomous council status would lead to statehood, as had happened in the northeast, helped cause the defeat of Anand Pathak's bill for self-government in Darjeeling in late 1985 and early 1986. Members of Parliament fretted that Pathak's bill was "Statehood in disguise, though you are calling it only as an autonomous district council" (Lok Sabha Debates 1985, 389). The Union government Home Minister noted that if the Darjeeling people's aspirations were not satisfied by autonomous council status, "then the second demand would be to ask for a Statehood . . . there are very dangerous implications, if we accept the proposal of this nature" (Lok Sabha Debates 1986, 359). The central government viewed " 'regional autonomy' . . . [as] nothing but a step towards statehood and the Centre was not at any cost prepared to amend the Constitution to make way for it" (Subba 1992, 180).

The dilemma for the national leaders was that granting self-government might encourage an escalation of demands for statehood, yet neglecting some kind of accommodation could foment divisive tendencies. As Kymlicka (1995, 10) has noted, "self-government . . . pose[s] a serious threat to social unity. . . . However, denying self-government . . . can also threaten social unity, by encouraging secession." What should be an easy solution in India's federal system, that is, establishing new states (Stepan 1997, 24), was not considered desirable. By default, a new administrative arrangement for self-government emerged.

The Darjeeling solution has become, in turn, a model for other geographically concentrated, culturally distinct minorities. In 1994, the Jharkhand Autonomous Area Council was created; the following year, the Ladakh Autonomous Development Council was established. There had even been discussion of granting self-government to Uttarakhand in Uttar Pradesh, a region where the culturally distinct minority are upper-caste Hindus, albeit poor.

State governments often are reluctant to "give up" areas to autonomous councils—as in the case of Bihar stalling on the Jharkhand autonomous council,
or the Uttar Pradesh government fighting against Uttarakhand autonomy—
but they are equally if not more opposed to granting statehood. Nevertheless,
in late 2000, primarily because of a new political configuration at the national
level, statehood was granted to Jharkhand and Uttarakhand (now called
Uttaranchal), as well as to the Chhattisgarh of Madhya Pradesh. The Darjeeling
area, however, was not considered for statehood.

Autonomous councils can be seen as another layer of federalism. "Mul-
tilevel federalism" in India received a further thrust forward in 1992 with the
adoption of the 73rd Amendment to the Constitution (Frankel 1997, 14).
The "Panchayat Raj" amendment has invigorated local government through
decentralization. In particular, it has empowered women by reserving seats for
them in local panchayat governments. The 73rd Amendment is not, however,
applied in locales governed by autonomous councils. The autonomous councils form, in essence, a parallel layer of decentralization. They are "an institutional innovation . . .effecting decentralization of power" (Ganguly 1997,
331). Although laudable, these decentralization processes seem to have emerged
in an ad hoc, unplanned manner. "The whole issue of inter-articulation of the
institutional arrangements and operational range under the Sixth Schedule
and the 73rd Constitutional Amendment Act 1992 [needs] to be carefully
examined and a substantially altered Sixth Schedule by synthesising the positive thrust of both will have to be evolved," warns Roy-Burman (1997, 132).
In a similar tone, Ganguly (1997, 333) argues that "a comparative analysis
of . . . ADCs [autonomous (district) councils] and the Panchayat Raj . . . is in
order."

Federalism enshrines the principle of multiple locales of power. In India,
the central government in the past has maintained the upper hand in any
power struggle with states. Likewise, state governments have maintained the
upper hand vis-à-vis autonomous councils (Nichols-Roy 1997, 324). Yet it is
the culture of federalism that allows the struggles even to occur, with the
outcomes not necessarily preordained. Within the parameters of federalism,
India appears to be muddling through toward greater decentralization.

DEMOCRATIC POLITICS

Politics determine the particular outcomes of "muddling through," for politics, in India, take place in a democratic environment whose primary manifestation is elections (Khilnani 1997), and electoral democracy constitutes a
further set of parameters constraining accommodation to cultural pluralism.

The Communist Party of India (Marxist) (CPI(M)) ruled uninterrupt-
edly in the state of West Bengal since 1977, with the indomitable Jyoti Basu

at the helm (until his retirement in 2000). By the time it came to power, the CPI(M) had already infiltrated the tea plantations of the Darjeeling area, but it was not until 1980 that it broke the hold of the All India Gorkha League (AIGL), a regional party, on the state legislative assembly seats in Darjeeling, because of the death of the AIGL's charismatic leader (Subba 1992, 125; Franda 1970). The CPI(M) competed as well with Congress(I). Both the CPI(M) and Congress(I) were mainstream parties, and their supporters in the Darjeeling Hills were referred to as "Nepalis." In contrast, AIGL supporters were called "Gorkhalis," and supporters of the AIGL's successor, the GNLF, were considered "Gorkhas." In this politicized atmosphere, Subba (1992, 71) notes, "all three terms—Gorkha, Gorkhali, and Nepali [all referring to the Nepali-speaking population of the Darjeeling area] have transcended their ethnic meanings and assumed political connotations." The "social" construction of ethnic identity had escalated to the political level. In the early 1990s, the GNLF even attempted to expunge from the electoral rolls voters whom they suspected claimed Nepali and not Gorkhali as their language in the census (Josse 1992; Samanta 1996).

Horowitz (1985) has analyzed the escalation of ethnic conflict resulting from political parties upping the ante in electoral competition. In the Darjeeling case, political competition opened the door to self-government through which stumbled both the CPI(M) and Congress(I). In December 1985, on the eve of the GNLF mobilization for its integrationist demands, the CPI(M) MP from the Darjeeling area, Anand Pathak, introduced his bill in Parliament to grant autonomous status to the Darjeeling hills. Subba (1992, 92) suggests that it was never the intention of the CPI(M) government in West Bengal to actually achieve the stated goal of self-government for Darjeeling—for the CPI(M) knew that such a bill would be defeated (Samanta 1996, 99–100). Instead, the intention was to put the ball in the central government's court, forcing Prime Minister Rajiv Gandhi to take a stand. According to a local source, "[t]here appears to have been no other object for moving the amendment except to embarrass the Congress-I" (quoted in Samanta 1996, 101). Congress(I) attempted to return the favor: while Pathak and his colleagues faulted the central government for failing to meet the aspirations of the people of Darjeeling, Congress(I) government ministers blamed the CPI(M) state government for inadequate administration and economic development of the area (Lok Sabha Debates 1985, 1986).

In the ensuing display of competitive politics during the debate over Pathak's bill, the electoral impact of various solutions to the Darjeeling crisis was weighed. Special representation rights, which Kymlicka would consider an appropriate liberal solution to minority demands for integration, were deemed too costly politically. According to Lok Sabha transcripts, when one MP endorsed special representative rights as a method to ensure that minority communities got their fair share of resources and benefits, by weighting their representation in state assemblies, his proposal was greeted with multiple "interruptions." Presumably the cause of the interruptions was the impact that special representation for Darjeeling would have on the existing makeup of the state assembly. Alternatively, self-government would add another elected representative body (the autonomous council), leaving intact the status quo of the state assembly. Indeed, a political "deal" was rumored to have been made between the CPI(M) and the GNLF. The GNLF would get the elected positions on the autonomous council in return for abstaining from contesting the state assembly seats from the Darjeeling area, which would go to the CPI(M) (Karat 1994).

Upping the ante between the CPI(M) and Congress(I) was clearly visible in the rhetoric both sides spouted on the "nature" of the GNLF agitation. Pathak's bill advocated self-government for Darjeeling—in order to stave off any secessionist threat. He argued that there were "reactionary and vested interests" that were exploiting the Nepali-speakers' legitimate demands that could lead to the "disintegration of the country" (Lok Sabha Debates 1985, 354). Congress(I) went further, suggesting that the Nepali speakers themselves harbored separatist tendencies. The Home Minister noted that, if accepted, Pathak's bill "would be interpreted . . . as another victory for separatist forces" (quoted in Samanta 1996, 99). Soon after, in Parliament, a prominent Congress(I) member lumped the GNLF together with "extremist groups" in Tripura, Nagaland, and Manipur (all in the northeast) and Jharkhand (a tribal area in Bihar) (quoted in Majumdar 1991, 77).

Once Pathak's bill was defeated, the CPI(M)'s rhetoric changed fairly dramatically. In a CPI(M) party pamphlet, the GNLF's activities in Darjeeling were now labeled a "secessionist agitation" that was succeeding in "misleading large number [sic] of people" (Ranadive 1986, 7). Ghising and the GNLF, it was now claimed, had demanded "a separate State of Gorkhaland separating from India" (ibid., 8). But unfortunately, so the CPI(M) argued, the central government was making the mistake of choosing a "conciliatory and compromising attitude towards hardened separatists"; the central government should instead "take a forthright stand and tell people that the secessionist movement must be contained by the unity of the people and wherever necessary by administrative actions" and "inflic[t] a political defeat on the secessionists" (ibid., 9). The CPI(M), in a very short period of time, had moved from arguing for self-government to advocating force to put down what was now described as a secessionist threat. In the meanwhile, violence erupted in the Darjeeling area, a good portion of it between CPI(M) supporters and GNLF activists. Indeed, "[t]he goriest violence in the Darjeeling hills . . . was between the supporters of the GNLF and the CPI(M) but ethnically belonged [sic] to the same group—Nepalis" (Subba 1992, 124). Anand Pathak, the sponsor of the self-government bill, was among those affected, with his home being "completely gutted by the GNLF supporters" (ibid., 128).

While the state CPI(M) government had moved from supporting self-government in late 1985 and early 1986 to subsequently opposing it, the Congress(I) central government moved in the opposite direction, from opposing Pathak's self-government bill to embracing the autonomous council solution. By September 1986, Prime Minister Rajiv Gandhi was describing the "Gorkha agitation" as not "anti-national" (i.e., it was not secessionist). Rajiv's statement was meant to keep in line local Congress(I) activists who had emphasized the agitation's secessionist tendencies (Subba 1992, 178). By November 1986, P. Chidambaram, Minister of State of Home Affairs, was claiming that "Subhas Ghising [the GNLF leader] has regretted any misapprehension or doubt. . . . He has made assurance of total loyalty of [sic] India" (quoted in Majumdar 1991, 11).

The contrasting trajectories of Congress(I) and CPI(M) rhetoric are striking. The Congress(I) central government, in early 1986, initially was apprehensive about the separatist tones of the Gorkha movement, but by late 1986 it had come to the conclusion that it was not a separatist movement. In contrast, the CPI(M) state government's rhetoric took the reverse course, seeing the movement as legitimate and benign in early 1986 but shifting to a strident view of the movement as secessionist and anti-national by late 1986. Some accused the Congress(I) central government of abetting Ghising and the GNLF as a political counterweight to the CPI(M), thus "collaborating" in the violence that ensued between 1986 and 1988 (Samanta 1996, 106–107). Rajiv Gandhi, it was suggested, had "used Ghising [the leader of the GNLF] as a stick to beat West Bengal Chief Minister Jyoti Basu" ("Encounter" 1992, 6).

The type of political and electoral competition that ensues in a democracy provided the momentum that in this case produced a fairly radical solution to integrationist demands made by a cultural minority. While neither the CPI(M) nor Congress(I) initially foresaw self-government as a desirable solution, they were locked in political sparring that inevitably led to the agreement to grant self-government to the Darjeeling area through the establishment of an autonomous council.

CONCLUSION

The success of the DGHC has been hampered by the very same constraints that enabled its advent. A major obstacle has been continued acrimony between the DGHC and the West Bengal state government. The ambiguity of "multilayered" federalism allows for the logic of electoral democracy to be played out by each party attempting to outbid the other. The DGHC claims that it has been unable to engage in serious economic development because of the CPI(M) state government's obstructions (Datta 1991, 240). The CPI(M)

retorts that the DGHC is incompetent in promoting growth and development. The tit for tat is nearly identical to that between the CPI(M) and the
Congress(I) Union government during the mid-1980s. Ghising and the GNLF
then upped the ante, calling for statehood (within the Union) at any cost and
rallying supporters with their stridency. And the CPI(M) tried to weaken the
electoral hold of the GNLF on Darjeeling by proposing to hold panchayat
elections in the area, despite the exemption of the 73rd Amendment in autonomous council areas (Chaudhuri 1994). As one political commentator
noted, "the fire on the [Darjeeling] hill[s] is being stoked" (Aiyar 1998, 27).
    Van Beek (1999), in his work on the Ladakh autonomous council, has
raised the issue of whether autonomous councils are destined to fail because
their liberal democratic premises lead to a fetishism of the notion of "community," reifying what are heterogeneous groupings of people as natural, given,
primordial communities (such as the CPI(M) "Nepali speakers" and the GNLF
"Gorkha speakers," assumed to be one homogeneous, undifferentiated community). He concludes that the autonomous council formula, in being a
liberal democratic one, does not offer a radical break from the dominant
paradigm of development and, therefore, it is bound to fail. In a similar vein,
I have argued elsewhere that by relying on a cultural definition of minorities
seeking redress, the liberal state frequently neglects to address the political
and economic dimensions of the minorities' plight (Sonntag 2000). In other
words, liberalism tends to confine the range of solutions to the cultural realm.
This makes it difficult for the adopted solution to successfully resolve underlying political and economic inequalities.
    The "muddling through" within the framework of liberal democratic
federalism that led to the DGHC experiment also impedes that experiment
from being replicated. The capacity of the Indian State to accommodate
immense diversity has been repeatedly demonstrated through its institutional
and administrative experimentation and variation. But coherency and consis-
tency have not been major features of India's brand of accommodating cultural pluralism. India may occasionally "get it right" but through, seemingly,
a "fit of absent-mindedness" (see Khilnani 1997, 34).

REFERENCES

Aiyar, Mani Shankar. 1998. "Fire on the Hill." *India Today International* (February 2): 27.

Baruah, Sanjib. 1999. *India against Itself: Assam and the Politics of Nationality.* Philadelphia: University of Pennsylvania Press.

Chaudhuri, Kalyan. 1994. "Tensions in the Hills." *Frontline* (September 23): 116–18.

Datta, Prabhat. 1991. "The Gorkhaland Agitation in West Bengal." *The Indian Journal of Political Science* 52:2 (April–June): 225–41.

————. 1993. *Regionalisation of Indian Politics*. New Delhi: Sterling.

Edney, Matthew H. 1999. *Mapping an Empire: The Geographical Construction of British India, 1765–1843*. Delhi: Oxford University Press.

"Encounter." 1992. Interview with Chhatre Subba. *The Independent*. Kathmandu ed. (November 11): 6.

Franda, Marcus F. 1970. "Intra-regional Factionalism and Coalition-Building in West Bengal." *Journal of Commonwealth Political Studies* 8:3 (November): 187–205.

Frankel, Francine R. 1997. "The Problem." *Seminar* 459 (November): 12–15.

Ganguly, J. B. 1997. "The Relevance of the Autonomous District Councils Today." Pp. 331–33 in *The Autonomous District Councils*, ed. L. S. Gassah. New Delhi: Osmons.

Gassah, L. S. 1997. "Introduction." Pp. 1–14 in *The Autonomous District Councils*, ed. L. S. Gassah. New Delhi: Osmons.

Ghurye, G. S. 1963. *The Scheduled Tribes*. Bombay: Popular Prakashan.

Government of West Bengal. 1986. *Gorkhaland Agitation: The Issues*. An information document. Calcutta: Director of Information, Government of West Bengal.

————. 1988. *Towards Formation of the Darjeeling Gorkha Hill Council*. Calcutta: Information and Cultural Affairs Department.

Harrison, Selig S. 1960. *India: The Most Dangerous Decades*. Princeton: Princeton University Press.

Horowitz, Donald L. 1985. *Ethnic Groups in Conflict*. Berkeley: University of California Press.

Josse, M. R. 1992. "Recognition of Nepali In India." *The Independent*. Kathmandu ed. (September 30 and November 11): 11.

Karat, Prakash. 1994. Personal interview. (February 10). New Delhi: CPI(M) Headquarters.

Khilnani, Sunil. 1997. *The Idea of India*. New York: Farrar, Straus Giroux.

King, Robert D. 1997. *Nehru and the Language Politics of India*. Oxford: Oxford University Press.

Kymlicka, Will. 1995. *Multicultural Citizenship*. Oxford: Clarendon Press.

Lok Sabha Debates. 1985. *8th Lok Sabha* 11:14–15 (December 6–9). New Delhi: Lok Sabha Secretariat.

————. 1986. *8th Lok Sabha* 14:11 (March 7), New Delhi: Lok Sabha Secretariat.

Magar, Harsha Bahadur Bura. 1994. *Is Gorkhaland a Reality or Simply Mirage?* Kathmandu: Mrs. Puspawati Bura Magar.

Majumdar, J. M., compiler. 1991. *Eastern Himalaya through Parliamentary Proceedings, 1985–1989*. Vol. 2. Darjeeling: Documentation Cell, Centre for Himalayan Studies, University of North Bengal.

Nichols-Roy, Stanley. 1997. "Autonomous District Councils—the Sixth Schedule." Pp. 323–26 in *The Autonomous District Councils*, ed. L. S. Gassah. New Delhi: Osmons.

Prakash, Amit. 1999. "Contested Discourses: Politics of Ethnic Identity and Autonomy in the Jharkhand Region of India." *Alternatives* 24:4 (October–December): 461–96.

Ranadive, B. T. 1986. *Gorkhaland Agitation: A Part of Imperialist Plot in the East.* Calcutta: Sushil Chowdhury, on behalf of West Bengal State Committee, Community Party of India (Marxist).

Roy-Burman, B. K. 1997. "Sixth Schedule of the Constitution." Pp. 15–38 in *The Autonomous District Councils,* ed. L. S. Gassah. New Delhi: Osmons.

Samanta, Amiya R. 1996. *Gorkhaland: A Study in Ethnic Separatism.* New Delhi: Khama.

Sarbadhikari, Pradip. 1991. "India's Subnationalism: The Gorkhaland Controversy." *Canadian Review of Studies in Nationalism* 18:1–2: 61–71.

Sonntag, Selma K. 1998. "Kymlicka Travels to India: National Minority Rights in the Himalayas." Paper presented at the Annual Meeting of the American Political Science Association (September 4–6), Boston.

———. 1999. "Autonomous Councils in India: Contesting the Liberal Nation-State." *Alternatives* 24: 4 (October–December): 415–34.

———. 2000. "Self-Government, Indigenity, and Authenticity: A Comparative Study of India and the United States." Paper presented at "Indigenous People—The Trajectory of a Contemporary Concept in India" workshop, Seminar for Development Studies, Uppsala, Sweden, April 7–9.

Stepan, Alfred. 1997. "Comparative Democratic Federalism." *Seminar* 459 (November): 16–26.

Subba, Tanka B. 1992. *Ethnicity, State and Development: A Case Study of Gorkhaland Movement in Darjeeling.* New Delhi: Vikas.

Timsina, Suman Raj. 1992. *Nepali Community in India.* Delhi: Manak.

Van Beek, Martijn. 1999. "Hill Councils, Development, and Democracy: Assumptions and Experiences from Ladakh." *Alternatives,* 24:4 (October–December): 435–60.

Young, Crawford. 1976. *The Politics of Cultural Pluralism.* Madison: University of Wisconsin Press.

Chapter 11

Politics of State Creation and Ethnic Relations in Nigeria

The Case of Former Bendel State

Paul G. Adogamhe

Nigeria, in its social and political engineering, has engaged in several waves of state creation (in 1963, 1967, 1976, 1987, 1991, and 1996) to accommodate its ethnic and cultural diversity. As a result, since gaining independence from Britain in 1960, the Nigerian federation has gone from three regions to thirty-six states (see Figure 11.1). While there seem to be persistent and politically irresistible communal pressures for the creation of new states and localities, there are now growing misgivings about further subdivision. At the same time, a number of arguments have been presented to justify the creation of even more states (Federal Republic of Nigeria 1987, 170–79). The dilemma facing Nigerian policy makers today is how many political units or states are optimal for the maintenance of stability. More broadly, understanding ethnic relations in a multiethnic country such as Nigeria will provide insights into the complex problems associated with diversity and integration in general and thus will make a contribution to the development of emancipatory ideas of cultural pluralism. This chapter will examine the impact of state creation on ethnic relations in Nigeria by using Bendel State as a case study. It postulates that the impact of the reorganization of the country, as employed by the federal government, has intensified ethnic competition and further agitation for more administrative revisions.

Let us begin first by reviewing the three main arguments used to justify further state creation. The first is cultural balance. Here the important issue is the persistence of religious, linguistic, historical, regional, ethnic, and economic differences. The effort is to create a federation that allows each cultural bloc a sphere of relatively autonomous operation and development within which to pursue its unique personal identity (Graf 1988, 143). As Chief Awolowo argued in 1960, the creation of states should be based on a criterion

195

Figure 11.1 Evolution of Administrative Map of Nigeria from Three Regions to Thirty-six States

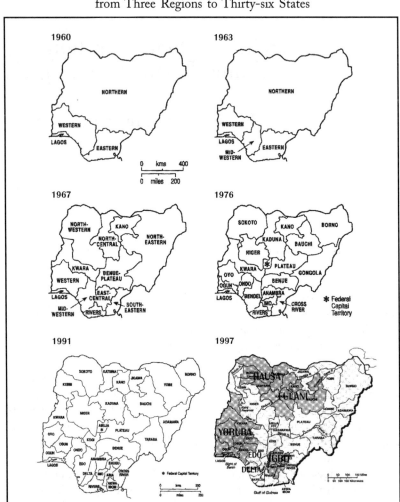

Source: Adapted from the *Atlas of African Affairs* by Leuan L. I. Griffins 1994

that "would enable each linguistic group not only to develop its peculiar culture and institutions but also to move forward without being unnecessarily pushed or annoyingly slowed down by others" (quoted in *African News* (February 14, 1983) 5).

The second argument is that the creation of states might correct the structural imbalance in the Nigeria Federation, and thus create greater stability and enhance the role of the federal government as the protector of minorities. In other words, the creation of states will enhance national unity and stability by removing potential areas of ethnic, religious, and other conflict (Okunmuyide 1996).

Finally, the Irikefe commission on the creation of states rightly concluded that the basic motivation behind the demand for new states is rapid economic development. All other reasons adduced by state agitators can be viewed merely as rationalizations to achieve this goal (Nigeria 1975, 10). This is because the revenue allocation formula employed by the federal government to apportion revenue from the Distributable Pool Account is based approximately one-half on the equality of states and one-half on population. It is the sum that is distributed equally that produces the agitation for more states.

ACCOMODATING CULTURAL PLURALISM

One of the major problems today in Nigeria is interethnic differences and tensions. Noted Nigerian historian Obaro Ikime (1979, 24–25) attributes much of this to colonial rule, as well as to the present practice of creating new states and new local government areas, for every creation throws up its own problems, and generates a new kind of intergroup relationship. It leaves some groups feeling cheated, even as others capitalize on their good fortune. Furthermore, in several countries in Africa and Asia, decentralization programs accomplished precisely the opposite of their stated goals–paradoxically increasing centralization. Nooi (1987), examining the effects of local government reforms in Malaysia, Thailand, Indonesia, Nigeria, Sudan, and Zambia, concludes that while local autonomy or democracy has been identified as the objective of restructuring in each country, instead, the centralization of power has increased. Thus any study of boundary making must bear in mind these problems and offer suggestions as to how these may be tackled.

Cultural pluralists are committed to the view that federalism mitigates ethnic rivalry and tension, since the federal form of association facilitates structural changes within the component units. But the Nigerian experience reveals that decentralization is a complex, contradictory, and constantly evolving policy strategy. Therefore, the creation of states and localities should not be considered a "quick fix," nor can it be expected to solve all of the country's administrative, political, and economic problems. According to Rondinelli and Nellis (1986, 20):

Decentralization must be viewed more realistically, however, not as a general solution to all the problems of underdevelopment, but rather as one of the range of administrative or organizational devices that may improve the efficiency, effectiveness, and responsiveness of various levels of government under *suitable conditions.* (emphasis added)

Rotimi Suberu (1966, 68–69) made an excellent point when arguing for a genuine decentralization program in Nigeria that would encompass both political and economic devolution. Politically, it would not only give minority communities the autonomy and security they needed to protect their rights from being eroded by the bigger ethnic groups, but it would divest the central government of many of its current "extraneous" responsibilities, thus transforming a barely concealed unitary system into a more authentic federation. Economically, he advocated a revenue-sharing arrangement that would not only devolve greater resources to the subnational authorities but would give greater weight to internal revenue generation efforts among these authorities. Such horizontal revenue sharing principles, according to him, would reduce the grievances of the oil producing areas and also encourage a greater degree of economic coherence and efficiency among Nigeria's financially anemic states and Local Government Areas (LGAs). The Oil Mineral Producing Area Development Commission (OMPADEC) was the most strategic intervention in this regard, but it has remained virtually moribund since its inception.

Although the Nigerian government's strategy for accommodating cultural pluralism has been to carve the country into a number of states and localities, the fact is that ethnicity still plays a major role in Nigerian politics (Nnoli 1995, 172). The problem of interethnic relations is significant, not only because it is a great stumbling block to the practice of democracy and peaceful coexistence among the ethnic groups, but also because it poses a potentially serious threat to the political stability of Nigeria as a country. Social relations (including ethnic relations) are unevenly distributed, so that political stability is ensured through domination.

According to Olzak and Nagel (1986), a political system can promote competition among ethnicities by adopting policies that emphasize ethnic differences based on shifts in administrative boundaries or policies that may create new ethnic boundaries. But the perception of unfairness in terms of differential access to the reward structure or the discriminatory allocation of resources to the different populations often increases tensions, rivalries, and unrest between groups (BeLanger and Pinard 1991, 448). Therefore, it can be postulated that deliberate changes in the system of reward distribution can contribute to specific changes in ethnic behavior patterns and, depending on the nature of the changes, can allow for more peaceful interethnic interchanges and cooperation or more competitive behavior and conflict (Perry 1995, 170).

The Quest for Political Balance

The problem of ethnic minorities in Nigeria dates back to the colonial era. The constitutional revision of 1947 created a federation of three regions, of which the North was spatially larger than the East and the West combined. At the same time, each of the regions had a majority ethnic group. The majority group of each region provided the bulk of electoral support to a dominant regional political party. The Yoruba came to be closely identified with Action Group (AG) in the West, while the National Council of Nigeria and Conventions (NCNC), which had a national focus at its inception, became an Igbo party in the Eastern Region, and the Northern People's Congress (NPC) received its strongest support among the Hausa/Fulani. The preponderant influence of the ethnic majorities in the politics of the regions caused great anxiety and apprehension among their respective ethnic minorities, because the governments of the three regions embarked on a policy of political oppression and intimidation, as well as economic and cultural discrimination, of the ethnic minorities within their regions.

A new constitutional arrangement, as well as the emergence of new political parties during the 1950s, sparked separatist agitations in several parts of Nigeria. During the constitutional conference of 1957, the three regions' ethnic minorities requested that separate states be created for them within the federation. The requests and agitations, which took the form of state movements, were spearheaded by political organizations. Notable among them were the Mid-West State movement in the Western Region, the Calaber-Ogoja-Rivers State movement in the Eastern Region, and the United Middle Belt-Congress movement in northern Nigeria. In response to these mobilizations, the 1958 Willink Commission was set up to inquire into "minority fears" and the means of allaying them.

The commission rejected their requests for the creation of states despite their popular support, in the belief that their creation would initiate fresh "minority problems." While the commission rejected the creation of states based solely on ethnic criteria, it did recommend taking some measures to balance political power within each region so that a majority would be less tempted to use power solely for its own advantage. These measures included the adoption of a unified police force, the insertion of fundamental human rights into the Constitution, the central control of prisons, and the establishment of an electoral body to handle the conduct of elections at both the federal and regional levels. After due consultation with the leaders of major delegations, the secretary for the colonies told the constitutional conference that the demand for new states was incompatible with the request for political independence and then agreed to insert state creation into the Independence Constitution (Nigeria 1958, 21–24).

The provisions of this constitution proved inadequate to safeguard the rights and interests of minorities. Given the political development that characterized the first Republic, there were renewed agitations for separate states. The opportunity came during the crisis in the Western Region when the NPC and NCNC wanted to extend their influence by weakening their mutual opponent, the AG Party, which controlled the Western Region (from which the Mid-West Region was created). The NCNC also wanted to reward the local head of the NCNC, Chief Osadebay. Together they helped create the Mid-West Region in 1963, following a plebiscite conducted that same year.

The creation of the Mid-West Region, while giving satisfaction to ethnic minority inspirations in the old Western Region, left the country's other minority problems substantially unresolved. It also intensified the overall imbalance in the structure of the federation (Suberu 1998). It is ironic that while the NCNC and the NPC actively supported the creation of the Mid-West Region (to protect minority interests in the Western Region), they fiercely opposed the creation of both the Calabar, Ogoja, River (COR) State (for the South-Eastern and Rivers peoples in the east), and the Middle Belt State (for minorities in the north).

In May 1967, when Nigeria's first constitution had been virtually nullified by two bloody military coups, and when it looked very likely that the Eastern Region might secede from the federation, Colonel Yakubu Gowon, then Head of State, promulgated a decree dissolving the four regions and replacing them with twelve states. One motive was to preempt Colonel Ojukwu's attempt to secede from the federation by giving minorities of the South-Eastern and Rivers Areas the right to manage their own affairs independently of the Igbo, who dominated the East Central State. Three days after Colonel Gowon's announcement of the new states, Colonel Ojukwu announced that the Eastern Region was seceding from Nigeria and that, henceforth, the old "Eastern Region" would be known as the Republic of Biafra.

The question of state creation was again raised by General Murtala Muhammed when he appointed the Irikefe Panel Commission to advise on the possibility of creating more states. Even though the panel thought the effect of additional states on overall national development would be neutral, it supported more states in the interest of political stability. Such new political entities were necessary to help foster participatory democracy, which ultimately is the bedrock of political stability.

The 1979 Constitution of the Second Republic provided detailed procedures for the creation of new states, and on February 3, 1979, General Muhammed announced the creation of seven new states, bringing the total number of states to nineteen. Two more states were added by Babangida's administration in 1987. On the eve of the collapse of the Second Republic, about thirty-eight requests for the creation of additional states had been received and processed by the National Assembly. Its Conference Committee subsequently recommended fifteen of these for referendum (Federal Republic of Nigeria 1979, 169). Then, in 1991, General Babangida's administration created nine additional states, which brought the total to thirty. He also expanded the number of local government areas (LGAs) from 301 in 1984, to 449 in 1989, and then to 589 in 1991. In 1997, General Abacha, following in the tradition of his military predecessors, created an additional six states and 182 more local governments (*West Africa* 1996, 1549). This brought the total number of states in the Nigerian Federation to thirty-six and the number of local government administrations to 771 (see Fig. 11.1).

As a result of these reorganizations, certain problems have become apparent. The initial establishment of a twelve-state structure in 1967 consolidated the unity of Nigeria at a critical period in the country's history. Since then, state creation has developed its own dynamics, becoming a self-perpetuating process over which various administrations have had little control. General Abacha's strategy for stopping the agitation for more states seems to have consisted of his extraordinary directive that the federal government would not allocate any special takeoff monies, federal grants, or assistance to the six states that he created. This was a major policy and strategy reversal on the modalities and convention for the creation of states. Rather, he insisted that the elites who clamored for the states should raise funds to provide the much-needed infrastructure for their takeoff. This remained his position until he died suddenly in 1998.

The subsequent military administration firmly excluded any further creation of states, but that has not stopped further agitations for more states. Even the rigid 1979 constitutional provisions for state creation were unable to prevent further agitations for more state and local governments from local elites and their representatives at the federal level. In addition, the creation of states and localities has been used by the various governments in Nigeria to create a political support base for their respective regimes. It is ironic that even the return to democratic politics has not stopped further agitations to reconfigure the political structure of the country.

POLITICS OF ECONOMIC DEVELOPMENT

The most remarkable thing about the agitations that preceded the 1991 and 1996 state creations is the prominence attached to the principle of accelerated development. It is this which may explain why Bendel State was divided into Edo and Delta states. Both major political parties in the Second Republic, the Unity Party of Nigeria (UPN) and the National Party of Nigeria (NPN), as well as others supported the creation of three states out of the former Bendel State—Delta, Edo, and Anioma states. The popular argument was development radiates from administrative headquarters, and that the more centers that exist, the faster the rate of national development. This view became pervasive after 1975, when the Irikefe Panel defined as one of the cardinal goals of the 1976 state creation exercise the need to promote accelerated, even development. The requests for all nine states created in 1991 and the six created in 1996 were predicated on the need for accelerated development.

The adoption of the Distributive Pool Revenue Allocation Formula and the principle of Federal Characters in 1979, both of which allocate federal appointments and resources on a state basis, made it expedient for communities, which had opposed state creation for fear of ethnic domination (such as the Itsekiri, Ekiti, Afenmai, and Esan communities), to abandon their position. Under the new arrangement, a state that was divided had its share of the national cake upgraded by the ratio of the number of states in the Federation. In contrast, a state that was left intact had its own share reduced. Consequently, the larger ethnic groups that had fought against the division of their state in the past were now willing to campaign for the fragmentation of their territories.

The defunct Bendel State represented a classic case of a state that was being disadvantaged by remaining intact. The strategy of sharing the national cake was needed to ensure the federal character of Nigeria. Federal employment and college and school admissions were allocated on the basis of state quotas. As new centers of growth and development were engineered in other parts of the country, through the state creation exercise, Bendel State received progressively less of the national cake. Worse still, Bendel suffered declining revenues from the "distributive pool," while federal revenues to the former western region for infrastructure rose from 8.33 percent in 1970 to 15.79 percent in 1976. This occurred for the simple reason that three states had been created out of one entity. During the same period, the revenue of Bendel state declined from 8.33 percent to 5.36 percent (Ministry of Information 1999). Bendel state, as one of nineteen states, could not hope to receive the same percentage of federally collected revenue as when it was one of four regions (1963–1967) or one of twelve states (1967–1976). Splitting Bendel State into two states was, therefore, a welcome and much-awaited political development.

Little attention has been paid to the economic viability of the newly created states, that is, to their ability to generate substantial internal revenue and consequently establish a certain degree of autonomy. Diamond (1987, 211) argued that the greater the number of states, the weaker and less viable individual states would become, with the direct consequence that the center would actually gather more power and initiative. This has in fact occurred in Nigeria, especially during the long years of military rule. This trend was likely helped by the federal government's control of the oil wealth, which has increased its distributive power. This has serious implications for the fiscal autonomy of state and local governments. Since the states and LGAs are the legitimate units of distribution, the ethnic groups clamor for more of these administrative units in order to receive more federal government benefits.

However, the various state agitators, when pressing their demands, typically stress common historical origins that are believed to contribute some degree of sociocultural unity. For instance, the supporters of the Anioma State movement told the government: "We are a homogeneous and indivisible entity within the present Bendel State and our long-standing demand for recognition for our geopolitical and cultural identity dates back to at least 1938 and in brief is informed by obvious affinities of a common language, a common culture and geographical continuity" (*Sunday Times* August 18, 1991, 15). In their request for the creation of Afemesa State (out of the present Edo State), the agitators also stressed their common sociocultural and historical background: "The proposed State, in spite of a few local dialectal variations, is a homogenous entity, made up of people, who are predominately Edo-speaking. . . . The people of Afenmai and Esan have had a long history of living together as one people under various administrative arrangements and expediencies" (Afemsan State Committee 1996, 2). Despite the bitter rivalry and tension between the Urhobo and Itsekiri communities, the advocates of Delta State also saw the need to inform the government: "There is age-long strong cultural linkage among various ethnic groups of the Old Delta Province, namely the Ijaws, Ndokwas, Isokos, Itsekiris and the Urhobos including widespread in the intermarriages"(*Sunday Times* June 14, 1987, 17). No one would argue that ethnicity is now absent from Nigerian politics. Since nearly every large ethnic group in the country had already gotten its own state by 1976, later state creation is seen not as a result of minority demands but of "marginal" demands, based on economic rather than ethnic interests.

Other factors, however, have contributed to make the aspiration for state creation irresistible. Some have argued that the primary motive for creating new states in Nigeria is based on calculations of self-interest by the ruling elites, directed solely toward maximizing their political and economic advantages. According to Graf, "the issue of state creation, affecting as it does both the immediate concerns of the population for material well-being and the sensitive areas of their self-esteem, identity and aspirations, here presents itself as an optimal ideological means of further entrenching elite rule" (1988, 146). Thus state creation presents the Nigerian elite, who have been excluded from traditional government appointment, with an opportunity to carve out spheres of influence for themselves. In addition to being governors in the new states, there would be numerous patronage possibilities in a new state bureaucracy, a multiplicity of advisory bodies and parastals, a judicial system, a state legislature, and delegates to the federal legislature. Hence, Nnoli argued:

The most ardent advocates of new states or regions have always been aspirants to high positions . . . who have failed to attain positions of prominence at the national, regional, [and] state levels and also hope to attain such heights in smaller constitutional entities. They rationalize their inordinate ambitions by pleading reason of national unity (1978, 161).

The restructuring of the Nigerian Federation was in no way based on an attempt to produce a fundamental socioeconomic transformation of the society. Rather, it emphasized the redistributive aspect of development. This is characteristic of the Nigerian elite: they prefer to rely on the manipulation of distributive processes rather than on production (Nnoli 1978). The irony of the Nigerian situation is that in spite of this territorial fragmentation the major ethnic groups (Hausa and Fulani, Yoruba, and Igbo) still dominate twenty-three of the thirty-six states and continue to demonstrate collective solidarity when competing in national politics. According to Bach, "the creation of states and the development of 'statism' have added—and not substituted—new patterns of cleavages to the preexisting ones" (Bach 1989, 234).

THE CREATION OF BENDEL STATE AND ITS ETHNIC RELATIONS

As we reflect on the dynamics of regional and state segmentation in the Federal Republic of Nigeria, the following process seems to be at work. The constitutional division of Nigeria into regions was an attempt to harmonize the ethnic pluralism of Nigerian society. The segmentation of the regions into states seemed to be a desperate attempt to save the Federal Republic of Nigeria from fragmentation into several sovereign states, when one of the regions decided to break away as the sovereign state of Biafra. In order to take a closer look at the complex nature of the problem, we will now examine the creation of Bendel State and its ethnic composition. Then we will discuss how these ethnic groups formed the basis for the agitation for Anioma State and for LGAs in Delta.

Sometimes the driving force in the rise of separatism is the urge of ethnic minorities to assert themselves vis-à-vis the major ethnic groups. In the Mid-West Region, the Yorubas were linguistically different and a major ethnic group. The agitation to create a Mid-West State dated back to 1947, when nationalist forces were organized to combat the "objectionable features" of the Richard Constitution. But it was not until 1948 that the Reformed Benin Community was formed to advocate separation. At the regional conference held in Ibadan in 1950 to discuss the Richard Constitution, representatives of the Benin and Delta provinces demanded a separate state. The Mid-West delegates complained to the 1957 Willink Commission about cultural and economic discrimination by dominant Yoruba ethnic groups. Specifically, they noted two problems with the regional government. First, its actions indicated a deliberate intention of obliterating the separate culture and institutions of the Mid-West, while it took no steps to preserve the legacy of the Benin Empire. Second, it was spending enormous sums of money on the development, production, and research of cocoa, while rubber, palm, and timber, grown in the Mid-West, were neglected. Regarding discrimination in the provision of public services, deliberate neglect of the Mid-West in the matter of roads, water supplies, hospitals, and schools was brought to the attention of the Commission.

The Willink Commission rejected the creation of a Mid-West Region but recognized the need to allow areas with distinguishable cultures within the region to preserve the elements of their cultures. Thus each of the designated minority areas, such as Edo, was to have a representative council to monitor the sociocultural progress of its area (Nigeria 1958, 96). The Mid-West Region (formed on August 9, 1963) was the first post–independence region to be created in Nigeria. It then became a state—one of the twelve states created on May 27, 1967, and it remained one of the nineteen states created in 1976—the only difference was that its name was changed to Bendel State. When the Federation was split further, into twenty-one states, in 1987, it was left intact and became the oldest state in Nigeria. Then, on August 27, 1991, when General Babangida increased the number of states to thirty, it was divided into Edo and Delta states. As one of the four regions, Bendel State's share of the national cake was one-fourth. This was reduced first to one-twelfth, later to one-nineteenth, and finally to one-twenty-first, before Bendel was split into two.

According to ethnologists, Bendel State was part of the Benin Empire, from where most of the component parts derived their origin. At the height of that empire, its boundaries extended to the present Benin Republic to the west, by encroaching upon the Yoruba-speaking areas, and to the east, by embracing many of the Igbo-speaking peoples west of the river Niger. The various ethnic communities of Bendel State include the Afenmais, Binis, Urhobos, Ijaws, Itsekiris, Isokos, Ishans, Ndokwas, and Igbos, all of whom migrated from Benin (see Figure 11.2). Even though several of these groups now speak a number of different languages, they retain similar customs, beliefs, and cultures, as manifested in their festivals, religious beliefs, diet, dress, marriages, ceremonies, traditions of kinship, and chieftaincy titles. Bendel State was estimated to have a population of well over 5 million when it was divided into two states, and a cursory look reveals that the dominant group is the Edo-speaking people (Bradbury 1973).

The majority of the people occupying the eastern flank of Bendel are Igbo-speaking. The Western Igbos and Onitsha in the east make various claims to Edo (Benin Kingdom) origin. During the reign of Esigie (c. 1520–1540), Bini

Figure 11.2 Ethnic Groups in Defunct Bendel State

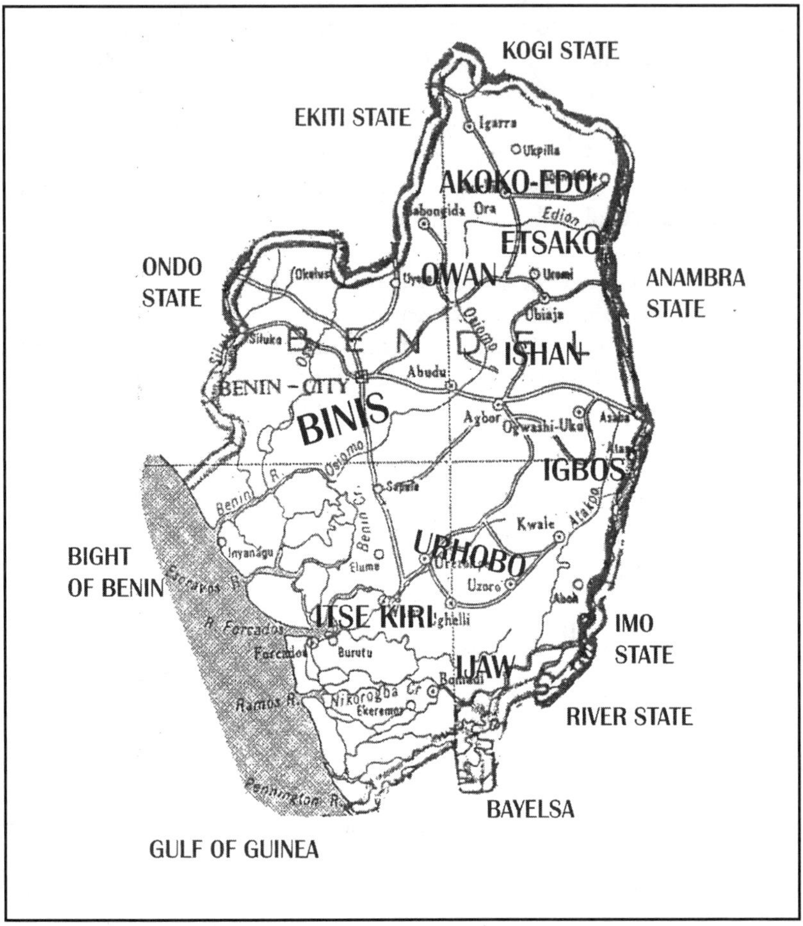

Source: Nigeria Federal Republic. 1978. *Official Handbook.* Lagos: Ministry of Information Publications, 19.

immigrants founded many communities, including Agbor, Isselle-Uku, Aboh, and Onitsha, which are described as Eboi country. They later developed many Igbo traditions and customs as a result of intermarriage with their neighbors across the Niger. The Itsekiri community in the Niger Delta speaks a dialect of Yoruba, though it includes a number of words borrowed from Edo, Portuguese, English, and other European languages (because of its early contact with these people). Both Itsekiri and Benin legends tell of Ginuwa, a Benin Prince, who traveled inland with a retinue of nobles (c. 1475) to found Warri, the capital of Itsekiriland. However, there is evidence from both oral and written sources to support the existence of political, commercial, cultural, ancestral, and even linguistic links between the various groups in the state. These cultural similarities are the product of the inter-relatedness of the people. However, in spite of the many languages and dialects, the people have enjoyed a long and stable period of historical, political, cultural, and socioeconomic relationships. Invariably, they have a myth of traditional significance that connects them to the Benin Kingdom.

Bendel State is generally perceived to be a microcosm of Nigeria because of the apparent complexity and diversity of subcultures. During Governor Samuel Ogbemudia's administration, Bendel had about twenty local government areas that were almost equal in size. This made the equitable distribution of resources relatively easy to work out. An equal number of roads were identified to be tarred in each of the local government areas every year, and the locations of cottage hospitals and modern school buildings also followed the same principle. Notwithstanding the economic waste inherent in the system, it worked admirably well for maintaining social and political stability (A. P. Sanda 1985). Another factor in the state's political stability was that no single group was large enough to hold another ransom, which meant shifting political alliances and the need to be very accommodating. Hence, in spite of its ethnic diversity, Bendel managed to hold its ethnic communities together and to create a durable identity and sense of statehood.

ETHNIC RELATIONS IN BENDEL STATE:
AGITATION FOR ANIOMA STATE

The request for Anioma State was presented to the National Assembly in March 1980 after the publication of a booklet, *The Case for the Creation of Anioma State*. Arguing for the creation of the Anioma State, Senator Nosike Ikpo, chairman of the movement for the state, said the request was based on a search for an identity for Bendel Igbos, for whereas the Eastern Igbos regarded the Western Igbos (Anioma) as Bendelites, non-Igbo-speaking Bendelites regarded them as Igbos (*Daily Times*, July 10, 1981, 14). The proposed state was to include the local government areas in the eastern flank of the state (i.e., Osimili, Ika, Aniocha, and Ndokwa).

In spite of the apparent homogeneity of the ethnic communities involved in the agitation for Anioma State (the majority were "Igbo-speaking" people), they exhibited both intraethnic and interethnic competition regarding who was to be included or excluded from the proposed state. The Lagos-based Ukwuani Society condemned as erroneous and ridiculous the idea that the Ukwuani are Igbos. It appears that the Ukwuani Society's opposition to the inclusion of Ndokwa in the Anioma State stemmed from the desire to be regarded as "non-Igbo" and to be disassociated from a movement purportedly advancing the interests of the Igbo-speaking areas of Bendel State. The people's claim to separate identity, although Igbo-speaking, is not unconnected, given the events of the civil war, during which their allegiance and sympathy for the federal military government were in question. This situation made it necessary for them to address a memo on their "non-Igbo" identity to the federal military government in July 1967 (*Daily Times*, March 25, 1978, 6). They preferred the security provided by a multiethnic state, but in another release, published in July 1980, a committee of Ndokwa citizens attributed their hostility to Anioma State to the wrong approach adopted by the protagonists of the state who took for granted that Ndokwa LGA could be associated with the state without taking their views into consideration. It noted with happiness that a change of heart had occurred in the agitators for the Anioma State, and that this change augured well for the realization of the proposed state. Although opinion was divided on the issue, a vast majority of Ndokwa people had unequivocally embraced the agitators on one fundamental condition that it felt constrained to publicize: the state's capital should be located at Kwale, the headquarters of Ndokwa LGA (*Daily Times*, August 23, 1980, 6).

The revenue allocation system in the Second Republic reserved a percentage of the national revenue to mineral- and oil-producing states. Ndokwa LGA was the only oil-producing area in the proposed state and, hence, its allocation from the federal government would have had to sustain the proposed state. It was obvious, therefore, that the attitude of the Ndokwa people was motivated by several considerations, including the question of leadership and the distribution of future benefits in the proposed state. The State Creation Committee could see that the Ndokwas, having emphasized their separate and non-Igbo identity, were comparatively not as anxious as the Osimili, Ika, and Aniocha local government areas to be excised from Bendel. Instead, the Ndokwas were focused on the benefits that could accrue to their area if it was included in the proposed state.

The Ika, another ethnic group that opposed the plan to create the state, also did so over the issue of where to place the capital. In a memo addressed to the Senate Committee on State Creation, an Ika Division Union expressed shock and dismay over the proposed selection of Kwale as the capital, for in its view it was completely out of consonance with the choice of the Anioma people. The memo also claimed that an earlier decision to locate the capital in Anioma City, a spot central to the four LGAs, had been confirmed in May 1981 and again in January 1983, when the Senate and the House of Representatives visited the area. It therefore appealed to the Senate to remove the issue, threatening that Ika people were prepared to pull out of the proposed state and remain in Bendel if Anioma City was not chosen as the capital. The move to restore Anioma City as the capital was rebuffed by the Ndokwa

Tactical Committee, which reaffirmed the "special position" of the Ndokwas in the proposed state, noting that without the Ndokwas, Anioma State would not be viable. The Senate's approval of Kwale as the capital was a victory for the Ndokwas; as the oil-producing area, it was difficult, if not impossible, to refuse their request.

While the Ndokwas were busy consolidating their position, another opposition to the movement emerged from the Isoko committees in Ndokwa LGA, which expressed surprise and embarrassment that, contrary to their wishes, the whole area inhabited by Isoko-speaking communities was put in Anioma. They had made their stand unequivocally clear in a memorandum submitted to the National Assembly Committee on the creation of states on April 23, 1981. They alleged that Ndokwa leaders had given them the impression that they were in support of Delta State, only to discover later that Ndokwa leaders had signed requests both for Anioma and Delta states but secretly had thrown their support behind Anioma. The Isoko viewed this action as a calculated act of bad faith and trickery, and as a result, they strongly demanded to be excluded from the proposed state. They also argued that they were a distinct people, whose language and culture were at variance with Anioma (*Daily Times* April 21, 1983, 15). The smallest ethnic group in the area of the proposed state, the Isoko, understandably was reluctant to be included in a state dominated by the western Igbos, particularly, as the petition suggested, since no effort was made to protect their interests. The strongest factor responsible for the hostility of the Isoko, however, would appear to have been a desire to be united with the Isoko of Isoko LGA, who opted for the proposed Delta State.

Even the agitators for Anioma State failed to agree on whether or not the Onitsha LGA, across the Niger River, should be incorporated into Anioma. In a document signed by His Highness Obi R. P. Onjetemu (The Asagba of Asaba), his chiefs and representatives of the various Asaba quarters requested, in June 1981, that their people in the Onitsha LGA be included in Anioma for purposes of stability and balance in the state. The request was justified because of cultural, social, economic, and political associations that had existed between them from time immemorial. This situation, it was further claimed, placed the Onitsha in Anambra on the same footing with Asaba in Bendel, that is, as fellow sufferers (*Daily Times* November 10, 1980, 8–9). The Obi of Iselle-Uku, the traditional Head of the Ezechime clan, also supported the inclusion of the Onitsha in the proposed Anioma State because of the socioeconomic and manpower benefits that they were bringing into the new state (*Daily Times* November 10, 1980, 8–9).

The stands of both the Asaba and the Ezechime were criticized by the Ika Division Union and the Ndokwa Tactical Committee. The former even threatened to seek appropriate constitutional remedies should the Ika be stampeded into an unholy association. If sections of the Anioma differed over the inclusion of the Onitsha in Anioma State, the Anioma State movement, as a body, was united in its opposition to the inclusion of the Onitsha. The National Assembly, therefore, was petitioned to reject the request to include the Onitsha, because Onitsha had no genuine need to join Anioma State. Notwithstanding the fact that this protest memo was signed by Senator Nosike Ikpo, National Chairman of Anioma's four LGAs, about forty traditional rulers from various LGAs presented a counter-memo to the Senate affirming support for the inclusion of the Onitsha in the proposed state. Underlying the disagreement was a desire of the traditional rulers, who had been banned from partisan politics during the Second Republic, to neutralize the power and influence of the leaders of the Anioma State movement. Meanwhile, the latter, who were mainly politicians, businessmen, academicians, professionals, and civil servants, wanted to exclude the Onitsha people to gain political power, administrative and government positions, and contracts in the new state. In June 1983, the Joint Conference Committee of the National Assembly adopted a resolution for the creation of twenty-eight states. Two of these were Anioma and New Anambra. The former included the Osimili, Aniocha, Ndokwa, and Ika LGAs. The latter included the Onitsha LGA and had Onitsha as its capital (*Daily Times* February 9, 1983, 1). Had the states been created, the bitterness that characterized the struggles for their creation would have had an adverse effect on the successful evolution of the states, and their ethnic relations.

ETHNIC RELATIONS IN DELTA STATE: CONFLICT BETWEEN THE ITSEKIRIS AND IJAWS OVER THE CREATION OF LOCAL GOVERNMENT AREAS (LGAs)

Delta State was created in 1991 from the former Bendel State, and its capital was located in the Osimili LGA, at Asaba—the hometown of the wife of General Babangida, the former head of the Nigerian government. The Itsekiris and Urhobos, who agitated for the creation of the state, wanted the capital to be Warri, a cosmopolitan oil city of strategic importance to Nigeria's economy whose populace is largely Urhobo, Itsekiri, and Ijaw. These three major ethnic groups have lived together for so long that they have developed mixed marriages and parentage. However, in spite of these close blood ties, Warri has experienced interethnic competition and conflicts between these ethnic groupings. The conflict usually was between the Urhobos, who were the majority ethnic group in the proposed Delta State, and the Itsekiris, who were the overlords (Ikime 1969).

But in 1997, fighting broke out between the Ijaws and the Itsekiris over the creation of a new LGA. At its inception, Delta had twelve LGAs, but within a month, the number was increased to nineteen; at present, there are twenty-five (see Figure 11.3). The Ijaws usually have been regarded as set-

Figure 11.3 Twenty-Five Local Government Areas and Ethnic Groups in Delta State

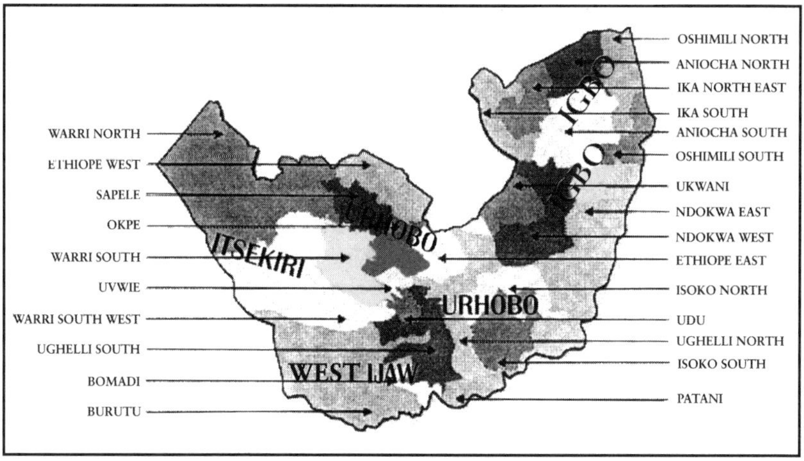

Source: "Local Government Areas and Ethnic Groups in Delta State" at http://www.deltastate.gov.ng/fact%main%20page.htm.

tlers, or "itinerant fishermen" and "market-stall holders," and they are found mostly within the settlements of Ogbe-Ijoh, Egbeoma, and Gbaramatu. The Itsekiris, who claimed to be landowners, spearheaded the call for new local government councils, arguing that dividing the old Warri local authority into two LGAs would bring them a larger allocation of federal funds and more assistance from oil companies. So, in 1991, Warri was divided into Warri North and Warri South LGAs. This made the Itsekiris an even smaller minority in their traditional homelands, and the attempt to remedy this created a bloody and disastrous ethnic crisis. The fighting stemmed from an incompetent attempt by the government to bring greater development by giving into demands for the creation of more LGAs. A few weeks before the 1997 local government elections, the military administrator of Delta State, Colonel John Dungs, announced that a new Warri Central local government with two wards would be carved out of Warri North and Warri South. The three wards excised from Warri South were mainly inhabited by the Ijaws, and the two excised from Warri North were mainly inhabited by the Itsekiris. The administrator's announcement was badly timed, as the election campaign in the existing LGAs had generated rivalry and bitterness among the ethnic groups. It also seemed to be unplanned, as the headquarters of the new local government area were to be in the government reservation area of the city—the heart of the existing Warri North LGA. A few days before the election, the administrator announced that the headquarters of Warri Central LGA would be at Ogbe Ijoh (Itsekiri for "the Ijaw quarters"). With Colonel Dungs' announcement, the Ijaws began to celebrate what they perceived as a victory, granting them control over the LGA.

The Itsekiris, in response, petitioned the administrator, who then announced that elections in the new LGA would be postponed, and that the headquarters would be moved to Ogidigben, a remote Itsekiri town. Ijaw wards would be further divided into nine, giving them a preponderance of councilors, while there were still just two Itsekiri wards—the Itsekiri were granted the headquarters and thus should be satisfied. The immediate result of the readjustment was violence between the Ijaws and the Itsekiris. The Itsekiris' protest march turned into a riot that killed more than sixty people in Warri City itself, and the house of a prominent Ijaw leader, Chief Edwin Kiagbodo Bekederereno-Clark, was burned, and some occupants were killed (*African Confidential*, 3–4). The conflict spread unremittingly into remote riverine creeks and estuaries, and it was reported that young Ijaws kidnapped oil workers and cut down oil installations in the creeks. They were said to have rocket launchers, grenades, and light assault rifles. The oil minister, Dan Etete, an Ijaw, warned that those fighting would face the military if they did not halt their attacks on oil installations. Many Itsekiris interpreted the minister's statement as federal support for Ijaw attempts to establish a permanent hold over territories where they traditionally had been tenants.

The fighting between the Ijaws and the Itsekiris in Warri threatened to halt oil production in Nigeria's most lucrative fields. It is estimated that more than one-third of Nigeria's onshore oil production is in the Warri region, or nearby (*African Confidential* May 9, 1987, 3–4). It is the site of one of the nation's three refineries, some of Shell's major storage and service installations, and the only petro-chemical plant in southern Nigeria. It also has the Aladja Steel Mill and a deep-water river port. In addition, the Warri district provided, as reported by *The Guardian* (April 28, 1997), no less than 60 percent of the internal revenue of Delta State. Therefore, a prolonged crisis definitely would undermine the budgetary projections and hamper the overall progress of the state. The fighting did not merely disrupt the oil industry, but many markets were burned down, and the agricultural activities of ordinary people were halted. The federal government was worried about oil, but for the average Ijaw, Itsekiri, or Urhobo, the oil industry could close down without making much difference in their lives. This situation in the oil-producing areas engendered alienation, frustration, and hopelessness, which encouraged the communities to resort to desperate, and sometimes anarchic, behavior.

A federal government's peace mission, under the leadership of the then Chief of Naval Staff, Rear Admiral Mike Akhighe, who was sent to assess the problem, was not impressed by the way local officials handled the issue, hence, the federal government appointed a Judicial Commission of Inquiry to look into the crisis and make recommendations.

The Ijaws found themselves increasingly marginalized in the struggle for development, even though they claimed to be Nigeria's fourth largest ethnic group. Their traditional areas around Burutu, Forcados, and other remote villages deep in the Delta had been incorporated into three mainly Ijaw LGAs, but oil companies had invested most heavily in Warri. The Ijaws have become convinced that they are the victims rather than the beneficiaries of the oil industry.

The Itsekiris, although few, were the overlords in the Niger Delta, because they were related to the Benin royal dynasty and because they were well armed (a result of being allied to the European traders). "In modern times the Itsekiris rely on diplomacy and alliances with the federal powers to hold onto their status in the Delta" (*African Confidential*, 1997, 3–4). Another contention among these ethnic groups is nonrecognition by the Urhobos and Ijaws of the Olu (King) of Warri as the traditional ruler of the entire region. They consider him to be only the Olu of Itsekiris. The present Olu of Warri, Atuwatse II, has been accused by some Ijaws not only of being biased and parochial but also of ignoring their grievances. They claim that while they supported his people in their quarrels with the Urhobos, their other neighbors (the Olu), have supported the Itsekiris in marginalizing them. The Itsekiris deny any desire to dominate anyone but conclude that the administrators' LGA restructuring exercise was planned to marginalize them, which they perceived as unfair. In the confusion, it became clear that Nigeria's economy was threatened by ethnic disturbances in the Niger Delta.

The involvement of the masses of Ijaws and Itsekiris in the conflict at the local level deserves some explanation. The restructuring of the local-level state institutions must be linked not just to changes in state-societal relations as a whole but also to changes in the overall form of capitalist social relations. The whole state creation exercise in the country is a product of the Nigerian state's underdevelopment and its floundering attempts to reconcile the contradictions of "accumulation and development" under the tutelage of international capitalism. The newly introduced political units in the Delta brought about all sorts of differentials and disharmonies. Obaro Ikime (1969, 25) argued that the differences in sociopolitical institutions between various ethnic areas often are used as an index of development, or lack of it, resulting in different treatment being meted out to each group, thereby creating new tensions among the ethnic communities. A prominent Ijaw leader, Chief Oromoni, asserted that the relocation could only have been done to further the political interest of the Itsekiris while undermining the interest of the Ijaw clans (*The Guardian* March 30, 1997, 3). According to Ikime, even if these administrative restructurings at the local level may be necessary, and ultimately beneficial to the groups, the government must enter into a close and even a prolonged dialogue with the people whose welfare it is its business to promote and protect. In Delta, the state military government did not measure up to that expectation, and its poor handling of the crisis, which likely changed the various types of resources, opportunities, expectations and perceptions of the inequities in the area, generated even more conflict between these two ethnic communities. Furthermore, given the history of mutual suspicion in the area, it was provocative to arbitrarily create and recreate, within three months, the same local council for the Itsekiri and the Ijaw communities.

CONCLUSION AND RECOMMENDATION

This chapter seeks to explain the phenomenon of state creation in the Federal Republic of Nigeria. Furthermore, it also examines the ethnic relations triggered by state creation in the multiethnic society of Nigeria. When the federal government conceded to demands for states from ethnic minorities, the majority ethnic groups demanded the segmentation of their more populous states in order to ensure an egalitarian distribution of federal government resources. Thus state creation became a never-ending process. The 288 ethnic groups of the country have so far been lumped into thirty-six states. The process of state creation has not only generated bitterness and ill feeling among the ethnic communities (about who was to be included or excluded in the proposed states), but each state-creation exercise has initiated fresh minority problems by playing up differences among communities, which were constituted into new states. Divisiveness and the inability to coexist are reasons stressed by communities to justify the creation of new states and LGAs. Underlying the conflicts were issues such as the location of new capitals; control of economic and political power among ethnic groups; the desire to escape from actual and anticipated economic rivalry or domination; and the preservation of ethnic identity and cultural affinity.

The ethnic disharmony caused by state creation in Nigeria has been replicated in Bendel State, in which eight ethnic groups were lumped together from 1963 to 1991. The segmentation of Bendel into Edo and Delta states seems to coincide with the problems involved in the creation of states in Nigeria nationwide, especially with regard to the ethnic rivalries and conflicts. The above case study demonstrates that there is no end in sight to the demands for more administrative units. The evidence suggests that the ethnic harmony and federal unity envisaged in espousing these measures have been compromised, if not totally undermined. Ethnic relations have escalated from being conflictual to violent. The rivalry between the Ijaws and the Itsekiris shows how territorial rearrangement generates new conflicts and competition over scarce resources, even to the extent of threatening peace and stability in the whole country.

No one can dispute the fact that Nigeria needs a federal form of government, but its experience of federalism provides three basic lessons. First, state creation does not necessarily mean greater equality and freedom for small ethnic groups, for even after creating many new states, the three largest ethnic groups still dominate the politics of the country. Second, the role of the federal government, as the sole owner of the oil resources of Nigeria and the sole distributor of oil wealth to the states and localities, has resulted in economic dependence on the federal government, a dependence that is inimical to economic development. The concentration of authority and resources at the federal level also has created apparent inequity in revenue sharing and intense competition among the federating states and ethnic groups. Even though it is typical of federations to distribute seats and resources, at least in part on the basis of the number of federating units, this can produce a bidding war to get more federal monies. Third, successive Nigerian governments have failed to devise a satisfactory formula for revenue allocation among the federating units. Reform of the revenue sharing formula, which either would give greater weight to the principle of derivation, or greater internal revenue generation powers to the subnational authorities (while at the same time taking into account other principles of population and needs), would be a logical solution for the country. Finally, the government should take measures to revamp its programs targeted at ameliorating the severe condition of economic insecurity in the oil-producing areas. If such measures were followed, it would not only give minority communities their autonomy vis-à-vis the larger ethnic groups, but it also would discourage the fissiparous tendencies that now seem inherent in the Nigerian Federation.

REFERENCES

Adejuyigbe, O. 1979. "Rationale and Effect of State Creation with Reference to the 19 States." Pp. 190–222 in *Redirecting on Federalism*, ed. A. B. Akinjemi, P. D. Cole, and Ofonagoro. Lagos: NIIA.

Adejuyigbe, Omolade, Leo Dare and Adepoju Adeventi, eds. 1982. *Creation of States in Nigeria: Review of Behavioral Demands and Problems up to 1980*. Lagos: Federal Government Printer.

Afemsan State Committee. 1996. *Request Document*. Auchi: Government Press.

Akinyele, R. T. 1996. "States Creation in Nigeria: The Willink Report in Retrospect." *African Studies Review* (September): 39: 2.

Anioma State Movement. 1980. *Two Cases for the Creation of Anioma State*. Lagos: Government Press.

Asiodu, Izoma P. C. 1993. "The Political Economy of Fiscal Federalism." *Daily Times* (February 19), 19, 36.

Ayomike, J.O.S. 1993. *Benin and Warri.* Benin City: Ilupeju Press.

Bach, Daniel C. 1989. "Managing a Plural Society: The Boomerang Effects of Nigerian Federalism." *Journal of Commonwealth and Comparative Politics* 27: 219–44.

Barbour, K. M. 1971. "North-Eastern Nigeria: A Case Study of State Formation." *Journal of Modern African Studies* 1: (September): 333-48.

Barth, Frederick, ed. 1969. *Ethnic Groups and Boundaries: The Social Organization of Cultural Differences.* Boston: Little Brown and Company.

Bates, Robert. 1983. "Modernization, Ethnic Competition and the Rationality of Politics in Contemporary Africa." Pp. 152–72 in *State Versus Ethnic Claims: African Policy Dilemmas*, ed. Donald Rothschild and Victor A. Oarunsola. Boulder: Westview Press.

BeLanger, Sarah and Maurice Prinard. 1991. "Ethnic Movements and Competitions Model: Some Missing Links." *American Sociological Review* 56 (August): 446–57.

Benjamin, Soloman Akhere. 1997. "Problems and Prospects of State Creation in Nigeria: The Case of Oyo and Osun States." *NISER Monograph Series* No 9. Ibadan: NISER Press.

Bradbury R. E. 1973. *Benin Streets.* London: Oxford University Press.

Brass, Paul R., ed. 1985. *Ethnic Groups and the State.* London: Crown Helm.

Coleman, James J. 1988. *Nigeria Background to Nationalism.* Berkeley: University of California Press.

Destores, Leo A., ed. 1975. Ethnicity and Resource Competition in Plural Societies. The Hague: Mouton.

Diamond, Larry. 1983. "Class Ethnicity and Democratic State: Nigeria 1958-66." *Comparative Studies in Society and History* 25:3: 467–80.

Diamond, Larry. 1987. "Issues in the Constitutional Design of a Third Nigerian Republic," *African Affairs* 86:3543 (April): 209–26.

Ekek, P. P., and E. E. Osaghae, eds. 1989. *Federal Character and Federalism in Nigeria.* Ibadan: Heinemann.

Federal Republic of Nigeria. 1987. *Report of the Political Bureau.* Lagos: Federal Government Press.

Graf, William. 1988. *The Nigerian State: Political Economy, State Class and Political System in the Post–Colonial Era.* Portsmouth: Heineman.

Griffins, Levan L. I. 1994. *The Atlas of African Affairs.* New York: Routledge.

Horowitz, D. 1984. *Ethnic Groups in Conflict.* Berkeley: University of California Press.

Igharevba, Jacob. 1960. *A Short History of Benin.* Ibadan: Ibadan University Press.

Ikime, Obaro. 1969. *Niger Delta Rivalry.* London: Longman.

———. 1979. "Through Changing Scenes: Nigeria History Yesterday, Today, and Tomorrow." Inaugural Lecture Series. Ibadan: University of Ibadan Press.

———. 1985. "In Search of Nigerians: Changing Patterns of Inter-Group Relations in an Evolving Nation State." Presidential inaugural lecture, delivered at 30th Congress of the Society, May 1.

Imoagne, Oshomha. 1990. *The Edo and the Neighbours of M. Western Nigeria* Ibadan: New Era Publishers.

Karim, Bazlul M. 1991. "Decentralization of Government in the Third World: A Fad or a Panacea?" *International Studies Notes* 6:2: 50-54.

King, Mae C. 1976. "State Creation in Federal System: A Quest for Unity." *West African Journal of Political Science* 2: 1, 2.

Kirk-Greene, A.H.M. 1983. "Ethnic Engineering and the Federal Character of Nigeria: Born of Contentment, or Born of Contention." *Ethnic and Racial Studies* 1: 4 (October): 457–76.

"Local Government Areas and Ethnic Groups in Delta State" at http://www.deltastate.gov.ng/fact%main%20page.htm.

Ministry of Information. 1999. The Visit of the Nigerian Head of State to Edo State, His Excellency, General Abdulsalam Abubakar. Benin City: Government Printing Press.

Nigeria. 1957. *Report by the Nigerian Constitutional Conference.* London: Allen and Urwin.

———. 1958. *Report of the Commission Appointed to Enquire into the Fears of Minorities and the Means of Allaying Them.* London: Willink Commission.

———. 1967. *Nigeria's 12 State Structure: The Only Way Out.* Lagos: Federal Government Printer.

———. 1975. *Report of the Panel Appointed by Federal Military Government to Investigate the Creation of More States and Boundary Adjustment in Nigeria.* Lagos: Federal Government Printer.

Nigeria. 1987. *Nigeria Year Book, 1987.* Lagos: Time Press.

———. 1991. *Official Handbook.* Lagos: Federal Ministry of Information.

Nigeria Federal Republic. 1978. *Official Handbook.* Lagos: Ministry of Information Publications.

Nnoli, O. 1978. *Ethnic* Politics *in Nigeria.* Enugu: Fourth Dimension Publishing.

———. 1995. *Ethnicity and Development.* London: Avebury Press.

Nooi, Phang Siew. 1987. "Local Government Reform: A Comparative Study of Selected Communities in Africa and Southeast Asia." *Planning and Administration* 14:1: 31-38.

Ogbumudia, S.O. 1991. *Fear of Challenge.* Ibadan: Heinemann Educational Books, Nigeria. PLC.

Okpu, U. 1977. *Ethnic Minority Problems in Nigerian Politics:* 1960–1965. Uppsala: Acta Universitatis Uppsaliensis.

———. 1986. "Conflicts in Agitations for More States in the Nigerian Second Republic," *Asia and African Studies* 20: 329–56.

———. 1983. "Nigeria's Dilemma Development on New Starter." *Africa* 38:2: (June): 193–203.

Okunmuyide, R. 1996. "The Confederal Option." *Guardian* (October 3): 4–5.

Olorunsola, Victor, ed. 1972. *The Politics of Cultural-Nationalism in Africa*. Garden City: Doubleday.

Olzak, Susan. 1992. *The Dynamics of Ethnic Competition and Conflict*. Stanford: Stanford University Press, 1-14.

Olzak, Susan, and Joanne Nagel. 1986. "Competitive Ethnic Relations: An Overview." *Competitive Ethnic Relations*. Orlando: Academic Press.

Osaghae, E. E. 1991. "Ethnic Minorities and Federalism in Nigeria." *African Affairs* 90: 237–58.

———. 1995. "True Ogoni Uprising: Oil Politics, Minority Agitation, and the Future of the Nigerian State." *African Affairs* 95: 325–44.

Otite, Onigu. 1990. *Ethnic Pluralism and Ethnicity in Nigeria*. Ibadan: Shaneson.

Perry, Mars. 1995. "State Intervention and Ethnic Conflict Revolution: Guyana and the Caribbean Experience." *Comparative Politics* 27:2 (January): 170.

Roberts, F.O.N. 1997. *Theories of Local Governments and the Nigerian Experience*. NISER Monograph Series. Ibadan: NISER Press.

Rondinelli, Dennis A. 1981. "Government Decentralization in Comparative Perspective Theory and Practices in Developing Countries." *International Review of Administrative Science* 2: 133–45.

———. 1983. "Implementing Decentralization Programs in Asia: A Comparative Analysis." *Public Administration and Development* 3:3: 181-207.

Rondinelli, Dennis A., and John R. Nellis. 1986. "Addressing Decentralization Policies in Developing Countries: The Ease for Countries' Optimism." *Development Policy Review* 4:1: 3-23.

Rothchild, D. C. 1964. "Safeguarding Nigeria Minorities." *Duquisne Review* (spring): 35–51.

Sada, P. O. 1976. *Ethnic Relations in Nigeria*. Ibadan: Caxton Press.

———. 1985. "The Nigerian Twelve State Structure: An Appraisal of Some Aspects of Politico-Geographical Visibility." *Nigerian Geographical Journal* 14: 23–24.

Smith, Brian. 1981. "Federal-State Relations in Nigeria." *Africa Affairs* 80: 373-79.

Suberu, Rotimi T. 1993. "The Travails of Federalism in Nigeria." *Journal of Democracy* 4:4 (October): 39-53.

———. 1998. "Federalism, Ethnicity and Regionalism in Nigeria." Pp. 341–60 in *Dilemmas of Democracy*, edited by Beckett and Young. Rochester: Rochester University Press.

———. 1996. *Ethnic Minority Conflicts and Governance in Nigeria*. Ibadan: Spectrum Books.

Tamuno, Tekena N. 1970. "Separatist Agitations Agiterional in Nigeria Since 1914." *The Journal of Modern African Studies* 8:4: 563–84.

Umorem, Joseph A. 1996. *Democracy and Ethnic Diversity in Nigeria*. New York: University Press of America.

Young, Crawford. 1976. *The Politics of Cultural Pluralism*. Madison: University of Wisconsin Press.

———. 1982. "Patterns of Social Conflict: State, Class, and Ethnicity." *Daedalus* 3:2: 71–88.

———. 1986. "Nationalism, Ethnicity, and Class in Africa: A Retrospective." *Cahiers d'Etudes Africaines* 26:3: 421-95.

Periodicals

African Confidential

African News

Daily Sketch

Daily Times

The Guardian

National Concord

Nigerian Chronicle

Nigerian Observer

Sunday Times

West African Magazine

Chapter 12

Ethnicity and Constitutionalism in Ethiopia

Assefaw Bariagaber

INTRODUCTION

Discourses on nationalism and ethnicity have recently crystallized around three schools of thought—primordialism, instrumentalism, and constructivism. Gone are the days when explanations of nationalism and ethnicity were sought almost exclusively in terms of liberalism and Marxism. The latter two perspectives, developed by generations of intellectuals, are being reevaluated, as the proliferation of studies on societal cleavages over the last thirty years indicates (Rabushka and Shepsle 1972; Geertz 1973; Young 1976; Hobsbawm and Ranger 1983; Anderson 1983; Smith 1991). Indeed, far from the predictions of both liberal and Marxist theorists, ethnicity and other societal cleavages, such as race, language, and religion, have become more enduring and a threat to the very fabric of the post–Westphalian state system. Perhaps more importantly, the recent revival of ethnicity has affected not only the newly independent postcolonial states in Africa and Asia but also many well-established states, including the former Soviet Union and Canada. States are thus looking for alternative—but balanced—ways to manage cultural pluralism. This includes maintaining state interests that are still based on an incessant search for uniformity while, at the same time, accommodating the objective needs of the community, which are more or less characterized by pluralism.

This chapter focuses on Ethiopia, a state that provides an interesting case study in the search for appropriate mechanisms to manage cultural pluralism. With the adoption of the new constitution in 1995, Ethiopia claims to have transformed itself from a centralized state into a federation of ethnic territories. Indeed, according to Article 39, (1), (2), and (3) of the 1995 Constitution:

> Every Nation, Nationality and People in Ethiopia has an unconditional right to self-determination, including the right to secession.

Every Nation, Nationality and People in Ethiopia has the right to speak, to write and to develop its own language; to express, to develop and to promote its culture; and to preserve its history.

Every Nation, Nationality and People in Ethiopia has the right to a full measure of self-government which includes the right to establish institutions of government in the territory that it inhabits and to equitable representation in the State and Federal Governments.[1]

The constitution also specifies the conditions under which the right to secession may be invoked, proceduralizes its implementation, and details the duties and responsibilities of the federal and state governments in a cessation. It is important to note that no other state's present constitution explicitly recognizes secession as a means of managing cultural pluralism. In this sense, Ethiopia provides reasons for a fresh look at the types of constitutions that were discredited after the death of the former Yugoslavia and the Soviet Union.

The novelty of such an endeavor is especially remarkable when contrasted to the way Eritrea—a newly independent country that remained part of Ethiopia until 1993—chose to manage its cultural pluralism. The 1997 Eritrean Constitution provides for a unitary government where "[t]he equality of all Eritrean languages is guaranteed" (Article 4, (3)). Although the Eritrean Constitution does not recognize any official state language, and that is a measure intended to accommodate cultural pluralism, because it puts all languages on an equal footing, it does not say much about self-government. Nonetheless, both the Eritrean and Ethiopian constitutions take into account cultural cleavages, though they are accorded different recognition. Also, both constitutional devices represent near anomalies, especially in light of current trends in world politics. Ethiopia's federation of ethnic groups, as some have argued, resembles the post–1945 Yugoslav Constitution, and many do not see much of a future in this endeavor. Eritrea's choice of a unitary and centralized government—in a world increasingly obsessed with the devolution of power—is also seen by many skeptics as an arrangement that has to change sooner or later in light of continuing demands for recognition by different segments of the society.[2] So despite cultural similarities anchored deep in historical time, their existence as a single political entity in the very recent past, and their almost identical levels of economic development at present, Ethiopia and Eritrea have pursued different approaches to group accommodation. In other words, a unitary state, such as Eritrea, remains an option in the Horn of Africa. The question, therefore, is why has Ethiopia abandoned strict control from the center in favor of devolution, especially given the zeal with which it pursued centralization for over 100 years? I apply the instrumentalist perspective to show how elites—especially elites from hitherto peripheral groups—

played a crucial role in elevating ethnicity to the zenith of political discourse in Ethiopia and, as a consequence, in devising a constitutional framework that weakened the center in favor of the periphery.

I have argued elsewhere why it was necessary for such similar states to adopt constitutions dissimilar in form and content (Bariagaber 1998). Certainly each constitution is a function of the ethnic trajectories traversed over time. Ethiopia's is the result of highly politicized ethnic cleavages, while Eritrea's came about as a result of the depoliticization of societal segmentation. In this chapter, I apply the probabilistic concept of political stability to argue that the Ethiopian Constitution provides a basic structure for stability in the next few years, because its provisions are likely to empower hitherto neglected but recently politicized cultural groups.

CONTEXTUAL VARIABLES IN THE MAKING OF CULTURAL GROUPS IN ETHIOPIA

There are more than seventy-five cultural groups in Ethiopia—the Oromo, Amhara, Tigray, Afar, Somalis, Gurage, and Sidama are the largest (Araia 1995), however, none of these has a demographic majority. Although some profess local religions, over 80 percent of Ethiopians are either Muslims or Christians. The Muslims and Christians are about equal in number, however, partly as a result of the myth associated with "Christian Ethiopia," the Amhara and Tigray, who are predominantly Christian, have maintained hegemony over the country for hundreds of years. This has remained a distinguishing feature of the Ethiopian state until recently. Some still insist that present Ethiopia, based on the federation of its ethnic constituents, is not fundamentally different from its predecessors.[3]

Religious rivalry is closely intertwined with economic rivalry between Amhara and Tigray Christians, on one side, and Afar and Somali Muslims, on the other. Economic dimensions of conflicts deep in the historical past include Amhara and Tigrayan encroachments into the bordering Afar lowlands to forcibly collect tribute and to subjugate the people. Similarly, in a very inhospitable environment, there were continued competitions between the Afar and Somalis for water and grazing land, Amhara incursions into traditionally Somali regions for more land resources, and the Oromo's northward migration into lands previously occupied by the Amhara, Afar, and Somali. Since each of these groups speaks a different language and possesses distinct social traditions, such conflicts also may be viewed as ethnically based.

More recently, Ethiopia became more centralized and relatively powerful after Menelik II became emperor in 1889, and Amhara forces occupied most of the Somali Ogaden and the rich agricultural lands of southern and western Ethiopia. By the early 1900s, traditional Ethiopia had expanded roughly fourfold and assumed its present size. It also became an empire-state, encompassing culturally distinct groups (Perham 1948; Jalata 1993; Lewis 1993). This continued under Haile Selassie I, and the hitherto autonomous or semi-autonomous regions of Ethiopia, including Tigray, lost whatever measure of self-governance they had and were placed under the central rule of Addis Ababa. With the modest expansion of the bureaucracy and the adoption of Amharic as the national language, the forced assimilation of the peoples in these newly incorporated regions continued for most of the twentieth century.

However, the Ethiopian state has never been strong enough to spread its centralizing tentacles and did not succeed in assimilating many of its constituent peoples. Indeed, despite claims of the pervasiveness of the Amhara/ Tigray culture, Haile Selassie's government recognized the fragility of the ties that bound the various cultural groups. It refused to consider even limited self-administration, because "Ethiopia [was] composed of different tribal groups which were far from regarding one another as members of the same nation." (Erlich 1983, 34). Strict control from the center was maintained to hold the empire together. Except for Eritrea, such determined state presence made it difficult for ethnic groups to mount effective resistance against the centralized state until Emperor Haile Selassie was overthrown in 1974.

These variables explain why the military government instituted in 1974 officially recognized the "question of nationalities" as one of the many pressing issues facing Ethiopia. This recognition, ostensibly made to neutralize opposition and to cast the regime as progressive and fundamentally different from its predecessors, opened the door for cultural elites, or "political entrepreneurs," as Rabushka and Shepsle (1972, 83) would put it, to help define and articulate ethnic demands. In an attempt to extract more government concessions, each ethnic group presented itself as having been the most oppressed under previous regimes. In response to spiraling ethnic demands and to pacify the population at a time when the center was weakened, the *Derg* (the Amharic term for the military committee that overthrew Haile Selassie) issued the National Democratic Revolution Programme (NDRP) to resolve the "question of nationalities." But it was "too little, too late." Moreover, it was not put into effect because of the Derg's repressive and inherently centralizing measures, first against class-based and later against ethnicity-based political parties. The program was at best only designed to buy time until the new regime consolidated power: it actually was adopted to isolate the increasingly powerful nonethnic parties that wanted nothing short of the transfer of power from the Derg.

Thus the Derg helped create high expectations of a truly democratic, multiethnic state. However, the regime also presided in suppressing the forces unleashed by such expectations. This dynamics only helped solidify ethnic-based movements that proliferated in many parts of the country to demand self-determination, many through armed revolt. Indeed, like the Soviet Union, whose policies prompted a powerfully conflicting *"expectations of belonging"* in the incipient successor states (Brubaker 1996, 54, emphasis in original), the Derg never issued and carried out a prudent statewide nationalities policy. This ultimately led to Eritrean independence and the near breakup of Ethiopia into several states. The regime change in 1974 was, therefore, directly responsible for awakening the hitherto dormant substate identities, representing an important variable that played a crucial role in crafting the 1995 Ethiopian Constitution.

The role of elites in providing leadership for mobilized groups had been minimal even during the tumultuous years of 1974 and 1975, when spontaneous expressions of ethnic awakening shook Ethiopia. Indeed, most elites took the Derg as being sincere in its attempts to redefine the very foundations of the Ethiopian state, and they expected satisfactory resolution of ethnic issues to come from the top. However, they became increasingly disillusioned as the regime became less accommodating and more centralizing and dictatorial. Among the many organized oppositions that sought self-determination through armed revolt were the Tigray People's Liberation Front (TPLF) and the Oromo Liberation Front (OLF). Their role in group identity definition, formation, and mobilization is especially instructive, because they played important roles in devising the 1991 Transitional Charter—a document that served both as an interim constitution and as a basis for the present constitution.

In its quest to mobilize the people of Tigray, the TPLF selectively employed many tactics. First, it stressed the Tigrayan character of Axum, the seat of ancient "Ethiopian" civilization and the entity with which *Geez*, the source of the Tigrigna and Amharic script, is associated. Second, it emphasized the role Tigrayans played in the Ethiopian victories over various outside forces, including the Egyptians, the Mahdists from Sudan, and the Italians in the latter half of the nineteenth century. Third, it attributed the poverty in Tigray directly to an Amhara policy of deliberate underdevelopment of the region (Markakis 1994). Fourth, in all of its communications, the TPLF employed the Tigrigna language rather than Amharic (which had been the means of communication in Tigray since at least the 1870s). It also conducted massive literacy campaigns in Tigrigna and took major initiatives to raise the cultural as well as political consciousness of the Tigrayan peasantry. Fifth, it rejected a significant part of the existing Ethiopian historiography because it was Amhara-centric, and it reconstructed a new one where Tigrayan contributions were given prominence. Through selective applications of certain symbols, such as Axum, the TPLF succeeded in creating a new or, as the case may be, an old, but revived, Tigrayan personality. For example, the Axum obelisk featured prominently in TPLF's insignia as if to emphasize that the present Tigrayans were the sole inheritors of the great Axumite civilization. Similarly, "because periods of hardships tend to be stronger forgers of identity than triumphs," the TPLF consistently reminded Tigrayans of the government's brutal suppression of the 1943 *Weyane* revolt in Tigray (Abbay 1997, 334). In fact, to link the present with past Tigrayan resistance, the TPLF called its campaign the "Second *Weyane.*" In other words, the TPLF understood the critical role that ethnic and historic markers play in effective ethnic mobilization. Indeed, it has been quite successful in incorporating the significance of such markers in its nationalist strategy.

The reconstruction of Tigrayan identity provides an interesting case of the way certain symbols are selected, manipulated, and even constructed by the elite in their struggle against ethnic others. For example, the historic rivalry between the Tigrayans and the Amhara occupied a central position in the discourse of Tigrayan nationalism. The emergence of the Amhara as the most dominant group was a direct cause of the poverty in Tigray. Hence, it presented Ethiopian political history of the past 100 years as essentially a zero-sum scenario, where the emergence of the Amhara as the most dominant national group was at the expense of all other groups. But rivalries between the Tigrayans and other groups (Afar, for example), which in antiquity were almost equally intense, are seen as irrelevant in the present political discourse. Treating this otherwise would not have advanced the elite goals of seizing the center by a periphery-based coalition. Thus by their selective manipulations of primordial sentiments and linking these with the present, the Tigrayan elite was simultaneously able to mobilize their co-ethnics and to prevent the formation of a potentially powerful coalition of other ethnic groups.

The OLF also employed various tactics in mobilizing the Oromo. However, instead of appealing to the Oromo's critical role in the making of modern Ethiopia, it turned to the social and cultural system of the Oromo prior to their incorporation into modern Ethiopia in the latter half of the nineteenth century. In an effort to have solid ethnic and cultural markers from the past, the OLF embraced the *gada*—"a 'republican' organization of assemblies, election, and rotation of officers, based on age grades"—as its rallying symbol (Lewis 1993, 170). To emphasize Oromo distinctiveness from other groups, especially the dominant Amhara and Tigray, it rejected the hitherto occasionally used Geez script for *Oromiffa* (the Oromo native language) in favor of the Latin script. Bulcha (1996) contends that the adoption of a non-Geez script made the sociolinguistic boundary of the Oromo more distinct and advanced the quest for Oromo national identity. Such steps represented a critical step at self-definition and the zenith of politicized ethnicity in contemporary Ethiopia.

As indicated earlier, unlike the TPLF, which wanted to capture the center, the OLF looked for ways to establish an independent Oromo state. Thus Oromo nationalist discourse emphasized the cultural unity of the Oromo and their presumed common ancestry (Jalata 1993; Baxter 1994; Bulcha 1996). It also emphasized how they differed from other groups, especially the dominant Amhara. In this way, the Oromo nationalist elite hoped to unite the peasantry (which may not have cared about a state, but certainly did care about culture) behind what Anderson (1983) would characterize as an "imagined" Oromia.

The selection of particular symbols is, of course, contingent upon both present realities and goals. For the TPLF, the goal was to seize state power, hence, the rallying symbols were selected and manipulated in a way that would not antagonize other groups. For the OLF, the goal was to exit from Ethiopia and establish a sovereign Oromo state, hence, their targets included the Amhara, Tigrayans, and the Somalis, who opposed the realization of this goal.

As mentioned earlier, other liberation movements also existed in Ethiopia. The sole issue that kept a semblance of intergroup unity in the 1980s was their determination to overthrow the Derg. After this was accomplished in 1991, negotiations about the future of the Ethiopian state and the type of government to be instituted became contentious; the "question of nationalities" was the sole issue when dozens of ethnic-based organizations debated the Transitional Charter in 1991, as was ethnicity when the present constitution was drafted in 1995. Indeed, throughout the latter half of the 1970s and 1980s, elites had stressed "the variety of ways in which the members of the group were similar to each other and collectively different from others" (Brass 1991, 21). In such a highly politicized ethnic environment, the constitutional stipulation of the generous devolution of power appeared to have been the only way to keep Ethiopia together, especially after Eritrea became de facto independent in 1991.

The fall of the Ethiopian government had helped transform ethnicity from one of several important issues into the only issue: as such, it constituted the only variable that directly influenced the nature of the new constitution. Indeed, the conquest of the center by the periphery provided the latter with the opportunity to devise a constitution that reconstituted the very foundations of the state, where no specific group enjoyed special claims.

THE CONSTITUTION AND GROUP
ACCOMMODATION IN ETHIOPIA

The previous section examined factors that had critical impact on the final draft of the 1995 constitution of Ethiopia. It argued that the ethnic vector traversed over time had an indelible impact on the present constitution, and that the constitution was a meaningful expression of the political reality in Ethiopia in the early 1990s. It also must be noted the 1995 Ethiopian Constitution was based on the 1991 Addis Ababa Charter, which had been approved by twenty-four ethnic-based movements and which had served as an interim constitution of the Transitional Government of Ethiopia (Abraham 1994). In line with the Charter, the Transitional Government "recognized the unconditional right of every 'nation' in the country to self-determination, including the right of self-governance, cultural autonomy, as well as secession" (Mengisteab 1997, 124). It is the only constitution in the world today that explicitly states the right to secede, thus it is a novel document intended to help resolve highly politicized ethnicity and, as stated above, it was adopted by a broad spectrum of ethnic elites. That latter fact alone constitutes a new and promising beginning.

The present Ethiopian Constitution, however, continues to cause controversy among opponents as well as supporters. For example, Engdayehu (1993) contends that ethnic federalism leads to demands for secession. Similar sentiments also have been expressed by such organizations as the All-Amhara People's Organization (AAPO) and the Council of Alternative Forces for Peace and Democracy in Ethiopia (CAFPDE). Others, such as the OLF, have accused the government of paying lip service to the rights enshrined in the constitution but of failing to show the necessary resolve to carry out the provisions of the constitution. In other words, they see the constitution as a cover that the ruling Ethiopian People's Revolutionary Democratic Front (EPRDF) and, in particular, the TPLF, a senior member of the EPRDF, use to control the political process. Beyond Ethiopia, ethnic federalism of the Ethiopian type continues to arouse interest in many parts of Africa, including Sudan and Nigeria. For example, many leaders of minority groups in Nigeria, especially those in the oil-rich Niger Delta region, are calling for a reconstitution of the Nigerian state along ethnic lines. Indeed, a communiqué issued by the Niger Delta Ethnic Nationalities Conference in February 1999 states that "ethnic nationalities must constitute the basic building blocks upon which a stable, virile, and prosperous future Nigeria must be built" (as quoted in Agbese 2000, 32). Ken Saro-Wiwa, the famous Nigerian executed by the Abacha regime a few years ago, also called for a federation of ethnic states. Thus examination of the current Ethiopian political system may have wider implications. The issue in this chapter is therefore whether or not the Ethiopian Constitution provides the basic structures for a stable political system in the immediate future.

When evaluating constitutions, there is a tendency to talk in terms of how long they have lasted. Thus Lijphart (1977) argues that consociational democracy, as a formula for governance in segmented societies such as Lebanon, was a relative success, because it lasted for a decade or more. Although the longevity of a constitution is certainly a good indicator of the degree of acceptance by the different segments of a society, it may not account for constitutional dispensations with shorter life spans. Constitutions also should be assessed in terms of their likelihood of peacefully accommodating common ethnic demands, including decentralization, individual and corporate rights, and resources allocation.

To that end, the probabilistic concept of stability can be applied as an analytical tool to assess the Ethiopian Constitution. Following Deutsch and Singer (1964, 390), the stability of a system is defined as the "probability that the system retains all of its essential characteristics; that no [ethnic group] becomes dominant [so as to form a government of its own]; that most of [the ethnic based-parties] continue to survive; and that large-scale [ethnic conflict] does not occur." Thus stability essentially means maintenance of the existing constitutional arrangement. I claim that the segmental representation in the Ethiopian Parliament, where all ethnic parties are proportionally represented and are potentially members of a governing coalition, contributes to the stability of the political system. Political stability, the dependent variable here, is explained in terms of the number of parties, the independent variable, via the intervening variable, and coalition interaction and opportunity. Assuming that each party is autonomous and in a competitive situation, a Party A monitors the strength of each party, especially those with a strong chance of being its coalition partners. Thus in a two-ethnic party scenario, there is only one possible coalition opportunity AB, where A and B are ethnic-based parties. In a three-ethnic party competition, there are three possible dyadic interactions, AB, AC, and BC, where A, B, and C are ethnic-based parties. In a four-ethnic party competition, there are six such dyads. In an N-ethnic party situation, there are $N! \ / \ (N-2)!2!$ possibilities.[4] Also, an ethnic party A cannot afford to limit itself to dyadic interactions only because of the need to garner the necessary majority in the Lower House, especially when there are numerous smaller parties. Hence, there exist additional "coalitional interactions" that have to be taken into account. For example in a four-party scenario, there are $4! \ / \ (4-2)!2!$, or six, dyadic interactions and $4! \ / \ (4-3)!3!$, or four, triadic interactions, giving a total of ten coalition possibilities. In an N-ethnic party system, the total number of possible interactions (dyad, triad, quatrain, etc.) is given by the formula $\Sigma \ [N! \ / \ (N=M)!M!]$, where N is the number of parties and M = 2, 3, 4, ... N-1, is the number of parties in a given coalition. Clearly, as the number of parties (N) is increased by one, A's total coalition opportunity increases dramatically.

In a competitive situation, each party's response to moves by other parties, or coalitions of parties, depends on the resources it can mobilize to counter such moves. Hence, the more ethnic parties there are, the more each party allocates human and material resources to assess what I call "the universe of possible coalitions" and, on the basis of its assessment, to respond accordingly. In a scarcity-ridden environment, this can only be finite. Since its total attention, understood in terms of the party's "information-processing and resource allocating capabilities," is limited due to the finiteness of its resource base (Deutsch and Singer 1964, 396), it has to divide its attention among all parties and all possible coalitions of parties. For example, in a two-ethnic situation, each party is potentially able to allocate 100 percent of its attention to monitor moves by the other; in a four-ethnic party situation, a party A must divide its total attention not only to monitor the moves of each of the three parties but also the moves by coalitions of those parties (depending on the actual or perceived threat that each of the possible coalitions may pose). In any case, it is safe to assume that the more parties there are, the more coalition opportunities there will be, and the less attention a party allocates to each of them. Indeed, the share of attention that a party allocates to other possible coalitions gets smaller with each additional party, and it is expected to drop precipitously when the number of parties is greater than four, mainly because the number of coalitions increases sharply for each additional actor. What is important here is not the rate of decrease in the share of attention (because some coalitions may not merit much attention), but the fact that more parties mean less attention. An ethnic-based party will be unable to monitor closely each of its individual competitors and possible coalitions thereof, and it will make decisions to minimize the range of all possible responses. Naturally, the need to govern, and its inability to govern alone, will push an ethnic-based party to look for partners. However, the party has to make itself an attractive coalition partner by moderating its position on various issues. Indeed, coalitions inhibit the freedom to pursue one's interests. All of this seems to "favor social stability" and to inhibit social cleavage (Deutsch and Singer 1964, 394). This is even more true if a party is a member of distinct coalitions at both the national and regional levels, for such memberships create crosscutting pressures on each coalition partner and are conducive to the moderation of the member's behavior. Therefore, a party's need to govern and the fluidity of coalitions that accompanies a large number of parties at both the federal and regional levels, coupled with limited resources, exert enough pressure to produce moderation and inclusiveness in the system.

How well does this analytical framework fit the Ethiopian case? As stated earlier, the constitution of Ethiopia provides for a parliamentary democracy, whereby a party that wins a majority in the House of Peoples' Representatives, or is able to assemble a majority, forms a government. It also provides for ethnic-based federal regions, each of which is proportionally represented in both houses of the Ethiopian Parliament. Because none of the ethnic groups constitutes a majority of the population, it is impossible for any regionally based party to form a government on its own. Hence, coalitions between different parties are sought. The number of coalitions that a party is potentially a member of depends on its relative parliamentary strength. Thus each party will have to evaluate "the universe of possible coalitions," but especially majority coalitions in which it has a chance to be a member.

There are about seventy-five linguistic groups and at least fifty registered ethnic parties in Ethiopia (Mengisteab 1997). Most ethnic groups have multiple ethnic-based parties competing in their regional base, and this adds to the fluidity of coalition politics at both the federal and regional levels. That is, the need to govern as part of a coalition, and the potential of abandoning the existing coalition in favor of another, contribute to the moderation that is essential in coalition stability. Although the Ethiopian Constitution does not have an explicit clause that prohibits national and nonethnic-based parties from competing in any region, or ethnic-based parties from competing in regions other than their own, the present environment of politicized ethnicity is such that the regions have become exclusive domains of specific ethnic-based parties. Thus far, only a few national parties have fielded candidates in such cosmopolitan areas as Addis Ababa and Dire Dawa. Moreover, because ethnic-based parties almost always compete in their own regions, candidates for office are overwhelmingly members of the dominant ethnic group in the region. This has produced roughly proportional ethnic representation in the Ethiopian Parliament, in which almost all groups are represented, either through their ethnic parties (none of which constitutes a majority), or through coalitions in which one's ethnic party is a member. It is almost impossible to find elected officials at the regional level serving in an ethnic region other than their own.

An interesting recent phenomenon in Ethiopia that illustrates the preceding discussion of system stability is that due to their limited resources, the smaller parties have rushed to form coalitions and/or unions of coalitions to maximize their influence in any governing coalition, especially at the federal level. The Joint Political Forum Party and the Ethiopian National Democratic Party are examples of unions of many parties. Moreover, many smaller ethnic groups have merged their previously separate territories into a single administrative unit to effectively compete against the larger groups. Thus only nine of the original fourteen ethnic regions now exist. As a result, both the cabinet of the Transitional Government and the present cabinet were composed of individuals belonging to nine ethnic groups (Abraham 1994).

Because of the coalition arrangement, reached among such groups, a cabinet member other than their own may represent some ethnic groups. Indeed, the question of who represents an assortment of smaller groups in a coalition is decided at the local level. This has the potential of transferring conflicts from the federal to the regional level, thereby contributing to the stability of the federal system. Also, some parties are members of coalitions at both the federal and regional levels; therefore, they act as bridges between the federal and regional governments and as potential mediators in times of discord. In the event that such mechanisms and safeguards fail and the largest ethnic-based parties exclude others from power—and that is possible, because the two or three largest parties can theoretically garner the necessary majority

in the Lower House—then the constitutional provision of the right to secession, at least in theory, may be invoked. This explicit right is intended to
protect the minority from the tyranny of the majority and, therefore, it contributes to the essential maintenance of a broad-based system. Looking at the
probabilistic theory of stability outlined above, it is difficult to imagine a
scenario whereby exclusionary politics would be widespread for *an extended
period of time*, especially when the option to secede is open to any group.

The above explanation of system stability is based solely on the electoral
system, with a particular focus on the number of ethnic-based parties. It
assumes that each party finds itself in a competitive environment, despite the
fact that most ethnic parties cooperated in the development and formulation
of the constitution, including such important provisions as proportional ethnic representation, "minority" representation, and corporate rights. Some have
pointed out that such provisions provide additional elements for system stability. This does not mean that there are no ethnic tensions in Ethiopia. The
OLF, for example, has not participated in the political process on the grounds
that the more powerful EPRDF has harassed OLF members and prevented
them from carrying out legitimate political activities. It has since resumed
armed opposition to win the rights provided by the constitution. Similarly,
there is continuing opposition in the Ogaden to "Abyssinian" rule, and the federal
government has yet to succeed in convincing the population that the present
political arrangement is in their best interest. So far, however, the activities of the
opposition groups have not significantly affected the system. Indeed, the system continues to maintain its essential characteristics, and the existing problems do not appear to be related to structural deficiencies in the Transitional
Charter or the constitution, but to the lack of democratic culture and transparency common to many developing nations (Young 1997). As Mengisteab
(1997, 127) has noted, "The hierarchical ethnic relations in the country are
now fundamentally gone and state building through assimilation has ended.
What remains is the development of civic culture that respects the will of the
people." And this may take a while, not because of the absence of institutional
mechanisms but primarily because of the insidious mistrust that exists between elites of the different ethnic groups.

The withdrawal of the OLF from the political process is a manifestation
of this mistrust. The TPLF is content with this, because the OLF's withdrawal gives the Oromo People's Democratic Organization (OPDO), a TPLF
partner and competitor against the OLF, more time to consolidate. But it is
a double-edged sword, because once such a partner becomes well established,
it also becomes more assertive and increasingly independent of the TPLF.
Indeed, like any political party—especially an ethnic-based one—the OPDO
and the OLF have to appeal to the same ethnic constituency, and this can
only be accomplished successfully if each assumes a more nationalist platform. Thus the OPDO will strive to outdo the OLF and to become as

independent of the TPLF as possible. Recent reports of a split within the OPDO and the disagreement between the Ethiopian prime minister (from the TPLF) and the Ethiopian president (from the OPDO) are a clear testimony to this. Hence, it is very likely that more assertive party politics, outside of the control of the TPLF, will continue to develop. The TPLF will have to come to terms with this, albeit reluctantly, because it knows its base of support does not extend beyond the northern part of the country. In other words, the institutional mechanism in place and a party's need to govern will push the political climate in Ethiopia toward more inclusiveness, even of the more assertive political parties.

CONCLUSION

At present, Ethiopia continues to face external as well as internal challenges. Externally, it has been wary of developments in stateless Somalia. For example, it has mounted periodic incursions into Somalia in pursuit of Al Ittihad, an Islamic group fighting for the independence of the Ogaden region of Ethiopia. It also has accused Sudan of fomenting opposition to the ruling EPRDF. Internally, it continues to face challenges from groups with diametrically opposed conceptions of an Ethiopian state. On the one hand, groups such as the Ethiopian People's Revolutionary Party (EPRP) dismiss the present constitution as a recipe for disaster and call for alternative federal arrangements. On the other hand, groups such as the OLF, while expressing support for the constitution, have accused the present government of heavy-handedness and, as a result, have opted for armed opposition to achieve rights enshrined in the present constitution. Generally, however, the demand of the opposition has centered on strict adherence to the letter and spirit of the constitution. The EPRDF may be getting the message. As a result, the political process is now more open than ever, and more political parties took part in the May 2000 elections. Of course, the EPRDF has been accused of harassing candidates from opposition parties, but given the nature of party politics in countries with little experience in democratic governance, this is not unexpected, and in spite of the risks involved, the opposition is becoming more vocal. Thus there is hope for such a plural society, contrary to Rabushka's and Shepsle's (1972) theory of democratic instability in plural societies.

The theory of democratic instability in plural societies suffers from two shortcomings when applied to Ethiopia. First is the supposed breakdown of oversized coalitions focused on coalitions formed during the struggle for independence from colonialism. Thus elites in colonial administrations had to prove that they were capable of working together; they came up with coalitions whose sole aim was to facilitate independence and to extract resources previously controlled by the colonial powers. Second is that the post–independence constitutions were adopted with the active participation of the departing colonial administrations and did not necessarily reflect local societal characteristics. In contrast, the Ethiopian Constitution is a product of a particular history that made ethnicity the sole variable in its crafting. In the extreme case that two or three of the largest parties form a governing coalition that excludes others—and that is possible but not probable—the constitutional provision of the right to secession provides a strong incentive for inclusiveness in the decision-making process. Thus the generous devolution of power already in place appears to be the best way to meet existing group demands.

Finally, it is important to emphasize that the Ethiopian constitutional mechanism is spatially and temporally specific: it was borne out of the particular experiences of the Ethiopian peoples and can only be generalized to other cases where cultural cleavages have become highly politically salient. Indeed, it was a means of holding the country together at a time when ethnic politics had hit its zenith. It may not even serve Ethiopia in the long term, because ethnic federalism may not be conducive to long-term internal economic integration (Mengisteab 2000). However, it will provide the necessary short- and medium-term stability that Ethiopia desperately needs.

NOTES

1. The terminology used in Ethiopia to refer to a cultural community is *nation, nationality,* or *people,* however, for no other reason except brevity, I have used terms such as *ethnic, cultural,* or *religious group* to refer to any collectivity, regardless of whether that group constitutes a nation, a nationality, or a people. Such terminology, as used here, does not in any way question the rights and claims that these groups make on the basis of that identification. In fact, the rights of such collectivities are identical, as indicated in the 1995 Constitution.

2. For example, in their programs the Eritrean Liberation Front-Revolutionary Council (ELF-RC) and the Eritrean Liberation Front-Abdallah Idris Group do not explicitly mention ethnicity or religion as being politically relevant. However, their call for constitutional recognition of Arabic and Tigrigna as official languages appears to be an implicit acknowledgment of the existence of two major cultural groups: lowland Eritreans, who are Muslims with links to Arabic, and highland Eritreans, who are Tigrigna-speaking Christians.

3. The ongoing opposition to the present government, dominated by the Tigray national group, is a case in point.

4. The mathematical symbol "!" is read as "factorial" and is a short way of writing a series of multiplications. For example $5! = 5 \times 4 \times 3 \times 2 \times 1 = 120$. Similarly, $3! = 6$, because it means $3 \times 2 \times 1$.

REFERENCES

Abbay, Alemseged. 1997. "The Trans-Mareb Past in the Present." *The Journal of Modern African Studies* 35: 321–34.

Abraham, Kinfe. 1994. *Ethiopia: From Bullets to the Ballot Box.* Lawrenceville: The Red Sea Press.

Agbese, Pita. 2000. "Ethnicity, Constitutions and Governance in Nigeria." Paper presented at the Conference Funded by the Ford Foundation on Government Policies, Constitutions and Ethnic Relations in Africa, Morehouse College, Atlanta, February 24–26.

Anderson, Benedict. 1983. *Imagined Communities: Reflections on the Origin and Spread of Nationalism.* London: Verso.

Araia, Ghelawdewos. 1995. *Ethiopia: The Political Economy of Transition.* Lanham: University Press of America.

Bariagaber, Assefaw. 1998. "The Politics of Cultural Pluralism in Ethiopia and Eritrea: Trajectories of Ethnicity and Constitutional Experiments." *Ethnic and Racial Studies* 21: 1056–73.

Baxter, P.T.W. 1994. "The Creation and Construction of Oromo Nationality." Pp. 167–86 in *Ethnicity and Conflict in the Horn of Africa,* ed. Katsuyoshi Fukui and John Markakis. London: James Currey; Athens: Ohio University Press.

Brass, Paul. 1991. *Ethnicity and Nationalism: Theory and Comparison.* New Delhi: Sage.

Brubaker, Rogers. 1996. *Nationalism Reframed: Nationhood and the National Question in the New Europe.* Cambridge: Cambridge University Press.

Bulcha, Mekuria. 1996. "The Survival and Reconstruction of Oromo National Identity." Pp. 48–66 in *Being and Becoming Oromo: Historical and Anthropological Inquiries,* ed. P.T.W. Baxter, Jan Hultin, and Alessandro Truilzi. Lawrenceville: The Red Sea Press.

Deutsch, Karl, and David Singer. 1964. "Multipolar Power Systems and International Stability." *World Politics* 16: 390–406.

Engdayehu, Walle. 1993. "Ethiopia: Democracy and the Politics of Ethnicity." *Africa Today* 40: 29–52.

Erlich, Haggai. 1983. *The Struggle over Eritrea, 1962–1978: War and Revolution in the Horn of Africa.* Stanford: Hoover Institution.

Geertz, Clifford. 1973. *The Interpretation of Cultures.* New York: Basic Books.

Gorman, Robert. 1981. *Political Conflict on the Horn of Africa.* New York: Praeger.

Hobsbawm, Eric, and Terence Ranger eds. 1983. *The Invention of Tradition.* Cambridge: Cambridge University Press.

Jalata, Asafa. 1993. *Oromia and Ethiopia: State Formation and Ethnonational Conflict, 1868–1992.* Boulder: Lynne Rienner.

Lewis, Herbert. 1993. "Ethnicity in Ethiopia: The View from Below (and from the South, East, and West)." Pp. 158–78 in *The Rising Tide of Cultural Pluralism: The Nation-State at Bay?* ed. Crawford Young. Madison: University of Wisconsin Press.

Lijphart, Arend. 1977. *Democracy in Plural Societies.* New Haven: Yale University Press.

Markakis, John. 1994. "Ethnic Conflict and the State in the Horn of Africa." Pp. 217–38 in *Ethnicity and Conflict in the Horn of* Africa, ed. Katsuyoshi Fukui and John Markakis. London: James Currey; Athens: Ohio University Press.

Mengisteab, Kidane. 1997. "New Approaches to State Building in Africa: The Case of Ethiopia's Ethnic-Based Federalism." *African Studies Review* 40: 111–32.

———. 2000. "The Role of the State in Politicizing Ethnicity: The Ethiopian Case." Paper presented at the Conference Funded by the Ford Foundation on Government Policies, Constitutions and Ethnic Relations in Africa, Morehouse College, Atlanta, Georgia, February 24–26.

Perham, Margery. 1948. *The Government of Ethiopia.* New York: Oxford University Press.

Quirin, James. 1993. "Ethnicity, Caste, Class, and State in Ethiopian history: The Case of the Beta Israel (Falasha)." Pp. 200–221 in *The Rising Tide of Cultural Pluralism: The Nation-State at Bay?* ed. Crawford Young. Madison: University of Wisconsin Press.

Rabushka, Alvin, and Kenneth Shepsle. 1972. *Politics in Plural Societies: A Theory of Democratic Instability.* Columbus: Charles E. Merrill.

Smith, Anthony. 1991. "The Nation: Invented, Imagined, Reconstructed?" *Millennium: Journal of International Studies* 20: 353–68.

Sorenson, John. 1996. "Learning to be Oromo: Nationalist Discourse in the Diaspora." *Social Identities* 2: 439–67.

Walta Information Center. 1999. *38 Political Parties Announce Their Candidature for May Election.* Addis Ababa: Walta Information Center.

Young, Crawford. 1976. *The Politics of Cultural Pluralism.* Madison: University of Wisconsin Press.

Young, John. 1997. *Peasant Revolution in Ethiopia: The Tigray People's Liberation Front, 1975–1991.* Cambridge: Cambridge University Press.

Part 5

Conclusion

Chapter 13

Afterword

Interrogating the Emancipation of Cultural Pluralism

Crawford Young

The editor of this book has chosen an evocative title: *Emancipating Cultural Pluralism*. The reader will at once wish to know why cultural pluralism requires emancipation. To what is it subjugated? How is its liberation to be accomplished? How can pluralism's positive aspects be nurtured and its sometime destructive force be contained?

Cris Toffolo, in her introduction, provides several responses. The lingering hold of a modern/traditional polarity upon the social scientific imagination and state agents is one oppressive legacy of "old thinking." Doubtless, she is right in pointing to a continuing subliminal imprint of such premises, reflected in the number of times one encounters in the media or even in academic analysis such phrases as "ancient tribal hatreds" as a *passe-partout* explanation of contemporary conflicts in former Yugoslavia, Rwanda, or elsewhere. The chapters in this book further discredit any equation of ethnic, religious, or racial identity with a traditionality, which the powerful solvent of modernity will gradually erase. In different ways, the chapters by Hoover, Abdalla, Christensen, B. Simon, and Adogamhe all nullify such an equation. On the contrary, nearly four decades of scholarship have firmly established the "modernity of tradition" (Rudolph and Rudolph 1967). The dramatic rise in the salience of cultural identities is intimately linked to the multiple processes of modernity (Young 1976, 1993).

Another dimension of emancipation, for Toffolo, is through contesting the contemporary moral validity or practical effectiveness of repressive nation-state responses to cultural diversity. At the apogee of the illusion of the nation as an integrative ideal in the 1950s, the belief was widespread that cultural difference was a "problem" for state managers, whose solution was marginalization or erasure. Such a vision readily translated into repressive measures of diverse sorts, from a ticket to the *gulag*, which "nationalist deviation"

239

guaranteed under high Stalinism, to the counterproductive throttling of the
scourge of "tribalism" in immediate postcolonial Africa, to the forcible dis-
patch of Indian or Aboriginal children to boarding schools or white families
to extinguish indigeneity in the United States or Australia.

Such repression was of several kinds. One form was simple denial of
difference; a classic case was the long insistence of the Turkish state that its
Kurdish minority were simply "mountain Turks." Buffington's chapter el-
egantly shows how the post–revolutionary Mexican national ideology of
mestizaje airbrushed the Indian from the citizenry, a doctrinal legerdemain
encountered in a number of other Latin American cases. This theme also is
referenced in Tilley's chapter (see also V. Tilley 1997). Forcible repression of
any public display of cultural difference was another response, for which the
examples are legion. The Algerian national idea sits uneasily with assertions
of Berber cultural rights that periodically break through the surface and often
have faced a repressive response. Indonesia displayed over the years a low
threshold of tolerance for militant resistance in Aceh, East Timor, and West
Papua to a text of "national integration," seen by some as Java centered. India,
although in many ways a positive model of the accommodation of difference,
did not hesitate to deploy its large army when national integrity was deemed
at risk—in Punjab, in 1984, off and on in the northeast, and regularly in
Kashmir, especially since 1990.

Some modes of denial are less overtly repressive but nonetheless vulnerable to the emancipation thesis. Classical liberalism often treated forms of
cultural plurality as acceptable in the purely private domain, but not in the
public square. With respect to the accommodation of religious difference,
such an approach in the Western world did tame religious difference among
Christian churches, after two centuries of bitter sectarian strife following the
Protestant Reformation revealed the fatal flaws in the *cujus regio, ejus religio*
doctrines. As immigration patterns made religious landscapes more complex,
such formulas became more problematic, as illustrated by the furor in France
over whether Muslim girls wearing head scarves in school violated the republican and laic principles of the secular state. Even more debatable was the
notion that cultural difference of ethnicity or race could only find legitimate
expression in the apolitical realm of folklore, or in private practice. In the
polity where a difference-denying liberalism had perhaps the strongest hold,
the United States, a close inspection of nineteenth- and early-twentieth-
century voting behavior reveals the enormous impact of sect and ethnicity,
not to mention race, in determining partisanship.

Yet another mode of implementation of such iconic state discourse as the
"indivisible republic" or *e pluribus unum* is through energetic assimilation
projects. Such homogenizing policies are not always resisted; France, for
example, has long effectively assimilated both substantial numbers of immigrants from elsewhere in Europe and the diversity in its own population stock

(Weber 1976). In the United States and other Western states, the assimilative socialization of schoolroom, place of employment, and dominant media usually has not encountered strong resistance among European immigrants, especially in the postimmigrant generations. But the "rising tide of cultural pluralism" makes a predominantly assimilative approach more problematic than in the past, a trend measured in the growing assertion of national minority and immigrant rights in Europe. When a perceived ambition of imposing a national identity is seen as being in deep contradiction to the collective self of many citizens, as with the Muslim Brotherhood's version of Islam, examined by Abdalla, the war of visions becomes total and intractable (Deng 1995).

Toffolo's titular claim that cultural pluralism merits emancipation from such forms of nation-state denial, repression, or erasure will doubtless evoke a nod of assent from most readers, many more than would have agreed four or five decades ago. But there are yet other forms of emancipation lurking in the title. Many of the chapters argue that cultural groups themselves hold moral value as arenas for human fulfillment. Toffolo and a growing chorus of others argue that the subject need not stand before state power as mere individual, unencumbered by intermediate cultural attachments. The human connectedness constituted by such affiliations is constitutive of the "social capital" that Putnam (1993) suggests is indispensable to a stable social order. In different ways, the Tilley, Hoover, and T. Simon chapters echo this theme.

This in turn leads to an interrogation of liberalism as foundational doctrine for the contemporary nation-state. With the collapse of communism, the diminished appeal of various corporatist doctrines (Wiarda 1981), and the earlier discrediting of fascism, liberalism and its political progeny, the rule-of-law state, today enjoy an unparalleled ascendancy. But the basic postulates of liberalism, whether in its contractarian, utilitarian, or Kantian forms, are firmly rooted in the individual as rights-bearing citizen, which today is the constitutive element of political society. The citizen in classical liberal theory enjoys an unmediated collective identity in the nation whose "people" are the ultimate fictive holders of the sovereignty exercised on their theoretical behalf by the state.

The compatibility of this philosophic rendering of state and society with the near universal reality of at least some degree of cultural plurality has evoked, since the 1980s, a widening debate, much of it well captured in the volume edited by Ronald Beiner (1999). The Tilley and Sonntag chapters express or imply skepticism about the compatibility of full liberalism and cultural pluralism; Hoover, T. Simon, and Bariagaber suggest ways that this might be achievable. Their debate is a microcosm of a larger controversy pitting the classical individualism of historical liberalism, defended by such scholars as David Hollinger (1995) or Abigail Thernstrom (1989), against the communitarians receptive to cultural diversity, such as Charles Taylor (1989) or Michael Walzer (1997). Noted liberal philosophers such as Will Kymlicka (1995) propounded a comprehensive elaboration of a multicultural liberalism, heavily grounded in a Canadian model. The dilemma of incorporation of a principle of cultural diversity into the constitutional superstructure of the liberal democratic state found discursive expression initially in Canada, which began to deploy the term *multiculturalism* as an official attribute in 1965. Since that time, in diverse formulations, multiculturalism has been appropriated as state discourse in a surprisingly wide range of sources, not only in Australia, the United Kingdom, and the United States, but also several Latin American states (Van Cott 1999). In 2000, Sultan Mohammed VI even declared Morocco a "multicultural nation" (in a visit to a Berber-speaking zone).

The semiotic impact of the spread of a doctrine of multiculturalism is well captured by Steven Vertovec (1996, 50–51):

Since the 1970s multiculturalism has emerged as a term increasingly called upon in parliamentary debates and political party manifestoes, the rhetoric of ethnic group leaders, the logic of local government structuring and budgeting, social scientific analyses, popular media, and commercial marketing. The term has had far-reaching impact on numerous professions; educationalists are inundated with texts, journals, conferences and debates concerning multicultural education, while health-care practitioners, social workers, police and other public professions are increasingly the focus of "multicultural awareness" training programmes.

Vertovec adds the important corollary that, "given such a wide range of actors and arenas, it is apparent that multiculturalism currently means no single thing; that is, it represents no single view of, or strategy for, contemporary complex societies" (Vertovec 1996, 50–51).

In reflecting upon the contributions to this book, some consideration is needed of the architecture enclosing and surrounding cultural pluralism, "nation" and "state," as well as their accompanying master narratives. Nationhood is embodied in the modern doctrine of nationalism, whose origins are variously situated from sixteenth-century England (e.g., Greenfeld 1992) to the French Revolution (e.g., Hobsbahm 1990). Roger Scruton (1999, 279) gives cogent summation to the appropriation of nationalism by the contemporary state as indispensable discourse of legitimation:

Nationalism is therefore the *ideology* of the modern state: the set of doctrines and beliefs that sanctify this peculiar local arrangement, and legitimize the new forms of government and administration that have emerged in the modern world. . . . There is no better ideology for persuading the common man that he owes his loyalty to educated and anonymous pen-pushers in the distant cities.

All contemporary states, in pursuit of their legitimation imperative (Young 1994), represent themselves as nations, if only in becoming. The universality of this discursive bonding of "state" and "nation" as "nation-state" is a remarkable fact of contemporary life. Like nationalism itself, this lexical marriage is recent, indeed, even more contemporary than nationalism itself, originating in the constitutional law lectures on "sovereignty and liberty" of French professor Léon Duguit in the aftermath of World War I. The war, he argued, pitted an "état-puissance" (Germany), where sovereignty belonged only to the state, and France, where the state was an organic expression of the sovereign nation (thus état-nation, whose sequence was inverted in English translation) (Arbos 1990, 61). Even more novel is the term *nation building,* which crept into the academic and state vocabulary only after World War II.

Whichever birth date one prefers, the idea of nation indisputably originated in Europe and became tied to a territorial state whose dominant ethnic group conferred its name upon the nation. During the first decades of the nineteenth century, the nation concept spread in two directions. Western hemisphere settlers absorbed the idea in the course of their independence struggles and their efforts to consolidate new states. Nationalism took on new coloration in the process (Anderson 1983); through its alchemy, the settler-ruling elites shed their metropolitan identity and donned new territorial consciousness. At the same time, a nation was initially a collective awareness of the settler component of the populace; those of African ancestry, slave or free, and the indigenous populations were excluded or marginalized.

The second new turn for nationalism was through its discovery by ethnic communities as a potent ideological claim for statehood. This could come either by assembling an array of small political entities sharing an identity ostensibly based on language, as with the German and Italian unification movements, or by asserting a right to separate from an existing imperial domain (especially the Austro-Hungarian, Ottoman, and Russian), because their national consciousness could not flourish in a subordinated status. "Nation" thus acquired an indissoluble link to the novel moral doctrine of self-determination.

The successful bonding of the idea of nation with the concept of self-determination opened the way for yet another mutation of nationalism. When in the aftermath of World War I the doctrine of self-determination won acceptance in the United Nations Charter, subjugated populations in the vast Asian, African, and Caribbean colonial domains found an invincible ideological weapon. By asserting a territorial identity as a people united by a shared history of oppressive subordination to alien powers, anticolonial nationalism obtained crucial traction in winning external as well as internal sympathy and support.

AFTERWORD

Through this historic itinerary, nation and nationalism acquired multiple forms and variable content, a point to which we will return. The point is the universality among state elites and large segments of their populations of the belief that "nation" is essential to the state itself. "State" is merely a cold, and an arid legal abstraction for the formal institutions of rule. "Nation" imagines the citizenry as holding a collective personality, a living human ensemble endowed with emotional properties. One is governed by a state, but one belongs to a nation. "Nation-state," as normative rendering of the sovereign political units held by the international juridical order to constitute the global order, is firmly embedded in everyday understandings, or what Billig (1995) imaginatively calls "banal nationalism." One would be hard pressed to iden-tify any contemporary state that does not represent itself as a "nation," even if imperfectly realized; what remains to accomplish is an imperative project; nor can one easily contest the assumption by state elites that some form of ideology representing the citizenry as a solidary collective community is in-dispensable to meeting the challenge of legitimation. Naturally they may err by choosing a text of nationhood of exclusionary content, which subverts, perhaps fatally, its own legitimating purpose. The challenge to statecraft is to fashion the ultimately malleable content of the nation transcript into a form that serves the ultimate aim of state legitimation.

From this follows the observable fact that in many countries there are numerous groups and population segments that contest the moral value of "nation" as authoritatively formulated by state managers and understood by dominant elements of the population. Their discontents resonate in several of the chapters in this book. The Tilley chapter ably argues that there is an "international template" that now inscribes its normative "na-tion-state" model upon the world state system, particularly its newer members, readily interpreted as requiring the infusion of the cultural personality of a dominant group into the nation template. This, however, was neither necessary nor inevitable, as one may observe in the contrast-ing patterns in different regions.

These contrasts are evident in the numerous new states that are a product of the final dismantling of colonial empires and the splintering of the former Soviet Union and Yugoslavia. All adopted the discourse and doctrine of nationhood, but gave it varying content. The new Balkan and Eurasian states immediately identified the state with a "titular nationality," giving varying degrees of reassurance to minorities; Russians stranded in the non-Russian republics have, for the most part, received respectful treatment. In Southeast Asia as well, postcolonial states bore the name of an ascendant ethnonational group, and the "template" of nation-state doctrine tended to peripheralize hill peoples. In contrast, in much of sub-Saharan Africa, the Caribbean, and the archipelagic republics of Southeast Asia, the idea of "nation" denies any ethnic connotation and is thus potentially inclusive.

One need also note that diverse cultural communities engaged in active or even armed challenge to their forced attachment into a "nation" whose collective representation they reject are equally committed to the idea of nation. Should such cultural groups as the Sri Lanka Tamils, the Spanish Basques, or Quebec nationalists succeed in their campaigns for separate sovereignty, there can be no doubt that they would vigorously inscribe nation-state doctrine in their newly created polities. In all likelihood, such projects would appear exclusionary to a segment of the citizenry.

Some perceive the nation-state as an archaic form of political organization, about to be swept away by the solvents of globalization. Appadurai, for example, asserts that the nation-state is on its last legs, unable to arbitrate globality or modernity, with its actual governing institutions "inclined to self-perpetuation, bloat, violence, and corruption" (Appadurai 1996, 19). The postmodern pallbearers for the nation-state may find that the casket is not yet ready for its presumed contents. On the contrary, one particularly salient recent trend toward some enhanced degree of democratization in much of the world may operate in the opposite direction. The state imperative of legitimation becomes more central in the democratic polity, since the existing unit renounces simple force and repression in sustaining itself. Cultural pluralism can only be accommodated by sustaining consent, because full democracy opens up to territorially concentrated groups a possible exit option. Thus in my view, to achieve the analytical objective of emancipating cultural pluralism, one needs to accept the empirical reality of the extant nation-state, singular and plural.

This leads us to the question of the state. In seeking emancipation of cultural pluralism, one collides with the paradox of the state: at once the historical source of cultural group inequalities and grievances, yet also the indispensable institutional framework for the accommodation of cultural diversity and remedy of past group injustice. Particularly in instances where the state in name and official historical narrative is linked to a defined cultural grouping, the vocation of nationhood inevitably clashes with the identity attachments and quest for self-preservation of minority groups. For states that represent themselves as territorial and civic, such as the "fragment states" born of European expansion in the Western Hemisphere, southern Africa, and Australasia, for much of the formative period the state project of nation building was suffused with a logic based upon the subordination, exclusion and erasure of a racial other, a thesis persuasively propounded by Anthony Marx (1998) for the United States, Brazil, and South Africa.

Tilley's chapter highlights that the state is never culturally neutral, for it inevitably reflects the interests and perspectives of the dominant elements of society. This important insight requires acknowledgment, even if the task of locating the "dominant segment" may be less simple than she implies: obvious enough in apartheid South Africa, but less clear in the age of "rainbowism," or in an India of ascendant state level political alignments of variable contours. I return to further explore this point later.

Yet another source of state framing of cultural pluralism as a "problem" is the incurable propensity of ruling institutions to engage in projects of codification of group identities and simplifications of patterns of collective consciousness. James Scott (1998) lays bare these tendencies in his seminal exegesis of the impact of a state vision of "high modernity" that leads to simplifying and sometimes obfuscating official classifications. To grasp the dynamics of state schemes for the management of cultural pluralism, one must begin by "seeing like a state." Definition of census categories is the most obvious site for the codification projects; the British Raj, in its impulse to classify and rank Indian castes, played a critical role in defining the boundaries of communal competition, initially for battling for higher status in the hierarchy. Postcolonial India, through its laudable efforts to efface past societal exclusion by special reservations for scheduled castes and tribes, eventually precipitated a reverse race down the ranking order, as the extension of these benefits to "other backward castes" created incentives to fit within this category (Jenkins 1998). The colonial state in Africa engaged in such identity codification on a large scale, imposing a "tribal" template of its own design. The resulting administrative structures, Mamdani (1996) eloquently argues, imposed upon the rural populace a status as ethnic subject, a distinction that carried over into a postcolonial division between educated, urban citizens and rural subjects. In part as a reactive denial of ethnic diversity, most African postcolonial states suppressed ethnic categories in their census exercises. Naturally this administrative erasure had little impact upon identity politics on the ground; Adogamhe's chapter chronicles the intense ethnic struggles triggered by the creation of new states and local government areas in contemporary Nigeria.

The state as nation beyond dispute merits the skeptical treatment accorded by Toffolo, Buffington, Tilley, and others. Yet analysis cannot end with this discovery. The emancipation of cultural pluralism is by no means self-enforcing. Only the state has the institutional capacity and ultimately the legitimate recourse to coercion to remedy injustices experienced by given identity groups within political society. The "group harms" carefully dissected in Thomas Simon's chapter can find resolution only through some overarching institutional framework within which claims can be identified and adjudicated, resources can be summoned as required, or authoritative rules can be redrawn to better assure group justice. Thus the nation-state looms over multicultural societies as both problem and solution, foe and friend.

Of course, there is no basis to assume that states will in fact choose the virtuous path of effective accommodation of cultural pluralism, deploying the culturally sensitive moral pragmatism to which the T. Simon and Hoover chapters beckon. However, there are some reasons to expect that more states will do so with greater sensitivity and skill than in the past. There are far greater incentives for empathetic multicultural behavior than at the zenith of national integration ideology four or five decades ago. At the international system level, a web of normative documents slowly accumulates, protective of the rights of national minorities, indigenous peoples, and minority religions; these ramifying codifications of a global moral discourse cognizant of group as well as individual rights contrast sharply to the 1948 UN Universal Declaration of Human Rights, which took normative notice of only the individual. Even though the infrastructure of global governance lacks enforcement mechanisms, the growing corpus of human rights international law and the existence of an expanding universe of active nongovernmental organizations campaigning for its application create important restraints upon state action. Indonesia's abandonment of East Timor under intense international pressure is one of many illustrations of the influence of a changing international normative order. The Organization for Security and Cooperation (OSCE) in Europe provides an important venue for making human rights of cultural groups a justiciable value (Held et al. 1999).

A wide variety of policy options is available to multicultural states to improve their performance with respect to cultural pluralism. In a pair of edited volumes (Young 1998, 1999), I and my contributors identify a number of policy spheres where multicultural statecraft has occurred: decentralization, asymmetric federalism, legal pluralism, ethnic preference on behalf of historically disadvantaged groups, and electoral systems that best assure group representation and provide incentives for intergroup cooperation, among others. We also explore a number of country cases, where at least arguably positive results in the accommodation of cultural pluralism are evident (e.g., Spain, Malaysia, Tanzania, and Mauritius). Bariagaber's analysis of the interesting and important Ethiopian constitutional experiment is another case in point, and an important innovation in Africa.

In an arresting conclusion, Ted Gurr (2000) finds that violent ethnic conflict, measured on a global basis, actually declined in the 1990s. He attributes this drop in part to a worldwide process of political learning. The much higher consciousness of cultural pluralism and its challenge to a just and harmonious society in recent decades produce a climate of policy experimentation and observation of multicultural formulas and outcomes in neighboring or similar states.

A particularly obvious domain for adjustment lies in the doctrine of nation itself. The historical trajectories by which successor states to the Soviet Union and Yugoslavia came into being make the assertion of the titular nationality, a notion redolent of the "nationality policy" conceived by Lenin and Stalin, as defining the collective personality of the new states (Brubaker 1996; Khazanov 1995; Bremer and Taras 1997). Yet the Soviet successor states and those former Yugoslav states coveting admission to the European

Union face strong pressures to assure minority rights. As noted earlier, a large number of states have formally adopted the discourse of multiculturalism. Several Latin American states have amended their constitutions to officially acknowledge a special status for indigenous peoples and, in the Colombian case, recognition of Afro-Colombians as a distinct community (Van Cott 1999). In Australia, Canada, and the United States, the idea of nation is much more inclusive than in the past. European states are gradually reconciling themselves to the permanence of the Turkish, North African, or African diaspora communities; Germany, for example, has begun to abandon its *jus sanguinis* restrictions on citizenship. In India, the original national integration doctrine based in elevating Hindi as the sole national language has long been abandoned, and a multilingual reality has been acknowledged. The chauvinistic *Hindutva* doctrine, asserting a construct of Hinduism as the core element in Indian nationhood, has in effect been heavily diluted by its political promoter, the Bharatiya Janata Party (BJP); the realities of exercising power and the necessities of coalition building at the state level erode any possibility of imposing an exclusionary conceptualization of Indian nationhood (Rudolph and Rudolph 2000).

Naturally these adjustments in national ideology do not automatically win full acceptance either by dominant elements of society or by those targeted for inclusion. A long history of marginalization and racism necessarily renders minorities skeptical about new claims to an enlarged idea of national community, but over time, such changes can impact the psychology of multicultural politics.

Beyond the two faces of the state, one also must examine the dual nature of cultural pluralism itself. Hoover stresses that group identities do confer a sense of moral worth and anchoring for the individual, yet cultural identity is in part constituted by the "other," often stereotyped in negative ways. Thus cultural diversity offers both a valuable basis for human fulfillment through communal affiliation and a ready line of demarcation for social competition and political conflict. Communal segments may be victims of group harm; they also may be its perpetrators. Along with admiration and respect for the struggle of national and racial minorities or indigenous peoples for recognition of historic wrongs and compensatory action, one needs to contemplate the ugly metal barricades separating Protestant and Catholic neighborhoods in Belfast, the mortal fear that Tutsi and Hutu have for each other in Rwanda and Burundi, and the dubious future of the multicultural state that the international community seeks to assure in Bosnia. Alongside the persuasive communitarian message of a Charles Taylor or a Michael Walzer, and the liberal multiculturalism of a Will Kymlicka, one must acknowledge the deadly ethnic riots scrutinized by Donald Horowitz (2001) and Paul Brass (1996).

Thus we may conclude that the emancipation of cultural pluralism requires careful examination of the nation and state, which provides the arenas within which cultural plurality exists. However, our task is not yet complete. In reality, nation, state, and cultural pluralism, although a common definition can be found for each, nonetheless are widely variant in their particular manifestations. Therefore our emancipatory project must take note of the wide difference and important contingency of the specific circumstances of liberation.

Nation and nationalism come in several quite distinct forms, and thus "national integration" projects also are varied. In nearly all of Europe (except Switzerland, Belgium, and the United Kingdom), and the northern tier of the Eurasian landmass, nation is linked to a nation-forming ethnic community, which historically has always dominated the state. A number of scholars (e.g., Gellner 1983; Greenfeld 1992) have argued that there is a sharp distinction between nationalisms in the East, which are ethnic in character and chauvinistic in content, and those to the West, which are more benign and civic in nature, a generous characterization often applied to American nationalism. This distinction is doubtless overdrawn, although there is an obvious contrast between the tolerance of Scandinavian forms of nationalism, or the universals of French "republican" principles, and the ethnic mythologies mobilizing Serbs and Croats.

A second major family of nationalisms is found in the Western Hemisphere and Australasia; I have already traced the ancestry and essential postulates of these settler-based formulations. Here one must underline the important evolution from a sometimes narrow Creole origin and/or the original colonial doctrine of racial castes to its suppression by *mestizaje* (or racial fusion) as the essence of the nation—the "cosmic race" in Mexico. So while Buffington's critique of *mestizaje* is persuasive, the doctrine is clearly more inclusionary than its predecessor.

A third large group of nationalisms is entirely territorial, and it originates most visibly in anticolonial independence struggles. The lack of an ethnic origin for nationhood does not preclude the construction of a historical master narrative extending beyond colonial occupation or its sources in more than a simple struggle against the imperial yoke. One classic example is the elegant text by Jawaharlal Nehru, appropriately titled *The Discovery of India* (1946). Steger's chapter explores the intellectual odyssey of the other towering figure in Indian nationalism, Mahatma Gandhi. Of upper-caste Hindu background, through his life and work he sought to find discursive and tactical ways of making the idea of "India" inclusive by rebaptizing "untouchables" as "*harijans*" (children of God) and by leading a protest movement against the disappearance of the Muslim caliphate. Partha Chatterjee (1993) highlights well the multiple and often subaltern sources of the nationalist text that was not simply a construct of the anticolonial intelligentsia.

The itineraries of "nation" in Africa also are more complex than sometimes assumed. They have both an African and a territorial component. The former originates in the pervasive racialization of the African as savage child, characteristic of all colonial states in Africa; the "native" subject was viewed as being devoid of civilizational attributes, heathen in religious belief, barbarian in social practice, incurably indolent, and thus deserving the firm, unsparing tutelage of the adult colonial master. This ascription invited a reaction in the form of African solidarity, eventually codified in the discourse of pan-Africanism. At the same time, a territorial discourse emerged, at first primarily among the permanent European residents and colonial agents. An emergent indigenous elite in the core zones of the colonial political economy absorbed these notions, and joined them to a deepening challenge to imperial rule, initially to its exclusionary racial practices and then to a demand for a full liberation, which in practice could only occur through the territorial template of the colonial partition.

The degree to which African nationalism has become naturalized in the popular consciousness is well illustrated by the persistence of states in the public imagination and in international law, even when they cease to exist over an extended period. Somalia, from 1991 until 2000, lacked even the pretense of a functioning government, yet its tenuous restoration in 2000 seemed a "normal" development. In Congo-Kinshasa, since 1998, the territory is loosely occupied, though not really ruled, by four different fragments, supported at different moments by seven foreign armies. Yet none of the contenders lay claim to anything other than a restored "Congo." Similar phenomena were observable for much of the 1990s in Liberia and Sierra Leone.

The internalization of nationhood has its negative aspects. One example is the disastrous 1998–2000 war between Eritrea and Ethiopia, seemingly over a few square miles of barren territory, yet with both sides appearing to enjoy popular support for their military confrontation despite tens of thousands of casualties. The launching of the ostensibly nationalist slogan of *Ivoirité* in the Ivory Coast in the 1990s by former President Henri Bédié has divisive implications, targeting the authenticity not only of presidential rival Alassane Ouattara but also northern Muslims, and the large, mostly Burkinabe, immigrant population (perhaps 40 percent).

Finally, unlike in the first two families of nations, identifying a "dominant society" in many such states is an elusive task. In those nation-states with a titular nationality, domination axiomatically rests with the group giving its name to the state. In those nation-states originating in settler-led revolts, the descendants of the Creole community, often absorbing other European immigrants over time, can be identified as dominant. But in the purely territorial nation-states of the third family, domination is much more fluid and contingent. There may well be a degree of domination defined by the cultural antecedents of the ruler, who in constituting an entourage may rely upon an inner circle of cultural affiliates. As well, the logic of survival of rulers frequently dictates an "ethnic security map" (Enloe 1980) in the command structures of the armed forces. But such ascendance is neither so pervasive nor permanent as in the first two instances. The advent of a new ruler scrambles the cultural cards and leads to a reworking of patterns of relative ethnic standing. Further, there are strong incentives to obscure or conceal a contingent ascendancy of a given ethnic or religious group, which is in flagrant contradiction to the discourse of nationhood necessary to the preservation of such states.

Our survey of the diversity of nationalisms is not exhaustive. The eighteen states that are both territorial and Arab are a category apart. "Homeland" states such as Israel, and originally Liberia, are a distinct breed; so perhaps is the scattering of island ministates in the Pacific and Caribbean. But the point to establish is that the emancipation of cultural pluralism from a possibly repressive version of nationalism is a variable project.

States also vary widely in their nature, as does the character of their hyphenation with the word nation. For a long time, until the late 1980s, the articulation of socialism as supreme legitimating doctrine seemed a possible pathway, even if it was irreconcilable with democratic practice. With the splintering of the Soviet Union and Yugoslavia, this form of nation-state as authoritative model all but vanished, lingering on in Chinese doctrine with respect to its minority nationalities and, to some extent (without the socialism), in the Ethiopian Constitution. If there is an international template, as Tilley suggests, by the 1990s this framing model was the liberal democratic state, however "illiberal" or merely "virtual" its democratic practices are at times (Joseph 1999). Yet other forms exist; in the Arab world, the most visible polities are best characterized as *mukhabarat* (national security) states.

States also vary widely in their degree of centralization. The politics of cultural pluralism operate quite differently in effectively federal states such as India or Canada than in predominately centralized polities such as France or South Africa. Their effective reach and capacity also influence the ways in which multicultural realities are experienced. With the emergence in the 1990s of the "failed" or "collapsed" state, especially in Africa but also in the former Soviet Union (Zartman 1995), the significance of a spectrum separating effectively governed polities from those with minimal claim to the Weberian attributes of stateness became evident. In reflecting upon the emancipation of cultural pluralism, one must consider the Hobbesian realities of life in Congo-Kinshasa, Sierra Leone, or Tajikistan, along with the culturally repressive actions in a number of the nation-states whose writ effectively runs.

Cultural pluralism itself is highly variable. If the most salient form of difference is racial, then the bedrock historical fact of "race," as constructed in circumstances of conquest and large-scale recourse to slavery and other forms of unfree labor, emerges. Thus race is a profoundly ranked system of differentiation. Ideologies justifying ranking and racial hierarchy have largely eroded or even disappeared, but the institutional, psychological, and social dimensions of racism prove very persistent and difficult to eradicate (among many sources, see Cornell and Hartmann 1998; Omi and Winant 1994). Further, race, unlike religion or ethnicity, is normally rooted in phenotype. Racial categories invariably originate in ascription by the dominant; they become internalized and authenticated by doctrines of solidarity and struggle by the subordinated. They are thus particularly resistant to denial or escape; ethnicity often may be chosen or concealed, but race and the social judgments that flow from it normally cannot. An important part of the social energy powering doctrines of multiculturalism arises in contexts such as the United States, where the cultural pluralism most needing emancipation lies in the group categories that are either wholly racial (African diaspora populations), or racialized (Latinos, indigenous peoples).

Ethnicity is more variable. Ethnic consciousness among voluntary immigrant populations is less intense than among territorially concentrated national minorities in a state with a titular nationality. Ethnicity in the immigrant setting, especially in the second generation and beyond, becomes an "ethnic option" (Waters 1990).

Another important distinction differentiates groups that characterize themselves only as ethnic communities, and those employing the discourse of nation. Nationalism invokes a much wider set of claims upon the multicultural polity than does ethnicity, joined as it is to the doctrine of self-determination and the possible claim to separate statehood, or at least full autonomy. Discourse in this domain is constitutive of practice, and the language of collective consciousness is of singular importance. In Africa, for example, in the first postcolonial decades, ethnic collectivities gradually repudiated the older designation as "tribes," a term redolent of primitivism, in favor of "ethnic group." Only in the 1990s did the term *nation* begin in some places to creep into intellectual vocabulary. In the influential words of the late, widely respected Nigerian scholar, Claude Ake, an authentic African democracy "will have to recognize nationalities, subnationalities, ethnic groups, and communities as social formations that express freedom and self-realization and will have to grant them rights to cultural expression and political and economic participation" (Ake 1996, 132).

Religious identity is a third distinct domain of cultural identity, overlapping with ethnicity in some instances where religion demarcates a group also possessing ethnic characteristics and self-consciousness (Jews or Armenians, for example). Since community is defined by theology, which in turn is elaborated on in sacred texts, the nature and demands of affiliation are quite distinct. The world religions enjoy sophisticated institutional structures for their perpetuation and reproduction, as well as anointed specialists for their leadership. The divine nature of their calling opens them to struggles over doctrine and frequent factional divisions, as well as to a recurrent temptation

to use political power to impose orthodoxy. Abdalla's chapter skillfully dis-
sects a contemporary manifestation of this age-old disposition in Sudan.
The modern nation-state appeared to have found a resolution to frequently violent struggle over religion by asserting its secularity. The entry of
significant numbers of Muslims, Buddhists, and Hindus into Western states
(who in fact have inserted a Judeo-Christian subtext in their secularity) raises
new issues. So does the rise of integralist or "fundamentalist" streams in all
major religions. A half-century after its birth, Israel remains unable to adopt
a constitution because of intense conflict over the degree to which Orthodox
understandings of Judaism should inform its content, and over the authenticity of the Judaism of a segment of its population that self-identities as Jewish.
The BJP ideology of *Hindutva* is another case in point.

More than the other two forms of identity, the degree of attachment to
a religious affiliation and the solidarity obligations flowing from it are widely
variable. The integralist vision of Islam enforced by the incumbent regime in
Sudan, as Abdalla shows, is rejected not only by the mostly non-Muslim
south but also by many, perhaps most, in the Muslim north. The rise of
religious division as a line of conflict in Nigeria poses an enormous threat to
civil order, as indicated by the recent wave of Muslim–Christian riots. Even
in Western Europe, where no more than 10 percent of the population regularly attends church services, such conflict has explosive potential, because
religious belief summons the divine authority of God's will and readily stig-
matizes the religious other as the enemy of God.

But racial and ethnic consciousness also is experienced with varying intensity. Though racial ascription may be binding unless phenotypical invis-
ibility is possible, the degree to which racism is experienced depends directly
on site and context. Racial identity, in turn, has a range of possible means of
expression, from the passively accommodative to the militantly combative.
Ethnic identity, to an even greater degree, holds different meanings for different individuals. For some, ethnic community may define the everyday
practice of social existence. For others, especially in environments where its
conflictual aspects are subdued, as in Switzerland, ethnicity may have little
significance for social interactions, or even for such life choices as marriage.

One may note an intriguing variation in the tonality of debates about
cultural pluralism, depending upon the region of focus. In the many states
where racial inequality and oppression have left a deep imprint upon society,
or where ethnonational minorities have been subjected to relentless assimilative pressures or political exclusion and repression, the norms of multiculturalism have particular resonance. In South Asia, where searing memories
of communal violence are still fresh, the texture of the debate is different. In
Africa, the long shadow of the Nigerian civil war and the Rwanda and Burundi
genocides temper perspectives toward cultural pluralism, tilting more to an
apprehension of its dangers than to an attraction for its blessings. It is no

accident that the three chapters in this book by African authors have a thrust that contrasts with the others.

In conclusion, the emancipation of cultural pluralism is, beyond dispute, advanced by the valuable chapters in this book. The fact that one may detect different signposts to this liberation is only natural when one takes due note of the large range of variation in the very meaning of nation, state, and cultural pluralism. In a new century of multicultural politics of many shapes and sizes, large dilemmas lie ahead. One such normative conundrum is whether the ultimate objective is the dissolution of the nation-state and subnational forms of consciousness in a more univeralistic community or the enhancement and celebration of cultural plurality. Steger (2000, 189) asks:

> Rather than engaging in the futile task of purging nationalism of its malign elements, shouldn't the adherents to a philosophy of nonviolence attempt to transcend nationalism altogether? Shouldn't they seek the realization of a nonviolent society according to a cosmopolitan vision that elevates universal human standards over national cultural traditions?

In a different vein, Valery Tishkov, Director of the Russian Academy Institute of Anthropology and Ethnology, and former Minister of Nationalities, enjoins states to "abandon the use of the word *nation* as an academically and legally meaningless self-ascription." "Ethnic group" belongs in the same trash can, as a "counterproductive" means of dividing human communities (Tishkov 2000, 646-47). However attractive these visions, one may wonder whether they are achievable. One also may add that the logic of Steger's aspiration implies a challenge to the emancipation of cultural pluralism.

Yet another difficult set of issues arises with respect to the extent and scope of cultural group rights. If cultural pluralism is emancipated, to what extent is the individual right to difference in jeopardy? Does the cultural group have a collective right to discipline its members and to impose conformity upon them? How can the compatibility of basic human rights and cultural group empowerment be monitored?

Emancipated cultural pluralism poses a number of dilemmas and necessary adjustments to the liberal consensus which, for the moment, does constitute a global "international template." The liberal ascendancy may well erode with the emergence of new forms of populist and collectivist ideologies, but for the immediate future, the reconciliation of the inherent individualism of the liberal value system with the claims of group rights inherent to emancipated cultural pluralism will frame macro-historical process. The degree of optimism permitted the analyst is more a matter of faith than empirical data. I prefer to err on the side of hope in the malleability of nation, state, and liberalism, and the possibility of civil accommodation of cultural diversity, but the wishful thought has an uneven track record.

REFERENCES

Ake, Claude. 1996. *Democracy and Development in Africa.* Washington: Brookings Institution.

Anderson, Benedict. 1983. *Imagined Communities: Reflections on the Origin and Spread of Nationalism.* London: Verso.

Appadurai, Arjun. 1996. *Modernity at Large: Cultural Dimensions of Globalization.* Minneapolis: University of Minnesota Press.

Arbos, Xavier. 1990. "Nation-State: The Range and Future of a Concept." *Canadian Review of Studies of Nationality* 17:1–2: 61–69.

Beiner, Ronald, ed. 1999. *Theorizing Nationalism.* Albany: State University of New York Press.

Billig, Michael. 1995. *Banal Nationalism.* London: Sage Publications.

Brass, Paul R., ed. 1996. *Riots and Pogroms.* New York: New York University Press.

Bremer, Ian and Ray Taras, eds. 1997. *New States, New Politics: Building the Post-Soviet Nations.* Cambridge: Cambridge University Press.

Brubaker, Rogers. 1996. *Nationalism Reframed: Nationhood and the National Question in the New Europe.* Cambridge: Cambridge University Press.

Chatterjee, Partha. 1993. *The Nation and its Fragments: Colonial and Post-Colonial Histories.* Princeton: Princeton University Press.

Colley, Linda. 1992. *Britons: Forging the Nation 1707–1837.* New Haven: Yale University Press.

Cornell, Stephen and Douglas Hartmann. 1998. *Ethnicity and Race: Making Identities in a Changing World.* Thousand Oaks: Pine Forge Press.

Deng, Francis M. 1995. *War of Visions: Conflict of Identities in the Sudan.* Washington: Brookings Institution.

Enloe, Cynthia. 1980. *Ethnic Soldiers: State Security in Divided Societies.* Athens: University of Georgia Press.

Gellner, Ernest. 1983. *Nations and Nationalism.* Oxford: Blackwell.

Greenfeld, Liah. 1992. *Nationalism: Five Roads to Modernity.* Cambridge: Harvard University Press.

Gurr, Ted Robert. 1993. *Minorities at Risk: A Global View of Ethnopolitical Conflicts.* Washington: United States Institute of Peace Press.

———. 2000. *Peoples Versus States: Minorities at Risk in the New Century.* Washington, D.C.: United States Institute of Peace Press.

Hall, John A. 1993. "Nationalisms: Classified and Explained." *Daedalus* 122:3 (Summer): 1–28.

Held, David, Anthony McGrew, David Goldblatt and Jonathan Perraton. 1999. *Global Transformations: Politics, Economics and Culture.* Stanford: Stanford University Press.

Hobsbawm, E. J. 1990. *Nations and Nationalism Since 1780*. Cambridge: Cambridge University Press.

Hollinger, David. 1995. *Postethnic America: Beyond Multiculturalism*. New York: Basic Books.

Horowitz, Donald L. 2001. *The Deadly Ethnic Riot*. Berkeley: University of California Press.

Jenkins, Laura Dudley. 1998. "Identity and Identification: Affirmative Action in India and the United States." Ph.D. diss., University of Wisconsin-Madison.

Joseph, Richard, ed. 1999. *State, Conflict and Democracy in Africa*. Boulder: Lynne Rienner Publishers.

Khazanov, Anatoly. 1995. *After the USSR: Ethnicity, Nationalism, and Politics in the Commonwealth of Independent States*. Madison: University of Wisconsin Press.

Kymlicka, Will. 1995. *Multicultural Citizenship: A Liberal Theory of Minority Rights*. Oxford: Oxford University Press.

Mamdani, Mahmood. 1996. *Citizen and Subject: Contemporary Africa and the Legacy of Late Colonialism*. Princeton: Princeton University Press.

Marx, Anthony W. 1998. *Making Race and Nation: A Comparison of South Africa, the United States and Brazil*. Cambridge: Cambridge University Press.

Omi, Michael and Howard Winant. 1994. *Racial Formation in the United States from the 1960s to the 1990s*. 2nd. ed. New York: Routledge.

Nehru, Jawaharlal. 1946. *The Discovery of India*. London: Meridian Books.

Pourtier, Roland. 1989. *Le Gabon*. 2 vols. Paris: L'Harmattan.

Putnam, Robert. 1993. *Making Democracy Work: Civic Traditions in Modern Italy*. Princeton: Princeton University Press.

Rudolph, Lloyd I. and Susanne Hoeber Rudolph. 1967. *The Modernity of Tradition*. Chicago: University of Chicago Press.

———. 2000. "Living with Multiculturalism." Annual Meeting of the American Political Science Association, Washington.

Scott, James C. 1998. *Seeing Like a State: How Certain Schemes to Improve the Human Condition Have Failed*. New Haven: Yale University Press.

Scruton, Roger. 1999. "The First Person Plural." Pp. 279–293 in Ronald Beiner, ed., *Theorizing Nationalism*. Albany: State University of New York Press.

Steger, Manfred. 2000. *Gandhi's Dilemma: Nonviolent Principles and Nationalist Power*. New York: St. Martin's Press.

Taylor, Charles. 1989. *Sources of the Self: The Making of Modern Identity*. Cambridge: Harvard University Press.

Thernstrom, Stephen and Abigail M. Thernstrom. 1989. *America in Black and White: One Nation, Indivisible*. Cambridge: Harvard University Press.

Tilley, Virginia. 1997. "Indigenous People and the State: Ethnic Meta-Conflict in El Salvador." Ph.D. diss., University of Wisconsin-Madison.

Tishkov, Valery. 2000. "Forget the Nation: Post-Nationalist Understandings of Nationalism." *Ethnic and Racial Studies* 23:2 (July): 625–50.

Van Cott, Donna Lee. 1999. *Friendly Liquidation of the Past: The Politics of Diversity in Latin America*. Pittsburgh: Pittsburgh University Press.

Vertovec, Stephen. 1996. "Multiculturalism, Culturalism, and Public Incorporation." *Ethnic and Racial Studies* 19:1 (January): 49–69.

Walzer, Michael. 1997. *On Toleration*. New Haven: Yale University Press.

Waters, Mary. 1990. *Ethnic Options: Choosing Identities in America*. Berkeley: University of California Press.

Weber, Eugen. 1976. *Peasants into Frenchmen*. Stanford: Stanford University Press.

Weinstein, Brian. 1966. *Gabon: Nation-Building on the Ogooué*. Cambridge: MIT Press.

Wiarda, Howard. 1981. *Corporatism and National Development in Latin America*. Boulder: Westview.

Yack, Bernard. 1999. "The Myth of the Civic Nation." Pp. 103–118 in Ronald Beiner, ed., *Theorizing Nationalism*. Albany: State University of New York Press.

Young, Crawford. 1976. *The Politics of Cultural Pluralism*. Madison: University of Wisconsin Press.

———, ed. 1993. *The Rising Tide of Cultural Pluralism*. Madison: University of Wisconsin Press.

———. 1994. *The African Colonial State in Comparative Perspective*. New Haven: Yale University Press.

———, ed. 1998. *Ethnic Diversity and Public Policy: A Comparative Inquiry*. Basingstoke: Macmillan.

———, ed. 1999. *The Accommodation of Cultural Diversity: Case Studies*. Basingstoke: Macmillan.

Zartman, I William, ed. 1995. *Collapsed States: The Disintegration and Restoration of Legitimate Authority*. Boulder: Lynne Rienner Publishers.

Contributors

Ismail H. Abdalla, Ph.D., is an associate professor in the Department of History at the College of William and Mary. He has written and published two books, *Islam, Medicine and Practitioners in Northern Nigeria* and *Bithrat Al-Khalaas*, and he has edited two others. In addition, he has published numerous articles and chapters on African and Middle Eastern issues. He currently serves on the editorial board of *Sudan Notes and Records*.

Paul Adogamhe, Ph.D. is an associate professor of political science at the University of Wisconsin-Whitewater. He specializes in international relations and comparative politics, with regional interest in African government and politics. Adogamhe also teaches in the Race and Ethnic Cultures Program. His research interest focuses on African politics, Nigeria's foreign relations, international organizations, and Third World development.

Assefaw Bariagaber, Ph.D., is an associate professor in the School of Diplomacy and International Relations, Seton Hall University. Prior to coming to Seton Hall, he taught at the University of Nebraska at Kearney and, during 1998–1999, he was a Visiting Research Fellow at the Center of International Studies at Princeton University. The author of numerous articles, Bariagaber currently serves as the associate editor of the *Eritrean Studies Review*.

Robert Buffington, Ph.D., is an associate professor of Latin American history at Bowling Green State University. His published works include a book, *Criminal and Citizen in Modern Mexico* and an edited volume (with Carlos Aguirre), *Reconstructing Criminality in Latin America*.

Ellen Christensen, Ph.D., is curator of architecture at the Chicago Architecture Foundation. She teaches architectural history for the Graham School at the University of Chicago.

Jeff Hoover, Ph.D., is an associate professor of philosophy at Coe College. His research and teaching focus on social and political philosophy, nineteenth- and twentieth-century Continental philosophy, German idealism and romanticism, feminist philosophy, and postmodernism. His articles have appeared in such publications as *Philosophy Today*, *Neues Athenaeum/New Athenaeum*, *Journal of Religion*, and *Constellations*.

259

Beth Simon, Ph.D., is an associate professor of linguistics and English at Indiana University/Purdue University. Her research and writing center on multilingualism, language loss and assimilation, and language gender and literacy. Her essays, fiction, and poetry appear in many journals.

Thomas W. Simon, Ph.D. and J.D., holds the Schulze Endowed Chair of Interdisciplinary Studies at the University of Northern Colorado. He also practices law. He has taught philosophy at Illinois State University and has served on the law faculty of the University of Ljubljana (Slovenia) as a Fulbright Fellow in 1999. For a number of years, he served as a consultant to the United Nations Working Group on Minorities and for the Central and Eastern European Law Initiative of the American Bar Association. He has worked on drafting the Albanian Constitution and on minority protection constitutional provisions for Belarus and the Ukraine. His publications include over forty articles and, most recently, a textbook, *Law and Philosophy.*

Selma K. Sonntag, Ph.D., is a professor of government and politics at Humboldt State University in Northern California. Recent publications include articles on language politics, and cultural pluralism in northern India. Her area of specialization is South Asia.

Manfred B. Steger, Ph.D., is an associate professor of political theory at Illinois State University. His many publications include *The Quest of Evolutionary Socialism: Eduard Bernstein and Social Democracy, Engels after Marx, Nonviolence and Its Alternatives: An Interdisciplinary Reader, Gandhi's Dilemma: Nonviolent Principles and Nationalist Power,* and *Globalism: The New Market Ideology.*

Virginia Q. Tilley, Ph.D., is an assistant professor of political science at Hobart and William Smith Colleges. Her professional interests include comparative politics of nationalism and economic development, the interrelation of international norms, state-building and economic development strategies with national ideologies, and the incidence of ethnic conflict. She has pursued research on ethnic conflict, principally in El Salvador, Guatemala, Israel, and the West Bank. Her articles have appeared in such publications as the *Latin American Research Review, The Journal of Latin American Studies,* and *Ethnic and Racial Studies.*

Cris Toffolo, Ph.D., is the Director of the Justice and Peace Program and an associate professor of political theory and comparative politics at the University of St. Thomas, St. Paul. Her areas of specialization include nationalism and ethnicity, contemporary political theory, and South Asia (in particular, Pakistan, human and women's rights, and political development). Publications include "Pakistan" (with Charles Amjad-Ali), in the *World Encyclopedia of Political Systems and Parties*. Toffolo also serves as a consultant for Amnesty International (USA).

Crawford Young, Ph.D. is the H. Edwin Young and Rupert Emerson Professor of Political Science at the University of Wisconsin-Madison, where he has taught since 1963. His numerous publications include *Politics in the Congo, The Politics of Cultural Pluralism, Ideology and Development in Africa, The Rise and Decline of the Zairian State* (with Thomas Turner), and *The African Colonial State in Comparative Perspective*. Young has taught in Uganda, Congo-Kinshasa, and Senegal, is a former president of the African Studies Association, and is a fellow of the American Academy of Arts and Sciences.

Index

Ethnic, 56, 57, 137, 195, 197, 214, 223, 226, 234n1, 239, 248–259; cleavages, 223; communities, 207, 214, 252–253; conflict, 197, 214; competition, 210, 195; consciousness, 252–253; decline, 90; demands, 224, 229; diversity, 207, 246; elites, 228; entrepreneurs, 45; environment, 38; immigrants, 184; inclusion, 15; inventory, 94; majorities in Nigeria, 199; movements, 227; neutral, 37; option, 252; parties, 229–232; pluralism in Nigeria, 195, 204, 214, 232; and race, 57; relative standing, 251; representation (Ethiopian), 231; revivalism, 19n6; security map, 251. *See also* Ethiopia, ethnicity, Eritrea, Croats, Serbs, Nigeria, race

Ethnicity, 4, 15, 29, 55–62, 73–75, 129, 155, 163–165, 198, 203, 221, 240; cleansing of, 14, 73–75; is contingent, 55, 59; defensive, 62; defined, 50, 57; deserves neither praise nor blame, 61; and diet, 90; and ethics, 13, 61; harmful, 55, 61; identity view of, 55; inclusion into state, 15; and Islam, 109; politicized, 227–228; strife view of, 55; suffering, 11; types of, 13; theories of, 14, 59; value of, 58, 75; versus, 252. *See also* Ethiopia, ethnic cleansing

Ethnization, 56–57
Ethnology, 88, 97
Ethnonationalist, 43, discourses, 43
Ethnos, 56, 58, 59, 60, 96; definition, 58
Eugenics, 15, 91, 94, 99, 100n10; and Mexican Revolution, 15; Second International Congress 91; in Mexico, 94; Mexican, 100; Second International Congress, 100
Europe, Eastern, 6
European Union, 247–249
Evil(s), 111; of alcoholism, 96

Evolution, 85, 92, 99; emancipation from, 12; social, 86; of populations, 94
Ezechime, 209

Factionalism, 111
Family, 29; values, 85
Fascism, 241; Italian, 95
Fasting, 138
Father, 170
Fatherland, 88, 89, 96; and Indians in Mexico, 84
Federalism, 183, 190–191, 195, 197–199, 200, 205, 247; Ethiopian, 18, 222, 228–231; ethnic, 234; Indian, 182, 185, 187; linguistic, 181; Nigerian, 204, 215; and secession, 228.
Ferri, Enrico, 95; fascist penal code, 95
Fighting words doctrine, 76n2
Fiqh, democratizing of , 108. *See also* shari 'a
Force, 118, 135; use of, 112, assimilation, 41
Forjando Patria, See Gamio
France, 251; Muslims in, 240
Franco Sodi, Carlos, 97, 98
Franco-Mexican Commission, 87
Freedom, 31, 110–111, 141, 252; and power, 7;
French Revolution, 242
French, 243; republican principles, 248
Fulani, 204
Fuller, 167, 170
Fundamentalism, Islamic, 166
Fundamentalist, 253
Fuqaha', 108

Gada, 226
Galindo, 96
Gamio, Manuel, 81, 82, 88–91, 99, 100n10
Gandhi, Indira, 168–170
Gandhi, Mahatma, 17, 130–143, 249; compared to Plato, 135, 136, 140; idealized vision of, 139; saintly personality, 137; on self rule, 15; in South Africa, 131–132; and spinning wheel, 138; *See also Hind Swaraj*

Identity, 32, 59, 61, 147–149, 153–
156, 170, 184, 195, 203, 207, 225–
226; Albanian 70; Arab, 47;
ascriptive, 6, 26; cards, 65; collective,
241; construction of, 147, 149;
cultural, 248; and custom, 11;
Charles Taylor's views on, 27;
defensive, 65; ethnic, 75, 184, 214,
253; groups, 149, 246; ideologies of,
149; in India 154, 158, 164; Islamic,
118, 153; language, 148, 155; Latin
American, 49; markers, 148; modern
need for, 27; national, 129; politics,
6–7, 9–14, 16–17, 19, 28, 60, 163–
165, 246; racial, 253; religious, 252–
253; search for, 32; sectarian, 137;
social, 149, 156; Tigrayan, 226
Ideology, 152, 244, 251, 254; daily
exercise of, 149; defined, 121; and
democracy, 8; and formation of social
identity, 149; and group identity; 29;
and Hinduism, 165, 175; Idioms,
158; national, 248
Idris, Ja'far Sheikh, (Sudan), 123n6
Igbo(s), 199, 204–205, 208; in Bendel,
207; Eastern, 207; Western, 207, 209
Ignatieff, 60
'ihya', 107
Ijaw(s), 203, 205, 210–214
Ijma', 111–113, 123n7
Ijtihad, 106, 108
Ik, 58
Ika, 208, 209
Ikhwan, 125n21, 22. See Muslim
Brotherhood
Ikime, Obaro, 197, 210, 213
Imam, 124n15
Immigration, 48, 49, 85, 241
Imperialism, 48–49, 110, 125n2, 137,
143n1
Incorporation, and Seri, 94; racial
improvement, 94
Independence, 130, 139; Mexican, 82;
India's, 141, 173, 181; struggles, 8
India(n), 130–139, 141, 147–162, 163–
180, 181–194, 246, 248–249, 251;

civilization, 136, 139–140; Constitution, 182–187, 191; Dar Commission, 186; the Emergency, 164;
Indian National Congress, 131, 134;
Indianness, 135, 136, 173; Indians,
136, 181–182; language identity, 6,
147, 153; nation, 137; nationalism,
131, 136, 139–143; Orientalism, 138;
partition, 165; patriotism, 134, 135;
reorganization of States Act, 181;
secular state, 174; unity, 133; urban,
148; virtues, 140. See also Ayodhya,
Bengal, Bhojpuri, Brahman, caste,
BJP, Darjeeling, DGHC (Darjeeling
Gorkha Hill Council), Gandhi,
Identity in India, Hind Swaraj,
Hindu-, language and India,
nationalism, nonviolence, self-
government.
Indians (Mexico), 49, 82–87, 89, 91–98
240; ancestors, 83; attacks on culture
of, 41, 90, 96, 97; contemporary, 83;
and crime, 92, 96, 97; degraded state
of, 82; influence of altitude on, 84;
integration, 82; Mayan, 45; measurement of, 92, 95; as national symbol,
83; problem of 81–83, 85, 96, 98;
resilience of traditions of, 97; status
of, 98; stereotypes, 98; rural, 85. See
also indigenous people, mestizos,
mestizaje, Mexico
Indians, (American), 59; treaties; 40–41
Indigenous people(s), 81–87, 90–91,
96–99, 243, 248, 250, 252; alcoholism among, 96; elite, 240; eradication
of, 49; and eugenics, 15; measurement of, 94; national development,
94, 98
Individual(s), 8, 18, 27, 99, 109, 140; in
Durkheim, 19n5; Indo-Aryan, 133;
ism, 241, 254, right, 254; subjectivity,
35
Indonesia, 240, 247
Industrialization, 5, 19n5
Inequalities, 245; legitimization of, 92
Instability, theory of, 233

ments, 112, 114, 115; minorities 112,
118; Republican Brothers, 125;
reconstruction of, 121; Second
Republic (1986–1989), 115; Sudanese
Brotherhood, 15; uprising of October
1964, 113. *See also* Christian(s),
Islam, Islamicists, Muslim Brother-
hood. *See also* Islam
Suffering, 11, 110, 137
Swaraj, *See Hind Swaraj*
Switzerland, 249, 253
Symbolic, 175, action theory, 164
Symbolism, 164, 167, 175, 227

Tab-Allah, Ali, 123n2
Tadayyun, 107, 108, 109
Tajdid, 120
Taji-Farouki, 117
Tajikistan, 251
Tala Kholo ("open the lock"), 170
Taliban, 35
Tamils, 245
Tanzania, 247
Tarascans, biotyping of, 96
Tarde, Gabriel, 92
Tariqás, 114
Tatwier, 107
Tawhid (divine unity), 107, 108, 109,
110
Taylor, Charles, 27, 241, 248
Temple, 163, 172; Rama temple
campaign, 164, 165, 166; correct
form for, 171; Hindu, 168
Teotihuacán, Valley of, 90
Territory, 149, 155; cultural, 157;
sacred, 139
Thawabit, 107
The Balkans, 64
Third World, development, 5; indepen-
dence, 5; theoretical issues, 6; de
colonialization, 8; thought, 7
Tigray People's Liberation Front. *See*
TPLF
Tigray(an), 223–226, 234n3
Tilak, B. G., 137, 139
Tilley, Virginia, 3, 14, 99n2, 240, 241,
244, 245, 246, 251

Toffolo, Cris, 6, 81, 99, 143, 163, 239,
241, 246
Tolerance, 137; a traditional Hindu
value, 136
Tonnies, 19n5
TPLF (Tigray People's Liberation
Front), 225, 226–228, 232–233
Tradition, 7, 8, 17, 99
Traditional, 19n5, 27, 239; identities,
81
Traditionalism, 20n11
Traditionalist, 123n7
Transitional Charter, 227, 232
Transitional Government, 231
Transnational movements, 50
Tribal, 239, 246; the Balkans, 66;
Ethopia, 224
Tribals, 166, 182–184, 224; in India,
182, 184
Tribes, 246, 252
Truth, 136, 140, 154, 172. *See also
satyagraha*
Turkey, 240, 248. *See also* Ottoman
Turks, 70
Turnbull, 58
Tutsi, 40, 41, 63–64, 70–72, 74, 75,
248; *See also* Rwanda
Twa, 70
Tyranny, 140

U.P., *See* Uttar Pradesh
Uchendu, 19n6
Uganda, 64, 72
Ukwuani Society, 207
Ulama, 121
Ummah, 106, 110–113, 118, 120
Underclass, 133; and Gandhi, 132
Underdevelopment, decentralization as
solution (Nigeria), 197
Unification, linguistic, 91
United Kingdom, 242, 249
United Middle Belt-Congress, 199
United Nations, 67, 72, 247
United States, 5, 42, 240–242, 245,
248, 252; white ethnic groups in, 41;
role in Rwandan genocide, 73
Unity Party of Nigeria (UPN), 201